DISCARD

ECONOMIC CHANGE IN THAILAND
1850–1970

ECONOMIC CHANGE
IN THAILAND
1850-1970

James C. Ingram

A new edition of
Economic Change in Thailand Since 1850
with two new chapters on developments
since 1950

STANFORD UNIVERSITY PRESS

STANFORD, CALIFORNIA

1971

In this edition Chapters 1–10 are reprinted substantially without change from *Economic Change in Thailand Since 1850* (Stanford, 1955). Chapters 11 and 12 are completely new, replacing Chapter 11 of the 1955 edition, and the statistics in the Appendixes have been updated.

Stanford University Press
Stanford, California
Copyright © 1955, 1971 by the Board of Trustees
of the Leland Stanford Junior University
Printed in the United States of America
ISBN 0-8047-0782-0
LC 70-150325

Preface to the 1971 Edition

In 1969 I had the good fortune to return to Thailand for a two-year stay—the first visit since 1952. I was pleased to find that the first edition of this book, long out of print, was still in use, and that a need for a second edition seemed to exist. At first, I considered a thoroughgoing revision of the entire book, with the addition of new chapters to deal with economic changes from 1950 to 1970. However, I was soon convinced of two points: first, that I could add little to what I had previously written about the earlier period, 1850 to 1950; and second, that a description and analysis of economic changes since 1950 was by itself a major undertaking.

Consequently, in this new edition I have left my account of the period 1850–1950 unchanged except for a few corrections and minor alterations to remind the reader of its 1951-52 perspective. At half a dozen places where such a reminder seems particularly important, footnotes have been added; elsewhere perhaps two dozen words like "today" have been changed to phrases like "as of 1950"; and the dates 1850–1950 have been added to the chapter titles and page heads of Chapters 3–10. In general, however, the present perfect tense and other technically ambiguous indicators of time perspective have been left without clarification.

My decision to leave Chapters 1–10 substantially unchanged does not mean that I am satisfied with them, or that no further work on the period 1850–1950 is needed. On the contrary, many aspects of this period deserve further study, especially from the Thai side, and recent historical and social science studies need to be taken into account. I hope this work will be undertaken by the growing number of Thai and foreign scholars who are interested in this period.

The new material in this edition is contained in Chapters 11 and 12, in which I attempt to provide a concise account of the principal economic changes in Thailand from 1950 to 1970. I found this to be an even larger undertaking than I had expected, and these chapters are therefore selective and synoptic, not comprehensive or exhaustive. The Thai economy has become more complex, many changes have taken place, and, in particular, the volume of data and documentation has increased greatly. Economic statistics are vastly more abundant, though reliability remains a problem, and a great many economic studies, reports, and analyses—both official and unofficial—now exist. These studies were a great help, but the limitations of time and space necessitated brief treatment of several topics, and complete omission of some others—notably the role of foreign aid and the impact of the United States military operation in Thailand. However, I hope the selection and emphasis I have made will provide the reader with a sense of the continuity of Thai economic development and indicate the nature and vitality of economic change in the past two decades. My own impression, from both the data and personal observation, is that Thailand's economy has undergone a "sea change" in these twenty years, that it has entered a new phase in which modern technology is being increasingly incorporated into the productive process, and in which a significant and growing fraction of the population will not only accept, but even press for, economic change in their lives and activities. Large parts of the economy are still static, dominated by tradition, and as yet relatively untouched by this new phase, but I think it would be a mistake to focus too closely on these areas if one wishes to understand Thailand's recent economic experience.

I am again indebted to a great many persons for their support, encouragement, advice, and direct assistance in the preparation of this edition. I wish particularly to express my appreciation to Dr. Puey Ungphakorn, Governor of the Bank of Thailand and Dean of the Faculty of Economics at Thammasat University, for inviting me to join his Faculty as a visiting professor for these two years, and to the Rockefeller Foundation for financial support which made it possible to accept. I wish also to thank Dr. Ralph K. Davidson, Deputy Director of the Social Science Division of the Rockefeller Foundation, for his counsel and encouragement.

For their comments and criticisms of one or more of the new chapters, and for much helpful discussion along the way, I am grateful to Professors Ammar Siamwalla, Forrest Cookson, Lawrence D. Stifel, and Delane E. Welsch, sometime colleagues at Thammasat University.

Many persons, too numerous to name here, in the Bank of Thailand, Thammasat University, the National Economic Development Board, the Department of Customs, and other agencies have generously helped me and supplied data not yet available in published form. To Miss Katalee Sombatsiri, Librarian of the Bank of Thailand, and Mr. Somsak Saengthongsuk, Department of Economic Research, I owe a special word of thanks. Miss Vipa Limsuwan ably assisted in certain phases of this work, and Miss Choosri Sastrayoungkul cheerfully and expertly typed the whole manuscript.

In some respects, Thailand has changed a great deal in twenty years, but the difference is most evident in Bangkok, where some of the costs and drawbacks of economic development have also appeared. For the future, I hope the Thai genius for compromise and adaptation will assert itself, and enable Thailand to preserve the charm and special quality of its style of life even as its measured income rises.

JAMES C. INGRAM

Bangkok
December 1970

Preface to the 1955 Edition

THE PRIMARY purposes of this study are, first, to describe the major economic changes in Thailand since that country was exposed to the influence of world trade and Western culture in the middle of the nineteenth century, and second, to seek interpretations, explanations, and generalizations about that experience in so far as it is found to be repetitive or amenable to the apparatus of economic analysis. Much the greater part of the book is concerned with the first purpose.

The scarcity and unreliability of data concerning the economy of Thailand will be mentioned in several places. Here I wish merely to observe that in the course of this study I made a systematic search for information in the files of the various ministries of the government of Thailand. Officials at all levels were cordial and co-operative, and they kindly gave me much time and assistance. In this way I obtained a considerable amount of information about recent events, but I found relatively few sources of historical information other than those already known. Only the Ministry of Finance possessed extensive files going back to 1890. These records, particularly the files of the Financial Advisers, contained much valuable information. In other ministries I found only occasional bits of information for the period prior to 1910.

I had hoped to find some data in the records of long-established banks and trading firms in Bangkok, but in this I was disappointed as the important concerns had lost their records either in the war or through fire.

An effort was also made to find information about economic changes in the writings of Thai authors. Some relevant material was found in such works, but on the whole I concluded that the Thai as private individuals have not written much about the economic problems facing their country.

These comments about sources may help to explain the use of some rather questionable sources, as well as to indicate the difficulty of the task undertaken here. Information is more plentiful for the more recent decades, however, and it appears likely to become more so in the future.

An earlier version of this study was submitted to Cornell University in 1952 as a doctoral dissertation. It has undergone considerable revision since that time, principally in the interests of brevity, and the final chapter has been added.

I am indebted to a long list of individuals and organizations for assistance with this study. I cannot list all who helped, but I particularly wish to acknowledge my debt to the following persons who gave me much encouragement, assistance, and advice: Mr. Sommai Huntragul, chief of the Research Division, Bank of Thailand; Dr. Puey Ungphakorn, then in the Ministry of Finance; and Mr. Prayad Svastixuto, Research Division, Bank of Thailand.

Dr. Flournoy A. Coles, Jr., economist for the MSA Mission in Bangkok, and Mr. Graham Quate, agricultural attaché of the United States Embassy in Bangkok, also gave me advice and information on several problems.

I am grateful to Professor Alfred E. Kahn, Cornell University, for his perceptive criticisms and suggestions; to Professor Edwin P. Reubens, City College of New York, for much friendly counsel and advice; and to Professor Lauriston Sharp, Cornell University, for his encouragement and support.

I wish to express my appreciation to the Social Science Research Council for a fellowship which made it possible for me to spend a year on research in Thailand, and to the Institute of Pacific Relations for financial assistance in the publication of this study.

Finally, I wish to acknowledge the aid of my wife, Alice Graham Ingram, whose contributions to this study have been many and varied.

JAMES C. INGRAM

Chapel Hill, North Carolina
May 1954

Contents

ECONOMIC CHANGE IN THAILAND

1850–1970

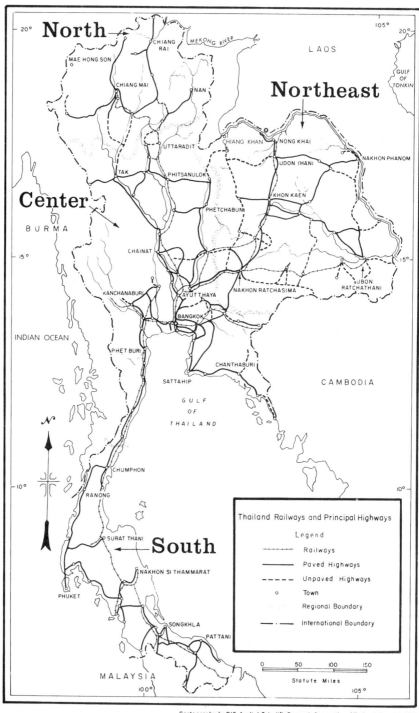

North

CHIANG RAI
MAE HONG SON
CHIANG MAI
NAN
MEKONG RIVER
LAOS

Northeast

GULF OF TONKIN

UTTARADIT
CHIANG KHAN
NONG KHAI
NAKHON PHANOM
UDON THANI
TAK
PHITSANULOK
KHON KAEN

Center

BURMA

PHETCHABUN

CHAINAT

NAKHON RATCHASIMA
UBON RATCHATHANI

KANCHANABURI
AYUTTHAYA
BANGKOK

INDIAN OCEAN

PHET BURI

CHANTHABURI

SATTAHIP

CAMBODIA

GULF OF THAILAND

CHUMPHON

RANONG

SURAT THANI

South

NAKHON SI THAMMARAT

PHUKET

SONGKHLA
PATTANI

MALAYSIA

Thailand Railways and Principal Highways

Legend

+++++	Railways
———	Paved Highways
- - - -	Unpaved Highways
o	Town
	Regional Boundary
-·-·-	International Boundary

0   50   100   150
Statute Miles

Cartography by RIG, Applied Scientific Research Corporation of Thailand, Bangkok, 1971

1

Introduction: Historical Background

THE AYUTHIAN PERIOD of Thai history came to an end in 1767 when Ayuthia, the capital city, was captured and sacked by the Burmese armies. But Thailand did not remain long under Burmese power. Even in 1767 Phya Taksin and his followers were regaining control of parts of Thailand, and by 1771 Phya Taksin controlled nearly all of the Thailand of the Ayuthian period. He was later crowned king. For several years he ruled wisely, but then allegedly began to show signs of madness, and in 1782 he was executed. His successor, also a general, was the founder of the present Chakri dynasty.

Besides their complicated court titles and names, the Thai kings of the Chakri dynasty are given the title of "Rama." For convenience we will refer to them as King Rama I, King Rama II, etc. The dates of the successive reigns of this dynasty follow:

King	Also Known As	Period of Reign
Rama I	Yodfah	1782–1809
Rama II	Lertlah	1809–24
Rama III	Nang Klao	1824–51
Rama IV	Mongkut	1851–68
Rama V	Chulalongkorn	1868–1910
Rama VI	Vajiravuhd	1910–25
Rama VII	Prajadipok	1925–35
Rama VIII	Ananda-Mahidon	1935–46
Rama IX	Phumiphon-Aduldet	1946–

The first three kings of the new dynasty had little to do with Western nations, although toward the end of the third reign it became apparent that the traditional isolation from the West could not long be maintained. The British approach in Burma and the opening of China made this very clear. There were Western missionaries and a few traders in Thailand during the first three reigns, but the principal official Western contacts were made through the missions of John Crawfurd (1821), Captain Henry Burney (1825), and Sir James Brooke (1850) for Great Britain, and the Roberts Mission (1833) from the United States. Burney and Roberts succeeded in negotiating treaties, but they were very limited ones.

Upon the death of King Rama II in 1824, it was expected that Mongkut would become king, but instead his half brother ascended to the throne, and Mongkut became a Buddhist priest. At the time he was twenty years old, and during the next twenty-seven years he remained a priest and became a scholar. When he became king in 1851, he had mastered several foreign languages and learned much of Western history and science. He is the king who employed Mrs. Anna Leonowens to teach his children.

The present study begins with the reign of King Rama IV, or King Mongkut, whose readiness to accept change made the tasks of Sir John Bowring (1855) and Townsend Harris (1856) much easier than they would otherwise have been. Most of the changes were set in motion through the leadership of King Mongkut and his son, King Chulalongkorn. A distinctive feature of the period covered by these two important reigns (1851–1910) was that the court and nation had to be led by the king to accept change and reform. The initiative came from the top. In later reigns this was less true.

Since the beginning of the Chakri dynasty, Thailand has had a period of comparative peace. The British conquest of Burma removed the major source of conflict, but the decline of the old enemy in the west was soon followed by the rise of a new one in the east. French colonial aspirations gave rise to border disputes along the whole of Thailand's eastern border which were not settled until 1907, and then only after Thailand had lost between 70,000 and 80,000 square miles of territory. The worst crisis came in 1893, when French gunboats forced their way up the Chao Phya River[1] and French troops occupied Chandaburi in the east. The British desire to keep Thailand as a buffer state between British and French possessions in Asia, together with British interest in the trade of Bangkok (then 70 percent in British hands), was largely responsible for the use of British diplomacy to preserve the independence of Thailand.[2]

That the Thai government, struggling with manifold abuses of extraterritoriality, hampered by fiscal limitations imposed by treaties, and trying to prevent the loss of territory without provoking open aggression, could at the same time (1890–1910) carry out administrative and social reforms, proceed with railway construction, and begin to plan scientific irrigation projects, is truly remarkable. The history of this period has not yet been adequately—or fairly—written.

Until 1932 the power of the king was absolute. In practice the king made use of state councils and administered the country through ministers, but the final authority lay in the hands of the king. Little or no progress toward self-government had been made, although King Rama VII had said in 1931 that

---

[1] Also known as the Menam River. Actually, the word "Menam" means simply "river" in Thai, but the Westerner, not bothering with all of "Menam Chao Phya," has corrupted the name to "Menam River."

[2] Cf. Great Britain [Foreign Office], *Correspondence Respecting the Affairs of Siam*, published by order of the House of Commons (London, 1894).

he approved of the idea of granting a constitution to the people. Quite suddenly in June 1932 a bloodless coup d'état was successfully staged by a small group of officials and militarists, among whose leaders were Nai Pridi Phanomyong, a Paris-trained lawyer, and Marshal Phibun Songgram, Prime Minister 1938–45 and 1948–57. The king agreed to accept the constitutional government, and for a time there was great hope for democratic government in Thailand. Space is not available here for a description of events since 1932;[3] suffice it to say that control of the government has remained in the hands of a small group, in which military men have been dominant, and that numerous coups and countercoups have been staged since the first one in June 1932. Progress toward a broadly based popular government has been virtually nil.

King Rama VII abdicated in 1935. The monarchy has been continued, however, and it has a powerful hold on the Thai people. King Rama VIII (the "boy king," Ananda) was revered by the people, and his death by violence in 1946 was a brutal shock to the entire nation. Early one morning he was found dead in the palace with a bullet through his head. The case has never been solved—theories of murder, suicide, and accident are widely held—and it is doubtful that it will be.

In 1941 the Prime Minister, Phibun Songgram, agreed not to resist Japanese occupation. Later on, Thailand officially declared war on Great Britain and the United States, an act which the United States government never recognized. M. R. Seni Pramoj, Thai ambassador to Washington, refused to transmit the declaration. Field Marshal Phibun was ousted in 1944, but when the Pridi government fell before a coup d'état in 1947, it was not long before Phibun again became Prime Minister. Since 1947 the government has become ever more tightly controlled by a small clique of army and police officers.

The reigning monarch, King Rama IX (King Phumiphon-Aduldet), came home in 1951 from Switzerland, where he had lived most of his life, to take the throne. The king has little real power at present, but his *position* has a great hold on the loyalties and affection of the mass of people. Apparently, the latest coup (November 1951) was largely designed to limit the authority of the king by readopting the 1932 constitution.

By and large, the government has been conservative ever since the 1932 coup d'état. Since World War II it has been strongly anti-Communistic, and Thailand has departed from its historic policy of neutrality. The country is orderly and peaceful, though reported incidents of insurgency increased in the 1960's.

The following points may be taken as footnotes which apply throughout this study:

1. When reference is made to the "Chinese" in Thailand, it is necessary

---

[3] For a narrative of events since 1932, see K. P. Landon, *Siam in Transition* (Shanghai and Chicago, 1939); Alexander MacDonald, *Bangkok Editor* (New York, 1949); and Virginia M. Thompson, *Thailand, the New Siam* (New York, 1941).

but difficult to know who is meant. Frequently, the reference is to the 3,000,000 people who are Chinese ethnically or by ancestry. Thus, if a man has a Chinese father and a Thai mother but has been brought up as a Chinese, he may be considered "Chinese" in many cases. Frequently, the word "Chinese" is used to mean only immigrants from China. Legally, any person born in Thailand is a Thai national, and thus most official statistics classify as "Chinese" only those not born in the country. This problem is important because of the division of labor along racial or national lines, and because of the growth of an anti-"Chinese" sentiment in Thailand in recent decades. In this study we shall use "Chinese" to apply to the entire ethnic group unless otherwise stated. Even this line is difficult to draw. Sometimes, for example, one son will be Thai while his brother is brought up a Chinese.

2. The Thai have always called their country Muang-Thai (land of the free), but its official name to foreigners was Siam until 1939, when Premier Phibun changed it to Thailand. When he was ousted near the end of the war the name was changed back to Siam, and when he returned to power in 1947 it was again changed to Thailand. The official name—Thailand—will be used throughout this study, except in the second chapter and in footnote references which have Siam in the original.

3. Until 1940 the year in Thailand ran from April 1 to March 31. In converting dates from the Buddhist Era to the Christian equivalent, we will show both the beginning and the ending year. Thus, B.E. 2475 will be referred to as 1932/33, meaning the period April 1, 1932, through March 31, 1933. Since 1940 the year officially begins on January 1, although dates are still expressed according to the Buddhist Era.

4. Frequent references are made to regions in Thailand. The definition of these has been determined largely by the availability of statistics. The map (p. ii) depicts the regional boundaries used. A full definition will be given in Appendix A. The country is divided into seventy-one *changwats* (or provinces) for administration. The capital city of each changwat bears the name of the changwat. Before the constitutional regime, the country was divided into larger units called *monthons or* "circles." These varied in number from ten to eighteen, and each monthon included several of the present changwats.

5. For the most part, Thai measures of area and weight have been used. The two most important measures are:

a) The *rai*. This is a measure of area, equal to 1,600 square meters or about 0.4 acres.

b) The *picul*. This is a measure of weight, equal to 60 kilograms or 132 pounds. Formerly it was equal to 133⅓ pounds. One metric ton is equal to 16.67 piculs.

6. The currency unit of Thailand is the *baht*, also known to foreigners as the *tical*. The baht is subdivided into 100 *satang*. Before World War II, the ex-

change value of the baht was fairly steady at about 11 to the pound sterling and 2.0–2.5 to the U.S. dollar, but inflation during and after the war drastically changed the exchange value of the baht. From 1949 to 1951 the free market rates were 21–23 baht to the U.S. dollar, and 50–57 to the pound, while official rates (valid only for specified transactions) were 12.50 baht to the dollar and 35 baht to the pound. The course of the exchange rate is examined in detail in Chapter 7. Here the primary point is that the drastic changes in the value of the baht since the war make the postwar value and price statistics appear startlingly different from prewar figures. This must be remembered in examining the tables in subsequent chapters.

7. For those not familiar with the literature on Thailand, we should mention the scarcity of data. The Thai as private persons have not written much about the facts and figures of their own economy. As a result available information comes mostly from government or foreign sources, and before 1900 government records are few and far between. The reliance on government records since 1900 is unfortunate but unavoidable. Only the government has collected and published the statistics which must be used in this study. Inadequacy of data has hampered every phase of this study, and many important aspects have had to be omitted because of a total lack of data.

The probable margin of error in the statistics used is often quite high, but the error cannot be estimated or allowed for. Throughout this study the assumption is made that the trend values are safer and more reliable than short-term or year-to-year comparisons. Wherever possible the analysis rests on trends.

8. Finally, there is little or no mention of corruption in this study. Corruption is an extremely important phenomenon in the Thai economy, particularly in the period since World War II, but no quantitative data can possibly be obtained. Systematized "squeeze" and the routine "tea money," as found in Thailand, become regular items of national income, and because of their location at strategic points in the government, they have great influence on the allocation of resources.

This kind of bribe is found not only in government, but also in many levels of business. Outside of its importance as a source of income (a "factor" share!), corruption has economic importance because it introduces a new element of uncertainty into economic calculations. Whether a venture will succeed or fail may depend on one crucial "permit" or "special purchase," or it may depend on a succession of them, as when a permit has to be renewed every month, or when the importer's comprador must be regularly persuaded to sell a scarce commodity. With the prospect of *total* failure always present, entrepreneurs must discount the future very heavily indeed. Fortunately, a kind of "standard" has developed even in corruption, and those who exceed the standard are (sometimes) exposed and punished.

2

The Economy of Siam in 1850

SIAM IN 1850 was an independent and virtually self-sufficient kingdom whose absolute monarchs had sedulously avoided much contact with the West for a century or more. Such an accessible region did not remain outside the developing world economy merely by accident. The flood of adventurers and explorers from Europe had not overlooked Siam. The Portuguese established some slight contact with Siam in the sixteenth century. During the seventeenth century Siam was brought much closer to the West, and the English, French, Dutch, and Portuguese set up trading posts in Siam. In the reign of King Narai (1657–88), the king's first minister was the fabulous and romantic Constantine Phaulkon, a Greek adventurer whose encouragements to France and French Catholicism ultimately provoked a rebellion at the court and his own execution by the triumphant rebels.

After the demise of the unfortunate Phaulkon, the new dynasty turned against the West, and not until the middle of the nineteenth century did Siam have any important contact with Western nations. From 1688 to about 1850, the kings of Siam deliberately discouraged commercial and diplomatic contacts with the West.

One of the remarkable features of Siamese history is that the weak and tiny kingdom was allowed virtually to close its borders against the West during the heat of the scramble for colonies. Some parallels between Japan and Siam are that both had their first Western contacts with Portugal, both entered into closer relations with the Dutch in the seventeenth century, both excluded Westerners and lived in virtual isolation from the seventeenth to the nineteenth century, and both were "opened to the West" at about the same time (1854 for Japan, 1855 for Siam). Yet Siam's isolation appears the more remarkable, since she was not an island, remote from the main shipping routes and centers of interest in Asia, as was Japan.

Whatever the secret of this success, it is true that Siam, unlike Japan, came within Western influence largely because her new monarch desired this change. Somdetch Phra Paramendr Maha Mongkut, fourth in the Chakri dynasty, came to the throne at the age of forty-seven after having spent twenty-seven years as a Buddhist priest. He was a scholar of ability, and he was convinced that his country would benefit from cultural and commercial contact with the West. His reign began in 1851, and in 1855 the treaty between Siam and Britain was negotiated by Sir John Bowring. The importance of this treaty in Siam's future development can hardly be exaggerated. Its terms were substantially unchanged for seventy years.

But before we begin to examine the changes which occurred, we need to look briefly at the economy of Siam in 1850 before the changes began.

SOCIAL AND ECONOMIC ORGANIZATION

Siam is a part of monsoon Asia. Her boundaries lie entirely within the tropics. The bulk of the country forms a wedge between Indochina and Burma, to which is attached a long slim peninsula ending at the Malayan border. The area of the country today is approximately 200,000 square miles, about the same as the area of France. All of the present area, and more besides, was part of the Siam of 1850, although it is not clear just what were the boundaries of the kingdom ruled by Mongkut. Since 1850, France and Britain have taken nearly 100,000 square miles of territory which was then more or less recognized as part of Siam.

Population

The population estimates by many travelers about 1850 vary widely. Bowring thought 4.5–5.0 million was a good guess, with no population growth for some time.[1] Pallegoix's estimate was 6 million, of which he said 1.5 million were Chinese.[2] It is not known when the Chinese immigration began in strength, but estimates in the seventeenth century put the number of Chinese in Siam at about 4,000–5,000.[3] By 1850 immigrants were coming in at the rate of 15,000 per year.[4]

We need not try to come to any exact conclusion about the population in 1850; a rough indication is sufficient for our purposes here. The population in 1911, according to the revised figures of the first census, was 8.3 million,[5] and there is no evidence of a *decline* in population from 1850 to 1911. Instead, it is likely that the population was slowly growing over this period, and we should not be very far off to take 5 or 6 million as the population in 1850. This would indicate a population density in 1850 of 25–30 per square mile. Thus, Siam in 1850 was rather sparsely populated. Considering the type and tech-

---

[1] Sir John Bowring, *The Kingdom and People of Siam* (London, 1857), I, 81–83. Other, more gullible travelers estimated population as high as 38 million. See Archibald R. Colquhoun, *Amongst the Shans* (New York, 1885), pp. 168–73.

[2] Mgr. Pallegoix, *Description du Royaume Thai ou Siam* (Paris, 1854), I, 7–8.

[3] John Crawfurd, *Journal of an Embassy to the Courts of Siam and Cochin-China* (London, 1828), pp. 450–53.

[4] H. G. Quaritch Wales, *Ancient Siamese Government and Administration* (London, 1934), p. 68. Original source of this estimate appears to have been D. E. Malloch, *Siam, Some General Remarks on Its Productions* (Calcutta, 1852), p. 6, who gives it as the estimate of a correspondent in Bangkok.

[5] Thailand, Department of Commerce and Statistics, *Statistical Year Book of Siam, 1936/37* (Bangkok, 1939), XIX, 48.

nique of agriculture employed, there was room for a large increase in the farming population.

Agricultural Production

The working population appears to have been almost wholly engaged in agriculture, and rice was the principal crop then as now. Rice was grown in river valleys which were flooded each year with a fair degree of regularity. Man-made irrigation was practiced mainly in the North, where the slope of the land was greater, or where the natural flood did not remain for a long enough period. Here the farmers developed ingenious co-operative systems for irrigating their fields, while in the Central Plain, where irrigation could have and later did extend rice cultivation over large and fertile areas, the inhabitants were content with the yearly inundation brought by the rains. At any rate they did not develop artificial means for controlling the water supply, although a number of canals had been dug which served to distribute the water, and some farmers made use of various devices to move water onto the fields from these canals.

Rice was the principal crop in the middle of the nineteenth century, but we have no statistics of the total area under cultivation, nor of the total annual output. The average area in paddy in 1925-29 was 18.1 million rai; the annual average yield of paddy in this period was 72.5 million piculs; and the average population was 11.0 million.[6] The average yield of paddy was thus 4.0 piculs per rai, and the area cultivated was 1.6 rai per capita. There has been little or no change in the technique of rice cultivation, so that we may provisionally assume that the yield per rai was the same in 1850 as in the base period 1925-29. If the area in rice per capita were also the same, the 6 million population would have cultivated 9.6 million rai. But in the 1925-29 period 40 percent of the crop was exported,[7] while in 1850 rice exports were quite small, as we shall see below. If we deduct 40 percent from the figure of 9.6 million rai, we obtain the figure 5.8 million rai as an estimate of total area in rice cultivation in 1850, an area which would yield 23.2 million piculs of paddy at the 1925-29 rate of yield.

This estimate may not be too far wrong. Available evidence since 1900 suggests that the yield per rai has fallen, however, and the estimate of production in 1850 may be low on that account. On the other hand, if yields were high in 1850 the population might have cultivated less land per capita, in which case the production estimate might be approximately correct but the acreage estimate too high.

An estimate of the total rice output could also be made from the demand

---

[6] *Statistical Year Book, 1936/37,* XIX, 417.

[7] Approximately 44 percent of *rice* was exported, but we use 40 percent here to allow for domestic utilization of husks, etc. Export figures are of clean rice (mostly), while our total output figures are of "paddy," i.e., unmilled rice.

side. Rice has been and still is the staple diet of the Siamese. It is quite likely that the rice produced in 1850 was—barring floods and droughts—sufficient to furnish the Siamese with about all the rice they needed.[8] The annual per capita consumption of rice has been estimated at 2.4 piculs, which in terms of paddy would be 3.4 piculs.[9] For a population of 6 million, total annual consumption would thus be 20.4 million piculs of paddy, compared with our above estimate of production of 23.2 million. It is possible that rice consumption per capita may have been larger in 1850 than it is today, but this is not known.

These computations may suffice to indicate the order of magnitude of rice production in 1850, but they are meant to yield only very rough approximations which can be used to show the later increase in production.

Fortunately, we do not have to rely entirely on such estimates to get an idea of the importance of rice in 1850. We may also look at the opinions of contemporary observers. Bacon says that in 1856 (the year before he arrived), "there was rice enough in Siam . . . to feed the native population and to supply the failure of the rice crop in Southern China. . . ."[10] Bowring quotes a missionary, one Grandjean, as saying that in the northern part of Siam cultivation was almost entirely limited to rice.[11] Bowring himself stressed the point that Siam had the capacity greatly to expand the cultivation and export of rice. Pallegoix, and later Van der Heide, also observed that rice had been the principal food of the Siamese ever since they became a sedentary people.[12] We may safely conclude that rice has long played an important role in the daily life of the Siamese. Indeed, the overwhelming importance of rice is unlikely to be questioned for any country of eastern Asia.

Information on the relative importance of other crops is more difficult to obtain. Compared to rice, of course, they were and are minor. Today, for example, some 95 percent of cultivated land in Siam is devoted to rice. Other crops may, however, have accounted for *more* than 5 percent of total cultivated land in 1850. The trend over the past century has been toward greater specialization in rice as well as toward a larger absolute area planted in rice. The peasant in 1850 grew only a little more rice than his family needed, and at the same time he was more self-sufficient. That is, in most cases he grew his own

---

[8] "Rice being the staple diet of the people, the Siamese freeman seems always to have possessed the right to demand from the state, under certain easily fulfilled conditions, as much rice land as he and his family could cultivate . . . ; and, until in modern times rice came to be grown for export, agricultural labors seem to have weighed but lightly on the people, for, as the Siamese proverb puts it, 'satiated kine stop grazing.' " Wales, *op. cit.*, p. 6.

[9] One picul of paddy equals about 0.7 picul of rice. The above estimate of consumption is found in Thailand, Ministry of Agriculture, National FAO Committee, *Thailand and Her Agricultural Problems* (rev. ed.; Bangkok, 1950), pp. 118–19.

[10] George B. Bacon, *Siam, Land of the White Elephant* (New York, 1892), p. 84.

[11] Bowring, *op. cit.*, II, 14.

[12] J. H. Van der Heide, "The Economical Development of Siam During the Last Half Century," *Journal of the Siam Society*, III (1906), 74–75; Pallegoix, *op. cit.*, I, 122.

tobacco, silk, cotton, sugar cane, fruit, betel nuts, coconuts, etc. There was some trade, to be sure, and every peasant did not supply all his requirements of all commodities, but in general it is valid to say that families, villages, and regions were more self-sufficient than they were to be in seventy-five years. Certainly the nation was.

Some crops declined in importance after 1850. The sugar plantations of Siam greatly impressed Bowring—so much so that he made his famous and faulty forecast that sugar would become Siam's major export.[13] He also stated that sugar was produced almost everywhere in the kingdom, and that Pallegoix had counted thirty factories, each employing 200–300 men. The sugar industry soon thereafter went into a decline; indeed it went into an eclipse, from which it is only now emerging.

Some indication of the importance of products other than rice may be obtained from Pallegoix's estimate of revenues of the king.[14] Ricelands were the source of only 2,000,000 baht, while "gardens" were taxed to the extent of 5,545,000 baht, and other agricultural crops (not including timber) accounted for approximately 1,800,000 baht. While this is not at all conclusive, since the government may have taxed the staple food relatively little, it does indicate that other crops were of substantial importance.

The production of textile fibers had to be considerable in 1850 to clothe the population even as skimpily as it was clothed. That the production of textiles was inadequate is quite likely, but some quantity of fibers appears to have been available to the people generally, to be worked up in households and in village industries.[15] Siam even used to export cotton in small quantities before 1855. One estimate (for about 1850) gives raw cotton exports of 450,000 baht, and cotton cushions and mattresses of 211,500 baht—together over 10 percent of total exports.[16]

Although the dress of the people was simple, their garments were not designed to use cloth sparingly. The principal garment for both men and women was the *phanung*, made by wrapping and folding a rectangular length of cloth about the waist and between the legs. It usually extended from the waist to the knees. The size varied of course, but a considerable amount of cloth was ordinarily used to fold and tie the phanung properly (the cloth used was 4–6 meters long and about one meter wide). In addition, women usually wore a jacket or scarf of some kind as a bodice. The women in some regions wore

[13] Bowring, *op. cit.*, I, 203–4.

[14] Pallegoix, *op. cit.*, I, 309–11. This revenue estimate, along with others for that period, is too much of a guess to be taken very seriously.

[15] "There certainly was a time, before the birth of foreign trade, when the inhabitants of Siam not only spun and wove all the cloth they used for their garments but also produced the raw material from which the cloth was made. Such material was chiefly cotton, and each community probably grew enough of it to supply its own easily satisfied requirements." W. A. Graham, *Siam* (3d ed.; London, 1924), II, 28–29.

[16] Malloch, *op. cit.*, pp. 34–51.

the *pasin,* a kind of skirt, instead of the phanung. Clothes were of both cotton and silk, and they were very durable.

Pepper has been a well-known product of Siam ever since the first Western contact with that country in the sixteenth century. The total acreage has never been very large, however, even though the high value per unit of weight made it an important product for trade. Total area has probably never exceeded 40,000 rai, but the area in 1850 cannot be estimated with any accuracy.

Graham says Siam used to supply its own requirements of tobacco, with perhaps a little left over for export, but that the Siamese came to prefer foreign tobaccos after 1850.[17] As we shall see, the local industry was later revived.

A wide variety of vegetables, fruits, and spices is grown in Siam, and nearly every villager has a garden. Although we cannot make quantitative estimates, it is probable that such gardens were also common in 1850, and that they were relatively more important at that time.

Considering all these things, it appears that the percentage of cultivated land used for crops other than rice probably was larger than 5 percent in 1850.

Techniques.—Agricultural techniques in the Siam of 1850 were quite primitive, as they still are. Except in the North, irrigation was not used. The peasant relied on the seasonal rains to flood the fields and thus provide water to nourish the grain. Some distribution canals were in use in 1850, but they could not change the supply of water furnished to the fields by rains and flood. Modern irrigation, in the sense of control over the amount of water supplied to the fields, did not exist.

Two major methods of planting rice have long been used in Siam, as well as in other parts of Asia. The first requires much labor but is the more productive. The rice is planted in a nursery plot and allowed to grow there while the fields are being plowed, harrowed, and flooded by rains or by water admitted through the terraces around each plot. As each field is prepared, the seedlings are transplanted to it by hand. In the second method the fields are prepared as before, but the grain is sown broadcast directly onto the field. This method uses less labor, but the yield per rai is smaller and more seed is required.

Little work is needed between planting and harvesting. Terraces have to be inspected now and then, granaries must be prepared, and as the grain ripens the birds must be kept away, but the cultivation itself is finished. The fate of the crop rests with the water supply.

In the harvest season the whole family is found in the fields. Reaping is done by hand with knives and sickles. The plants are cut and bound into sheaves, and then threshed, either by hand or with the aid of buffaloes.

The tools employed in rice cultivation are extremely simple. The plow is little more than a pointed stick, although it may be tipped with iron. The harrow is also of wood. Other tools include a hoe and a knife or sickle for reaping. Graham says that with some reaping tools "each individual straw

[17] Graham, *op. cit.,* II, 24–25.

is pressed separately against its cutting edge by the thumb of the operator and so cut through,"[18] but in most of the country a small sickle, capable of cutting several stalks at one stroke, is used.

The water buffalo, which works well in flooded fields, is the principal draft animal used for rice cultivation all over Siam. In regions outside the Central Plain, bullocks are used to pull the sturdy two-wheeled carts. These carts are not often found in the Central Plain because the network of canals and streams requires the use of water transportation.

As a part of the method of production, we should mention the custom of communal planting and harvesting. A single farmer often asked his neighbors to help in these activities, and the event became a community outing, with the host providing refreshments for his volunteer force. Such a system was possible because planting and harvesting dates varied for different varieties of rice and for different localities. When each farmer planted only as much paddy as his family required, no one was likely to be abused by this system. Later, when production for sale increased, the system had less to commend it and its use declined.

Rice was also grown by hill tribes who practiced what is known as "shifting" or "fire-field" cultivation. Under this system a section of forest was cut down, allowed to dry, and burned just before the rainy season. Rice was then planted in the burned-over field for two or three years, or until yields diminished, after which the cultivators would move on to another place. It is doubtful that this form of agriculture was quantitatively significant in 1850. It is still practiced in some regions and is a source of concern to the conservation officers of the Forestry Department, but agriculture officials informally estimate that the area so cultivated is very small in relation to total riceland.*

Land tenure.[19]—Though all land was the property of the king, custom and tradition of several centuries had given the so-called freeman the right to take as much land as he and his family could cultivate, an amount which usually did not exceed 25 rai. Various regulations established procedures he must follow, and some of these (such as having documents drawn up and notices proclaimed) cost him money, but his basic right was not challenged. The freeman could take possession of uncultivated land as long as he went about it properly. In all parts of the country there was an abundance of unused land which needed only to be cleared and cultivated.

Once he had fulfilled requirements, the applicant had full rights over the land, although in theory his right remained that of a usufructuary. Nevertheless, the freeman could sell or mortgage his land. The king could take it back for public purposes, or if it went uncultivated for three years.

---

[18] Graham, *op. cit.*, II, 16.

* This statement, written in 1952, is still valid, but shifting cultivation by hill tribes in highland areas is regarded as a serious problem in 1970.

[19] The following sketch of land tenure and social organization is based chiefly on Wales, *op. cit.*, Chs. 3 and 5, and Graham, *op. cit.*, I, 229–49. See also Virginia M. Thompson, *Thailand, the New Siam*, Ch. 19.

All people were chattels of the king, and the freeman was obliged to per-form personal services for him during a specified period of time, as well as to turn over a part of his produce.[20] In practice, by 1850 the freeman generally fulfilled these obligations to his patron, who received them in the king's name. The patron frequently would be called on to supply numbers of men for a period of time on public works, but a large part of the personal service un-doubtedly was performed to the patron's private advantage.[21] The same applies to produce.

The relation between the patron and freeman was personal, not territorial. This was an essential part of the feudal system of Siam after the fifteenth cen-tury. Every freeman had to have a patron to whom he was obligated for produce and services, but the freeman could choose his own patron and could move from place to place. In return, the patron had the duty of protecting his clients (as in matters of justice) and of lending them money when they needed it. If he did not do the latter, they might sell themselves into slavery, in which case the patron lost their services completely.

Slavery was widespread in the Siam of 1850. Estimates of the number of slaves vary greatly because the line between slavery and forms of debt bondage was extremely hazy. Commenting on the description of slavery in Bowring, Lasker says:

> The account is interesting in that it points to the diversity of forms of slavery as outcomes of different social and historical origins. The range of causes of enslave-ment includes at one extreme a self-submission little different from a voluntary contracting out of labor and, at the other, but much more rare, a harsh traffic in human beings treated impersonally as investments.
>
> From the middle of the 17th to the beginning of the 19th century Siamese legis-lation on the subject of slavery was for the purpose of its regulation and humaniza-tion rather than its abolition.[22]

There was an organized slave market with fixed prices. Slaves fell into two chief categories, redeemable and nonredeemable. Slaves who had sold them-selves, or who had been sold for less than their full value, could regain freedom at any time merely by repaying to their masters the sum the latter had paid. Slaves who had been sold outright for full value were not redeemable.[23] The redeemable slaves were not exempt from the *corvée*, although their masters

---

[20] Wales, *op. cit.*, p. 45. Graham, however, says the population was divided into Lake Sui (those who had to turn over produce) and Prai (those who were subject to *corvée*). Graham, *op. cit.*, I, 235–36.

[21] The patron had a right to the services of 10–20 percent of his clients, as a sort of commis-sion for supervising the remainder. See Prinz Dilock von Siam, *Die Landwirtschaft in Siam* (Tübingen, 1907), p. 45.

[22] Bruno Lasker, *Human Bondage in Southeast Asia* (Chapel Hill, 1950), p. 58.

[23] Graham, however, says that any debt slave was redeemable, and that he could change mas-ters merely by persuading someone to pay the old master the amount of the debt. Graham, *op. cit.*, I, 237.

sometimes paid this obligation in money in order to have full use of the slaves. Nonredeemable slaves were not subject to the *corvée*.

Between the king and the mass of the people were the nobles and officials who administered the country. When feudalism was put on a personal basis, these classes were broken away from their territorial holdings to become patrons of the freemen choosing them and to become functional administrators. By thus preventing the growth of semiautonomous territorial units within the kingdom, the power of the king was strengthened and that of the feudal nobles weakened.[24]

The titles of nobles in Siam were not permanent. Even the descendants of the king became commoners after the fifth generation, because the title dropped one rank with each succeeding generation and there were five ranks. There was thus little danger of a challenge to the king from entrenched nobles. The danger was further reduced because nobles often sent their most attractive daughters to be wives of the king. These wives became both agents of their families and hostages ensuring good behavior.

Even after the feudalism of Siam changed from a territorial basis, the nobles and princes sometimes held extensive areas of land which they cultivated with slaves and with their share of the services rendered to them by freemen. The land might either be purchased or received as a gift from the king. Nobles could acquire large tracts by claiming the right to take as much unused land as they could cultivate, and by counting their retainers as part of their families for this purpose. For several centuries prior to the reign of King Rama V it was the custom for the king to make grants of land to officials, nobles, and other persons. Grants of land varied according to a system of ranks known as the Sakdi Na grades, which ranged from 25 rai (commoners) to 10,000 rai (Chao Phya's of highest grade).[25] Many large holdings of land undoubtedly came into existence through this system. It was discarded by King Rama V, although the system of ranks was retained.

Because people living in the outer provinces could not conveniently be called to perform personal services, they gradually began to send produce instead. This practice was extended as the king found himself unable to utilize so much labor efficiently. The produce thus acquired became the basis of the king's trade with foreigners, and the fact that he received these payments in kind may account in part for his desire to monopolize foreign trade. This basis disappeared as money came to be substituted for produce, while at the same time the feudal structure was weakened as it became primarily a tax-

[24] The accuracy of this description varies for different regions of the country. In the dependent Laos and Malay states of the North and South, the power of the local chiefs or princes remained much greater than in Siam proper. Furthermore, their power prevailed over fairly cohesive territorial units. Indeed, it was not until the early twentieth century that the Laos states became firmly governed from Bangkok, while by 1909 some of the dependent states on the South and East were lost to England and France respectively.

[25] W. A. R. Wood, *A History of Siam* (London, 1926), p. 85.

collecting organization. The commutation of feudal obligations had gone quite far by 1850 and this, together with the changed organization and the practice of calling nobles to Bangkok to live near the court, had succeeded in weakening the feudality so much that it constituted no danger to the crown.

Rent paid in contract for the *use* of land does not appear to have been important in the Siam of 1850. A landowner could not demand such contractual rents because unclaimed land was free for the taking. The payments made by the peasant were based on his subjection to the king—a matter of status and not of contract. The payments differed from rent also in that the cultivators of more fertile lands do not appear to have had heavier obligations. If a percentage of the produce was taken they paid more, but the obligation for personal services was not adjusted to the quality of the land held.

Some writers have asserted that because land was so abundant it could have no exchange value, and because it had no value no rent could be charged. Therefore, they say, some other system had to be devised whereby a part of the produce could be appropriated by the ruling class.[26] Whatever the merit of this hypothesis, it is true that contractual rents were not important in Siam before 1850.

A portion of his produce was, however, sometimes taken from the cultivator as an interest charge on money borrowed in a year of poor harvest, or perhaps for ceremonial consumption, as for cremations or weddings. Interest rates were high (30 percent and up),[27] and often the peasant either sold his children to pay his debt or was himself made over to his creditor as a debt slave. Lasker says that insolvency was the reason for most slavery in Siam.[28]

We have little or no evidence on the average size of farms in 1850. The upper limit of 25 rai for the ordinary peasant seems to be generally accepted, as does the existence of many large estates ranging up to 10,000 rai. We cannot be certain, however, that the peasants in general did exercise their right to cultivate 25 rai. It seems likely that many may not have wanted to work so much land, either because they preferred leisure or because they had no opportunity to exchange the added produce for goods they wished to have. The reports of contemporary writers suggest an average holding of considerably less than 25 rai.

In summary, the social organization of agricultural production, extremely complex in details, seems in its broad outlines to be quite simple. The great mass of peasants held their land from the king and, although they had virtually full rights of ownership, they had to supply a portion of their produce and their time to the king. These payments were collected in the name of the king by officials and nobles, each of whom collected from those peasants who

---

[26] Van der Heide, *op. cit.*, pp. 3–4. Also Virginia M. Thompson, *Labor Problems in Southeast Asia* (New Haven, 1947), pp. 214–20.

[27] Bowring, *op. cit.*, I, 188, puts the average at 3 percent per month.

[28] Lasker, *op. cit.*, pp. 57, 150–54.

had chosen him as patron. An unknown fraction of the payments of produce and services ultimately reached the king, or was applied to his projects. In addition to this structure, a large number of slaves of different grades cultivated the land of their masters or otherwise served them.

Other Industries (Besides Agriculture)

Compared with agriculture the other industries in the Siam of 1850 were minor. These early beginnings may be important for our purposes, however, because they contain the roots of modern industries.

Fishing.—The people of Siam traditionally have had two basic foods: rice and fish. The fish they procured both from the sea and from inland streams, ponds, and lakes with the aid of an immense variety of ingenious nets, traps, and other devices. Many travelers have described this equipment, which ranges from simple contrivances fashioned by one man in a few minutes to huge permanent traps erected at a cost of several thousand baht.[29]

No estimates of the volume or value of the total catch can be made for this early period, yet it is clear that fish formed an important source of protein in the Siamese diet. Fish were dried and preserved and were thus available throughout the year, and practically every Siamese is said to have eaten some fish every day.

Siam has long exported dried fish to China and other near-by places. The exports were chiefly the product of sea fishing that went on along the Gulf of Siam. A boating enthusiast, H. Warington Smyth sprinkled his two-volume work with frequent references to the excellent workmanship and design of Siamese boats in general and of fishing boats in particular. It is probable that sea fishing was the full-time occupation of a considerable number of people along the Gulf of Siam, and that practically the entire inland population devoted a part of its time to fishing.

Forestry.—Little is known of the forestry industry in 1850. The teak industry had not developed for export at that date, although the native population made much use of teak for the construction of houses, temples, bridges, boats, etc.[30] The teak industry was largely in the hands of Chinese operators who paid Laos princes for the right to work the forests. Logs were sawed by hand into planks in Chinese sheds.

The early traders were interested in woods of a higher unit value, such as sapanwood, and this trade was of minor importance. There was little domestic trade in the forest products. Most people could satisfy their own needs from the near-by jungle with little trouble, and public requirements were probably met largely with *corvée* labor in the forests. Thus, while forest products played an important part in the life of the people, they did not form the source of

[29] H. Warington Smyth, *Five Years in Siam* (New York, 1898), I, 87–89.

[30] Crawfurd, *Embassy to Siam*, p. 427.

much money income or full-time employment in the Siam of 1850, except possibly for internal trade in teak.

Mining.—The most important mining activity in Siam has long been the mining of tin. The Chinese were attracted to the tin mines of Southern Siam many centuries ago and, until the Europeans appeared, they had the field to themselves.[31] They performed the entire mining operation, furnishing labor, capital, and management, and in addition operating their own smelters.

In the seventeenth century some Europeans got involved in tin mining, but in 1850 the Chinese still dominated the industry. The Siamese had shown little or no interest in it, while the government had been content with a tax on the output of the mines.

Crawfurd thought iron ore must have been abundant in Siam because iron was so cheap in Bangkok. Whether ore was abundant or not, several mines were being worked at the time of his visit, although the total output was probably small. This industry was also in the hands of the Chinese. Crawfurd wrote:

> At present [1821], a considerable quantity of malleable iron is produced, and at Bangkok there are several extensive manufactories of cast-iron vessels, wholly conducted by the Chinese.[32]

Salt was produced on the Gulf of Siam and in the Korat Plateau, and then shipped into Northern Siam and abroad. Its high value per unit of weight made it an ideal commodity for the trade of the time.

Handicrafts and manufacturing. — Outside of the categories discussed above, most production in Siam can be classified under the general heading of "handicrafts." These handicrafts were partly pursued by specialists who devoted their full time to their crafts, but by far the most important part of such production was carried on as a part-time activity, or "household industry." Because of the self-sufficient nature of the economy, these handicrafts were an important part of the economic life of the nation.

Full-time specialization existed chiefly in the households of wealthy nobles, where artisans were employed to produce the luxuries desired by their masters. Artisans were retained in such skills as metalwork, lacquer gilding and inlaying, gold- and silversmithing, and jewelry.

These artisans were not entirely free. An element of compulsion was involved, and once a man showed talent in a craft he might be compelled to become a specialist in the lord's household.[33] Compulsion might be introduced through the *corvée*—perhaps by calling a man for his term of service in the planting and harvesting seasons and thus forcing him to labor for his rice.

---

[31] Thailand, Ministry of Commerce and Communications, *Siam, Nature and Industry* (Bangkok, 1930), pp. 107–8.

[32] Crawfurd, *op. cit.*, p. 323.

[33] *Ibid.*, p. 322.

Once a man became an artisan, moreover, his sons were also required to acquire and practice his craft, and this hereditary obligation, together with forced service, is thought by some to have stifled initiative and creative impulse in the craftsman, and to have undermined his self-respect.[34] Lasker also thinks the hereditary bondage may have accounted for the Chinese usurpation of the skilled crafts from the Siamese.[35] The skilled crafts were thus degraded in the eyes of the people.

Yet in spite of the social stigma involved, there were quite a few craftsmen in the Siam of 1850, although many of them were already Chinese. King Mongkut boasted that he hired 600 goldsmiths to work on his brother's tomb, and Bowring said that glass manufacturers were numerous and gold beaters abundant, and he praised the ingenuity of copper and iron founders.[36] Graham says that one type of porcelain developed in Siam was a blend of Siamese and Chinese design and skill, and that it was even shipped to China. This porcelain, said to be of a high order of artistic merit, later disappeared so completely that there was "scarcely a piece of later date than 1870 A.D."[37] Skilled craftsmen along the Chao Phya River built the great junks of the China trade, as well as smaller vessels.[38]

Important as they were, these full-time crafts probably were relatively minor when compared with the part-time activities carried on in nearly every household and village. Through such household industries the mass of the people secured almost all that they had of material things.[39] The women performed most of the part-time skills. They spun and wove the cloth and made it into garments. Even around Bangkok a great deal of clothing was spun and woven by the women. According to Crawfurd, "the manufacture of silk and cotton fabric is . . . abandoned wholly to the women, and very little skill is displayed in either."[40]

Women also dyed cloth, made the crude pottery used in households, made hats and paper, and did a great deal of basket and lacquer work. Silkworms were grown chiefly in the North and Northeast, but silk weaving was an occupation of women everywhere, including even the wives of nobility.

Quantitative data on the volume of products produced by the handicraft

[34] Lasker, *op. cit.*, p. 284; Thompson, *Thailand, the New Siam*, p. 600.

[35] Lasker, *op. cit.*, p. 103.

[36] Bowring, *Siam*, I, 237–40.

[37] Graham, *Siam*, II, 171–72.

[38] F. A. Neale, *Narrative of a Residence in Siam* (London, 1852), pp. 42–45. We have already mentioned the admiration H. W. Smyth had for Siamese boatbuilders. See also Smyth, *op. cit.*, I, 92–94.

[39] This view is held by a number of writers. To give only one example, Mom Luang Dej Snidvongs, *Die Entwicklung des siamesischen Aussenhandels* (Bern, 1926), p. 90, says that before the 1855 treaty the clothing needs of the country were largely filled by the home industries, and that these industries were even capable of exporting considerable quantities of textiles to Burma and Annam.

[40] Crawfurd, *Journal of an Embassy to the Courts of Siam and Cochin-China*, p. 323.

industries cannot be obtained. These products must have represented an important part of the standard of living of the mass of the Siamese, however. Most of the people grew their own rice, fruit, and vegetables, caught and preserved their own fish, made their own clothes, and constructed their own houses. There was some trade through barter and some money exchange, of course, but the production was largely in household industries and handicrafts. Furthermore, it seems that no entrepreneurs had appeared to finance and supervise the production of goods in the household industries. Each household made its own decisions, by and large, and most of them probably chose large amounts of leisure in preference to added output. Undoubtedly there was much seasonal unemployment or underemployment. Rice cultivation took only five to eight months of the year, depending on the type of rice, and even during the rice season there were many days when the farmer was not kept busy—e.g., between transplanting and harvesting.

Farmers and their families worked just long enough to supply themselves with the necessities of life, and custom, habit, and climate kept the requirements at a modest level.

Internal Trade

Most of the internal trade of Siam in 1850 was probably carried on through barter entirely within the villages. The movement of goods between villages and between regions must have been relatively small. Inadequate and costly transportation would partially account for this, although a more important reason may have been that every region could easily produce the basic items entering into the standard of living. On the main rivers and in the Central Plain, trade was probably brisker because of the better transportation by water.

By 1850 the Chinese seem to have gained almost complete control of the interregional trade of Siam.[41] They carried goods into the regions accessible by water transportation and, to a lesser extent, even into the remote interior villages, exchanging them there for money or for the produce of the people. Among the Siamese the women were the traders. They carried their products to the market and bargained with itinerant Chinese traders.

In 1850, as in later years, the Siamese seem to have made little effort to compete with the Chinese. Nor did Western traders give the Chinese much competition. The traders who went into the interior usually operated on such a small scale, and had to do so much haggling and bargaining over each transaction, that Westerners simply did not wish to compete. Furthermore, the Chinese were allowed to move around freely in the country, while the government tended to regulate the activities of Western traders much more closely, even to the point of prohibiting them from going outside the limits of Bangkok. Graham says that in the years before 1850, "the Chinese traders, having

41 Bowring, *The Kingdom and People of Siam*, I, 85–88.

no treaty, were bound by no obligations, and secured all the privilege they wanted by the simple process of buying every official who had anything to do with the matter."[42]

The Chinese also had an advantage in that most transactions were on a barter basis. The native produce acquired through such barter was brought to Bangkok and either sold there or exported. To the extent that the goods were exported, the Chinese advantage lay in the greater number and frequency of calls made by the Chinese junks which plied between China and Southeast Asia.[43] The close connections between Chinese traders and officials of the court also gave the former an advantage in disposing of their goods in Bangkok.

Another important reason for the supremacy of the Chinese is found in the government practice of granting monopolies in the trade of certain items. When the monopolies were granted to Chinese, as they usually were, the monopolists could make arrangements with each other for sharing and cooperating in the trade of different regions. Outsiders would find it extremely difficult to break into such friendly arrangements.

Before the monopolies were sold to the Chinese, it appears that they were *royal* monopolies. The king reserved to himself the right to trade in certain items. Usually this applied to the import and export trade in these items. It was during the reign of King Rama III (1824–51) that the royal monopolies began to be sold to Chinese traders, and the practice of farming out taxes to individuals—also Chinese—became important.[44] Neither arrangement served to encourage the Siamese people to engage in trade.

Native produce was thus exchanged for the goods of other regions and other nations through the medium of the traders. This flow of goods based on interchange was, however, probably exceeded in importance by the one-way flow of goods from the interior to Bangkok in payment of taxes. Although taxes were increasingly converted into money, in 1850 many taxes were still being collected in kind. When taxes were farmed out to Chinese monopolists, the trader may also have been the tax collector. Whether he took the tax in produce or first bought the produce and then took the money, the end result was the same. Goods flowed from the interior to Bangkok, where they were used to maintain the court. The taxpaying provinces of the interior did not receive much in return for the taxes paid, unless we count the general protection afforded through the maintenance of order and the defense against foreigners. When public works in the provinces were deemed necessary, labor and materials were furnished by the people through *corvée* and requisition.

[42] Graham, *Siam*, II, 96–97.

[43] Of 332 vessels which arrived in Bangkok in 1850, only four were English and American, according to O. Frankfurter, "King Mongkut," *Journal of the Siam Society*, I (1904), 197. Most of these vessels must have been Chinese junks.

[44] Wales, *Ancient Siamese Government and Administration*, pp. 204–8.

This one-way movement of goods to Bangkok is not exactly "trade," but it represented an important part of the interregional economic activity in the Siam of 1850. The villages were virtually self-sufficient centers of production which, under the existing institutional arrangements, were required to send a portion of their produce to maintain the court and the city of Bangkok. This necessity of supplying Bangkok must have represented a sizable drain on the countryside. The population of Bangkok was 8 to 10 percent of the total, and nearly all the surplus produced in Siam probably went to maintain this unproductive segment of the population. On the other hand, the lavish court may have been essential to the preservation of law and order all over the kingdom.

FOREIGN TRADE

In 1850 the foreign trade of Siam was carried on primarily with neighboring Asian countries. European trade was a relatively small part of the total. After a period of rather close contact in the seventeenth century, relations with the West were almost completely broken off until the beginning of the nineteenth century. Trade with other countries did not cease, however. From 1700 to 1850 Siam was carrying on a brisk trade with China and her neighbors in Southeast Asia.

In our attempt to describe the conduct and composition of trade in 1850, we will make use of any available information concerning trade *prior* to 1850. We do not hope to give a precise estimate of trade in a given year. Instead, our object is merely to obtain a general idea of Siam's capacity to export, of imports available to her, and of the conduct of trade before 1850.

Exports

Three generalizations appear to be possible concerning Siam's exports. They consisted largely of unprocessed natural products; they were chiefly items of high value per unit of weight; and they usually exceeded imports in value, the difference being made up by the import of treasure.

Perhaps the best estimate of exports in the middle of the nineteenth century is that given by D. E. Malloch, an official of the British East India Company, whose list of exports is given in Table I. Two important things about this table are the low figure for rice exports and the absence of teak exports. Otherwise, it is interesting to note that the list includes everything of importance which Siam exports *even today,* except for rubber. No important new exports have been added to the list, although the relative importance of some items has changed drastically.

We are especially interested in the volume of rice exports prior to 1855, a matter about which there is some controversy. Malloch gave the export of rice as only 200,000 piculs, but he noted that it could "be had in great abundance

TABLE I
Siam's Exports About 1850

Commodity	Baht	Commodity	Baht
Bark	110,000	Rice	150,000
Birds' nests	172,800	Pepper[a]	99,000
Cardamoms	124,000	Tobacco	100,000
Raw cotton	450,000	Tin and tin utensils	253,500
Cotton cushions and		Sticklac	254,000
mattresses	211,500	Sugar	708,000
Fish	213,500	Lard and fat	146,000
Iron and ironware	180,000	Sapanwood	350,000
Dried meat	120,500	Agilawood	100,000
Oil	101,000	Other items[b]	1,127,200
Hides, horns, and skins	503,000		
Ivory	80,000	Total exports	5,585,000
Gamboge	31,000	Total imports	4,331,000

[a] Malloch says the price of pepper was 12–20 baht per picul and that 61,500 piculs were exported. If these figures are correct, the value should be at least 700,000 baht instead of 99,000 as shown in the table.

[b] These "Other items" include a number of products, no single one of which was very large.

Source: D. E. Malloch, *Siam, Some General Remarks on Its Productions* (Calcutta, 1852).

cheaper than in any part of the world, and is exported in large quantities to China and the Malay coast, with the permission of the Government."[45]

The question of the volume of rice exports is confused by the tendency of many writers to conclude that, because rice exports increased after the Bowring Treaty in 1855, there must have been a prohibition on the export of rice before that date which, when removed, enabled the production and export of rice to increase. This view appears too simple. There is evidence that rice was exported in the first half of the nineteenth century and also in the seventeenth century, sometimes in considerable quantities. Records of the Dutch and British East India companies in the seventeenth century contain frequent references to shipments of rice from Siam. The Dutch appear to have imported Siamese rice to Java and Malacca, although they were constantly having difficulty with the capricious and suspicious Siamese kings. Messages to the home office report the arrival of ships from Siam laden with rice and sapanwood, and one such message (1654) complained that the king had forbidden the "usual measurers to measure any rice for the Company."[46] These early records indicate that the export of rice depended on the weather, the state of

45 Malloch, *Siam, Some General Remarks on Its Productions*, p. 7.

46 *Records of the Relations Between Siam and Foreign Countries in the 17th Century*, copies of papers preserved at the India Office, printed by order of the Council of the Vajiranana National Library (Bangkok, 1916), II, 9–18.

war or peace in Siam, and the temper of the king. There are frequent references to complete prohibitions on rice exports because Siam was at war or
because of drought or flood. Some of the dispatches hint that the king limited
the export of rice because he thought the Dutch in Java were dependent on
imports of rice, and that he hoped to extort a monopoly profit from them.

An agent of the British East India Company wrote to the home office in
1660 to urge that a trading center be established in Siam. In his list of "plentiful commodities" of Siam, rice was included.[47] A summary of Siam's trade
in 1679, supposedly written by George White, contains this interesting passage:

> The more vulgar commodities wherein all persons have liberty to trade are:
> iron, rice, Jaggarah, Timber, Salt, coconut oil, Cheroon, Raw hides.
>
> This country is the general granary for the adjacent parts, equalling if not ex-
> ceeding any part of the world in abundance of Rice, wherein the neighboring Ma-
> layan Coast is yearly supplied as far as Malaccah, and when it happens to be scarce
> and dear about Java, as it did anno 76–77, the Dutch and other transport several
> ships lading thither.[48]

The Emperor of China is said to have commanded the importation of
300,000 piculs of rice from Siam in 1722. Furthermore, by 1735 the rice trade
between China and Siam was well established, and in 1751 Chinese import-
ing over 2,000 piculs of rice from Siam were rewarded with a mandarin
button.[49]

Crawfurd did not give a specific quantitative estimate of rice exports, but
he obviously thought the volume was considerable. "Outside of Bengal," he
wrote, "Siam unquestionably exports more rice than any other country in
Asia." He was also impressed by the fertility of Siam's riceland and the de-
pendability of the rich harvests, and was led to make this statement:

> The conviction of this fact [certainty of yield] has produced a salutory influence
> even upon the jealous and arbitrary government of Siam, which, in opposition to
> the practice of other Asiatic states, generally permits the free exportation of rice, no
> doubt from a long habitual experience of the safety of this policy.[50]

Whatever the size of rice exports, the British were not participating in the
trade because the Burney Treaty of 1826 specifically forbade the British to
export rice. This prohibition appears to have been rather strictly enforced,
although Burney says he agreed to the article "when the Phra Klang assured
me that of course in seasons of plenty if British Merchants applied to export
grain, they should receive permission to do so."[51] Apparently the Siamese
did not interpret the treaty as Burney expected.

Throughout the literature on the subject of rice exports there are frequent

[47] Ibid., p. 28.   [48] Ibid., pp. 205–6.   [49] Bowring, op. cit., I, 77–78.
[50] Crawfurd, Embassy to Siam, pp. 420–21.
[51] The Burney Papers, printed by order of the Committee of the Vajiranana Library (Bangkok, 1910), I, 336.

references to regulations specifying that rice could not be exported unless a certain amount—usually three years' supply—was available in Siam. Wales says that "in the third reign [1824–51] export of rice had been prohibited unless there was a three years' supply of grain in the country."[52] Such a regulation could very easily have been abused by the king. If he forbade rice exports on this ground, no one could prove him wrong, and it is not unlikely that he may have used the regulation to stop exports whenever it suited him to do so. As a matter of fact, storage facilities in the tropical climate probably did not permit the keeping of a three years' supply anyway, and certainly there was no way to prove that such a supply did or did not exist.

The weight of evidence seems to justify the conclusion that rice was a common item of export in Siam before 1850, but that the volume of exports was erratic, depending as it did on conditions in Siam as well as on the nature of the foreign demand. Siam's foreign trade transactions, in rice as in other commodities, probably were the outcome of a complicated process of bargaining which had many of the attributes of bilateral monopoly. The Siamese government was the sole buyer and the sole seller of many products in Siam, and the king probably looked upon trade as an integral part of state policy. It is, therefore, not possible to give a single estimate of rice exports in the years preceding Bowring's treaty of 1855. All we can say is that if the harvest was a good one, if the king were willing, and if near-by countries had need of rice, Siam could probably have exported several hundred thousand piculs (perhaps as much as 1.0–1.5 million). Despite this lack of precision, the evidence seems adequate to refute the impression often given in the literature that rice exports were virtually nonexistent until 1855, after which they rose rapidly. To give only one example, we may quote Thompson:

> The export of rice was started almost a century ago [1850?] by Chinese millers, who were rapidly followed by European firms. . . .
> The accession of Mongkut . . . brought a radical change. Siam's resources, *even the export of rice,* were opened to foreign trade.[53]

There is substantial agreement on the other articles of trade, although reliable estimates of volume are not available. Table II gives the comparative lists of exports of different observers. The commodities exported do not appear to have changed a great deal over the period involved. The lists also support our earlier remark that Siam's exports were made up primarily of raw materials which received little or no processing before shipment.

Imports

Even in this early period Siam's imports consisted mainly of manufactured articles, and most were consumption goods. Information on the volume of

---

[52] Wales, *op. cit.*, p. 207.
[53] *Thailand, the New Siam*, pp. 361, 421. Italics supplied.

imports is even scarcer than for exports, but it seems clear that total commodity imports were smaller in value than total exports, the difference being made up by the import of treasure.

Seventeenth-century records of the East India companies are full of references to commodities which could be sold in Siam. The most frequently mentioned article is cotton textiles. These early records also indicate that gold and silver were shipped to Siam in payment for at least a part of the exports.

TABLE II

COMPARATIVE LISTS OF EXPORTS NAMED BY DIFFERENT OBSERVERS[a]

Commodity[b]	White (1679)	Crawfurd (1821)	Pallegoix (1850)	Malloch (1850)	Bowring[e] (1855)
Rice	x	x	x	x	x
Teak	x		x		x
Sugar	x	x	x	x	x
Coconut oil	x	x	x	x	
Sapanwood	x	x	x	x	
Salt	x	x	x	x	x
Pepper		x	x	x	x
Cardamoms		x	x	x	x
Sticklac		x	x	x	x
Iron	x	x	x	x	
Ivory	x	x	x	x	x
Gamboge		x	x	x	x
Hides and horns..	x	x	x	x	x
Benjamin			x	x	x
Dried fish		x	x	x	x
Rosewood		x	x	x	x
Agilawood	x	x	x	x	x
Areca nuts	x	x			x
Tin	x	x	x	x	
Cotton		x	x	x	x
Tobacco			x	x	x

[a] The lists are designed to show that there was a considerable amount of uniformity in Siamese exports over this period.

[b] None of the lists include *all* of the commodities listed by the different authors.

[e] The list given for Bowring refers to the export commodities specified in the treaty negotiated by Bowring.

Sources: White, in *Records of the Relations Between Siam and Foreign Countries in the 17th Century*, II, 204–6; Crawfurd, *Embassy to Siam*, pp. 405–15; Pallegoix, *Description du Royaume Thai ou Siam*, I, 327–28; Malloch, *Siam, Some General Remarks on Its Productions*, pp. 34–51; Bowring, *The Kingdom and People of Siam*, II, 224–26.

Bowring quotes Gutzlaff as saying that in the junk trade between Siam and China, Siam's principal imports "consist of various articles for the consumption of the Chinese, and a considerable amount of bullion."[54] Crawfurd describes Siam's trade with several different countries and regions, and from all of them came imports of cotton or silk textiles and of gold, silver, or copper. In one place, speaking of imports from China, he says:

The staple articles of import are coarse chinaware, coarse teas, and raw and wrought silks; but the imports do not equal the exports without including a quantity of Chinese silver in ingots.[55]

Neale describes the imports of Siam, and he too stresses the quantity of silks from China, and of "common cloths" from India and the Straits.[56] The *Bangkok Calendar* for 1847 reported that people were becoming more fond of European goods, and that principal imports were cotton piece goods, prints, muslins, red cloth, twists, silks, hardware, and crockery.

Perhaps the best estimate of the total trade of Siam is that of Malloch. He said exports were valued at 5,585,000 baht, imports at 4,331,000 baht. Part of the excess of exports was probably settled through the import of treasure.

Before we turn to the conduct of foreign trade, we should mention that Siam appears to have occupied the position of an entrepôt for the trade of the South China Sea. Goods were collected and shipped to Bangkok from the Malay Peninsula, India, Cambodia, Manila, and other near-by places, after which they were shipped out again to China and Japan. Similarly, goods from China and Japan were brought to Bangkok and then distributed to other countries. Several of the writers cited above have mentioned this role of Siam.[57] We can only conjecture about why and how Siam came to fill this role. The sailing range of the junks may have had something to do with it, and so might the attitude of the Chinese toward foreign trade. In any case, the picture of Bangkok as an entrepôt—even in a minor way—offers a startling contrast to her later passive role in foreign trade.

The Conduct of Foreign Trade

The exact nature of the organization of trade prior to 1850 is obscure, but broadly it appears that trade was monopolized either by the king and his court or by individuals to whom monopolies of specific commodities were sold. There is some evidence that the trend was away from the former and toward the latter form in the first half of the nineteenth century.

Seventeenth-century records describe the king of Siam as an absolute

[54] Bowring, *op. cit.*, I, 246–47.

[55] Crawfurd, *op. cit.*, p. 412.

[56] Neale, *A Residence in Siam*, p. 176.

[57] *Records of the Relations Between Siam and Foreign Countries*, II, 206–12; Crawfurd, *op. cit.*, pp. 413–15; Neale, *op. cit.*, Ch. 11.

monarch who absolutely controlled trade. Private traders were sometimes allowed to trade freely in certain "vulgar commodities" such as rice, hides, and timber, but most export products were "engrossed by the King and exposed to sale by his factors, all others being strictly prohibited the buying of them from other hands."[58] Import trade was similarly controlled by the king.

Visitors to Siam in the first half of the nineteenth century found that trade was still largely in the hands of the king. Finlayson asserted that in 1821 "the king and his ministers still continue to be the sole merchants, retaining in their own hands the monopoly of all articles of consequence, and holding it contraband for any others to intermeddle."[59]

When Bowring arrived in 1855, he found trade largely conducted through monopolies held by the king, nobles, and Chinese. This was true of both foreign and domestic trade. Pallegoix's account gives the impression that monopolies held by individuals were far more important than royal monopolies. This interpretation is accepted by Nunn, who asserts that farmed monopolies represented a stage in revenue collection in which "the government was at last reaching out for control and had definitely abandoned state trading."[60]

King Mongkut himself wrote a short description of the system of trade in the first four reigns of the Chakri dynasty.[61] He said that in the first and second reigns (1782–1824) the kings themselves engaged in trade and got most of their revenues from the profits of trade. Certain articles were monopolized by the king, while others were denied to traders until the king had as much as he wanted to buy. The kings built junks and exported produce to China, bringing back Chinese immigrants as passengers. During the second reign, possibly because of the decreased profit, the king gave more freedom to traders but established an inland tax. Thus began the shift from state trading to taxation as a source of revenue. At the beginning of the fourth reign (1851–68), state trading was abolished and more use was made of taxes, some of which were farmed to private tax monopolists.

One writer has expressed the unusual view that before 1855 Siam put no restrictions on foreigners, and that they enjoyed complete freedom in trading with and in Siam.[62] This author tries to show that there was no *need* for extraterritoriality, and that Western nations wanted it only as a means of securing special privilege. This may well be true, but it is difficult to accept the notion that Siam was a free-trade nation. Although the king had full

---

[58] *Records of the Relations Between Siam and Foreign Countries in the 17th Century*, II, 202.

[59] George Finlayson, *The Mission to Siam, and Hué, the Capital of Cochin-China, in the Years 1821-2* (London, 1826), p. 166. Crawfurd and Burney also support this description.

[60] W. Nunn, "Some Notes upon the Development of the Commerce of Siam," *Journal of the Siam Society*, XV (1922), 99.

[61] Translated and published in *The Siam Repository*, I (April 1869), 67–68, 111. Cf. also Wales, *op. cit.*, pp. 204–6.

[62] Luang Nathabanja, *Extraterritoriality in Siam* (Bangkok, 1924), Chs. 2 and 3.

jurisdiction over aliens, Nathabanja says that there were absolutely no restraints on them. "The doors of Siam, both on land and sea, were kept wide open to receive all who desired to enter. They were allowed to travel, to explore, and to establish trading posts in any place throughout the realm." Furthermore, he says, the foreign merchants "were satisfied with local law and with the conduct and treatment of the local officers."[63] They were not, as in China, clamoring for the protection of extraterritoriality. Indeed, when extraterritoriality came in 1855 it was in response to the demands of governments themselves and not merchants.

It is difficult to evaluate this argument, especially the part which is relevant to the present discussion: namely, that the king of Siam did in fact allow "complete freedom" to the traders of all nations. No documentary evidence is adduced to support that position. The preceding pages indicate that there was a considerable amount of kingly interference with and control of traders, but many of those observers might have been as biased as we may suspect Nathabanja of being.[64] But even if we suspect the Western accounts of exaggeration or bias, their similarity nevertheless makes a compelling case for the conclusion that trade was monopolized, restricted, and controlled. It is probable, however, that Westerners objected to the conduct of trade less because its volume was limited than because they were unable to make such large profits. They preferred to deal as monopsonists with a large number of small native sellers. "A royal monopolist . . . could better make them comply with his desire."[65]

The Chinese appear to have been more successful in securing a working agreement with the Siamese government than were Western traders. Not only did they pay lower import duties, but they were also given special privileges and encouragements to trade. Many observers have been impressed with the industry and position of the Chinese in Siam, even before 1850. For example:

> They have sown the seeds of commercial enterprise. They have created commerce where none previously existed, and with their own hands, they have, as it were, called into existence some of the more valuable objects of commerce.
> . . . it is not to be wondered at, if that people should enjoy privileges denied to European and other nations. Chinese traders are accordingly subjected to less vexatious proceedings in their commercial transactions. . . .[66]

---

[63] *Ibid.*, pp. 31–35.

[64] The present writer does not intend to imply any judgment of Nathabanja's argument about the *need* for extraterritoriality. We are speaking solely of the freedom of trade before 1855.

[65] J. H. Van der Heide, "The Economical Development of Siam During the Last Half Century," *Journal of the Siam Society*, III (1906), 6–7. Van der Heide argues that trade could have been expanded even *with* the old system of controls, but that the Westerners would have had to share the gain with the government.

[66] Finlayson, *op. cit.*, pp. 166–68.

Crawfurd substantially agreed. He remarked that the Chinese, unlike Europeans, were allowed to buy and sell without inconvenient restriction.[67]

Relative Importance of Foreign Trade

Foreign trade appears to have been of relatively small importance to Siam in 1850. Except for a few commodities such as pepper, sugar, and ivory, exports were a rather small part of total production. We estimated rice production to have been 20–23 million piculs, while the upper limit of our estimate of rice exports was only 1.0–1.5 million piculs, or about 5 percent. The ratio probably was ordinarily less than 2 or 3 percent. The percentage exported of other basic items, such as fish, fruit, and timber, was also probably rather small. Only a few commodities, of lesser aggregate importance, were largely exported.

Similarly, the goods imported probably represented only a tiny fraction of total consumption, with some exceptions. Cloth of various kinds was a major import, but compared to the total annual consumption of cloth, imports must have been small. Most imports probably got no farther than Bangkok, being intended for the court or for the officials and merchants residing in Bangkok. It is probable that most of the proceeds of export sales also remained in Bangkok, since most of these goods were shipped to Bangkok in payment of taxes or other customary obligations. Little money needed to be sent to the interior in payment for these goods.

Even if the total foreign trade was a relatively small proportion of the annual produce of Siam (including therein all items produced and consumed within the family), it still may have been a significant part of the total *money* transactions in the nation. We will try to show, however, that foreign trade grew in relative importance after 1850, and that this growth has constituted one of the major economic changes in Siam.

PUBLIC FINANCE

Nature and Size of Revenue

A brief account of the organization of the government has already been given above. Here we will examine only its finances. In general the government's revenues came from three main sources: the tax on land and gardens, the monopolies, and the *corvée*. In addition, there were various minor sources. In the years leading up to about 1850–55, there was a tendency toward the conversion of taxes from payments in kind to payments in money, and at the same time the government sought new sources of money revenues.

Estimates of total revenue are both scarce and unreliable. One problem is to value the payments in kind and services; another is to figure how much

---

[67] Crawfurd, *op. cit.*, pp. 175–76. Cf. also Neale, *A Residence in Siam*, p. 174, and R. A. Moore, "An Early British Merchant in Bangkok," *Journal of the Siam Society*, XI (1914–15), 21–39.

of the revenue eventually reached the central government. No systematic attempt has been made to do this for the early period, nor can it be done with exactness.

Wales thinks the total *money* revenue in the reign of King Rama II amounted to about 2,260,000 baht, and the total revenue in money and kind to about 5,200,000 baht.[68] This last is Crawfurd's estimate, to which he added 20 million baht for the *corvée*, making a total revenue of 25.2 million baht.[69] Wales thinks the conversion of taxes into money was rapid during this period, and that in the third reign (1824–51) money revenues alone amounted to about 25 million baht. Pallegoix's estimate was 27 million baht for about 1854, of which 12 million baht represented money payments in lieu of personal service; 2 million, the Chinese poll tax; and 7.5 million, the tax on riceland and gardens.[70] The remainder, about 5.5 million baht, came from a variety of sources, most of them royal or farmed monopolies. Malloch's estimate of the money revenue in 1850 was 32 million baht.[71]

These estimates of money revenue are probably greatly exaggerated. Even in 1892, after rice cultivation had been considerably extended and the conversion of taxes from kind to money had proceeded further, money revenues were only 15 million baht. Pallegoix estimated the land tax at 7.5 million baht in 1854, while in the 1890's, with substantially the same tax rates, the land tax yielded between one and two million baht. Similarly, Pallegoix thought the money payments in lieu of personal service brought in 12 million baht, but in the 1890's the capitation tax yielded one million or less. These observers apparently were dazzled by the splendor of the Siamese court, and thus were led to put their estimates of its revenue unreasonably high.

Four principal sources of revenue are given by Wales. They are:

1. Payments in lieu of personal service, either in kind or in money. Payments in kind had long been allowed for those who could not conveniently be called for labor services. Men were also allowed to pay money in lieu of serving in the *corvée* as long ago as the late seventeenth century. Wales cites La Loubere, who says such commutation was well established in the reign of King Narai (1657–88). From the time La Loubere wrote to the first half of the nineteenth century, the period of service was shortened from six to three months, but the money payment to secure exemption was raised from 12 to 18 baht. This, Wales says, reflects the government's increasing need for money.

The favored position of the Chinese is indicated by the fact that they were not subject to the *corvée*, while the poll tax collected from them once every three years was raised from only 1.5 baht in the second reign (1809–24) to

[68] Wales, *Ancient Siamese Government and Administration*, p. 214. This section is based largely on Wales, Ch. 9.

[69] Crawfurd, *op. cit.*, p. 387.

[70] Pallegoix, *op. cit.*, I, 309–11.

[71] Malloch, *op. cit.*, p. 14.

4.25 baht in the fourth reign (1851–68) of the Chakri dynasty. This tax load was considerably lighter than that of the native population, which suggests that the government wanted to encourage Chinese immigration.

2. Produce taxes. The people had the hereditary obligation not merely to furnish personal services, but also to turn over a share of their produce to the king. The tendency here also was to substitute money for payment in kind. The tax on riceland was a money tax in La Loubère's time, but in a later reign the government apparently was in need of rice for the army and payments in kind were again required. From 1824 to 1851 the producer was allowed to pay in kind or money, as he chose. The money tax rate was 0.375 baht per rai. In 1854 the tax was collected in money only, and the rate remained 0.375 baht per rai.

Another tax of long standing was that on fruit trees and gardens. Wales says garden crops were taxed at the rate of one baht per rai until the reign of King Rama IV, who reduced it to 0.375 baht per rai. Pepper was not taxed until the reign of King Rama III, Wales says, because its cultivation was encouraged by the government. Fruit trees were taxed at so much per tree.

Taxes were also levied on various other products and activities such as distilled arrack, fishing (tax based on the equipment used), gambling, and prostitution. It was these taxes which first began to be farmed out in the reign of King Rama III. Many new taxes were introduced because of the pressing need for money in the government. Such taxes were farmed to Chinese, and they began increasingly to replace the revenue from royal trading.

3. Customs and inland-transit duties. Both export and import duties had long been charged on the trade of Siam. The import duty was usually a flat ad valorem rate, although the rate was higher for ships which called infrequently from strange countries than for the Chinese. Export duties were charged according to a tariff of rates for each kind of product. In addition to these taxes, ships calling at Bangkok had to pay a duty based on the width of the beam. This duty was higher for the ships of distant countries than for Chinese ships. In his treaty of 1826 Captain Burney was able to reduce this duty only to 1,700 baht (then £212) per fathom for English ships.

Inland-transit duties were duties on goods moving about inside Siam. The rate was 10 percent, Wales says, and the tax was collected by customs houses on the land and water routes of the country.

4. Profits from government trading. The government monopolized some articles of both export and import trade, but the number of articles monopolized seems to have varied a good deal from reign to reign. As we mentioned above, the trend was toward less direct government monopoly of trade.

The tax collection system was organized in such a way that there was plenty of chance for corruption, oppression, and abuse of privilege. The tax farmer usually had to produce a given sum in a year. His own profit was whatever he could collect over and above that. Such a system was inevitably abused. The inland-transit officials were not paid, and it is likely that a considerable part of what they took from the passing boats stayed in their hands. The revenues which finally reached the central government were probably only a small part of the total amount collected from the people.

Expenditures

The principal expenditures of the government, outside of those necessary to finance wars, were made for religious buildings and the maintenance of the court. The *corvée* system furnished a vast supply of unpaid labor for the construction of temples and other public works.

The money revenues of the crown were largely spent on the maintenance of a large court. The king gave handsome annual allowances to a large number of individuals, mostly members of the royal family or officials who had won royal favor. Various ceremonies, such as coronations, cremations, and weddings, also consumed large sums of money.

One form of public works received attention from the early rulers of Siam. That form was irrigation works. Canals for irrigation and transportation had been dug since early times, particularly in Central Siam. Wales says the canal which cuts across a big bend in the Chao Phya River, and on the lower end of which Bangkok is now located, was constructed in 1534. "In all several thousand kilometers of canals were dug since that period, and tens of thousands of acres of unproductive land were made fit for cultivation by irrigation."[72]

The Monetary System

The currency of Siam consisted almost entirely of silver and cowrie shells, the latter being used only for very small purchases. The basic unit of money was the baht or tical. This was a bullet-shaped lump of silver with the king's seal stamped on it. The rupee was much used in Northern Siam because of the commerce with Burma. We have absolutely no information on the amount of money in circulation. Bowring does tell us that most of the circulation was the silver coin itself, although the government issued some promissory notes which circulated at par.

The king's personal finances were inextricably combined with the public treasury. Some type of mint was operated—probably it was operated intermittently by silversmiths—to mint the silver which was imported. Later on, Mexican and other coins were imported, but they did not circulate freely until the king put his stamp on them.

There is no evidence to suggest that the king endeavored to accumulate gold and silver, or that the restrictions on trade were deliberately designed to produce an import of bullion. The effect of Siam's favorable trade balance

[72] Wales, *op. cit.*, p. 230.

on the money supply is not discussed in the literature of the period prior to 1850. Presumably the inflow of silver was partly or wholly converted into money, since the king does not seem to have accumulated much of a stock of it, but we have no information about the effects of this.

The rate of exchange in 1850–55 was fairly steady at 8 baht to £1. This rate was determined by the weight of the baht coin and the world price of silver.

THE BOWRING TREATY

Because of its great importance in the seventy years following its adoption, we will briefly describe the provisions of the treaty negotiated by Sir John Bowring in 1855. The treaty went into effect in April 1856.

King Mongkut came to the throne in 1851, with the apparent conviction that Siam must learn to live with the Western nations if she was to survive as an independent nation. Only a few years before he became king, China had been forced to open her borders to the Western traders by the use of naval power, and the spectacle of this great nation falling victim to the Western barbarians must have had a profound influence on King Mongkut. Yet such reflections on power politics do not appear to have been the sole—perhaps not even the major—considerations determining Mongkut's friendliness to the West. He seems to have been convinced that Siam would benefit from closer relations with the Western nations, and he deliberately and voluntarily sought to develop such relations.[73] Bowring thus had a far easier task than did his predecessors, who had to deal not only with a hostile and unwilling group of nobles and officials, but also with a king who sought to thwart their efforts at every turn. Bowring may have had difficulties with the members of the court, but the king was on his side from the start. In a monarchy so absolute as the Siamese, this was a tremendous advantage.

Relations between Siam and Great Britain were still guided by the Burney Treaty of 1826. Bowring took this treaty as his starting point. From his point of view certain of its articles were still adequate, others needed only to be enforced, and a few needed to be changed. Specifically, he wanted to get rid of:[74]

1. "The repugnant clause" which placed British subjects in Siam entirely under the jurisdiction of Siamese law,

2. the clause permitting Siamese officials to forbid British merchants to build, hire or buy shops and houses,

---

[73] Since this point will come up again later on, we will pause only to note that King Mongkut voluntarily reduced the measurement duty on ships calling at Bangkok, removed the ban on rice exports, and abolished a number of government monopolies. These things were done *before* the Bowring Treaty was negotiated, and they were done without any request for a *quid pro quo*. See Malloch, *op. cit.*, p. 26; M. R. Kukhrit Pramoj and M. R. Seni Pramoj, "The King of Siam Speaks," pp. 4–5, 95–97; and Prinz Dilock, *Die Landwirtschaft in Siam*, pp. 66–67.

[74] Bowring, *op. cit.*, II, 201–4.

3. the clause empowering provincial governors to prevent British merchants from trading in each locality,

4. the clause making opium an item of contraband, and

5. the clause requiring a measurement duty of 1,700 baht per fathom to be paid by British ships entering the port of Bangkok. This clause also prohibited the export of rice and paddy.

In addition Bowring had the general goal of concluding a treaty which removed all restrictions on trade. He was remarkably successful in all his aims. Actually, King Mongkut had voluntarily made important concessions to Western trading interests.

The following provisions are the ones of principal economic importance in the treaty as finally signed in 1855:

1. British subjects were placed under consular jurisdiction. Thus, for the first time, Siam granted extraterritoriality to foreign aliens.

2. British subjects were given the right to trade freely in all seaports, and to reside permanently in Bangkok. They were to be allowed to buy and rent property in the environs of Bangkok; namely, in the area more than four miles from city walls but *less* than twenty-four hours' journey from the city (calculated at the speed of native boats). British subjects were also to be allowed to travel freely in the interior with passes provided by the consul.

3. Measurement duties were abolished and import and export duties fixed.

   a) The import duty was fixed at 3 percent for all articles, with two exceptions: opium was to be free of duty, but it had to be sold to the opium farmer; and bullion was to be free of duty.

   b) Articles of export were to be taxed just once, whether the tax was called an inland tax, a transit duty, or an export duty.

4. British merchants were to be allowed to buy and sell directly with individual Siamese without interference from any third person.

5. The Siamese government reserved the right to prohibit the export of salt, rice, and fish whenever these articles were deemed to be scarce.

6. A most-favored-nation clause was attached.

The crucial provisions were those establishing extraterritoriality, free trade, and import and export duties. As clear-cut as this treaty was, however, the chief reason for its success in the ensuing years was probably the willingness of King Mongkut to enforce its provisions in spirit as well as in letter. A great loophole was left in the article allowing the prohibition of rice exports "whenever a scarcity may be apprehended," and King Mongkut's predecessors would have found many more occasions than he did to invoke that clause.

The treaty represented a substantial surrender of sovereignty by Siam, and not only in the matter of jurisdiction over British subjects. The 3-percent ceiling on import duties and the specified export duties took the control of customs out of the hands of the Siamese government. Sixty-four commodities, including practically all major and minor products of the country, were enumerated in the tariff attached to the treaty. Of these, fifty-one were not to be subject to inland taxes of any kind, whether on production or transit, and were to pay a fixed export duty specified in the tariff. The remaining thirteen commodities were not to pay any export duty, but were to be subject to certain inland or transit duties (but not both), the rates of which were also specified in the treaty. Thus, a large part of the public revenue system of Siam was permanently frozen by the terms of an international treaty.

The treaty also put an end to state trading and trading monopolies of all sorts. Monopolies for the collection of taxes, for the sale of opium, and for the operation of gambling establishments were *not* eliminated by the treaty, however.

Bowring was aware of the drastic changes signified by this treaty, as were the members of the commission appointed by King Mongkut to negotiate the treaty. The commission included two powerful men who were vitally interested in the existing system and who had fought against any concessions to the British and American envoys who had preceded Bowring. That King Mongkut could put such men on the commission attests the absoluteness of his power.

Bowring said:

. . . it was clear that my success involved a total revolution in all the financial machinery of the government,—that it must bring about a total change in the whole system of taxation,—that it took a large proportion of the existing sources of revenue,—that it uprooted a great number of privileges and monopolies which had not only been long established, but which were held by the most influential nobles and the highest functionaries in the State.[75]

The Bowring Treaty set a pattern which other countries were quick to follow. The following countries concluded treaties with Siam, all of them similar in most respects to the first:

United States	1856	Norway	1868
France	1856	Belgium	1868
Denmark	1858	Italy	1868
Portugal	1859	Austria-Hungary	1869
Netherlands	1860	Spain	1870
Germany	1862	Japan	1898
Sweden	1868	Russia	1899

Thus was Siam opened rather abruptly to the West. The economic changes which occurred in the ensuing century will be the subject of the rest of this study. We will concentrate on the growth of trade because most changes were introduced through trade with foreign nations.

[75] Bowring, *op. cit.,* II, 227.

3

The Growth of Rice Exports
1850–1950

THE BROAD OUTLINES of the changes which have taken place in the Thai economy since the Bowring Treaty are quite simple, although detailed evidence of these changes is sometimes difficult to find, and the causal sequence is often unclear.

If we look at the main trends of the entire century, we see a marked growth in the volume and value of exports, accompanied by a roughly comparable growth in total imports. The exports were composed of a few primary products, while the list of imports included a wide variety of manufactured goods. The population of Thailand, which was itself increasing, tended to specialize more and more in the production of one major crop (rice) and a small number of other primary products, selling these products for money, and using the money to buy various articles of consumption. Money thus came to play an increasingly important role in an economy in which it had formerly been of but minor significance. When Western traders were freed by the Bowring Treaty to put such products as cheap cotton prints on the Thai market, the people bought these products and, if they could not buy, they sought a source of money income. Money could most easily be acquired by producing some commodity for the export market. As villages and households turned to the production of money crops, and as they began to purchase bright-colored garments from the traders, the household crafts declined. Cotton fields were perhaps used for rice or abandoned in favor of land suitable for rice. With the money income earned through the export market, the farmer bought the goods he had formerly made for himself.

The rate of change toward a money economy was uneven, both chronologically and geographically. In some decades the change was slow, in others it was rapid; and some regions of the country were affected much less than others. Indeed, as we examine the course of the century more closely, we will find that many of the characteristics of the Thailand of 1850 are still retained even in the Central region, and in some regions change has not been great.*

In general, therefore, Thailand changed from an almost self-sufficient economy to an economy which specialized in a few products and sold these to buy its requirements of other goods. For the nation as well as for many individuals the specialization went quite far. The nation produced little for export

* This statement applies to the situation about 1950. See Ch. 11 for developments since 1950.

besides rice, tin, teak, and (later) rubber. Large numbers of farmers were almost completely specialized in rice, and it was often their sole money crop.

With the development of an exchange economy, important new economic functions had to be performed—namely, the functions of taking the farmer's produce from him, transporting it to the seaports, selling it to foreign buyers, and then buying other goods to take back to the farmers. These middleman functions were performed by the Chinese, who of course had already begun to do so in 1850. Western merchants participated in these activities, especially at the wholesale level, but the Chinese were by far the most numerous. The Thai participated hardly at all.

One of the outstanding features of the period since 1850 has been the general willingness of the Thai to leave the entrepreneurship function to foreigners. This was true not only in the case of the middleman organization. In any new development which required the application of business methods and the use of individual initiative and entrepreneurship, the Thai were rarely to be found. Another striking feature of this period of Thailand's history was the existence of a supply of foreign entrepreneurship which was willing to flow into the country, and which was allowed to. The classical assumption of immobility of factors between nations was not found here, where a stream of labor and entrepreneurship flowed into Thailand in significant quantities.

These changes were accompanied by an increase in the population, slow at first and then quite rapid. The increase in population occurred in all regions, and did not vary with the degree of commercialization.

For two or three decades prior to 1950, there was a slowly awakening desire for economic diversification on the part of the Thai government, and perhaps also in the private sectors. As this desire gathered force, it brought with it the beginnings of industrialization in Thailand—a movement still in its infancy, but of increasing importance.

Statistics of Rice Exports

The biggest story in the period we are examining is the growth of rice exports. It was shown above that some rice was being exported prior to the Bowring Treaty, but the fact that such exports existed does not detract from the importance to Thailand of the growth of exports since then. During most of the century under examination, rice cultivation was the chief occupation for 80-90 percent of the people, and rice exports consistently represented 60-70 percent of total exports.

The summary facts of the increase in volume and value are set forth in Table III and Chart I. These figures, averaged over five-year intervals to smooth the yearly fluctuations, emphasize the steady increase in the physical volume of rice exports over most of the century we are examining. After a slow erratic rise up to 1870-74, the volume rose rapidly to a peak of 25.7 million piculs in the period 1930-34. This 25-fold increase—over the probable maximum volume at the time of the Bowring Treaty—which took place while

TABLE III

VOLUME AND VALUE OF RICE EXPORTS[a]

Period	Average Volume per Year (Thousand Piculs)	Average Value per Year (Thousand Baht)	Average Price per Picul (Baht)
1857–59	990		
1860–64	1,840		
1865–69	1,630		
1870–74	1,870	5,110	2.70
1875–79	3,530	10,110	2.90
1880–84	3,580	9,610	2.70
1885–89	5,320	15,080	2.80
1890–94	7,250	23,780	3.30
1895–99	8,000	36,410	4.60
1900–1904	11,130	61,280	5.50
1905–09	14,760	81,020	5.50
1910–14	15,220	81,230	5.30
1915–19	15,790	108,140	6.90
1920–24	17,680	115,350	6.50
1925–29	23,390	169,600	7.20
1930–34	25,720	91,240	3.50
1935–39	25,370	94,570	3.70
1940–44	13,250	99,320	7.50
1946	7,580	267,340	35.30
1947	6,535	384,605	59.00
1948	13,540	1,255,335	93.00
1949	20,260	1,869,410	92.00
1950	24,820	1,996,190	80.00
1951	26,290	2,223,610	85.00

[a] All figures represent the total of rice and paddy. Paddy comprises a very small percentage of the total, however.

Figures prior to 1920/21 refer to the Port of Bangkok only, but Bangkok ordinarily exports over 95 percent of the total.

Prior to 1940, many of the years concerned run from April to March.

There are wide variations in the estimates of postwar exports made by different agencies. In 1946–48 there was a great deal of smuggling to avoid exchange control and fixed prices, and the figures for these years are low on that account. The values given for 1946–51 are based on the foreign-exchange proceeds converted at the *official* exchange rates, which have been well below the free rates. See Ch. 7.

Sources: 1857–64 incl., J. H. Van der Heide, "The Economical Development of Siam During the Last Half Century," *Journal of the Siam Society*, III (1906), 82; 1865–99 incl., *Annual Diplomatic and Consular Reports from Her Majesty's Consuls in Siam, 1864–1900*, Great Britain, Foreign Office (London, 1865–1901); 1900–1944 incl., *Statistical Year Book of Siam*, 1916–44, Thailand, Dept. of Commerce and Statistics (Bangkok, 1917–50), I–XXI; 1946–51 incl., Exchange Control Division, Bank of Thailand.

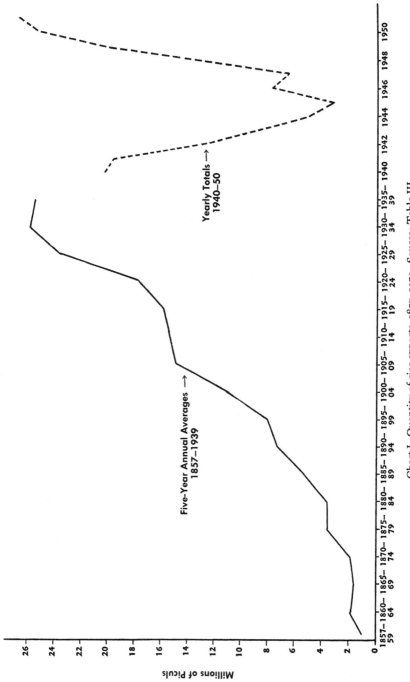

Chart I. Quantity of rice exports, 1857–1950. Source: Table III.

the population roughly doubled itself, represents the major economic change in Thailand since 1855. In no other productive activity have the Thai themselves been so deeply involved, nor is there any other productive activity which has concerned such a large part of the population.

Like all the statistics we will deal with, the figures for rice exports are of questionable accuracy. One useful rule to follow in considering any of the statistical material in this study, including rice exports, is never to place much weight on close year-to-year comparisons. The reliability of such comparisons is much less than that of the longer-run trends. In spite of this qualification, however, the rice export series is probably one of the most accurate series available for Thailand. Customs figures before 1920/21 included the trade of Bangkok only, but very little rice has been exported overland or through any other port. The Bangkok shipments probably accounted for 95–99 percent of the total rice exports.

The figures in Table III represent the combined volume of rice and paddy. This need cause no concern, however, since nearly all exports consist of milled rice and because the proportion of rice in the total is fairly stable.[1] Another difficulty arises from the fact that the unit of measurement, the picul, has not been entirely standard. It was officially changed from 60.48 kg. (133½ lbs.) to 60.0 kg. in 1923, but the new picul was not adopted quickly or uniformly. The picul has varied much more than that in different parts of the country, but we are here concerned mainly with the standard used in Bangkok by the customs officials. No adjustment has been made to take account of the official change to the new picul of 60 kg. because the customs figures are not accurate to a one-percent tolerance anyway.

The drastic increase in the baht price of rice in the years since 1940 calls for some comment. The severe wartime inflation increased domestic prices to about 1,200 percent of the prewar level.[2] During the same period, the exchange value of the baht declined from 11 to 35 baht per pound sterling and from 2.0–3.0 to 12.5 baht per U.S. dollar.[3] Thus the price of rice expressed in foreign currency increased much less than the price expressed in baht.

Nevertheless, the world price of rice did increase sharply in the postwar years. The failure of exports from Burma and Indochina to return to prewar levels, coupled with acute shortages in rice-deficient areas such as Malaya, resulted in high postwar prices.[4] As a matter of fact, Thailand sold much of

[1] There will be a slight upward bias in *value* figures from about 1890 to 1910 because during this period newly established mills in Bangkok began to mill a larger proportion of "white" rice and less "cargo" rice. The former brings a higher price per picul than the latter.

[2] Price indexes in Thailand are not very trustworthy, but all available attempts to construct indexes indicate a rise of twelve to fourteen times the prewar level.

[3] The postwar rates given in this comparison are the *official* rates after September 1949.

[4] Prior to World War II, Burma exported about 3.0 million metric tons of rice, Indochina 1.6 million tons, and Thailand 1.5 million tons. After the war, Thailand has been the largest exporter, even though her exports did not reach 1.5 million metric tons until 1949. Largely be-

her rice at prices considerably below the world level in the postwar years because she accepted the prices fixed by international allocating authorities. In recent years the spread between Thailand's average price and the world price has narrowed, however.

Source of Demand

A major factor in the growth of rice production was the introduction of a steady money demand for rice in Bangkok. The source of this increased money demand was foreign. A powerful economic force, originating outside the Thai economy, began to exert an influence on the structure of production. Before the increase in external demand, the peasant had had no reason to extend the production of rice much beyond his own requirements for food and taxes, plus perhaps a small surplus for sale or barter. The demand for Thailand's rice in the neighboring countries was erratic, depending as it did on the success of the crop in those countries. It was erratic also because the king might at any time limit or forbid the exportation of rice. Thus, even if Thailand could easily have produced an export surplus, the effort was not regularly made and, in the years prior to 1855, large exports probably occurred chiefly when a bumper crop in Thailand happened to coincide with a poor crop elsewhere. Such "large exports" were comparatively small, as we have seen.

The source of the increased money demand must have been external since the domestic population probably was already consuming about as much rice as it desired. Nor was there any increase in domestic money incomes which could have been directed toward the purchase of rice and thus have encouraged its production. Finally, the increased output of rice was very largely sold to foreigners as the rice-export figures themselves show. Exports rose from about 5 percent of the total crop in 1850 to about 50 percent in 1907.[5] As the growth in population proceeded, domestic consumption of rice had to increase, but the bulk of the population continued to supply its own demand for rice. This domestic demand would thus not involve the exchange mechanism or much increased money demand.

The importance of increased foreign demand as a cause of the increased production and export of rice has been stressed by Van der Heide. He points out that there had never been a *regular* foreign demand for rice in the old days, and that the peasant thus had had no stimulus to increase his production. Van der Heide says that it was modern transportation which "created a regular and increasing demand for bulk commodities like rice and teak. In consequence of the regular demand for rice, the production became stimulated and increased."[6] He considers the treaty provision which abolished the prohibition

---

cause of the reduced export from Burma and Indochina, world rice exports since the war have been only about 40 percent of the prewar level.

[5] The 1850 figure was estimated in Ch. 2. See Table VII for the 1907 figure.

[6] "Economical Development of Siam During the Last Half Century," *Journal of the Siam Society*, III (1906), p. 83.

on rice exports to have been purely secondary, because increasing production would soon have made the prohibition of exports unnecessary anyway.[7]

Thompson, among others, has stressed the importance of the development of steam transportation and the opening of the Suez Canal (1869) in making possible the mass export from Southeast Asia of bulky commodities such as rice.[8] It is impossible to evaluate with certainty the influence of the Suez Canal and the European market on the expansion of rice cultivation in Thailand. The statistics of rice exports by destination do not reveal the total amount shipped to Europe because the bulk of Thailand's rice exports went to the entrepôt ports of Hong Kong and Singapore. Rice shipped to Hong Kong probably would not be reconsigned to Europe, however, because of the distance involved. We might assume, therefore, that European shipments included direct shipments plus a portion of the Singapore shipments. There is no sound basis for estimating the share of Singapore shipments which was reconsigned to Europe, but the bulk of them were probably consumed in Singapore, Malaya, or other parts of Asia. Direct shipments to Europe comprised 4 percent of Thailand's rice exports in the period 1870-74, 7 percent in 1880-84, and 9 percent in 1900-1904. During the same periods Singapore took 20 percent, 50 percent, and 36 percent of the total.[9] These figures are not very reliable, and the share of Singapore shipments reconsigned to Europe is unknown. Nevertheless, the figures given may suffice to show that there was no sudden surge of European demand for Thai rice upon completion of the Suez Canal in 1869, and that exports to Europe did not increase significantly faster than exports to the rest of the world.

The Suez Canal may have had an important indirect influence on the market for Thai rice, however, in that Burmese rice exports may have been diverted from Asian to European markets, thus increasing the demand in Asia for Thai rice. But it would take a study of the entire pattern of world rice trade to settle this matter. The foreign demand for Thai rice may perhaps be better explained by the development of cheap ocean transportation which

[7] Apparently Van der Heide was thinking of the ban on rice exports as a measure to protect the food supply of the domestic population, which may well have been its original purpose. He thought the incentive given to production by a regular money demand for rice in Bangkok would have so increased the total output of rice that the *need* for prohibition would have been removed. This is what did happen, except in years of severely abnormal water supply. For a similar view, see also Prinz Dilock von Siam, *Die Landwirtschaft in Siam*, pp. 66-67.

[8] Virginia M. Thompson, in Rupert Emerson and others, *Government and Nationalism in Southeast Asia* (New York: Institute of Pacific Relations, 1942), pp. 134-35. See also J. S. Furnivall, *Colonial Policy and Practice* (Cambridge University Press, 1948), pp. 50, 84-85, for a discussion of the importance to Burma of the Suez in providing "a certain and profitable market for as much rice as people could grow." Before the opening of the Suez, rice exports had been relatively small and erratic, but after it was opened Burma's rice exports rose even faster than did Thailand's.

[9] Figures derived from *Annual Diplomatic and Consular Reports on Trade and Finance from Her Majesty's Consuls in Siam*, Great Britain (London, 1865-1910); and *Statistics of the Import and Export Trade of Siam*, 1900-1904, Thailand, His Majesty's Customs.

enabled Thailand to compete in Asian markets and by the development of economies in Asia which depended on large regular imports of rice, e.g., Malaya.

Developments in ocean transportation cannot properly be considered as changes in the conditions of supply as far as the economy of Thailand is concerned. They were external developments, and if they succeeded in bringing to Bangkok an effective foreign demand for rice, we should treat this as a change in demand rather than in supply. The increased demand from abroad then brought about a response—an adaptive change—in the Thai economy.

This distinction between the causal role of demand and supply cannot be pushed too far. The discussion would soon lose its value. As we examine the supply side, however, we may look for innovating changes which could have started the tremendous growth in exports after 1870. Once the production of rice for export became a well-known and commonly accepted part of Thai life, the distinction between changes originating on the demand and on the supply side tends to break down. The insistent pressure of a buoyant foreign demand may have *caused* this socioeconomic change to take place in the last half of the nineteenth century, but once the change was made we cannot single out changes in demand or supply as being responsible for further changes. They become inextricably mixed together in some such event as the rise in exports from the 1920's to the 1930's. In the initial increase in the mid-nineteenth century, on the other hand, the new factor seems clearly to have been the foreign buyer and his willingness to pay money for large quantities of rice.

The Expansion of Production, 1850–1950

In response to the external demand for rice and the lure of foreign goods, the area planted in rice increased greatly during the course of the century beginning in 1850. By 1905/6 the area had risen to 9.1 million rai, an increase of 3.3 million over our estimate for 1850 of about 5.8 million rai. The increase was even greater during the next forty-five years, and the total rose to a peak of 34.6 million in 1950. Statistics are set forth in Table IV.

This vast extension of rice cultivation was carried on almost entirely by the Thai themselves. The Chinese and other immigrants did not become rice growers in competition with the Thai. Furthermore, the land was brought under cultivation by individuals acting on their own initiative, and not to any significant extent by government or private resettlement programs. As they saw the possibility of earning cash incomes by growing rice, individuals began to clear and plant new land.

As we shall see, the government assisted and encouraged this activity, but most of the initiative came from individuals. Thus the extension of rice cultivation forms a notable exception to the general statements that the Thai left entrepreneurship to others and that change and reform were brought about

TABLE IV

AREA PLANTED IN PADDY

(Millions of Rai)

Period	Center	All Other	Total
1850			5.8[a]
1905–9	6.8	2.4	9.2
1910–14	7.2	4.3	11.5
1915–19	8.2	5.7	13.9
1920–24	9.6	6.7	16.3
1925–29	10.9	7.2	18.1
1930–34	11.8	8.3	20.1
1935–39	12.0	9.2	21.2
1940–44	14.1	11.4	25.5
1945	12.1	11.4	23.5
1946	13.1	11.8	24.9
1947	14.6	15.6	30.2
1948	15.8	16.8	32.6
1949	16.3	16.6	32.9
1950	16.7	17.9	34.6

[a] Estimated.

Sources: *Statistical Year Book of Siam*, XIII, 432; XIX, 417; XXI, 466–71. Data for 1945 through 1950 supplied by the Department of Agriculture, Bangkok.

from the top. Here the Thai as individuals took the lead, and it is significant that they responded to what was essentially a money incentive.

The land most accessible to transportation was the first to be taken up. During the last half of the nineteenth century this meant land in the Central Plain, where the existing network of canals and streams provided a cheap and convenient means for transporting rice and paddy to Bangkok, the major port. This broad, almost perfectly flat plain, through which flows the Chao Phya River, could be supplied with water for irrigation and transportation more easily than could any other region of similar size because of its flatness and because it was crisscrossed with streams. Some canals had previously been constructed there, either for transportation or irrigation (or both), and the land served by these was probably the first to be settled when the foreign demand for rice made itself felt.

In a very interesting and valuable calculation made for the year 1905/6, Van der Heide estimated that rice exports originating outside the Central section amounted to no more than 2 percent of the total exports for that year of 14 million piculs.[10] He arrived at this result by obtaining estimates of the

[10] Van der Heide, *op. cit.*, p. 90.

quantities of paddy coming past Paknampo (a check station on the river from the North) and from Korat in the Northeast on the newly constructed railway. Paddy could scarcely reach Bangkok from the North and Northeast by any other means of transportation. To the extent that population had increased in the outlying regions, the area in rice probably increased between 1850 and 1900 in those regions, but most of the increase in rice acreage from 1855 to 1905 probably occurred in Central Thailand, from which region virtually all exports originated in 1905. Nearly every traveler came away with this opinion. Observers who left a record of their impressions were unanimous in speaking of the extension of cultivation in the Central Plain, which they contrasted with the subsistence agriculture of the North and Northeast.

Since 1905 the extension of rice cultivation has proceeded considerably faster in the outer provinces than in the Center. At least that is the conclusion which emerges from the official statistics of land planted in paddy. The comparison is as follows:

AREA PLANTED IN PADDY[11]

(Millions of Rai)

Region	1903–7	1948–50	Percentage Increase
Center	6.5	16.3	151
All other	2.2	17.1	678

According to these figures, the absolute increase was somewhat greater outside the Center—9.8 million rai in the Central section, and 14.9 million in all other sections—while the *rate* of increase was over four times as great outside the Center. This result comes as a surprise, since the very strong impression given by most accounts is that very little change had been taking place in the outer provinces in comparison with the changes in the Center. We now find that from about 1905 to 1950 these backward, subsistence sectors were outstripping the commercialized Center in the extension of rice cultivation. Table IV contains more detailed statistics of regional changes up to 1950. (See Ch. 11 for changes since 1950.)

It remains to be shown that the North and Northeast also began to export rice in significant quantities. Perhaps the increased cultivation of rice was required merely to feed the growing population of these regions. The population figures of the official censuses given in Table V indicate that the population outside the Center doubled between 1911 and 1947, while the area in rice increased by about six times between 1903–7 and 1948–50. Even after allowing for substantial errors in both figures, it would appear that a surplus of rice

---

[11] Figures for 1903–7 derived from *Statistical Year Book of Siam*, XVI, 402 ff. Figures for 1948–50 supplied by Department of Agriculture, Bangkok. See Appendix A for a definition of the Center, as used here.

TABLE V
POPULATION AT OFFICIAL CENSUS DATES
(000 Omitted)

Date	Center Population	Center Index	All Other Population	All Other Index	Total Population	Total Index
1911	3,267	100	4,999	100	8,266	100
1919	3,520	108	5,687	114	9,207	111
1929	4,582	140	6,924	139	11,506	139
1937	5,748	176	8,716	174	14,464	175
1947	7,000	214	10,317	206	17,317	209

Sources: *Statistical Year Book of Thailand.*

must have been produced in the outer provinces. (Yields will be discussed below.)

The Center still remained the major granary of Siam, however, as can be shown by comparing the riceland per capita there and in the outer provinces:

RICELAND PER CAPITA[12]

Region	1903–7	1948–50
Center	2.0 rai	2.3 rai
All other	.5 rai	1.7 rai

The dominance of the Center is also shown by the available figures on total output of paddy:

AVERAGE YEARLY OUTPUT OF PADDY[13]
(Million Piculs)

Period	Center	All Other
1921–24	41.8	32.8
1930–34	46.0	32.7
1940–44	47.4	33.6
1948–50	63.6	49.2

Van der Heide indicated that the Center was able to export nearly 14 million piculs of rice in 1905/6. Since then the population has doubled, but the

[12] The per capita figures are derived from the statistics presented above. We are using 1911 population together with 1903–7 acreage figures, so the beginning per capita figure will be on the low side.

Van der Heide figured 3.0 rai per capita in the Center in 1905–6, but his population figures were even more questionable than ours. Furthermore, his "Center" was slightly different from ours, and he may have subtracted the population of Bangkok before computing his average, as we have *not* done here.

[13] Derived from *Statistical Year Book,* except for 1948–50 figures which were supplied by Department of Agriculture, Bangkok.

land per capita has remained about the same in the Center. Aside from possible declines in yields, therefore, it would seem that the Center would still be the major exporting region.

Nevertheless, the ability of the North and Northeast to export rice has also improved. Railways constructed to the North and Northeast have facilitated the delivery of rice in Bangkok, and the extension of cultivation in these regions has enabled them to become rice exporters along with the Center. When the railway to Korat was completed in 1900, shipments of rice and paddy began to move from the vicinity of Korat to Bangkok. In the beginning the amount was small, but by 1905 some 200,000 piculs were involved, and when the Northeastern railway was extended in the 1920's the shipments increased rapidly. Each year the farthest town reached by the railway became an important center for rice and paddy shipments because it drew on the supplies farther away. By 1925 some 1,700,000 piculs were coming from the Northeast, and by 1935 the total reached about 4,600,000 piculs,[14] nearly 20 percent of total exports.

The northern railway also carried considerable quantities of rice and paddy. We have placed the northern limit of the "Central" region so far north, however, that most of the rice and paddy shipments have originated within the "Center" so defined (see Appendix A).[15] The railway reached and passed Utaradit in the 1920's, and shipments originating north of that point have since increased considerably, amounting to about 650,000 piculs in 1925 and about 1,300,000 in 1935.

During the last several decades a larger and larger proportion of the total railway shipments has consisted of milled rice. In 1925, for example, practically all grain shipped from points north of Utaradit was in the form of paddy, but by 1935 about 35 percent was milled rice. Similarly, in 1925 only 10 percent of shipments from the Northeast were milled rice, but by 1935 the figure was 42 percent. This indicates the spread of rice mills over the country.[16]

It appears, therefore, that regions outside the Center began to contribute increasing quantities to the total rice exports of Thailand, although the Center remained the major source of exports. Since most of the rice grown in the North and Northeast has traditionally been glutinous rice, the increase in shipments from these areas takes on added significance. Glutinous or "sticky" rice is not exported to any considerable extent, although Central Thailand buys

[14] In the years since World War II, shipments from the Northeast have been smaller than they would otherwise have been because of the shortage of railway cars.

[15] Some paddy was sent by boat from the North to Paknampo and then shipped the rest of the way by rail. There are no exact estimates of the quantity involved, however. Thailand, Ministry of Communications, *Annual Report on the Administration of the Royal State Railways*, 1923/24, pp. 7–8.

[16] The facts and figures in the above three paragraphs are derived from *Annual Reports on the Administration of the Royal State Railways*, Thailand, 1897/98–1936/37. There is some error in these figures because some shipments were to intermediate points and not to Bangkok. The margin of error on this account is extremely small, however.

some for use in sweets. Apparently, therefore, the money demand for rice and the availability of rail transportation have induced producers in these regions to switch part of their output from glutinous to ordinary rice. This is another indication of an adaptive response to economic incentives.

We have so far not dealt with the questions of yield per rai and the technique of production. No quantitative data can be produced on the latter question, but all observers agree that there have been no significant changes in technique. The rice farmer clings to the methods and techniques handed down from generation to generation. He uses about the same instruments of production, prepares his fields in the same way, and harvests the grain by hand, just as his father did. The principal implements used are a wooden plow (with metal share), a wooden harrow, and knives for reaping. The construction of irrigation projects represents an improvement in technique on a national scale, and in the affected areas the farmers may obtain increased yields through improved water control, but the operations performed by the individual farmer have remained much as they were in 1850.[17]

The extension of rice cultivation without improved techniques has led to a long-run decline in yield per rai.[18] This decline indicates that poorer land, or land less well provided with water, was brought under cultivation. The following figures illustrate the declining yield:

AVERAGE YIELD OF PADDY ON PLANTED AREA[19]

Period	Piculs per Rai
1906–9	4.88
1914–18	4.07
1921–24	4.50
1930–34	3.91
1940–44	3.13
1948–50	3.37

We should mention that the official estimates of total production used in computing the yield figures have been seriously questioned by several writers, notably by V. D. Wickizer and M. K. Bennett.[20] Without making any great claim for the accuracy of the official statistics, we use them here in the hope

[17] See Thailand, Ministry of Agriculture, *Thailand and Her Agricultural Problems,* pp. 1–20.

[18] Unless otherwise stated, all yield figures given in this chapter are based on area *planted* rather than on area harvested. Each year a varying quantity of land is damaged by flood or drought. This factor is responsible for much of the variation in yields. This discussion of yield per rai applies to the period ending 1950. For yields since 1950, see Ch. 11.

[19] *Statistical Year Book of Thailand,* I–XXI; 1948–50, supplied by Department of Agriculture, Bangkok. Even the four- and five-year averages given here are strongly influenced by poor crops, and the apparent trend may be just the chance variation of good and bad crops. The year 1919 was omitted because of the drastic crop failure. The 1942 crop was badly damaged by high flood.

[20] *The Rice Economy of Monsoon Asia,* Institute of Pacific Relations, Food Research Institute (Stanford University, 1941), pp. 196–200, 219–20. These writers were examining the relation between population, area cultivated, and total production, and they doubted that secure inferences could be drawn from the official figures.

that long-run trends will be sufficiently clear and reliable for our purposes, even though year-to-year comparisons are highly unwise.

The apparent decline in yield per rai lends some support to the hypothesis that an unchanging technique was applied to a larger amount of land, and that the increments of cultivated land were of poorer quality *for rice growing*. The decline in yield per rai took place primarily in the outer provinces, where cultivation was rapidly extended without benefit of irrigation. The division of output between Center and "All Other" is unfortunately not available prior to 1920. Since then, the trend has been as follows:

ANNUAL AVERAGE YIELD OF PADDY[21]

(Piculs per Rai)

Period	Center	All Other
1921–24	4.24	4.90
1930–34	3.91	3.90
1940–44	3.37	2.95
1948–50	3.90	2.88

The decline in yields outside the Center has, of course, limited the export surplus of paddy available from those regions. Thus, the total output outside the Center increased only 50 percent from 1921–24 to 1948–50, while the area cultivated increased 150 percent. This sharp decline in yields is a serious matter for Thailand. Since, as far as we know, the number of man-hours required to cultivate a given area of paddy land has not declined, the reduced yield suggests that marginal increments of labor and land are producing ever smaller marginal physical products. One solution would be to try to increase the yield of rice by irrigation or seed selection. Undoubtedly there is much room for improvement in the areas concerned. A second solution is to help the people to find other crops or other industries in which the marginal productivity is greater. Because of traditions, customs, and inadequate knowledge of the alternatives, the people may not *themselves* be able to weigh the alternatives in any realistic way. Therefore, they may pass up many excellent opportunities in favor of the familiar employment of growing rice.

As we have said, the yield per rai has been fairly well maintained in Central Thailand. One reason is that as new (and often less fertile) lands have been brought under cultivation, irrigation facilities have been extended over larger areas. Better water supply has tended to offset the use of poorer land, and in some cases the provision of irrigation has enabled rich lands to be brought under cultivation for the first time. The advantage of superior irrigation facilities is mitigated by the fact that canals rapidly fill up with silt and must be redredged to retain their effectiveness.

Outside the Center, yields have not uniformly declined. In the North, in-

[21] Derived from *Statistical Year Book of Thailand* and tables given above.

deed, yields have remained even higher than in the Center. The reasons for this include: a less rapid expansion of the area planted in rice; fertile soils; extensive use of small-scale, co-operative irrigation schemes; and proximity to the stream that is the source of water (unlike much land in the Center whose water supply must come from a stream several miles away).

It is in the Northeast, where an immense increase in the area cultivated has taken place, that yields have declined the most. When it is realized that today the Northeast alone has some 35 percent of *total* paddy land (and 70 percent of that in what we have called "All Other" sections), the importance of the following yield figures is apparent:

NORTHEAST ANNUAL AVERAGE YIELD OF PADDY[22]

Period	Piculs per Rai
1920–24	4.30
1931–34	3.22
1940–44	2.54
1948–50	2.47

The declining yield we noted in the "All Other" section is predominantly influenced by the trend in the Northeast. Soils in the Northeast are poor and not well suited for paddy. Furthermore, the water supply is not good. Nevertheless, the area in paddy increased from an annual average of about 3,900,000 rai in 1920–24 to over 12,000,000 rai in 1948–50. Unless yields can be greatly improved in this region, there is an urgent need for developing other, more productive employments and for inducing the people to undertake them.

Rice has long been grown on nearly all of the cultivated land in Thailand. For as long as acreage statistics have been collected and published by the government, about 95 percent of the cultivated area has been devoted to rice. Other crops for which figures are published, such as maize, tobacco, cotton, coconuts, and peas, together account for less than 5 percent. The official statistics of "other crops" are highly unreliable. Yearly figures fluctuate wildly for many single crops, and some crops are still not reported. Yet it is clear that the combined total is relatively insignificant when compared to rice. Some estimates of the area planted in other crops are given in Table VI.

Generally, the area planted in other crops appears to have been relatively constant (in total) until the outbreak of World War II stimulated production of crops such as cotton, sugar cane, and tobacco. The growth of knowledge about legumes and other subsidiary crops has resulted in a further increase in acreage in the postwar years. Nevertheless, even in 1948 the total area of other crops was only 1,550,000 rai compared to 32,600,000 rai of paddy land, or less than 5 percent of the combined total.

[22] Figures for 1920–44, *Statistical Year Book of Thailand*; 1948–50, supplied by the Department of Agriculture, Bangkok.

TABLE VI
AREA PLANTED IN CROPS OTHER THAN RICE[a]
(Thousand Rai)

Crop	1911/12	1918/19	1928/29	1938/39	1944	1948
Coconuts	—	—	338	313	332	271
Soybeans	—	—	—	39	—	64
Peanuts	—	—	—	—	—	240
Mung beans	—	—	—	—	—	151
Peas	30	14	—	87	94	—
Cotton	22	28	23	30	325	191
Tobacco	71	54	62	56	82	142
Sugar cane	41	53	—	—	—	271
Sesame	—	—	—	11	—	70
Maize	40	39	46	55	97	137
Castor beans	—	—	—	—	—	12

[a] Dash indicates that figure is not available.

Sources: 1948 figures supplied by the Department of Agriculture, Bangkok. Sugar area for 1911 and 1918, "Monograph on Sugar in Siam," *The Record*, Thailand, Department of Commerce, II (January 1922), 9. All other figures, *Statistical Year Book of Thailand*.

The area of crops other than rice is likely to increase in relative importance in the future. Government encouragements through tariffs and government-sponsored industries such as sugar and tobacco, as well as the spread of knowledge among farmers, will tend to bring this result. By 1950 the area planted in the crops listed in Table VI had already risen to 2,100,000 rai from the 1948 figure of 1,550,000 rai, according to Department of Agriculture estimates.

Three important agricultural crops are omitted entirely from the above official figures. Two of these have long been important, the third has grown rapidly in recent decades. The first two are fruits and vegetables, two major items in the Thai diet. Most farmers have a few fruit trees and a patch of vegetables, and many supplement their incomes by selling part of the crop. Comparative figures of the area in fruits and vegetables are not available, however. An estimate of the Department of Agriculture for 1937 put the area in fruits at 1,900,000 rai, mostly in the Central and Southern regions; and the area in vegetables at 105,000 rai, mostly in the Central region. The third crop is rubber. Accurate statistics of acreage are difficult to obtain, but a recent estimate put the area in rubber as high as 2,000,000 rai in 1950.[23]

More will be said of the rubber industry when we discuss other exports. Rubber and rice are the only agricultural crops which are important exports, and rubber is a relative newcomer. Thailand has been largely a one-crop coun-

[23] Rubber Division, Department of Agriculture, Bangkok.

try as far as exports are concerned and, even allowing for fruits and vegetables, the overwhelming majority of cultivated land is devoted to rice [1950].

The Ratio of Exports to Total Production

The expansion of rice exports, coupled with declining yields and a steady growth in population, raises a question about the welfare effects on the domestic population. It would appear that exports could be maintained in such circumstances only at the cost of a reduction in domestic per capita consumption.

The figures given in Table VII suggest that such a drop in consumption did take place from about 1910 to 1940. Since 1940, conditions have been rather disturbed, but the figures available suggest that domestic consumption has regained its former level.

Although official estimates of the total production of rice are not available before 1907, it appears that the percentage exported increased from about 5 percent of total production in 1850 to 50 percent in 1907–9. During the whole of the period from 1907 to 1940, exports ranged from 40 to 50 percent of the total rice production.[24] From 1920 to 1940, the export percentage rose from 39 percent to 50 percent, and at the same time population steadily increased and yields declined. As a result of these trends the retained rice per capita fell during this period from 2.8 piculs to 1.7 piculs of cleaned rice. The "normal yearly requirement" of cleaned rice has been estimated at 2.4 piculs per capita, so that if the data in Table VII are accurate, the domestic population reduced its consumption of rice far below the "normal" level in the decade of the 1930's.

During and since World War II, however, exports have formed a much smaller share of total production, and the amount retained has exceeded the normal per capita consumption. This suggests that additions have been made to internal stocks since the beginning of the war. For example, in 1948–50 only 26 percent of the total crop was exported and the amount retained was 3.0 piculs per capita as compared with normal consumption of 2.4 piculs. That the situation could improve so markedly in the face of a declining yield per rai was possible only because the area cultivated has increased faster than the population since 1930. This conclusion cannot be firmly established, however, because of the probable inaccuracy of the basic statistics. For example, the indicated additions to internal stocks of rice in 1948–50 (10 million piculs per year) are too large to be reasonable. One possible explanation is that the shortage of transportation and the hampering influence of the Government Rice Monopoly have restrained the export of rice. Another possibility is that the relative prices of rice and meat have caused more rice to be used for feed than formerly.

---

[24] The yearly variation was much greater than these five-year averages. In years such as 1919 and 1920 the ratio exported dropped sharply because of crop failure.

TABLE VII

CONSUMPTION AND EXPORT OF RICE

Period[a]	Percentage of Exports to Total Production[b]	Average Yearly Retained Rice (*Piculs per Capita*)
1907/8 –1909/10	51	1.8
1910/11–1914/15	42	2.4
1915/16–1919/20	42	2.4
1920/21–1924/25	39	2.8
1925/26–1929/30	44	2.5
1930/31–1934/35	48	2.2
1935/36–1939/40	50	1.7
1940–44	23	2.7
1945–47	11	2.7
1948–50	26	3.0

[a] These periods refer to the years of export, and it has been assumed that exports are made from the production of the *previous* years. Therefore, exports are matched against production of the preceding year in each case.

[b] Paddy has been converted to cleaned rice by the factor 0.70.

Sources: Production and export figures from 1907/8 to 1944 are from *Statistical Year Book of Thailand*. Figures for 1945–50 were supplied by the Department of Agriculture, Bangkok.

Official statistics of production, export, and population thus lead to the conclusion that domestic consumption per capita declined rather sharply from 1920–24 to 1935–39, while since 1940 consumption has risen to (or above) the normal level.

These conclusions of course depend on the accuracy of the basic statistics, and there is reason to doubt that the statistics are sufficiently accurate to be used for such analysis. For one thing, the wild fluctuation of the yearly figures are partially obscured by the five-year averages in Table VII. For another, the methods of compiling production figures leave much to be desired and cast doubt on their accuracy. Furthermore, export statistics do not reflect the quantity of rice smuggled out. This has been an important but unknown factor in the post–World War II period, and it has also been important in other years, such as 1919 and 1920. Finally, no estimates of internal stocks are available to use in checking the results suggested by the statistics.

At least three attempts have been made to deal with the problem raised in this section. In 1935 a statistician employed by the Thai government, David S. Green, used production and export statistics, together with various assumptions concerning consumption and inventories, in an effort to explain the relationships for the period 1919–34.[25] He concluded that, until 1927, pro-

[25] Mr. Green's analysis is published in Thailand, Ministry of Agriculture, *Thailand and Her Agricultural Problems*, National FAO Committee, pp. 120–27.

duction exceeded exports plus normal consumption (he used 2.3 piculs per capita), thus increasing internal stocks. After 1927 stocks were drawn down because production fell short of consumption plus exports.

The same method was used in a more recent computation which covered the period 1918-47.[26] Assuming "normal" consumption to be 2.4 piculs per capita, the production and export data showed a steady increase in internal stocks until 1927, after which they dwindled away. In 1935 internal stocks reached zero, and until 1941 the amount of rice available for domestic consumption remained well below the normal level. Apparently domestic consumption was curtailed in order to maintain exports at a high level. The rice farmer seems to have found it necessary to sell a larger share of his production than he had previously sold, and necessary also to reduce his own consumption below the normal level. From 1941 to 1947 consumption was back up to the normal level and a small stock was accumulated.

The third treatment of the problem is by Wickizer and Bennett,[27] who found that consumption per capita appeared to decrease from the 1920's to the 1930's because of increasing pressure on the rice farmer to export his crop even in the face of declining yields. Wickizer and Bennett were skeptical of the basic statistics, however, and they said no secure inferences could be drawn. They were particularly skeptical of population and production figures. The 1947 census has again confirmed the rapid increase in population, and the trend in yield per rai continues the trend observed by Wickizer and Bennett, but other than that we have no basis for trusting the official figures any more than they did.

Entrepreneurship and Labor

The vast expansion of rice cultivation after 1850 was achieved by the indigenous population of Thailand. Most of the increase in labor was supplied by the increase in population, which rose from 5 or 6 million in 1850 to about 7.3 million in 1900 and to 17.3 million in 1947. Even this rapid population increase did not match the increase in riceland. The labor supply for producing rice may also have been augmented by a shift of labor from other employments. It is difficult to document this statement but, considering the decline in other employments, it is likely that there was a long-run shift of labor into rice cultivation. The relative importance of this increment could not have been very great, however, since the overwhelming majority of the occupied population was already engaged (at least part time) in the cultivation of rice.

The supply of labor probably received important additions as the existing rice growers gave up leisure (at least during a part of the year) and chose instead to spend time in the cultivation of more land. We have suggested that the initial cause of this may have been the assurance of a market for addi-

[26] *Ibid.*, pp. 112-19.
[27] *The Rice Economy of Monsoon Asia*, pp. 194-202.

tional rice—i.e., that an increased money demand, made effective through developments in transportation and the willingness of the king to allow exports, induced the rice producer to produce more than enough for his own needs. Whatever the causal sequence, the fact that the area cultivated increased faster than the population means that the ratio of land to labor was rising.[28] The gradual elimination of various forms of slavery and forced labor (to be described below) also provided additional labor services for the expansion of ricelands. Since there has been little or no change in the technique of rice cultivation, we may assume that man-hours per rai per year have remained constant, and it then follows that the increase in the ratio of land to population means that more man-hours per person per year have been devoted to rice growing. That is, the long-run trend has been for the agricultural population in general to give up leisure and other occupations for the additional income earned by working longer hours per day and more days per year in order to produce more rice.[29] Part of the additional rice production has been sold in order to get money to buy consumers' goods.[30]

Regional shifts in population do not appear to have been very important since 1850. People did not migrate from one region to another to any great extent.[31] The rate of population increase has been roughly the same in all sections of the country, and it is this natural increase which has supplied the bulk of the labor to extend the area of riceland. One reason for the absence of regional shifts is that all regions have had unused land which could be brought under cultivation as population expanded and as individuals desired more land. Even in 1950 only about 10–11 percent of the total area is cultivated.[32] Of course there are great variations in fertility, ease of clearing, and suitability for growing rice.

The extension of riceland has been the major entrepreneurial achievement of the Thai themselves. As we will see, they have left most other entrepre-

[28] We refer here to the land *per person*. We do not mean to imply that the man-hours per unit of land were decreasing. The amount of labor services (man-hours) applied per unit of land could have been maintained or even increased by a shift from other employments and by a substitution of labor for leisure on the part of the existing rice producers (and their families).

[29] The farmer's work load is concentrated in the planting and harvesting seasons, and it is mainly in these seasons that he and his family have had to work harder and longer. During the peak of the planting and harvesting seasons, a number of seasonal workers leave their city jobs and work in the rice fields.

[30] The above discussion does not imply a fall in per capita real income. Indeed, it leaves room for an increase, since it is possible that the added man-hours per capita in rice production may have been more than offset by the decline in man-hours per capita in other employments and/or that the total material income may have risen in consequence of the change. The data are obviously inadequate to settle this question, however.

[31] There is only negative proof to support this statement. Nowhere in the literature is there much mention of interregional shifts other than the agricultural workers who came to the Central Plain in the rice season (and of course the Chinese, who did not grow rice). None of the people interviewed in the course of this study thought any important migrations had taken place.

[32] The total area is about 330 million rai, of which 33 to 36 million are in crops. Another 60 to 70 percent of the total area is still in forest. Much of the remainder is not arable under present conditions, however.

neurial functions to foreigners. The cultivation of rice is an ancient and honorable occupation to the Thai, however, and they seem to have preferred it to all others. The explanation of such an occupational preference is outside the scope of this study, but the existence of the preference is of great importance. The Thai has preferred the communal life of the village, and it is not easy to break the ties of culture and tradition which have induced him to become a rice farmer (or to remain one, since by the time he is old enough to strike out on his own he is already experienced in the art of rice cultivation). This preference has probably been one of the most important determinants of the pattern of the economy which has developed in Thailand. The Thai have been willing to undertake the arduous labor of clearing land of jungle; they have risked their savings (or borrowed money) to develop the land; and they have learned to make money calculations of cost and profit. Thus they have been entrepreneurs in rice cultivation, but not in other lines of economic activity. Their unwillingness to compete in other ways appears to be the overwhelmingly significant factor involved in any study of economic development in Thailand, but it simply cannot be satisfactorily analyzed by the economist. We may suggest some possible reasons for it and discuss the effects of it, but the preference itself cannot be explained in economic terms.

An episode which occurred in 1917–18 illustrates the reluctance of people to leave the land and to undertake other kinds of work. Disastrous floods had left large areas destitute in the Central Plain, and as a relief measure the government provided jobs on the irrigation works (Prasak South). Free transportation to the place of work, living accommodations, and first week's rations were provided, and the going rate of wages was paid. In spite of the seriousness of the floods, the average daily attendance was only 330 men and 100 women, and many who came stayed only long enough to receive their first week's free ration.[33]

The preference for rice farming and village living has, together with the supply of unused land, kept nonagricultural wages relatively high in Thailand. Workers have had to be lured away from their agricultural pursuits, and most of the nonagricultural jobs have been filled by Chinese immigrants. The pressure of population has not forced labor to leave land to seek employment elsewhere. Instead, as was written in 1904, "the vast extent of land suitable for agricultural operations offers . . . a more attractive career than toiling for a daily wage."[34] Before World War II high wages were necessary to induce labor to stay in the cities, and workers "tended to gravitate back to more congenial rural areas and cultivation of soil."[35] Since the war this tendency seems to be less strong.

---

[33] Thailand, Royal Irrigation Department, *Administration Report for the Period 1914/15–1925/26* (Bangkok, 1927), pp. 17–18.

[34] A. Cecil Carter (ed.), *The Kingdom of Siam* (New York, 1904), p. 264.

[35] Virginia M. Thompson, *Labor Problems in Southeast Asia,* p. 244.

The fact is that almost all wage labor outside of agriculture has been performed by the Chinese. The Chinese population has steadily increased over most of the century since 1850, and restrictions on immigration have been imposed only in recent decades.[36]

It is not possible to compare the wages of hired labor with the earnings of rice farmers in any over-all way. Factors which operate to make such a comparison difficult include: the sectional variations in wages and in prices of items entering into the budget, the inadequate records of these magnitudes, and the problem of imputing a value to items produced and consumed in the household.

Judging from the number of complaints about the scarcity and high cost of labor which appear in the literature of the last half of the nineteenth and the first part of the twentieth centuries, wage rates were probably relatively higher than the earnings of the great majority of small rice farmers. But this cannot be definitely established. The Thai did not respond to high wage rates, and the principal increases in the supply of nonagricultural labor came from Chinese immigration.

The most important form of wage labor in which the Thai participated was agricultural labor. As the production of rice for sale increased, greater use was made of hired labor. At the same time, the old system of communal planting and harvesting tended to decline. These changes took place gradually, but they were appearing in the Central region early in the twentieth century.[37] Commercialization and the use of hired labor had gone further by the 1930's, when Zimmerman and Andrews made their studies, but even then—as now—the regions outside the Center continued to practice predominantly subsistence farming, with labor supplied almost exclusively by the family unit and by communal efforts.

Available statistics on the occupational distribution of the labor force may help to indicate the importance of rice cultivation:[38]

Year	Total Labor Force	Number in Agriculture, Forestry, and Fishing	Percentage in Agriculture, Forestry, and Fishing
1929	7,520,000	6,330,000	84
1937	6,825,000	6,045,000	89
1947	8,990,000	7,625,000	85

[36] K. P. Landon, *The Chinese in Thailand* (New York, 1941).

[37] Dilock, *op. cit.,* pp. 102–8.

[38] Figures for 1929 and 1937, *Statistical Year Book of Thailand*; 1947, *Monthly Bulletin of Statistics*, Thailand, National Economic Council, Central Statistical Office, No. 1, June 1952, p. 28. These figures are all based on censuses taken in the years concerned. Definition of the "labor force" and the classifications used have varied from year to year. This accounts for the odd decrease in total employment from 1929 to 1937.

The great bulk of the people engaged in "Agriculture, Forestry, and Fishing" were rice farmers. In 1947 only 61,000 of them were in forestry and fishing, and the number in other forms of agriculture probably would have been less than 150,000. Of course the rice farmers had subsidiary crops and occupations, but their *primary* occupation was the cultivation of rice. The above statistics are very imperfect, but it is nevertheless clear that the population of Thailand has very largely specialized not only in agriculture but in one special form of it—rice cultivation. Nearly all of the rice farmers are Thai, as they have always been.[39]

Note on the Development of Personal Freedom

Because rice cultivation has been the principal occupation of the Thai people throughout the period we are examining, we may well discuss the long movement toward personal freedom at this time. This movement was an important accompaniment to the expansion of rice cultivation, and it was substantially completed by 1905—just thirty to forty years after it began in earnest. The movement was of great importance to the development of a nation of small farmers in Thailand. In 1850 a large percentage of people were slaves of one sort or another, and almost the entire male population was subject to the *corvée*. Yet, according to law, by 1905 all forms of slavery had been eliminated and the *corvée* system had been given up in favor of paid labor, although vestiges of both these institutions remained for a long time. As people were freed and especially as their *children* became free, they sought their own land. Fortunately there was enough land for all who would clear and cultivate it. And, since not many people were willing to work for wages, most farms were small enough to be worked by the farmer and his family.[40] Freedom from the *corvée* obligation also encouraged individuals to strike out on their own, for they could no longer be called, as in the past, to work for the king or his representative just when their own crops needed them most.

The *corvée* system was already on the way out when King Mongkut came to the throne in 1851. Men were allowed to pay a money tax in lieu of working for the required period, and it appears that they were increasingly taking advantage of this opportunity. King Mongkut took the next step, which was to order that, when free labor was available, men should not be forced to work for nothing.[41] Later the state began to pay for conscripted labor at a fixed

---

[39] The 1937 census showed that some 98.5 percent of cultivated land was owned and cultivated by Thai (rubber was not included in this calculation). Chinese growers of sugar, pepper, and vegetables probably made up the difference. "Statistics, Memoranda, and Documents Submitted to the Fund and the World Bank Missions, 1949–50" (mimeo., Bangkok), p. 4.

[40] The provision that only as much uncultivated land could be claimed as the farmer and his family could cultivate also served to prevent large estates from being carved out of the public domain.

[41] Thompson, *Labor Problems in Southeast Asia,* pp. 214–20.

wage.[42] Beginning with the fourth reign, one major form of public works—canal building—was done with wage labor, and the labor was largely Chinese.[43] In a passage translated after his death, King Mongkut said he reduced the requisitioning of labor by half, and that such things as wood, brick, lime, and construction work were paid for out of taxes instead of being obtained with forced labor.[44] Chinese were hired to do the work.

During the last two or three decades of the nineteenth century the *corvée* system continued to be unpopular, and it was clear that its abolition was merely a question of finding the means to replace it. The scarcity of wage labor caused the government to move slowly, but it gradually became understood that paid labor was far more productive than conscripted labor. Thus in 1871, "many [Siamese officials] . . . , when they have any real work to do, prefer to compound with the men told off to do it; and with the money thus obtained, hire labour at the market rates."[45] Other evils of the *corvée* system came to be recognized (e.g., that it stifled initiative), and the report just cited stated that "all, or nearly all of those who, in the course of a very few years, will in all probability administer the Government of this country are quite aware of its great evils, and are anxious to free their countrymen."

Nevertheless, the *corvée* system and abuses of it continued to exist for the rest of the century. For example, officials imposed heavy labor assignments in order to receive a bribe for dispensing with the labor service,[46] and men were called for service during the busy part of the rice season, a hardship they could escape by paying a bribe.[47] The extent of the abuses must have varied a good deal from place to place and region to region. Indeed, this was one of the disadvantages of the system. It was arbitrary and the severity of enforcement rested with minor officials throughout the country.

Finally, in 1899 a law was enacted replacing *corvée* with a head tax.[48] The amount of the tax varied from 1.5 to 6.0 baht per year, depending on the prosperity and fertility of the region. The tax was enforced by the patrons, just as the *corvée* had been, although in the provinces near Bangkok the king provided for payment of the tax directly to the government. The new system was of course not immediately put into effect in all parts of the country. In

[42] H. Warington Smyth, *Five Years in Siam*, I, 284–85. Writing in the 1890's, Smyth said the government had "long since" established a regular rate of wages for conscripted labor.

[43] Chao Phya Wongsa Nuprapath, *History of the Ministry of Agriculture* (Bangkok, 1941), pp. 126–64. (In Thai language.)

[44] *The Siam Repository*, I (April 1869), 68.

[45] *Commercial Report from Her Majesty's Consul-General in Siam for the Year 1871* (London, 1872), pp. 1–2.

[46] *Commercial Report by Her Majesty's Acting Consul in Siam for the Year 1885* (London, 1886).

[47] Holt S. Hallett, *A Thousand Miles on an Elephant in the Shan States* (Edinburgh, 1890), p. 244.

[48] Dilock, *op. cit.*, pp. 53–56.

many places men were still required to work for their patrons long after the new law was enacted. Many of the references to the use of *corvée* labor after 1899 should, however, note that such labor was in *lieu* of the payment of the money tax. A law of 1901/2 provided that defaulters could be called for 30 days' service. Later (in 1919/20) this power was repealed, but when the proceeds of the capitation tax fell off sharply, the power to require services from defaulters was restored (1925/26) and fixed at 15 days.[49] Finally, the capitation tax was eliminated in 1938.

The elimination of the *corvée* system freed a significant amount of labor services, which could then be available for hire or devoted to the land of the cultivator himself. The argument had been advanced that because the Thai had to work for the government three months out of twelve, they could not compete for wage-paying jobs on equal terms with the Chinese. After 1900, however, there was no significant increase in the relative number of Thai wage laborers.

It is a curious fact that the new law still required Thai nationals to pay a much larger head tax than the Chinese. The Thai paid 6 baht per year (less in the poorer regions) while the Chinese paid only 4.37 baht once every three years. This tax advantage allegedly helped the Chinese to dominate the wage-paying jobs in Thailand.[50] In any case, the unequal tax rates remained in force until 1910, when the Chinese were subjected to the same tax as the Thai, whereupon they rioted and went on strike (but were suppressed).[51] There is no evidence that Thai wage laborers became relatively more numerous after 1910, however—at least not until recently.

Thompson says that *corvée* labor represented an intermediary stage between free and slave labor.[52] If she means that the *corvée* system was a milder kind of restriction of personal liberty than slavery, her statement is correct. But if she means that the *corvée* system was an intermediate stage in the transition from slave to free labor, the statement is incorrect. The *corvée* obligation derived from the ancient obligation of every freeman to perform services for his king. It was essentially a relationship between the people and the king, while slavery was a relationship between individual members of the population, arising in a number of different ways.[53] The *corvée* obligation was converted into an obligation on the part of male citizens between 16 and

---

[49] "Report Suggesting the Basis for Raising Revenues for the Year B.E. 2475 (1932/33) and Probably Future Years," Thailand, Fiscal Committee (temporary) (Bangkok, 1931/32), pp. 38–42.

[50] Dilock, *op. cit.*, p. 57.

[51] Victor Purcell, *The Chinese in Southeast Asia* (London, 1951), pp. 152–53. Dr. Purcell erroneously states that the Thai were taxed at the rate of 50 baht per year.

[52] *Labor Problems in Southeast Asia*, pp. 214–16.

[53] It is true that the *corvée* obligation could lead (through debt) to slavery, especially if the patron (i.e., the person who received *corvée* services in the king's name) abused his position. This relationship between the *corvée* and slavery is emphasized in the article, "Marking the People," *The Siam Repository*, V (1873), 340–44.

60 years of age to pay a head tax. Thus the duty to the king remained. The movement to eliminate slavery, on the other hand, sought to destroy the very basis of it by changing the laws and customs supporting it. Finally, the *corvée* system was eliminated in 1899 (according to law), some six years before slavery was finally eliminated (according to law).

Slavery was widespread in 1850 and there were a great many forms of it, but in general it appears that the slavery was a far milder form than that known to Westerners. Even so ardent an opponent of slavery as Samuel J. Smith wrote that slavery in Siam was generally humane, and that people were not reduced to "mere chattels."[54] Some writers have stressed the fact that slaves had established rights which were protected by law and custom. Thus, "in King Mongkut's time slavery was not a system whereby one or more human beings were subjugated by another. It was, strangely enough, the right of free men to sell themselves into bondage which, in most cases, was exercised with the object of extricating these persons from financial difficulties."[55] A man could also obtain a degree of security by selling himself into slavery, since the owner had to provide food, clothing, and shelter without any increase in the debt owed. On the other hand, the work performed represented interest on the debt and did not decrease that debt.[56] In addition to economic security the debt slave received the security of an assured status and the protection of his master. These things must have been important in 1850 when about all a small rice farmer could hope to do was to win a modest living for himself and his family from his land. In an early proclamation King Mongkut mentions his hope that the increase in trade following the treaties with the West will mean that "the poor may find better employment than to sell themselves into bondage."[57] Nevertheless, it appears probable that more people were attracted to some form of bondage by the security and protection it provided, than were driven to it by dire economic necessity. Land was freely available and any man with average luck who was willing to work could not have had much difficulty in making a living. Only by noting the *attractions* of bondage can we explain the situation which puzzled Hallett; namely, that debt slavery could be so prevalent when "a labourer's wages are such as to enable him to subsist on a fourth of his earnings."[58]

In general, it appears that the lot of the debt slave was not too unpleasant in comparison with his countrymen, and that many people were probably "slaves" more or less through choice. There was an extremely complicated

[54] *The Siam Repository*, IV (Bangkok, 1872), 380–81.

[55] Pramoj and Pramoj, "The King of Siam Speaks," p. 31.

[56] Dilock, *op. cit.*, pp. 33–34. Dilock also says that the word "slavery" in the Western sense hardly applied to debt slavery.

[57] "Proclamation Concerning Treaty Farangs," in Pramoj and Pramoj, *op. cit.*, p. 46.

[58] Hallett, *op. cit.*, pp. 243–53. Gambling and taxation probably contributed also, as Hallett pointed out. Hallett wrote of the 1880's, but *The Siam Repository* for 1873 (V, 482), also noted that the "most common day laborer can save two-thirds of his earnings."

body of law governing the rights and status of the different kinds of slaves, the status of children, and the legal prices. It was through a series of changes at different places in this body of law that King Chulalongkorn effected the elimination of slavery.[59]

The first important attack on slavery came in 1874, when King Chulalongkorn assumed direct control of the government after his second coronation ceremony. He had become king in 1868 at the age of 15, but until 1874 the country was actually governed by a regent and council. In 1874 a decree was issued containing the following provisions:

1. The fixed scale of prices for slaves was changed. For those *born* into slavery after October 1, 1868, the price was made zero at the age of 21.

2. People born into slavery after October 1, 1868, were to become free on their 21st birthday.

3. People who were born into slavery after October 1, 1868, and who were freed on their 21st birthday, could afterward neither sell themselves nor be sold by others into slavery.

4. Children born to freemen after October 1, 1868, could be sold only with the consent of the child after he reached the age of 15.

5. No one born after October 1, 1868, who had reached 21 years, could either sell himself or be sold into slavery.

The provisions of this decree alone were sufficient to promise the eventual elimination of slavery. If it were rigorously enforced, as soon as all those born *before* October 1, 1868, were dead, the entire population would be free. The decree wisely allowed a considerable amount of time for people to adapt to the new system. It also avoided a sudden destruction of wealth in the form of slaves.

When the first of the slaves born after October 1, 1868, began to claim their freedom, some wealthy owners brought "a considerable amount of pressure to bear on his Majesty to reform the law," but he and the judges remained firm.[60]

Upon his return from a trip to Europe, King Chulalongkorn issued another decree providing that no one born after December 16, 1897, could either sell himself or be sold by others. This decree was intended mainly for certain groups not covered by the earlier decree (e.g., children of prisoners of war) and for regions in the North to which the 1874 decree had not been applied.

Finally, slavery was abolished completely in 1905. Characteristically, this was done by a system which cost the masters little and the government nothing.[61] It was decreed that no new persons could become slaves, and that

---

[59] The following account is based largely on Dilock, *op. cit.,* pp. 30–42. See also R. Lingat, *L'Esclavage Privé dans le Vieux Droit Siamois* (Paris, 1931), Ch. 6.

[60] *Diplomatic and Consular Reports on Trade and Finance, Siam, Report for the Year 1887,* Great Britain, Foreign Office (London, 1888).

[61] P. W. Thornely, *The History of a Transition* (Bangkok, 1923), pp. 155–56.

debt slaves must be credited with four baht per month until their debts were paid off and they became free.

The gap between legislation and enforcement was undoubtedly large. Even as late as 1910 the slavery laws were not fully enforced in the Laos states, although we are told that slavery was decreasing there as Siamese rule became more direct.[62] Nevertheless, the net achievement was an impressive one to have been won at such a small cost in internal friction. Slavery was gradually and effectively eliminated from the social fabric of the nation, even though custom and practice lagged behind legislation.

The suggestion has been made that the relatively painless elimination of slavery was possible because the wealthy class could, after trade began, receive income from the rent of land, while before trade began land had no value and could earn no contractual rent, and the wealthy class had to receive its income from slave labor.[63] It is certainly true that the price of land increased during the last half of the nineteenth century and the first decades of the twentieth, and that there was an increase in tenancy by contract, but for neither of these facts is there much detailed evidence. We cannot offer much analysis of the above hypothesis, therefore, except to say that the known facts are consistent with it, although there is no evidence to prove (or deny) that any section of the population was ever motivated by the consideration.

The elimination of slavery and the *corvée* was an important factor in the expansion of rice cultivation. King Chulalongkorn deserves much credit for the skill with which he effected this reform.

Capital

The extension of rice cultivation required little money expenditure by the cultivators. Uncultivated land was free to anyone who would clear and cultivate it. The only charge made was a small fee to cover registration and the necessary paper work. The government also encouraged the extension of rice cultivation by giving tax favors to newly cultivated land (see below). The labor of clearing the land and preparing it for cultivation was the major cost involved, and this labor was usually supplied by the cultivator himself, although in some cases hired labor was used.

The cultivator also had to have seed for the first crop, the necessary tools for clearing and cultivating the land, and one or two draft animals. The amount of seed required would vary considerably since it depended on the type of rice and the method of sowing. To give an idea of the investment involved, we may take the estimate of 0.233 piculs of seed paddy per rai.[64]

[62] J. H. Freeman, *An Oriental Land of the Free* (Philadelphia, 1910), p. 101.

[63] Van der Heide, "The Economical Development of Siam During the Last Half Century," *Journal of the Siam Society*, III (1906), 74–101.

[64] This is the estimate of the Thai Department of Agriculture, as cited in *Thailand and Her Agricultural Problems*, p. 115.

A man who undertook to cultivate 20 rai of land would thus require about 4.7 piculs of paddy for seed. Using the average export prices of *rice* given in Table III and roughly converting them into *paddy* prices,[65] the cost of seed for 20 rai was as follows:

Period	Paddy Price per Picul (*Baht*)	Cost of Seed for 20 Rai (*Baht*)
1870–74	.90	4.20
1900–1904	1.90	8.90
1920–24	2.25	10.60
1935–39	1.30	6.10

Very little money needed to be spent on tools. The plow and some sort of knife for harvesting were the most important items, and the farmer could have made all of his tools except the knife blade and a metal tip for his plow. In 1910 a plow cost from 4–5 to 8–10 baht, depending on the wood used, and a metal tip cost only 25 satang.[66] Most farmers bought only the tip.

Little or no fertilizer is used in rice cultivation as practiced in Thailand, and no expenditure was required on that account.

The new farmer could probably get by with one buffalo or, if he lived in a region where bullocks were used, two bullocks. The purchase of these draft animals probably represented the largest money outlay made by the farmer. Prices varied widely from one region to another and from year to year, but an idea of the relative importance of this item of expenditure may be given by the following estimates:

	Price in Bangkok Vicinity[67]	
Period	Buffalo (*Baht*)	Bullock (*Baht*)
1890	40–50	15–32
1895		30
1902		64
c. 1905	70–120	70–80
1925–28	74	64
1937–40	41	32

[65] One picul of paddy is equal to approximately 0.70 picul of cleaned rice. We have arbitrarily assumed that the price of paddy seed in the village is 50 percent of the price of the paddy equivalent of cleaned rice, F.O.B. Bangkok.

[66] Yai S. Santitwongse, *An Outline of Rice Cultivation in Siam,* Thailand, Ministry of Agriculture (Bangkok, 1911).

[67] Figures for 1890, *Diplomatic and Consular Reports on Trade and Finance, Siam, Report for the year 1890,* Foreign Office (London, 1891), p. 41; 1895 and 1902, *Diplomatic and Consular Report for 1902,* Great Britain, p. 11; 1905, Dilock, *op. cit.,* p. 168; 1925–28 and 1937–40, *Statistical Year Book of Thailand,* XXI, 549 (these are export prices F.O.B. Bangkok).

Many items which would require money expenditures in other countries do not require them in Thailand because they may be obtained from common property or government lands. Thus in most sections the forests, swamps, and canal banks yield cattle feed, wood for farm implements, materials for the construction of dwellings, and the like.

It appears that a small amount of money would have been sufficient to enable a man to strike out on his own as a rice farmer. The figures given are likely to be on the high side for the country as a whole, because in the less accessible regions money prices tended to be much lower than in the vicinity of Bangkok (except for abnormal conditions), and because a large part of the country was not readily accessible by rail or water for much of the period since 1850. That the capital requirement for rice cultivation was relatively small may be demonstrated by comparing it with the value of the surplus rice which could have been produced in a single year by a single farmer. If a family of five cultivated 20 rai, and if the average yield were four piculs of *paddy* per rai, the yearly surplus would be about forty piculs of *rice*.[68] If the farmer sold his surplus at one-half the export price, his money income for a year would have been as follows:

Period	Baht
1870–74	54
1890–94	66
1910–14	106
1920–24	130
1930–34	70
1948–50	1700

Comparing these figures with those described above, it appears that the capital expenditures required to cultivate 20 rai of land in rice would have been about equal to only one year's money income. This calculation makes no allowance for nonmonetary costs such as labor for clearing or making tools. Even at interest rates of 30 to 50 percent, the new farmer should have been able to repay any money he borrowed to begin farming. The trouble was that the system of advances and repayments in kind sometimes concealed a much higher interest rate, and the farmer remained permanently in debt. Because they did not maintain sufficient cash resources, farmers were also plunged into permanent debt by crop failures.

Unfortunately we know very little about where the rice farmer obtained the small sum of money he needed to cultivate new land. Many young men were probably set up by their families, possibly with help from the bride's parents. Others received advances in kind or money from friends and relatives, and some borrowed from moneylenders and/or paddy buyers. The studies of

---

[68] A total yield of 80 piculs of paddy, less 20 piculs for family consumption, less one-third for loss in milling, equals about 40 piculs of milled rice.

Zimmerman and Andrews indicate that the major part of the agricultural debt in the 1930's was owed to relatives and friends, and carried no interest. Andrews concluded that absentee landlordism was found mainly in the Center, while in the other regions the landlords and tenants generally lived in the same village.[69]

The very small cash outlay required probably served to encourage the expansion of rice cultivation, and also made it easier for the cultivator to become an independent owner-farmer. The low capital cost of rice cultivation, compared with that required for fruit and vegetable gardens, has been cited as one reason for the increasing dominance of rice.[70]

With available statistics it is not possible to say much about the trend in tenancy and debt, but most observers have concluded that except for certain regions these problems are much less acute than in other countries of Asia. Dilock (writing about 1905) said that tenancy was of minor importance in Thailand because the right to claim land from the state plus the *duty* to cultivate it had kept the holdings fairly small.[71] He said the great landholdings were mostly near Bangkok, where rent could be charged. Elsewhere, people could take land from the state instead of renting it. Generally, it seems that tenancy and debt were most prevalent in the commercialized sections, especially in the heart of the Central Plain. Zimmerman (in 1930/31) found tenancy to be greatest in the Central region, and he noted that the percentage of tenancy varied from place to place.[72] Andrews (1934) substantially agreed.[73]

The problems of tenancy and agricultural debt excited a great deal of attention in the 1920's and 1930's. The severe crop failure of 1919/20 and the depression of the 1930's not only increased the debts of the farmers, but also made existing debts more onerous. Certainly the foreclosures of the 1930's accentuated the social problems of the debt burden. There was endless discussion of these problems in the government during the last years of the absolute monarchy and the first years of the constitutional regime. Many plans were formulated and committees appointed, but very little was done. The price inflation during and after World War II has greatly reduced the burden of the original debt, and the high prices of paddy have enabled many farmers to pay off their debts, but tenancy and debt remain a problem in the commercialized sections, especially in the Central Plain and in the region around Chiengmai. A sample survey of 26 changwats in 1947 showed the percentage of tenant-operated lands to be quite low in the South and Northeast, and highest in the Center.[74] In 1950–51 the consensus seems to be that tenant-

---

[69] James M. Andrews, *Siam, 2nd Rural Economic Survey, 1934–1935* (Bangkok, 1935), Ch. 5.

[70] Dilock, *op. cit.*, pp. 153–55.

[71] *Ibid.*, pp. 95–101. As slavery was abolished, Dilock says, nobles were unable to cultivate their large holdings, many of which reverted to the state according to law.

[72] Carle C. Zimmerman, *Siam, Rural Economic Survey, 1930–31* (Bangkok, 1931), p. 18.

[73] Andrews, *op. cit.*, pp. 100–103.

[74] "Statistics, Memoranda, and Documents," pp. 6–9.

operated farms are a very small proportion of the total and that tenancy is important in only two or three regions which have special characteristics.[75] (See Ch. 11 for a discussion of changes in tenancy rates since 1950.)

Even where tenancy is found, it is not necessarily an indication of maladjustment. Rents are roughly adjusted to the productivity of the land. Thus, in the prosperous Chiengmai region, where soils are fertile and two crops are often possible, tenancy is widespread and rents are high. As early as 1900 Van der Heide noted that people were willing to pay high prices and rents for land in the Rangsit area even though free land was available for the taking.[76] Obviously, fertility and access to markets influence rents and land values.

Underlying the problems of tenancy and debt is the problem of interest rates. The legal maximum is 15 percent, but it is common knowledge that private loans carry rates up to 36 percent, while loans involving payment in kind sometimes carry interest rates of 60 to 120 percent. On the other hand, many loans obtained from relatives and friends carry no interest at all. As noted above, Zimmerman and Andrews found such noninterest-bearing loans to be the rule in the three self-sufficing regions, and also common in the Center. It is difficult to generalize about conditions which vary so greatly even within a district or village. One farmer may get an interest-free loan while his neighbor has to take an advance on his crop which involves paying 100 percent interest. No doubt a part of the problem is to educate the farmers to make calculations of alternative costs and profits, because they frequently accept the advances offered by the middleman without really understanding the price they are paying; but there is also the problem of the supply of capital in agriculture. No adequate system of agricultural credit has ever existed in Thailand. Commercial banks have not been prepared to make loans to farmers, and the government has never made a serious effort to establish a farm-bank system. The "legal maximum" interest rate has not been enforced, nor could it be.

The moneylenders are both Thai and Chinese. Popular opinion has long been that the Chinese moneylenders hold most of the agricultural debt and charge high interest rates, but Andrews concluded that they charged lower rates than did the Thai professional moneylenders, and were on the whole less important.[77]

---

[75] This opinion has been expressed by a number of expert observers in and out of the Thai government, and it is also stated in Richard Pringle, "Report on Cooperatives in Thailand," U.S. Special Technical and Economic Mission to Thailand (mimeo., Bangkok, 1951), and in Dr. Flournoy A. Coles, "Aspects of Land Reform," U.S. Special Technical and Economic Mission to Thailand (rev. ed., mimeo., Bangkok, 1951).

[76] J. H. Van der Heide, *General Report on Irrigation and Drainage in the Lower Menam Valley* (Bangkok, 1903), p. 62.

[77] Andrews, *op. cit.,* Ch. 5.

For the long-run solution to the problems of agricultural credit, including tenancy, debt, and interest rates, the government has put its faith in the cooperative system. Started in 1916, the co-operative movement in Thailand made little progress until 1932, but since that time it has been pushed forward much more rapidly. In 1951 there were 8,151 co-operative societies of all kinds with a total of 249,175 members. Of these, 7,763 were *credit* societies with a membership of 145,603.[78] It is estimated that 5 percent of all farmers are members of some type of co-operative. Because the co-operative movement is still quite small relative to the whole problem, we will not try to describe it in detail. To give an idea of the recent growth of the movement, it is enough to say that although the first society was founded in 1916, by 1932 there were only 150 credit societies, while by 1941 the number had grown to 2,851; by 1948, to 6,196; and by October 1951, to 7,763.[79]

From the beginning, the co-operative movement has been a government-sponsored institution. Control and initiative have come from the central government rather than from the farmers themselves, but in spite of the central administration of the system the co-operatives have been very carefully nurtured. On the whole the credit co-operatives have operated with remarkable success. In thirty-five years of operation only 3 societies have failed.

Credit societies are the most important type of co-operatives. Members have unlimited liability for their own and the society's debts, and loans to members are fully secured by real property. (There was a debate in the 1920's over the question of real versus personal security. It was won by the adherents of real security.) The number of members in each society has been kept small —in 1951 the average was about 19—and members are carefully selected. With the exception of a few high-grade tenants, membership is limited to owner-farmers. Until 1947, long-term loans at 9 percent interest and short-term loans at 12 percent were made to members from funds borrowed by the societies at 6½ percent. Since 1947, when a "Bank for Co-operatives" was established, the interest rates to members have been reduced to 8 percent for long-term and 10 percent for short-term loans.

So far, the credit societies have had little success in mobilizing capital locally. Instead, they have been financed almost exclusively with funds supplied by the central government. This has been one reason for the small size of the co-operative movement, although a more important reason has been the need to build up the system slowly and carefully.

Other types of co-operatives in Thailand include Land Hire–Purchase, Colonization, Land Improvement, Consumers', Marketing, and Producers'

---

[78] Pringle, *op. cit.,* p. 4.

[79] *Report of the Financial Adviser Covering the Years 1941 to 1950,* Thailand, Ministry of Finance (Bangkok, 1951), pp. 32–40 (except for the 1951 figure which is from Pringle, *op. cit.,* p. 4).

co-operatives. Most of these were organized during and since the 1930's, and they are still few in number. (The total number of societies other than Credit Co-operatives was 388 in October 1951, and 209 of these were Consumers' Co-operatives.)

There are many abuses of and weaknesses in the present co-operative system. One of the greatest needs is to develop a spirit of joint effort. Too many farmers look upon the system as a paternal organization. Others take advantage of it—e.g., by borrowing for 8 percent on long term and relending to nonmembers at much higher interest rates.

If it can be expanded successfully, the co-operative movement promises to be of great benefit to agriculture in Thailand. The Department of Co-operatives, a part of the Ministry of Agriculture since 1932, has recently been raised to the status of Ministry of Co-operatives, and the government has stated that it intends to continue the expansion of co-operatives. Because of the shortage of trained men to administer the program and the lack of education in business methods at the village level, rapid expansion poses many problems and dangers to the co-operative movement, but it is still the only direct attack being made on the related problems of tenancy, debt, and high interest rates.

As we have seen above, agriculture in Thailand uses very little capital equipment. Zimmerman observed that, as commercialization proceeded, farmers tended to spend more money for labor, but not for labor-saving devices.[80] As agriculture became commercialized the use of capital goods became more, rather than less, extensive. The commercialized farmers use about the same tools and techniques as farmers in self-sufficient districts, but use more labor and land. One reason for the small amount of capital goods has been the technical difficulties of producing machines which can work effectively in flooded fields. Another reason has been the small area of individual fields and holdings. And, although tractors suitable for plowing and preparing the land have been developed, the farmer then does not have enough labor to harvest the area he can efficiently plant in paddy.[81] There must be a sort of balance between the labor required for planting and that required for harvesting. Until harvesting machines are technically possible, agriculture in Thailand cannot be mechanized. Even then, the small average size of farm and the division into small fields will limit the use of machines. Other practical obstacles to mechanization include the necessity for better water control, the necessity to use rice varieties which lend themselves to mechanized methods, the high cost of motor fuel relative to farm labor, and the relatively low paddy prices paid to the farmer under the present marketing system.

The expansion of rice production was accompanied by capital investment in rice mills. Formerly each family milled its own rice by hand but, with the

[80] Zimmerman, *op. cit.*, pp. 74–77.
[81] *Thailand and Her Agricultural Problems*, pp. 13–14.

increase in production for sale, machine milling developed into one of the major industries of the country. At first the new rice mills were concentrated in Bangkok, but as railways penetrated into the North and East there was a tendency toward smaller mills dispersed throughout the rice-growing regions.

The first steam rice mill in Thailand was constructed in 1858 by an American firm.[82] The mill was not an immediate success and it changed hands several times, finally ending in Chinese ownership. By 1867 there were only 5 important rice mills in Bangkok, but the number increased to 23 in 1889, 25 in 1892, 27 in 1895, 59 in 1910, 66 in 1919, 71 in 1930, and 72 in 1941.[83] Since 1910 the number of mills in Bangkok has thus not increased very much.

The mills in Bangkok are mostly run by steam, and they are much larger than the upcountry mills. The capacity of the Bangkok mills, which we call "large," is 100 to 200 tons of paddy per day. The country mills have a capacity of 30 to 40 tons per day.

The number of mills outside Bangkok has increased greatly in the last three or four decades. As early as 1877, mills were being located in the rice-growing districts,[84] although there are no estimates of the numbers involved. The first "modern" mill in Korat was built in 1915, and by 1931 there were 33 mills (mostly small) in the Northeast.[85] In the entire country outside of Bangkok, there were about 500 mills in 1930 and about 800 in 1950.[86] Most of these were of 30- to 40-ton size. A very recent development is the use of small, portable mills with a capacity of only 8 to 12 tons per day. In early 1952, it was estimated that as many as 4,000 of these portable mills were operating. They provide keen competition to the larger mills.

The trend toward a large number of small mills scattered over the country has changed the marketing pattern. Formerly, farmers sold their surplus paddy and kept the rest at home, where they milled it by hand. Now, the farmer more frequently takes his entire crop to the mill and receives a certain percentage of cleaned rice in return. This he either eats or sells.

From the beginning, rice mills in Thailand have been owned principally by Chinese and other foreigners, and the labor employed in them has been largely Chinese. Of the 23 steam mills in Bangkok in 1889, 17 were owned

[82] *Seventy Years Trade in Bangkok, 1856–1926* (Bangkok, 1926).

[83] For rice mill figures, see: 1867, *Annual Diplomatic and Consular Report, 1867*, Great Britain, p. 318; 1889, *Annual Diplomatic and Consular Report, 1889*, Great Britain; 1892, Jacob T. Child, *The Pearl of Asia* (Chicago, 1892), pp. 145–46; 1895, *Annual Diplomatic and Consular Report, 1895*, Great Britain; 1910, G. E. Gerini, *Siam, Its Production, Arts, and Manufactures* (Hertford, England, 1912), p. 163; 1919, H. F. McNair, *The Chinese Abroad* (Shanghai, 1926), p. 48; 1930, *Siam, Nature and Industry*, Ministry of Commerce and Communications (Bangkok, 1930), p. 212; 1941, Virginia M. Thompson, *Thailand, the New Siam*, p. 447.

[84] *Annual Diplomatic and Consular Report, 1877*, Great Britain, Foreign Office.

[85] Siam, Ministry of Commerce and Communications, *The Economic Conditions of North-Eastern Siam* (Bangkok, 1932), p. 12.

[86] The 1930 figure is from *Siam, Nature and Industry*, p. 212; the 1950 figure, from Department of Agriculture, Bangkok.

by Chinese; of 66 in 1919, 56 were owned by Chinese. Rice mills have been operated by the large European firms in some years but these have had difficulty competing with the Chinese. By 1919, for example, the European-owned mills had either been sold to the Chinese or closed down.[87] The small up-country mills are also predominantly in the hands of the Chinese.

The two biggest threats to Chinese control are government ownership, e.g., through the Thai Rice Co., a government concern which took over 10 large Chinese mills in 1938; and the tiny portable mills which are increasing in numbers so rapidly. Oddly enough, the recent trend in rice milling in Thailand has been toward smaller mills, dispersed over the country, rather than toward large, central mills.

Marketing and Trade, 1850–1950

When exports expanded after 1850, the system of marketing and exporting rice and paddy quickly acquired the basic characteristics which it was to retain for a long time. Indeed, except for certain innovations made since the end of World War II, the system has changed very little in recent decades.

For many years the big rice mills along the Chao Phya River near Bangkok processed almost all rice exports, and even in 1950 the great bulk of rice exports still passed through them. The purpose of this section is to describe the marketing system which was developed to get paddy from grower to mill and from mill to outbound ship.

The first point is that neither the grower nor the miller has performed the function of moving paddy from the producing areas to the mills. Instead, this function has been performed by independent middlemen. A second point is that nearly all of these middlemen have been Chinese. The middlemen go into the country, buy paddy directly from the grower, and ship it to Bangkok for sale to millers. Until well into the twentieth century nearly all rice for export came from the Central Plain. Middlemen went out on canals and rivers to the rural villages, bought the paddy, and brought it to Bangkok in river boats. Rarely did the growers themselves bring their paddy to the mills or the millers send their own buyers into the country. Sometimes, when competition was unusually keen among the millers, they sent their buyers up the rivers and canals to meet the paddy boats, but they bought for delivery in Bangkok and ordinarily did not undertake to transport the paddy themselves.[88]

As far as the paddy milled in Bangkok is concerned, the general practice still is for millers to buy only from middlemen, but the several thousand small

---

[87] Report on the Commercial Situation in Siam at the Close of the Year 1919, Great Britain, Foreign Office (London, 1920), pp. 18–19.

[88] Graham, op. cit., II, 78–82. One author, Octave Collet, Étude Politique et Économique sur le Siam Moderne (Bruxelles, 1911), p. 103, wrote that millers were buying paddy directly from growers in an effort to ensure a steady supply for their mills. This is an exceptional account, however, and may reflect a temporary situation.

upcountry millers frequently deal directly with the growers. Rice shipped to Bangkok from the upcountry mills is usually handled by the middlemen, however.

Many of the agricultural problems of Thailand are tied up with the system and methods of middlemen. These men not only buy and sell paddy; they also lend money, advance supplies, own and rent land, sell imported merchandise, and transport goods in both directions. The various functions are so mixed together that it is impossible to estimate the cost of any single function. The problem is further complicated by the seasonal variations in the price of paddy, the cost of storing it to take advantage of off-season prices, and the varying standards of quality and volume used in selling it.

The farmer's lack of knowledge of prices and markets, together with his lack of liquid assets, have made him peculiarly dependent on the middleman. This is especially true of tenant farmers, who frequently do not have much security to offer against loans, but who are compelled to sell their crops at harvest time (when prices are lowest) in order to repay advances made at high rates of interest. The middlemen cannot exactly be blamed for the high interest rates, however, because middlemen account for only a small part of the loans at high rates. The basic problems are risk and the scarcity of loanable funds, and until these are solved professional moneylenders, both Thai and Chinese, will continue to demand high rates for poorly secured loans.

The middlemen themselves are also powerless to remedy other situations in which they appear in unsavory roles. Thus they are often pictured as villains because they buy paddy in the harvest season and hold it until just before the next harvest. Actually, the cost of storage, the risk, and the foregone interest on the money value of paddy make this a costly operation, and a burden which the farmer may be unable or unwilling to assume. Similarly, the middlemen individually can do little to standardize the grading of paddy or the containers used for measurement. Because of such variations the farmer has been able to make little use of the small amount of information on prices and markets which has been available to him.

Regardless of their lack of responsibility for the system, the army of middlemen has taken a large part of the profit in rice exporting. The over-all share of the export proceeds which has been taken by the middlemen cannot be estimated with any accuracy, but it has probably been rather large. The Financial Adviser, Mr. Doll, estimated in 1937 that about 50 percent of the export price of rice was required to pay the miller, exporter, and middleman.[89] Of all the intermediaries, the middlemen between grower and miller probably took the largest share.

Competition has long been keen in the rice-milling industry. If contemporary accounts can be trusted, there has been a persistent tendency toward ex-

---

[89] *Report of the Financial Adviser for B.E. 2480 (1937/38).*

cess capacity in rice mills ever since 1875, and the pressures of overhead costs have forced millers to engage in intense competition for the paddy coming down from the country. Even so, the mills have not been able to operate steadily throughout the year. Under such circumstances it is strange that millers have not used agents to buy paddy directly from growers. Some attempts to do this were made, but they were not very successful. In one case the government interfered. This was in 1931–32 when the East Asiatic Company (Danish) began to buy paddy directly from growers and to make advances to them at 10 percent interest on the security of mortgages. An elaborate system of organization was developed, but violent objections in some sectors of the government ended in abandonment of the project. The government was willing to see Chinese middlemen and moneylenders replaced, but not by other foreigners.[90] The chief fear was that foreign companies would obtain possession of large amounts of riceland through foreclosure. The scheme was also opposed on the ground that it competed with the co-operative movement and might destroy it.

Millers have usually purchased paddy at the mill, and they have often sold the rice there also, thus restricting their own function to the milling itself. The practice in this respect varied from year to year, however. Sometimes the millers themselves handled most rice exports, and sometimes they sold to local trading firms and the latter handled the export trade. Generally speaking, Chinese millers have handled exports to Hong Kong, China, Singapore, Malaya, and other Asian markets on their own account, while exports to Europe, South America, and non-Asian markets have been handled by European trading firms in Bangkok. (This statement refers to the period prior to World War II.)

Thus the Thai have participated in the rice trade only as growers, and their lack of knowledge and experience in markets, prices, and business methods, plus their lack of cash reserves, has meant that a rather large share of the export proceeds of rice has been taken by the various middlemen. The government has made some efforts to improve the position of the farmer and to enlarge the role of the Thai in the rice trade, but with only limited success. There is a legal maximum interest rate, but it cannot be enforced. Standards of weights and measures were established in the 1920's, but the government had no way to ensure their adoption. Consequently, the market information disseminated by the government was not as useful to the farmers as was hoped. We have already seen that the co-operative movement, though sound in principle, was too small to have much effect on the total picture. The government has periodically announced plans for a system of storage silos throughout the country, but so far little or nothing has been done. Finally, in the late 1930's

---

[90] Source: correspondence and memoranda in files of Financial Adviser, Ministry of Finance, Bangkok.

the government announced plans to enlarge its role in the milling and trade in rice, but eventually the newly formed Thai Rice Co., a government organization, took over only ten of the large Chinese mills. This company has operated the mills successfully so far, although it has enjoyed some favors from the government. At the present time it is nominally controlled by the co-operative societies, which own 73 percent of the stock.

None of the above government measures did much to alter the marketing system for paddy. In the next chapter we will describe some changes in rice marketing that occurred after World War II.

4

The Role of Government in the Rice Industry 1850–1950

To EXPAND the cultivation and export of rice was an expressed goal of the government in the years following the Bowring Treaty. There was still some concern about the supply of rice for domestic consumption, to be sure, and in the treaty the right to prohibit rice exports in years of poor harvest was preserved, but in general the government was willing to trust the trade mechanism to safeguard the interests of the country. King Mongkut was the leading spirit in promoting and encouraging this new attitude. On one occasion he issued a "Notification Concerning Rain and False Rumors," in which he defended himself for not having prohibited the export of rice on the strength of rumors that a drought was coming.[1] "The volume of rice export will decrease of its own accord," he said, "should the price be too high." This suggests a clear willingness to trust the price mechanism. In denying that foreigners bought Thai rice out of a desire to harm Thailand, he urged the advantages of trade itself: "Their money will come into our pockets, which is better than to let our rice rot, or our peasants abandon their rice-fields."

King Mongkut saw that the interests of consumers and producers might come into conflict as rice exports increased. In the edict of 1855 which removed the ban on rice exports, he explained that the ban had been beneficial to those consumers who did not grow their own rice, since they had enjoyed low prices of rice.[2] The producers felt otherwise, however, and they suffered so much from the low prices in years of good harvest that they ceased to cultivate all their land, preferring to return part of it to the state. The state thus lost the revenue from land tax. Furthermore, when a poor season came along, the harvest from the reduced acreage was scarcely enough to feed the domestic population, and as a result the price rose greatly. The ban on exports therefore did not prevent distress in years of poor harvest, as it was designed to do. King Mongkut thus recognized the conflicting interests of two large groups within the nation, and he concluded that the general welfare would be best served by allowing the export of rice. In explaining this decision he also noted that the state would receive more revenue. The export duty was fixed by treaty at 4 baht per *kwien* of about 25 piculs, and the rates of land tax could

---

[1] Cited in Pramoj and Pramoj, "The King of Siam Speaks," pp. 78–79.

[2] Dilock, *op. cit.*, pp. 66–67. Actually, rice exports were not completely banned before this edict. See Ch. 2.

not be conveniently increased. To increase its revenue from the staple article of the kingdom, the government had to increase acreage and exports. At the same time, the consuming group was not ignored. In a "Notification Forbidding Collection of Rice Land Tax in the First Year of Cultivation," King Mongkut expressed his desire to expand the cultivation of rice in order to prevent the price from rising high enough to harm the nonfarm group: "Wherefore, it is the wish of His Majesty that more jungles be opened up for rice cultivation with a view to increasing the quantity of rice and lowering the price thereof, without prejudice to the interests of the peasants and merchants."[3]

The actions taken by the government to encourage rice production will be described in the following pages. We have already discussed the gradual elimination of slavery and the *corvée*, a movement which itself aided the expansion of cultivation because it increased the number of independent farmer-families whose natural inclination was to grow rice. We have also mentioned the government-sponsored co-operative movement and the statutory limit on interest rates. Other government actions fell into two groups: legislation concerning ownership and taxation of land, and capital expenditures designed to develop agricultural production. A third section of this chapter will describe the role of the government in the rice trade from 1945 to 1950.

Legislation

The tax on riceland from 1850–1900 was definitely designed to encourage people to bring new land under cultivation.[4] The inducement was in the form of an incentive land tax which granted exemptions for newly cultivated land.

In 1854/55 a law was promulgated in which two kinds of fields were defined: *Na Kuko* and *Na Fang Loi*.[5] The tax rate for both was 0.375 baht per rai, and the tax was collected in money, not in kind. In response to protests from farmers holding Na Kuko lands, the tax on that class of field was reduced in 1855/56 to 0.25 baht per rai.

In 1857/58 King Mongkut decreed that newly cultivated land should receive special treatment. He said that "although export of rice from the country has been encouraged, with the benefit of high price going to the peasants and merchants, . . . people . . . who are not occupied in rice cultivation suffer greatly from the high and rising price."[6] The solution was to expand the cultivation and thus to decrease the price, and to accomplish this purpose it was decreed that "no tax shall be collected from rice land cleared from the jungle

[3] Cited in Pramoj and Pramoj, *op. cit.*, pp. 67–68.

[4] The following discussion of the land tax is based largely on Police-Lieutenant Sthier Lailaksana (ed.), *Annual Collections of Laws*, 52 vols. (in Thai language, Bangkok, 1935–40). The writer is indebted to Nai Prayad Svastixuto of the Research Division of the Bank of Thailand for his assistance in compiling and interpreting this information.

[5] On *Na Kuko* the tax was levied on the whole of the area held by the farmer, while on *Na Fang Loi* the tax was levied only on the cultivated portion.

[6] "Notification Forbidding Collection of Rice Land Tax in the First Year of Cultivation," dated 1857/58, cited in Pramoj and Pramoj, *op. cit.*, pp. 66–68.

for the first year of its cultivation . . . in consideration for the special labour employed in clearing the jungle."[7] Furthermore, the tax was collected at a reduced rate for two or three more years, as follows:

Year	Tax per Rai	
	Na Kuko (*Baht*)	Na Fang Loi (*Baht*)
1st	No tax	No tax
2d	0.125	0.250
3d	0.125	0.250
4th	0.250	0.250
5th and thereafter	0.250	0.375

King Chulalongkorn made the inducement even greater in 1874/75 by charging *no* land tax on new lands for the first three years of cultivation. Beginning with the fourth year the rates remained 0.25 baht for Na Kuko and 0.375 baht for Na Fang Loi.

A new tax law in 1900/1901 retained the same rates for the two types of land, but the exemption for newly cultivated land appears to have been dropped. Thus for about 43 years (1857–1900), the tax incentive remained in force, and during the same period the basic tax rate was unchanged. The latter was no accident. The Bowring Treaty provided that tax rates applied to land held by British subjects could not be changed and, since the Thai government was unwilling to levy higher taxes on its own subjects than those of Great Britain (which included some Asian subjects), the rates were left as they were. Around the turn of the century Great Britain finally agreed to modify the treaty provisions to allow land held by her subjects to be taxed at rates not exceeding those charged on *similar land in Lower Burma*.[8] This concession paved the way for a complete revision of the land tax, which occurred in 1905/6.

The revised law increased the tax rates and provided for a method of fixing the tax according to the fertility of the land. Using yield per rai as the chief criteria, all paddy land was put into one of five classes. The distinction between Na Kuko and Na Fang Loi was retained, and a third type of land was defined; namely, land which was *claimed* by an individual but not yet cultivated. The tax rates were as follows (baht/rai):[9]

Class	Na Kuko	Na Fang Loi	Reserved Fields
I	1.00	1.20	.12
II	.80	1.00	.10
III	.60	.80	.08
IV	.40	.60	.06
V	.30	.40	.05

[7] *Loc. cit.*

[8] W. J. F. Williamson, "Finance," in A. Wright and O. T. Breakspear (eds.), *Twentieth Century Impressions of Siam* (London, 1908), p. 112.

[9] Actually, these are the rates fixed in the law of 1909/10 when the old unit of currency (the *att*) was abolished and the tax expressed in *satang*.

The tax rates fixed in 1905 remained in force until the 1930's, when they were reduced across the board because of the depression. Finally, in 1938 the land tax was abolished upon the adoption of a new National Revenue Code.

The incentive-taxation device did not appear in the tax law of 1905, although newly cultivated land may have fallen into Class IV or V for the first few years because of low yields. If so, it would have been lightly taxed. Furthermore, the farmer could claim new land and spend the first year or two in clearing it because during this time he would have to pay only a nominal tax (the rate shown above for "reserved fields").

Whatever effect the tax incentives which existed from 1857 to 1900 may have had on the extension of cultivation was limited to the Central and Southern provinces because the tax laws concerned were not applied elsewhere. In Northern Thailand (Monthon Bayab) the land tax was collected in rice from 1782 to 1882. Rates varied according to the quality and location of the land. Approximately in 1882 (perhaps earlier) the tax was changed to a money tax. Not until several years after 1905 was the Law of 1905 enforced in the North. The Northeastern provinces paid no land tax to Bangkok until well into the twentieth century. In 1927 the Financial Adviser sent a memorandum to the Minister of Finance in which he stated that the whole of the Northeast was exempted from payment of the land tax.[10]

By 1932 the land tax had been imposed in only four changwats in the Northeast.[11] Originally the lack of transport facilities was given as the reason for not taxing the Northeastern provinces, but by 1932 the railway served a large area which was still not taxed. The Northeast appears to have been favorably treated as far as the land tax was concerned.

Land taxes in Thailand have been lower than in other countries of the Far East. From 1857 to 1905 the highest tax was 0.375 baht per rai, while the value of the rice produced per rai varied from about 4.0 baht to 8.0 baht. The tax thus varied from about 10 percent in the 1850's to 5 percent about 1900. Even after rates were increased in 1905, the ratio of taxes to value of output remained low (10 percent or less) until the sharp drop in rice prices in the 1930's. Such rates are markedly lower than the 30 to 50 percent commonly reported for other Far Eastern countries.

Two further points are of interest regarding incentive taxation. First, when the *corvée* obligation was converted into a capitation tax, the amount of the tax varied from 1.5 to 6.0 baht. To encourage people to take the risk of cultivating new land in the less fertile regions instead of packing together in the fertile regions, the tax was lowest in poor and undeveloped regions.[12]

---

[10] "Memorandum on the Burden of Taxation," Files of Financial Adviser, Ministry of Finance, Bangkok.

[11] "Report of the Fiscal Committee of the Cabinet (Budget) Sub-committee," dated May 1932. Files of Financial Adviser, Ministry of Finance, Bangkok.

[12] Dilock, *op. cit.*, pp. 53–54. The lower rates probably were also simply *recognition* of the unequal ability to pay in the different regions.

In the poorest regions no tax was collected. Second, the nominal tax on un-cultivated holdings (the "reserved fields" mentioned) was designed to prevent individuals from claiming large areas of land and holding it for speculative or other purposes.[13] This is in accord with the consistent policy of the government to dispose of state lands to the cultivators themselves rather than to landlords, and to encourage small holdings.

As we have seen, an ancient custom gave every man the right to take as much land from the state as he and his family could cultivate—an amount usually figured to be around 25 rai. This right continued to exist throughout the period covered in this study. The land so claimed had to be registered and a small fee paid, and it had to be cultivated for three years before it became the property of the cultivator. No doubt there were some exceptions to the rule that those acquiring new land had to cultivate it to retain possession. Until the reign of King Chulalongkorn, grants of land were made to nobles and officials in lieu of salaries. Another source of large holdings was the practice of granting a part of the land along a canal to any private individual who would undertake to dig it. Frankfurter wrote in 1895 that this was a long-established custom, although he also said that if the land were not cultivated it reverted to the state.[14]

The Consolidated Land Act of 1908 did not specify an exact amount of land, but gave people the right to take as much land as they could "turn to profit." In practice the amount varied from 20 to 50 rai. The Land Act of 1936 specified 50 rai as the amount which could be taken. Both laws provided that the cultivator was to receive title to the land after he had cultivated it for three years.

These laws and customs concerning the distribution of land have been of great importance in Thailand. They have prevented the growth of a class of great landowners, and they have encouraged the growth of a nation of small, independent owner-farmers. Farmers have lost their land, and tenancy does exist, but the land laws have tended to prevent these problems from becoming as acute as in countries such as Burma. Together with tax laws, the land laws have encouraged the extension of cultivation.

Public Works

The two most important forms of public works undertaken by the government to assist the production of rice, directly or indirectly, were irrigation projects and railways. The desirability of irrigation had long been recognized in Thailand, and by 1850 a number of canals were already in use in the Central Plain, while the Northern farmers utilized ingenious co-operative

---

[13] Letter (with enclosures) from H.H. Prince Vivadhanajai to Sir Edward Cook, Financial Adviser, dated September 12, 1929. Files of Financial Adviser, Ministry of Finance, Bangkok.

[14] Dr. Oscar Frankfurter, *Die Rechtlichen und Wirtschaftlichen Verhaltnisse in Siam* (Guben, Germany, 1895), p. 15.

schemes of water control. King Mongkut continued to expand the system of canals in the Central Plain. These were used both for transportation and for distributing floodwaters over the paddy fields. The *Bangkok Calendar* for 1871 describes five great canals dug in the fourth reign. These canals, each 17 miles long or longer, went through "thousands of acres of the richest rice fields." The construction of canals, mostly in the Central Plain, continued during the reign of King Chulalongkorn. Most of the canals were constructed under government auspices, but a few were built by private individuals who were given part of the adjoining land in return.[15] During the reign of King Mongkut a shift was made from unpaid Thai laborers (obtained through the *corvée*) to paid Chinese labor. The Chinese workers were paid by the cubic measure of dirt excavated. Often the people who owned land along a new canal were required to pay a certain amount per rai toward the cost of construction.

Canals were thus constructed off and on throughout the fourth and fifth reigns (1851–1910). In many years no work was under way, however, judging from the frequent comments about the absence of any public works in certain years. For example, the British Consul reported that in 1880 nothing was done to provide new facilities in transportation and irrigation, and that the existing system was not even maintained.[16] Similar comments may be found for other years.

On the whole, irrigation and transportation facilities were extremely inadequate in the Thailand of 1890. A contemporary writer[17] compared the situation in Thailand with that in Burma and found that:

— the plains around Bangkok were as rich as those around Rangoon,
— water communications were equally easy in Bangkok,
— world markets were as accessible to Bangkok,
— the people of Thailand were as industrious,
— the land tax was even lower in Thailand.

In spite of all these favorable signs, the export of rice had increased only one-third to one-half as much as that of Burma during the period 1860–90. The writer concluded that the difference was to be found in the unequal provision of public works for irrigation and reclamation of land. Around Rangoon large sums were spent on such projects, while in Thailand "trade has developed by the unassisted resources of the country."[18] This judgment is unnecessarily harsh, but comparatively the Thai government had done little. The govern-

---

[15] Chao Phya Wongsa Nuprapath, *History of the Ministry of Agriculture* (Bangkok, 1941), pp. 126–54. (In Thai language.)

[16] *Commercial Report by Her Majesty's Agent and Consul-General in Siam for the Year 1880,* Great Britain, Foreign Office (London, 1881).

[17] Robert Gordon, "The Economic Development of Siam," *Journal of the Society of Arts,* XXXIX (March 6, 1891), 283–98.

[18] *Ibid.,* pp. 292–93.

ment had borrowed no money from abroad to use in capital developments, nor did it have any over-all plan for the development of agriculture.

In the last two decades of the reign of King Chulalongkorn (1890–1910) a beginning was made toward systematic irrigation, and considerably more than a beginning was made in public discussion of the subject. The first large-scale irrigation project in Thailand (the Rangsit scheme) was not under-taken by the government but by a private concern, the Siam Canals Land and Irrigation Co., which secured a concession in 1889 to dig canals in a vast tract of flat and swampy land northeast of Bangkok.[19] The company was to be allowed to sell the land thus opened up. The canals dug by the company were merely distribution channels; they could not increase the supply of water delivered to the fields in years of low rainfall. Nevertheless, land in the concession area was quickly taken up as the canals were completed, and by 1910 about 100,000 people were living in the area, where no one lived before.[20]

The scheme was not an unmixed success, however. Besides the legal wrangles over titles, there was a great deal of hardship in the district in years of low water supply, especially when the canals began to silt up. The culti-vators had in many cases bought or rented this land from speculators, and they were saddled with a heavy burden of rent or interest and taxes. Further-more, the water supply was so poor that of the total cultivated area of 900,000 rai only about 40 percent was ever actually matured.[21] The Minister of Agri-culture, Chao Phya Devesr, inspected the region in 1899 and submitted a report in which he recommended that an irrigation engineer be obtained as an adviser to the government. As a result of his report a Dutch irrigation expert, J. H. Van der Heide, was hired in 1902 to draw up an over-all irriga-tion plan for the nation. This was the beginning of *irrigation,* as opposed to mere distribution of flood waters, in Thailand (with some exceptions).[22]

Two circumstances provide the basic rationale for irrigation in the Central Plain.[23] First, the total rainfall during the growing season is normally less than the amount of water required to produce rice as it is grown in Thailand. The difference has to be made up by inundation caused by rivers spilling over. Second, the record of flood levels which has been kept at Ayuthia (a city some 50 miles north of Bangkok in the heart of the Central Plain) showed in 1930 that of the last 99 years, the water supply in only 32 was "distinctly good." In 22 years the supply was average (meaning that irrigation could have im-

[19] Thailand, Ministry of Commerce and Communications, *Siam, Nature and Industry* (Bang-kok, 1930), pp. 185–203.

[20] J. C. Barnett, *Report of the First Annual Exhibition of Agriculture and Commerce* (Bang-kok, 1910), p. 73.

[21] Siam, Royal Irrigation Department, *Administration Report for the Period 1914/15–1925/26* (Bangkok, 1927), pp. 1–3.

[22] The following brief description of what was *done* about irrigation leaves out the financial aspects and most of the controversy concerning proposed projects. For these aspects, and for a discussion of the economic case for irrigation, see Ch. 9.

[23] *Siam, Nature and Industry,* pp. 185–203.

proved the yield of rice), in 30 years the river level was low enough to cause considerable damage to the crops, and in 15 years the water was too high. Thus in only one-third of the recorded years was the water supply ideal. The water supply in the remaining years was not so poor as to cause crop failures as drastic as that of 1919/20, when exports were prohibited to protect the domestic food supply, but irrigation could help to stabilize the rice harvest and thus to safeguard the major source of foreign exchange for the nation and of money income for the bulk of the population.

Van der Heide made an exhaustive study of the existing network of canals and rivers and of the economy and geography of Thailand. He published his report in 1903.[24] This document contains an elaborate plan for irrigating the whole of the Central Plain. The plan hinged on construction of a barrage across the Chao Phya River at Chainat, a project which would bring that great river under control. Van der Heide's full scheme also included projects in the North and elsewhere, although his principal emphasis was on projects for the Central Plain. The estimated cost of the entire system was 47 million baht, to be spread over 12 years. The maximum cost in any one year was to be 5.5 million baht. Generally speaking, Van der Heide's report was a brilliant statement of the irrigation needs of Thailand and the solutions for them. Van der Heide himself was a famous irrigation engineer with experience in Java, Holland, and elsewhere and, although he may have misjudged the willingness of farmers in the Central Plain to pay money for water and land, his report is both an eloquent statement of the advantages of irrigation and a sound statement of the engineering problems involved. The cost figures given above represent the estimated capital expenditures; they make no allowance for the direct and indirect benefit which would accrue to the state. These benefits were carefully pointed out by Van der Heide. Indeed, the most unpopular features of his plan (sale of water and public lands) were included in an effort to make the capital investment pay for itself directly. These features could have been easily removed or modified, however.

Van der Heide pointed out that besides the improved yields of rice, the reduction in crop failures, and the improved quality of rice, irrigation would also enable each family to cultivate a larger amount of land. The farmer could regulate the softening and flooding of his fields and thereby increase the number of days available for cultivation of rice. Without irrigation the work load was dictated by the rains. The farmer worked furiously when he worked, but he could not begin until the rains came. A staggered harvest would also help, although the farmer achieved this to some extent by using seed of varying maturities. Furthermore, proper drainage would enable villages to cultivate fruits and vegetables and to engage in cattle breeding, while without

[24] J. H. Van der Heide, *General Report on Irrigation and Drainage in the Lower Menam Valley.*

it the floods made such activities, and even normal village life, practically impossible because the entire Central Plain is turned into a vast lake for several months each year. Houses have to be elevated and nearly all movement is by boat. Under such conditions large-scale cattle raising is impossible, as are fruit and vegetable gardens. Irrigation, said Van der Heide, would also enable farmers to use the long idle months of the dry season to advantage by cultivating crops which require little water. Irrigation could supply the necessary water even in the dry season. Finally, the construction of roads would be facilitated because the embankments of canals, being dry and permanent, could serve as road beds.

Through consideration of such valuable social by-products of irrigation, in addition to such direct benefits as increased land tax and export duties, Van der Heide tried to show the advantages of irrigation to the economic development of Thailand. Not the least of these advantages was a greater stability of total production—a fact which was repeatedly demonstrated in the next forty years.

The over-all scheme was rejected by the government. A reduced scheme, to cost 28,000,000 baht, was also "postponed." Instead, the newly formed Department of Irrigation was allowed only to dredge the existing canals and to install locks and sluices in the south Central region. Van der Heide remained in Thailand as Director of the Department of Irrigation until 1909. During this period he drew up a number of plans on a smaller scale for irrigation projects which would eventually fit into the over-all system. All of these were rejected. Early in 1909, after a damaging flood in the year 1908/9, after a final scheme was rejected, and after the government announced that it was postponing irrigation works indefinitely, Van der Heide resigned and went home. The Department of Irrigation was abolished in 1912, but circumstances were soon to force its revival.[25]

Another year of high flood occurred in 1909/10, and 1910/11 and 1911/12 were years of drought. "During these years hard times were experienced by the people in general, and want of irrigation was the thought of everyone at the moment."[26] King Rama VI made a speech from the throne in which he said that the government intended to carry out irrigation and drainage works. Sir Thomas Ward, a British irrigation expert then in India, was brought to Thailand in 1913 to draw up a plan. His four-volume report, published in 1915, outlined a number of projects and the recommended sequence of construction. The Department of Irrigation was re-created to administer the work, and in 1916 the first project (though not the one given first priority by Sir Thomas) was begun. Work went slowly, however, partly because the

[25] Siam, Royal Irrigation Department, *Project Estimate for Works of Irrigation, Drainage and Navigation to Develop the Plain of Central Siam* (Bangkok, 1915), III, Ch. 14.
[26] *Loc. cit.*

war made procurement of supplies and equipment very difficult. The war also increased costs considerably.

Although his plan contemplated eventual control of the Chao Phya River and an integrated system for the entire Central Plain, Sir Thomas did not design the entire scheme as one "package deal." Instead, he proposed a number of separate projects which would ultimately be brought together, and he said that Thailand was not yet ready for the biggest job—the barrage across the Chao Phya. In his opinion the population was not large enough to utilize the cultivable land made available by the full scheme, nor were financial resources available. The cost of the full scheme was estimated at 100 to 120 million baht, while the five projects he especially recommended were estimated to cost a total of 23 million baht.

The Rangsit concession area was the locale of the first real irrigation project in Thailand. This project, number three on the list recommended by Sir Thomas, was preferred by the government because conditions in that region were serious and because the government did not want to develop an unpopulated area which would tend to draw farmers away from their present holdings and thus "disturb existing arrangements of landlord and tenant in the Rangsit area and elsewhere."[27] The project, known as the South Prasak Canal Project, was completed in 1922 at a cost of 16,000,000 baht, compared to the original estimate of 11,500,000 baht. (Wages and materials rose considerably in the war years.) The total area commanded and the irrigated area in 1925 were 754,000 and 450,000 rai, respectively.

Funds for irrigation were still meager in the 1920's. Not even the costly crop failure of 1919/20 had persuaded the government to give priority to irrigation expenditures. Two small projects were sanctioned, however, and by 1930 the cumulative capital outlay on irrigation reached about 30,000,000 baht.[28]

Since 1930 additional irrigation works have been constructed. Most of the capital expenditure continued to be made in the Central Plain, where the separate projects subsidiary to the over-all scheme for control of the Lower Menam Valley were steadily pushed forward. Smaller appropriations were made for irrigation in the North and for several small projects in the Northeast. During World War II not much was accomplished because the necessary imports of material and equipment were not available, but since the end of the war the irrigation program has been pushed with redoubled vigor. In 1948 there were fifteen projects under construction, the total remaining cost of which was estimated at about 195,000,000 baht.[29] Large annual budget appropriations are being made in order to complete these projects. In addition,

[27] Siam, Royal Irrigation Department, *Administrative Report for the Period 1914/15– 1925/26.*

[28] This figure does not include expenditures made before 1915.

[29] United Nations, FAO, *Report of the FAO Mission for Siam* (Washington, 1948), p. 51.

the government has at last undertaken the great Chainat project, which will bring several separate projects in the Central Plain into one huge system of water control. A loan of U.S. $18,000,000 has been obtained from the International Bank for Reconstruction and Development to cover the foreign-exchange costs of this project, which will include a barrage across the Chao Phya River, several new canals, and a hydroelectric plant. Thus Thailand is in sight of the goal which in 1903 Van der Heide thought could be attained in twelve years for a total cost of 47 million baht.

According to estimates made for the Economic Commission for Asia and the Far East, the potential irrigable area in Thailand is 40,000,000 rai, while the area irrigated was 2,750,000 rai in 1938 and 4,050,000 rai in 1950.[30] The area of projects under construction and being planned was 9,100,000 rai in 1950. Thus when all these planned projects are completed, the area irrigated will be about 13,150,000 rai of the potential irrigable area of 40,000,000 rai.[31]

Railway construction in Thailand was not undertaken primarily to encourage and assist the expansion of rice cultivation; instead, political considerations were ascendant.[32] Nevertheless, construction of railways to the North and Northeast served to encourage the expansion of rice cultivation in those regions and also facilitated the import of foreign goods. These results may have been expected, but they were not the primary reason construction was undertaken.

As early as 1887 the government contracted to have a survey made for a railway to the North. The first railway opened to traffic was a private one, however. A twenty-kilometer line from Bangkok to Paknam was built in 1891–93 by the Paknam Railway Co. Its principal business was passengers, and it was a financial success.

In the meantime the government contracted to have a line built to Korat in the Northeast. The contract went to a Scottish firm after bitter competition, complete with political overtones, between British and German firms. Many difficulties were encountered by the winning firm, including the supervision of German engineers, and eventually the contract was canceled. An international court of arbitration awarded the contractor damages of 2,800,000 baht.

After this unhappy introduction, railways in Thailand have been built and operated by the government, although with the assistance of foreign engineers and technicians. The Korat railway (264 km.) was completed in 1900. In the next ten years a beginning was made on lines to the North and South. Foreign loans were obtained in 1905, 1907, and 1909 to help finance the exten-

---

[30] United Nations, ECAFE, *Economic Survey of Asia and the Far East, 1950* (New York, 1951), pp. 22–24.

[31] The "potential irrigable area" is merely a technical potential, considering rainfall, catchment areas, etc., and does not represent a practical goal.

[32] See Virginia M. Thompson, *Thailand, the New Siam,* pp. 497–506, and W. A. Graham, *Siam,* II, 141–53, for a description of the period of railway building and the difficulties involved.

sion of the railways. When war came in 1941, the system included lines to Chiengmai in the North, to the Malayan border in the South, and extensions from Korat to Ubon and Udorn in the Northeast. The following table indicates the progress made:

By the End of:	Kilometers of Open Lines	Capital Expenditures (Cumulative) (*Baht*)
1900	264	21,000,000
1910	932	67,000,000
1920	2,253	143,000,000
1930	2,922	194,000,000
1940	3,130	217,000,000

The southern railway did little to encourage rice exports, and until the northern line was carried beyond Pitsanulok it also did little to encourage farmers to cultivate more rice. As far north as Pitsanulok farmers could ship their paddy by river, while the rather small surpluses of peninsular provinces could be transported by coastal shipping. The northeastern railway (to Korat and other points) and the extension from Pitsanulok to Chiengmai did bring cheap transport to these regions for the first time, however, and stimulated the cultivation of rice for export. Both regions are separated from the Central Plain by mountains. Furthermore, the rivers of the Northeast drain to the south and east rather than toward Bangkok, while river transportation from Chiengmai was difficult and expensive because of rapids. Before the railways came, therefore, rice could not be profitably exported through Bangkok from either the North or the Northeast. Even in the Central Plain the railway began to carry much of the rice and paddy, which suggests that water transportation was more expensive.

The railway system was heavily bombed by Allied planes during World War II, and the lack of adequate supplies for maintenance accentuated the damage to rolling stock, buildings, and the roads themselves. At the end of the war the carrying capacity of the system was greatly reduced. This was one reason for the low rice exports in the postwar years (though not a major reason). The government made efforts to rehabilitate the railways, but by 1950 the job was not finished, while demand for transport had increased considerably. In 1950 a loan of U.S. $3,000,000 was granted to Thailand by the World Bank to assist the rehabilitation.

The provision of railways and irrigation works represents the major government effort to encourage rice production and export. The government has been severely criticized for not having done more to promote and improve agriculture, especially under the old regime (before 1932). In her description of the vicissitudes of the Ministry of Agriculture, Thompson says that "the Government did not seem to realize that in Siam agriculture should be the main concern of the state."[33] It is certainly true that the government did not give enough active and constructive attention to the problems of agriculture. It did little or nothing to improve the methods of cultivation and seed selection; it did nothing to improve the marketing structure or to standardize the quality of the grades of rice; it did not study soils and crops; nor did it effectively perform the function of *informing* the farmers about prices and marketing alternatives. Much more could have been accomplished in all these things, and without very large expenditures, too.

The nation would also have benefited from a more adequate system of irrigation works. With hindsight it is perfectly clear that if Van der Heide's irrigation schemes had been pushed forward rapidly, using foreign capital when necessary and domestic revenue where possible, the investment would have proved a sound one for the nation. The crop failure of 1919/20 alone cost the nation more than the entire cost of the works.

Such comparisons with what might have been should not lead us to underestimate the real achievements of the government. The railway and irrigation projects, the incentive land taxes, and the liberal land policy all had much to do with the increase in the cultivation of rice. They made it much easier for individuals to produce crops for sale than it would otherwise have been.

The Marketing of Rice, 1945-51

Since the end of World War II, the government has enlarged its role in the rice trade through a control system which involves very little effort but very large profit to the government. This system developed out of the postwar experience in rice procurement, and a brief discussion of that experience may be helpful.[34]

Immediately after the war, most of Southeast Asia outside of Thailand was in desperate need of rice. At the initial peace talks Thailand agreed to supply 1,500,000 metric tons of rice free of charge as a sort of indemnity for her part in the war. This undertaking was made part of the formal agreement signed by Great Britain, India, and Thailand on January 1, 1946. As it turned out, the government of Thailand was unable (some would say unwilling) to fulfill this agreement. The punitive provisions were later modified but, until they were finally and completely eliminated in August 1947, they hampered the recovery of rice exports and contributed to political disturbances in Thailand.

From the very beginning, the postwar agreements made the government responsible for procurement and delivery of rice. During the period in which

---

[33] *Thailand, the New Siam*, p. 376.

[34] A detailed account of the postwar events is given in *Report of the Financial Adviser for the Years 1941-50*, Thailand, Ministry of Finance, pp. 18-28, and the next four paragraphs are largely based on that account.

Thailand was supposed to supply rice free of charge, the government offered a fixed price (27.85 baht per picul, or £11/11/0 per metric ton at 40 baht per pound sterling) for white rice containing 35 percent broken grain.[35] At this price rice deliveries were small, and from September 1945 to March 1946 only 150,000 tons were made available for export. The rapid rise in domestic prices, the shortage of imported consumers' goods, and the high world price of rice all led to the hoarding of paddy. There was no incentive to sell it.

Furthermore, when a new agreement in 1946 provided for the purchase of rice by the contracting nations, the price was fixed at a very low level: £12/10/0 per metric ton of 35 percent white rice, ex mill and unbagged. Various government measures were taken to prevent hoarding and smuggling of rice and paddy, but they did little good. The incentive to smuggle was enormous when the black-market price in Singapore reached the amazing level of 600 pounds sterling per ton. The official price was increased in January 1947 to a basic rate of £23/12/5 per metric ton, but deliveries remained small. Indeed it is surprising that as much as 40,000 tons per month were delivered during this period.

On August 31, 1947, the Tripartite Agreement came to an end. Government-to-government contracts were continued in use, however, and Thailand undertook to export rice in accordance with allocations made by the International Emergency Food Committee. From this date Thailand began to receive the same basic price as other exporters, although this was still well below the free-market price of rice. After this date, therefore, no part of the punitive provisions remained. As a result of these changes, plus an increase in the government's internal buying price, exports rapidly increased in 1948, 1949, and 1950.

In order to meet its contract commitments, as well as to obtain control over the price of rice to domestic consumers, the Thai government declared a monopoly on rice trade at the end of the war. This monopoly enabled the government to appropriate a large part of the high prices received for rice exports. Surplus rice had to be sold to the Government Rice Office at prices fixed in baht. Mills were allowed to sell rice for local consumption, but the entire surplus over domestic needs had to be sold to the government, which resold it to foreign buyers. Internal transport of rice and paddy was strictly controlled, and provincial surpluses of milled rice were delivered to warehouses in Bangkok.

The government did not control the price of paddy. It merely bought milled rice for export, and the paddy price was determined by the competition of millers and middlemen, the willingness of growers to sell their paddy, and the rice prices paid by the Rice Office. Because the rice prices paid

---

[35] There are numerous grades and qualities of rice. The basic price was fixed for 35 percent rice in the postwar agreements and appropriate differentials established for other grades.

by the government were fixed for long periods, farmers had a better idea of the price they should get for paddy than they used to have. They began to hold their paddy for better prices, presumably because they were able to build up reserves. As a result they squeezed down the margins of the middleman.[36]

The government bought rice from the miller ex mill, and immediately sold it to shipping agencies ex mill.[37] The shipper was responsible for the expense of moving the rice from the mill to the ship. The government incurred little expense in the transaction, which was very profitable.

Government profits arose in two ways. First, the Rice Office sold rice to shippers for about 20 percent more than the price it paid to the millers. This trading profit was considerable because both the purchase and sale by the government were paper transactions involving little expense. Second, a *potential* exchange profit arose from the fact that the export price was expressed in foreign exchange. The Rice Office figured its accounts at the official rate of exchange, and the price in foreign currency was fixed at such a level that even when converted at the official rate the Rice Office could buy rice from millers and still make a 20 percent profit on the transaction. The foreign-exchange proceeds were turned over to the Bank of Thailand. The Bank in turn might sell part of the foreign exchange at the official rate, e.g., for certain imports, but it also sold part at the open-market rate of exchange. On this portion it made an additional profit equal to the difference between the two rates.[38]

An example may help to clarify the picture. In 1951 the export price of white rice, 15 percent broken, was U.S. $124.30 per metric ton including export duty but excluding gunnies. The price paid to the miller was 1,306 baht per metric ton. The operations of the Rice Office would show the following results for one ton:

Sale price ($124.30 @ 12.50)	=	1,554 baht
Purchase price	=	1,306
Gross profit	=	248 baht

The foreign-currency proceeds were turned over to the Bank of Thailand and could have been sold at the open-market rate of about 21 baht per U.S. dollar. This would yield an additional profit of $124.30 times (21.0 — 12.5), or 1,056

---

[36] Exact data on this point are lacking, but most observers agree that both millers and middlemen now receive a much smaller share of the export proceeds than they used to.

[37] On government-to-government contracts each contracting government appoints an agent in Bangkok through whom rice is purchased. The Siam Rice Agency, a consortium of five British firms, handled all rice exports to British territories, for example.

[38] If the Bank of Thailand had sold the entire foreign exchange proceeds from rice exports on the open market, it would undoubtedly have caused the open-market exchange rate to rise (i.e., the baht would have appreciated in terms of sterling and dollars). Therefore, the "potential" profit described above is overstated, but we have no way to compute what it might have been.

baht. The entire transaction, if figured at the open-market rate, would look like this:[39]

Net price to miller	1,256 baht
Export duty	50
Gross price to miller	1,306
Trading profit to government	248
Exchange profit to government	1,056
Total export proceeds	2,610 baht

As a matter of fact, the Bank of Thailand had not, by the end of 1951, sold dollars at the open-market rate, although some dollar exchange was sold at the official rate to encourage certain imports. The exchange profit we have described above was thus earned only on the sale of pounds sterling, and on only a part of such sales. The above account thus refers to the theoretically maximum profit of the government.

Clearly, the government took advantage of postwar exchange control and government-to-government contracts to appropriate for itself a large part of the export proceeds of the major export of the nation. Only the profit of the Rice Office is included in the revenue budget, however. The realized portion of the exchange profit accrued to the Bank of Thailand, and remained unused at the end of 1951.

From 1948 through 1950, the procurement scheme worked rather well. Rice exports rose from 812,000 metric tons in 1948 to 1,489,000 tons in 1950, and most exports were shipped against government allocations. The price of paddy adjusted itself to the prices paid to the millers and left an adequate margin for the millers and the middlemen, although these margins were said to be much narrower than they were before the war. There were some complaints about quality and sometimes deliveries lagged because the millers complained of being squeezed between the fixed buying prices of the Rice Office and the swings of the competitive paddy prices, but deliveries were not far short of contract commitments. Another hindrance to exports was the acute shortage of railway cars in the North and Northeast. Rice and paddy could not be moved to Bangkok and, as a result, upcountry prices were much below the Bangkok price, while railway cars brought high premiums which sometimes went into the private pockets of officials who had authority to allocate the available cars.

In 1951, although government-to-government contracts were again concluded for most of the estimated surplus, the Ministry of Commerce began to issue a number of permits to export rice against commercial contracts.[40]

---

[39] The exchange profit was somewhat less in the case of exports sold for pounds sterling because the spread between the official and open-market rates is less than for the dollar.

[40] Even with such permits, the exporter must still purchase rice from the government at the

Since the world price of rice was still above the prices fixed in government contracts, exporters were eager to obtain the private permits, and a lively market for permits sprang up. During 1951 the black-market price for such permits reached U.S. $35 per ton! Furthermore, shippers began to have difficulty in getting rice from the rice mills, even though they possessed export permits. As a result they began to offer premiums and bonuses to the millers for prompt delivery of rice. Millers also began to shade the qualities delivered, especially for shippers who did not pay the bonuses.

As a result of these complications, deliveries against government contracts began to lag. For 1951, such deliveries fell short of contract commitments by nearly 200,000 tons, even though rice exports exceeded the expected surplus by over 300,000 tons. Officials were obtaining permits for export against commercial contract and promptly selling them in the market. A permit for 10,000 tons meant $30,000 even at the low price of U.S. $3 per ton, and when the price hit $20–$30, the temptation to bribe the crucial officials was enormous. Millers were eager to get a cut also, and they were reluctant to make rice available unless they got some kind of a premium.

According to officials in the government, the milling problem has arisen because the millers have begun to lose money as a result of increases in the price of paddy at a time when internal rice prices remained fixed by the government. It is said that growers are prosperous and willing to hold stocks of paddy, while millers are driven by overhead costs to bid up the price of paddy in order to continue operating. They then try to cover their losses by delivering poorer qualities or by securing premiums and bonuses from buyers.

As long as the world price of rice is higher than the official export prices of the Thai government, it will be possible for millers to demand bonuses and for commercial permits to find a market. This margin has steadily fallen in recent years, however, and sooner or later the government may have to increase its buying prices in order to maintain exports at a high level. Furthermore, if the spread between the official and open-market rates of exchange is narrowed, the exchange profit will decrease.

In the meantime, the government is strengthening its finances and increasing its revenues through the operations of the rice monopoly and exchange control, and at the same time the internal price of rice is kept at a low level, thus benefiting domestic consumers of rice. The largest share of the burden has no doubt fallen on the rice farmer, who received in 1951 about one-half of the paddy price which he probably would have received in a free market.[41] Middlemen, millers, and exporters would also fare somewhat better in a free

---

fixed selling price, and he must also surrender 100 percent of the export proceeds to the Bank of Thailand at the official rate. The difference is that he can sell his rice for the prevailing world-market price.

[41] This comparison does not allow for the fact that, if there were no exchange control, the exchange rate would settle somewhere between the official and market rates.

market. Other groups—for example, the consumers of favored imports such as fuel oil and all families who must buy their daily rice—are benefited by the present system. It is also probable that the controlled rice and paddy prices have kept the production and export of rice lower than would have been the case in a free market. Markedly higher prices would have stimulated producers and restrained consumption, and exports would have increased for both reasons. Even at existing prices the area planted has expanded greatly, however, and it is doubtful that much more land could have been cultivated with existing techniques and irrigation facilities.

According to some observers, the postwar system has had the effect of increasing the number of Thai middlemen and exporters. The fixed buying price of the Rice Office introduced a degree of stability into the paddy market and enabled Thai middlemen to compete with the Chinese. Formerly, the price of paddy fluctuated wildly from place to place and from month to month because of the variety of measures used in buying it, because of seasonal variations, and because of the many transactions involving merchandise or loans. Thai middlemen did not have the working capital, the experience, or the trading ability to compete with the Chinese under those conditions. But when the millers' buying prices became fixed within narrow limits for long periods, the middleman function was greatly simplified. No doubt other factors were involved, but people in the rice trade consider the greater stability of prices to be of major importance in the rise of Thai middlemen.

Thai exporting firms have also become more important, largely because they have been favored by the government in its allocation of permits to export rice on commercial contract, but these firms frequently do not want to do the necessary work and merely sell the permits to other exporters.

There has been much criticism of the government rice program, and no doubt many of the stories of corruption in official circles, of underweight and underquality deliveries, and of costly administrative delays are true. Nevertheless, the government has sold rice ever since the war at prices considerably below world market prices and has successfully made deliveries against contracts (at least through 1950). This has been a great boon to the rice-importing nations of Asia. On the other hand, the system has kept the price of rice to domestic consumers quite low in comparison to world prices. This has been a powerful factor in stopping the postwar inflation which threatened Thailand.

The full extent of the tax on the rice farmer which the present system involves does not seem to be widely understood in Thailand. Actually, the effect of the postwar system has been to *reverse* the prewar policy of reducing the tax on the farmer, who now bears an extremely heavy tax.

5

The Growth of Other Exports
1850–1950

WHEREAS RICE is a product which plays an intimate part in the life of the great bulk of the Thai nation, the other major exports—tin, teak, and rubber—have been rather remote from the life of the people. Rice is the main food—and its cultivation, the major livelihood—of the majority of the people, but tin and teak (and rubber to a lesser extent) have been produced largely by foreign labor, foreign capital, and foreign enterprise. Furthermore, the number of people involved has been relatively small, in spite of the fact that these industries have long produced a significant portion of total exports. Although these industries have remained on the periphery of the social and economic life of the nation, the money value of their output has been so important that we must briefly describe their development.

Tin and teak have long been important export commodities, while rubber is a relative newcomer. Exports in 1850 were quite varied and no single product accounted for a very large part of the total. After 1850, rice and tin became the first products to dominate the export list. Teak became important in the latter part of the nineteenth century, while rubber has become a major export only in recent decades.

These four commodities have consistently represented 80–90 percent of total exports for several decades (see Table VIII[1]). If anything, the share of the big four is understated in Table VIII because a large quantity of teak floated down the Salween River into Burma is not included in the export figures, and because tin exports before 1920 are probably understated since the regular customs administration was not extended to the tin-mining peninsular districts until that date. Available estimates of tin exports (before 1920) appear to cover only a part of the tin-producing region. Of all the exports not included in the table (because they were outside the customs net), it is probable that well over 50 percent consisted of rice, rubber, tin, and teak.

In any case the table clearly shows that Thailand specialized in a comparatively small number of exports. These, as well as most smaller items of export, are primary products which have received very little processing before export. In this respect exports have changed very little from 1850 to 1950.

---

[1] The years selected before 1920 were largely dictated by availability of estimates of tin exports. These years are fairly representative of the general pattern, however.

93

TABLE VIII

PERCENTAGE OF TOTAL EXPORTS ACCOUNTED FOR BY FOUR COMMODITIES

Period	Per-centage Rice	Per-centage Rubber	Per-centage Tin[a]	Per-centage Teak[b]	Per-centage of All Four	Per-centage Total Exports[c]
1867	41.1		15.6		56.7	100
1890	69.7		11.1	5.5	86.4	100
1903	71.3		6.4	10.4	88.2	100
1906	69.1		11.0	11.2	91.3	100
1909/10	77.6		7.8	6.4	91.9	100
1915/16	70.1		15.9	3.9	89.9	100
1920–24	68.2	0.8	8.6	4.5	82.1	100
1925–29	68.9	2.3	9.0	3.7	83.9	100
1930–34	65.4	2.0	13.8	3.9	85.1	100
1935–39	53.5	12.9	18.6	4.2	89.2	100
1940–44	60.5	12.1	11.6	1.6	85.9	100
1947	35.3	7.0	11.8	5.1	59.2	100
1948	50.5	13.4	5.9	3.4	73.2	100
1949	62.7	8.3	5.3	3.7	80.0	100
1950	50.8	21.8	6.7	3.8	83.1	100
1951	48.0	30.1	5.1	3.3	86.5	100

[a] Before 1920, customs figures apply only to the port of Bangkok, while tin exports do not pass through Bangkok. Estimates of tin exports have therefore been added to the total exports of Bangkok. No effort has been made to value exports other than tin which did not pass through Bangkok, but the error thus introduced is not large, since around 80 percent of total exports are from Bangkok and tin accounts for a large part of the remaining 20 percent.

[b] Teak floated down the Salween River into Burma and the Mekong River into Indochina is not taken into consideration here. This is the only important omission from the table. No estimates of value are available, however, and it is impossible to handle this item as tin was handled (see Note a).

[c] Total exports do not include exports of treasure in the above computations.

Sources: The percentages have been derived from figures in the *Annual Diplomatic and Consular Reports on Trade and Finance from Her Majesty's Consuls in Siam, 1864–1909*, Great Britain, Foreign Office (London, 1865–1910), and *Statistical Year Book of Thailand, 1916–44*, I–XXI. Figures for 1947–51 are from Exchange Control Division, Bank of Thailand. Estimates vary widely for these postwar years.

Export Statistics

The statistics of total production and export are even less reliable for tin, teak, and rubber than for rice. The figures presented in the following tables are, in the author's judgment, the best available estimates. Data from the *Statistical Year Book* have been used whenever possible. Even after allowing for a wide margin of error, it is clear that there have been wide fluctuations in the volume of these exports, and that the steady growth we saw in rice exports does not characterize the export of these commodities. For example, the peak volume of teak exports came in 1905–9.

A few comments are needed on the nature of the figures presented in Tables IX and X. Tin was exported mainly in the form of tin ore, but we have

TABLE IX

ANNUAL VOLUME AND VALUE OF EXPORTS

Period	Tin Metal		Rubber	
	Volume (*Thousand Piculs*)	Value (*Million Baht*)	Volume (*Thousand Piculs*)	Value (*Million Baht*)
1867		1.2		
1884	82.5			
1890		3.9		
1891		3.6		
1892		4.4		
1893	60.0	3.6		
1895	60.0			
1903	83.0	11.4		
1904/5	66.5			
1905/6	70.0			
1906	79.0	12.9		
1908	83.0	8.5		
1909/10	78.0	8.6		
1915	151.0	19.9		
1920–24	117.0	14.6	25.0	1.3
1925–29	143.0	22.1	121.0	5.6
1930–34	183.0	19.2	153.0	2.8
1935–39	235.0	32.8	643.0	22.9
1940–44	107.0	18.4	325.0	19.8
1947	120.0	129.1	362.0	76.1
1948	154.0	146.8	1,584.0	332.7
1949	167.0	155.9	1,582.0	247.3
1950	241.0	259.6	1,878.0	856.9
1951	172.0	238.0	1,828.0	1,407.2

Sources: Tin—Figures for 1867, 1904/5, 1905/6, 1906, 1908 from *Annual Diplomatic and Consular Reports, 1864–1909*, Great Britain; 1884 from H. Warington Smyth, *Five Years in Siam* (New York, 1898), I, 319; 1890, 1891, 1892 from *Correspondence Respecting the Affairs of Siam*, Great Britain (London, 1894), p. 108; 1893 from Smyth, *op. cit.*, II, 298; 1895 from W. A. Graham, *Siam* (3d. ed.; London, 1924), II, 73; 1903 from A. Cecil Carter (ed.), *The Kingdom of Siam* (New York, 1904), p. 242; 1909/10 from G. E. Gerini, *Siam, Its Production, Arts, and Manufactures* (Hertford, England, 1912), p. 181; other figures from the *Statistical Year Book of Thailand*, except 1947–51 from Exchange Control Division, Bank of Thailand.

Rubber—*Statistical Year Book of Thailand*, except 1947–51 from Exchange Control Division, Bank of Thailand.

TABLE X

ANNUAL AVERAGE TEAK EXPORTS[a]

Period	Volume (Thousand Cubic Meters)[b]	Value (Million Baht)
1873–76	5.6	0.25
1883–87	27.0	1.10
1890–94	37.0	1.30
1895–99	62.0	4.10
1900–1904	78.0	6.90
1905–9	122.0	11.90
1910–14	90.0	5.90
1915–19	68.0	6.90
1920–24	83.0	7.60
1925–29	92.0	9.20
1930–34	67.0	5.40
1935–39	85.0	7.50
1940–44	27.0	2.70
1947	36.0	55.70
1948	53.0	85.20
1949	77.0	110.80
1950	92.0	140.00
1951	99.0	154.00

[a] Table refers to exports through Bangkok only.
[b] Ton of 50 cu. ft. equals 1.39 cu. m.; ton of 50 cu. ft. equals 20 piculs.
Sources: Figures for 1873–87, *Annual Diplomatic and Consular Reports*, Great Britain; 1890–94, Smyth, *op. cit.*, II, 270–71, 278. The volume figures that Smyth recommends as more reliable than customs have been used. 1895–99, Smyth, *op. cit.*, II, 278; J. H. Van der Heide, "The Economical Development of Siam During the Last Half Century," *Journal of Siam Society*, III (1906), 82; *Statistical Year Book of Siam*, XIII, 424; 1900–1944, *Statistical Year Book of Thailand*; 1947–49, *Annual Report for the Year 1950 to the Food and Agricultural Organization of United Nations*, Thailand, Ministry of Agriculture (Bangkok, 1951), p. 15; and *Report of the Financial Adviser, 1941–50*, p. 11; 1950–51, *Annual Report for 1951, Bank of Thailand*.

calculated the tin-metal equivalent on the assumption that ore contained 70 percent pure metal until 1923, and 72 percent thereafter. In some of the earlier years the source does not specify whether the estimate given is ore or metal. Tin is exported from several changwats in the peninsular South, but before customs control was extended to this region in 1920, estimates of exports were sometimes made for only a part of the tin-producing areas, and some of the figures may not refer to *total* exports.

Rubber is also produced in the peninsular South and, like tin, most of the amount produced is or used to be shipped to Malaya for transshipment. Estimates of rubber exports vary widely. The large number of small producers, imperfect border control between Malaya and Thailand, the inducements to smuggling during the cartel period of the 1930's, and inadequate government control of the industry have all contributed to the inadequate statistics. The figures given here for 1920–44 are those of the *Statistical Year Book*. The figures for the interwar years were later dropped from the published series because of unreliability, but they are included here because they do indicate the rapid growth of production.

Teak exports have been reported in piculs, tons (of 50 cu. ft.), and cubic meters. The quantities in Table X are expressed in cubic meters. Thailand's teak forests are in the North, from which region the logs are floated down the Chao Phya River to Bangkok, or down the Salween River into Burma. The figures given here include only the exports of teak through Bangkok. In some years the logs floated into Burma were about equal in number to those floated down to Bangkok, but the value of the Bangkok exports was greater because the logs were milled in Thailand before export.

Source of Demand

The production of tin and rubber was undertaken because of the stimulus of a favorable world-market price and to satisfy an external demand. Virtually the entire output of tin and rubber has always been exported. Domestic consumption is a negligible part of the total product, and the small amount consumed is usually embodied in imported manufactured products rather than processed domestically.

Before World War II, almost all tin and rubber was exported to Malaya for further processing and re-export. In 1940–41 there was an increase in rubber exports through Bangkok to Japan and the United States. Japan alone took 12 percent and 50 percent of Thai rubber exports in 1940 and 1941. Since the war, direct shipments of both tin and rubber to the United States have greatly increased. In 1947 and 1948 about 75 percent of tin exports (metallic content) went to the United States, but in 1949 and 1950 the amount dropped to 41 percent and 29 percent.[2] The balance continued to go to Malayan smelters. All of the tin produced is still exported.

The war gave an impetus to the manufacture of rubber products in Thailand, and the production of some products (such as footwear, bicycle tires, and hot-water bottles) has increased since the war. There is talk of producing automobile tires. In 1950, however, local manufactures consumed less than 1,000 tons of rubber yearly—less than one percent of total production.

The case of teak is different. Substantial amounts of this wood are used in Thailand for furniture, shipbuilding, houses, etc. Teak forests have long been exploited in a small way to satisfy the domestic demand and, even after large-scale exploitation of the forests began in the late nineteenth century under

[2] These percentages were supplied by the Department of Mines, Bangkok.

the stimulus of a world demand, foreign and domestic markets have competed for the yearly output. In 1891, for example, the low teak exports were attributed among other things to the lively local demand in Bangkok "which was able to keep the three European steam mills fully employed."[3] In spite of the long-standing domestic demand for teak, however, it was not until Burmese forests were nearing exhaustion that systematic large-scale exploitation of Thailand's forests began. The foreign capital, entrepreneurship, and labor used in this expansion of production came initially to produce for foreign markets although, once established, the output was sold to any buyer. Of the logs floated down to Central Thailand from 1919 to 1926, it was estimated that 37 percent was consumed domestically.[4] Similar estimates of domestic consumption were 45 percent in 1930 and 60 percent in 1949.[5]

In general, it is clear that production of tin and rubber was undertaken in response to external demand, and that external demand was a major cause of the expansion of teak production. At the same time, changes in the conditions of supply, especially in the supply of labor and in technique (for tin mining), influenced the expansion of production. As in the case of rice, changes in demand and supply are inextricably mixed in explanation of later changes in production, but the *initial* change seems clearly to have been the appearance of an external demand for tin, teak, and (later) rubber.

The Expansion of Production, 1850–1950

In spite of its small size, Thailand divides rather sharply into regions. With one exception, each region specializes in one of the four major export products. Teak is produced in the North, for example. Rubber and tin are produced almost entirely in the peninsular South and, as we have seen, the Central region is still the primary source of rice exports, although exports from the North and Northeast have increased in recent decades. The great Northeastern Plateau is thus the only one of the four regions which does not produce a major part of any of the four big exports as of 1950.

Tin.—The production of tin in the Thai portion of the Malay Peninsula remained almost entirely in Chinese hands until the first decade of the twentieth century. The "tin" island of Phuket was the principal center of tin mining, as it had been for several centuries, although production varied greatly from time to time. H. Warington Smyth, onetime Director of the Department of Mines in Thailand, noted that Captain Low in 1825 had found little tin mining and practically no Chinese there.[6] At the time of Smyth's visit

---

[3] Smyth, *op. cit.*, II, 279.

[4] "Review of the Teak Market," *The Record*, Thailand, Department of Commerce, No. 22 (October 1926), p. 379.

[5] *Siam, Nature and Industry*, Thailand, Ministry of Commerce and Communications, p. 138; *Annual Report for the Year 1950 to the Food and Agriculture Organization of United Nations*, Thailand, Ministry of Agriculture, p. 15.

[6] Smyth, *Five Years in Siam*, I, 315–28.

(about 1894) the island was again in a slump, with a yearly output of only 43,000 piculs of tin and a mining population of about 20,000. In between these dates there was a period of great activity in Phuket, and as late as 1884 the Chinese population alone was around 50,000 and the output of tin was 86,000 piculs.

Chinese miners also operated crude smelters in which they smelted a large part of the ore mined. As late as 1907 the Monthon Phuket exported 44,000 piculs of slab tin and 54,000 piculs of tin ore.[7] Most of this output came from the island of Phuket, and both mining and smelting were done by Chinese, who used methods which were very crude in comparison with those used in Malaya. Writing about 1904, Carter says that "generally speaking, all the mining is in the hands of Chinese; the labor is Chinese, and the smelting is done locally by Chinese methods."[8] By the turn of the century Malayan smelters appear to have been cutting into the business of the small Chinese charcoal smelters, but a substantial amount was still smelted in Thailand.

A large number of the small Chinese mines operated in southern Thailand. Very little capital was used. Tools were simple, and the largest item of fixed capital equipment was usually that required to supply water to the mine. In all tin mining the tin-bearing earth had to be washed in order to separate the tin ore. Water was essential, and some expensive and ingenious devices were employed to supply and utilize water effectively. Chinese immigrants were brought in as laborers during the nineteenth century. The Thai were involved in the tin industry only through the government, which charged a royalty on tin produced and operated a crude system of licensing. The royalty paid by the Chinese was 10 percent in some years and 16 percent in others.[9]

Apparently the government did not grant mining rights to Westerners on the same basis as it granted them to the Chinese. The British Consular Report for 1870 said hopefully that British subjects might be allowed to work the mines if the Thai government were convinced they had adequate capital to develop the mines. The system of licenses and royalties was revised in 1892 to give the government more effective control over tin-mining operations and, incidentally, to encourage Western firms to undertake mining operations, but foreign entrepreneurs did not respond for several years.

The influx of Western firms roughly coincides with the introduction of dredges into tin mining in Thailand. The first dredge was put into operation in 1907 by the Tongkah Harbour Tin Dredging Company, an Australian

[7] *Annual Series, Diplomatic and Consular Reports, Siam, Report for the Year 1907 on the Trade and Commerce of the Monthons of Saiburi and Puket,* Great Britain, Foreign Office (London, 1908).

[8] A. Cecil Carter (ed.), *The Kingdom of Siam* (New York, 1904), p. 242.

[9] The royalty was given as 10 percent in *Commercial Report from Her Majesty's Consul-General in Siam for the Year 1870,* Great Britain, Foreign Office (London 1871), p. 3. In 1895 H. W. Smyth said the royalty was 16 percent (*Five Years in Siam,* I, 315–28). In 1899 it was again reduced from 16 to 10 percent (*Bangkok Times,* January 23, 1899, p. 3).

firm which had secured a rich concession in Tongkah Harbor. The operation was highly successful and by 1921, in spite of high prices and the difficulty of procuring machinery during the war, the Tongkah Harbour Co. had 5 dredges in operation. Furthermore, several other large-scale mining ventures had been launched and were using a total of 8 more dredges.[10] In 1930 there were 38 dredges in operation or under construction, and by 1940 there were 45.[11]

Wartime damages and lack of maintenance brought dredge mining to a standstill during the war. In the postwar years attempts were quickly made to rehabilitate the dredges and, by 1950, 31 were in operation.

Since the advent of Western firms using the new dredging equipment, there has been an erratic increase in the production of tin. The movements of production have been largely in response to world price and demand conditions. It is important to note, however, that the expansion of output was not achieved solely by the large firms with dredging equipment. The small Chinese miners also maintained or expanded their output. The 1906 output of 79,000 piculs was virtually all produced by the Chinese mines, while in other years the situation was as follows:[12]

TIN METAL PRODUCED
(Piculs)

	By Nondredging Means	By Dredge
1906	79,000	
1916/17	99,000	48,000
1926/27	85,000	38,000
1936/37	84,000	139,000
1950	64,240	114,000

Thus the expansion of dredge mining did not greatly reduce the amount of nondredge mining. In 1950 there were 324 tin mines in operation, of which 25 employed dredges.[13] Of these 25, three were Thai companies, the rest British and Australian. The remaining 299 were mostly small Chinese-owned mines.

The output of tin mines has been exported in the form of ore since about 1907, at which date over half of the total output was smelted locally by the Chinese. By the early 1920's virtually no ore was smelted in Thailand; it went

[10] Thailand, Royal Department of Mines, *Notes on Mining in Siam with Statistics to March 31st, 1921* (Bangkok, 1921).

[11] *Siam, Nature and Industry*, p. 114; "Mining Statistics of Thailand for the Months of March, April, May 1951," Thailand, Department of Mines (mimeo., Bangkok), p. 8.

[12] Derived from *Statistical Year Book of Siam, 1936/37*, XIX, 488. Most of the tin produced by methods *other than* dredging is the product of the small Chinese mines. Figures for 1950 supplied by Department of Mines, Bangkok.

[13] "Mining Statistics of Thailand," 1951, p. 17.

instead to Malayan smelters. Local smelting revived during World War II, but died out again after the war was over. By 1950 no smelting was being done in Thailand. The local output has not been large enough to support a modern smelter, and the primitive small-scale smelters of the Chinese could not compete. [In the 1960's, a modern smelter was installed in Phuket.]

The amount of capital employed in tin mining cannot be determined accurately. In 1928 the Siam Chamber of Mines was formed, consisting of twenty-five European companies with a paid-up capital of 50 million baht (then equal to about £4,500,000).[14] These firms probably represented the bulk of foreign capital other than Chinese. Chinese investment was much smaller because of the nature of their operations. During the 1930's the government tried in various ways to increase the amount of Thai capital in the industry, but with little success. The bulk of the industry remained in foreign hands. In 1950 the *listed* capital of the foreign companies which had resumed operations was estimated to be £5,900,000.[15] This figure is almost meaningless for 1950, however, because the assets of the companies had little relation to the prewar capital stock.

In Western mines, as in the smaller Chinese ones, Chinese labor has been employed. Formerly, Chinese workers were recruited and brought directly from China to work in the tin mines. Descriptions of the mining industry written during the last century nearly always refer to the dominance of Chinese labor. Recent employment statistics are not directly comparable with the earlier descriptions, however, because the employment figures classify as "Thai" all workers who were *born* in Thailand, regardless of ancestry or degree of assimilation. In 1950 there were 13,500 workers in the tin mines, of whom 10,000 were "Thai" and 3,500 foreigners, mostly Chinese.[16] Thus the industry was still below its prewar level of employment. There were about 17,200 workers in 1937—9,000 Thai, 7,500 Chinese, and 700 "other."[17]

Rubber.—Thailand produced little or no rubber before World War I, in spite of the fact that the region bordering on Malaya is well suited for rubber trees. There was a brief rubber boom around the turn of the century, but it was mostly in the three dependent Malay States ceded to Great Britain in 1909. Until recently there has been comparatively little interest in rubber on the Thai side of the new border.

Estimates of the area in rubber have been made, although they are admittedly very rough. The following figures are merely one set taken from the many available (and widely divergent) estimates:[18]

[14] Virginia M. Thompson, *Thailand, the New Siam*, p. 460.

[15] "Statistics, Memoranda and Documents Submitted to the Fund and the World Bank Missions," 1949–50, p. 461.

[16] International Tin Study Group, *Statistical Bulletin*, IV (October 1951), 42.

[17] *Statistical Year Book of Thailand*, XXI, 75.

[18] For 1920, H. G. Callis, *Foreign Capital in Southeast Asia* (New York, 1942), pp. 59–70;

AREA IN RUBBER
(Thousand Rai)

Year	Mature	Immature	Total
1920			150
1929	88	287	375
1934	500	415	915
1940	748	300	1,048
1944			1,100 (1/6 to 1/3 immature)
1950	1,720	280	2,000

With full recognition of the shakiness of these estimates, it still seems clear that a remarkable percentage increase has taken place in rubber acreage in the last thirty years.

The expansion in rubber was brought about primarily by small holders. There are relatively few large rubber plantations in Thailand. Landon, writing in the late 1930's, said that most of the small planters had 2,000 to 3,000 trees, and that only a few estates had as many as 10,000 trees.[19]

The following figures summarize available data on the size-distribution of rubber holdings in recent years:[20]

Number of Holdings	1944	1950
250 rai and over	213	241
50–249 rai	1,970	3,426
Less than 50 rai	72,817	87,780
Total	75,000	91,447

Area in Holdings	1944 (Rai)	1950 (Rai)
250 rai and larger	167,000	156,000
50–249 rai	180,000	502,000
Less than 50 rai	755,000	1,316,000
Total	1,102,000	1,974,000

Average Size of Holdings	1944 (Rai)	1950 (Rai)
250 rai and larger	784	647
50–249 rai	91	146
Less than 50 rai	10	15
Over-all average	14.7	21.6

1929, 1934, 1940, P. T. Bauer, *The Rubber Industry* (Cambridge, Mass., 1948), pp. 2, 29, 379–80; 1944, *Report on Indochina Rubber Industry and Siamese Rubber Production Outlook*, U.S. Department of Commerce (Washington, D.C., 1946); 1950, supplied by Rubber Division, Department of Agriculture, Bangkok.

[19] K. P. Landon, *Siam in Transition*, pp. 70–73.

[20] For 1944 the figures are from the Thai Ministry of Agriculture, as cited in *Report on Indochina Rubber Industry and Siamese Rubber Production Outlook*; for 1950 the figures were supplied by the Rubber Division, Ministry of Agriculture, Bangkok.

That the bulk of rubber production is in the hands of small holders is evident, as the *average* holding was only 14.7 rai in 1944 and 21.6 in 1950, and 87,780 out of 91,447 holdings were less than 50 rai in 1950 (these holdings averaging only *15 rai*). Only 8 percent of the total area was in plantations of 250 rai or larger, and these 241 holdings averaged only 647 rai. Large-scale plantation cultivation is not important in Thailand.

As might be expected from the dominance of small holders, Western capital and entrepreneurship have not played an important part in the Thai rubber industry. Cultivation has been largely in the hands of the Thai (including Malays) and the Chinese. The latter were drawn to the rubber-growing regions quite early, both as entrepreneurs and as laborers. The following figures of ownership of rubber holdings are based on *nationality* rather than ancestry:[21]

OWNERSHIP OF RUBBER HOLDINGS IN 1949

(*Area in Rai*)

Nationality of Owner	Holdings, Under 50 Rai		Holdings, 50 Rai or More	
	Number	Area	Number	Area
Thai	77,845	1,058,507	1,716	267,934
Chinese	5,752	143,050	1,858	326,638
Other	151	2,503	67	20,368

It is roughly estimated that about *half* the total rubber area is owned by persons of Chinese ancestry, but there are no official statistics on this point. It is worth noting that immigrant Chinese own over half the holdings of over 50 rai but only 7 percent of those under 50 rai, and that Chinese-owned holdings under 50 rai averaged nearly 25 rai, compared to only 14 rai for Thai-owned ones. For the most part the Thai rubber grower is a very small operator.

Not a great deal of capital is needed to develop and operate a small holding at the present time. Thai nationals are entitled to claim unoccupied land from the state for a nominal fee, just as in the case of paddy land. Ordinarily the new owner works as a tapper for someone else while he gets his land cleared and planted. Sometimes the rubber planters also grow rice for their families, but usually they must buy their rice and other food. The seedlings require about six years to reach tappable age, and during this period the planter has to have some means of support. Seeds or seedlings of the ordinary sort may be obtained free from a neighbor, but if a better variety of high-yielding stock is desired it can be purchased from the Rubber Division for 10 satang per seed for selected domestic stock, or 1.0 to 2.5 baht per seed or seedling for foreign stock. The latter is flown in by the government. From 40 to 100 trees are planted per rai, and the cost of seed per rai may thus vary from zero (for ordinary domestic stock) to 4–10 baht (for selected domestic stock) to 40–250 baht

---

[21] Supplied by Rubber Division, Department of Agriculture, Bangkok.

(for foreign stock). Too often the cheapest alternative is taken. Besides seeds, the small holder must have equipment to collect and process the liquid rubber. The grower with only two or three rai may rent his neighbor's equipment or sell his rubber in liquid form, but ordinarily even the small holder of 15 or 20 rai processes his own rubber into sheets. It is estimated that the (1952) cost of the necessary tools and equipment for a small holder is about 2,000 baht.

Small holders usually sell their rubber in the form of raw rubber sheets and the buyers do the smoking on a large scale. The larger owners operate their own smokehouses, and they may also have equipment for washing, congealing, and rolling the rubber on a larger scale. The rubber merchants who buy the raw or smoked sheets also sort, grade, pack, and export it. Some of the larger plantations operate crepe-rubber rolling factories and export the crepe rubber directly, but all smoked sheets are exported by the rubber merchants. Nearly all these merchants are Chinese. Thai rubber has a reputation for a rather poor quality, and it is frequently said that the fault lies with the Chinese merchant who does not grade and sort it properly. No doubt this is part of the problem, but the establishment of standards has also been hindered by the processing methods of the small holder. He needs to learn to clean and prepare the rolled sheets properly.

A large number of tappers are employed by the larger rubber growers. It is estimated that a small holder can cultivate up to 10 rai by himself, and by using family labor even more can be cultivated without hiring labor. The larger plantations have to use hired labor, however. About 50,000 or 60,000 tappers are employed in rubber cultivation. As a rule they are paid a wage of 50 percent of the selling price of the finished sheets produced. Under this system the tapper has to process the rubber he collects. Less often the tapper may simply collect and deliver the liquid rubber, receiving a wage equal to 30–40 percent of the local price of the equivalent in dry rubber. The plantation owner must then process the rubber. In addition there are some workers who are paid a monthly wage to work in crepe factories and smokehouses. Much of the labor is Chinese. Since the war the earnings of labor have been much higher in the rubber-producing regions than in the rest of the country, and there has been some movement of labor in that direction. Generally speaking, however, laborers—especially Thai laborers—have not been very responsive to the high wage rates. One reason has been the high cost of living in the South, but ties of family and culture have probably been more important.

The rubber industry affords employment to about 150,000 persons, including 91,000 planters, 50,000 to 60,000 tappers, and an indeterminate number in factories and the trade. In 1951 it was the second largest source of foreign exchange to the nation and is likely to remain so in spite of the subsequent price slump. In time, rubber production could be greatly expanded through increased yields as well as increased area. Yields in Thailand are relatively low and the quality poor. Both can be improved. No survey has been made but it is roughly estimated that there is at least an additional 1,000,000 rai of land which could be planted in rubber.

At prices prevailing in 1951, the cultivation of rubber was considerably more profitable than rice cultivation. Assuming the price to the grower to be 50 percent of the export price of around 15 baht per kilogram (a rough average for all grades), even the low yield of 60 kilograms per rai produced an income to the grower of 450 baht per rai, compared with about 200 baht per rai in the case of paddy (4 piculs per rai at 45 baht per picul). Rubber prices could fall to half the inflated 1951 level and rubber cultivation would still be competitive with rice.

Production has not increased as steadily as has the acreage of rubber. Producers seem to have responded roughly to price changes. Production was undertaken during World War I, when prices were high. After that war the output fell off but picked up again during the high prices of the 1920's. Then when rubber prices dropped so low in the depression, the output again declined. With recovery and with the introduction of the cartel, prices rose and output increased steadily from a low of 57,000 piculs in 1932/33 to 815,000 piculs in 1941. The high prices following World War II resulted in an unprecedented rubber boom in southern Thailand, and in 1950 exports reached 1,900,000 piculs.

Teak.—The production of teak has not steadily increased since large-scale exploitation was undertaken in the late nineteenth century. Instead, it has fluctuated rather widely without showing a secular trend. The industry in general—and the export side of it in particular—has been largely in the hands of foreigners during the whole of the period covered in this study. Until the 1880's the Chinese and Burmese were dominant; since then a small number of European firms, using European capital and management and employing Chinese, Laos, and Burmese labor, have largely controlled the industry.

Thailand's teak forests are located in the Laos states of the North. Until the 1880's the forests were worked by Chinese and Burmese who obtained rights and leases from the Laos princes. Burmese foresters came into the Thai forests as Burmese forests became exhausted. Teak logs were sawed by hand in the Chinese sheds, a practice which continued to exist long after steam sawmills were introduced. Indeed, hand sawing is still found in many parts of the country. Production was principally for the domestic market, and until 1883 the value of exports had not exceeded 630,000 baht in any single year.[22] Little capital was employed in the industry, and methods were crude.

The lack of European participation before the 1880's is explained partly by the fact that Europeans were busy with the Burmese teak forests, partly

---

[22] *Annual Diplomatic and Consular Reports, 1869–1886,* Great Britain. This refers to exports through Bangkok only.

by the poor reputation of Thai teak, and partly by restrictive regulations of the Thai government and especially the Laos chieftains. Europeans were forbidden to cut timber themselves; they had to buy the logs from native foresters. But although this was changed by treaty in 1883, not until 1888 was a forest worked by a European company.[23] It was after the Burmese forests were closed in 1885 that European firms became really interested in Thai teak.

Once started, the influx of foreign capital and the exploitation of the teak forests proceeded rapidly. From an average yearly export of 27,000 cubic meters valued at 1.10 million baht in 1883–87, exports rose to a yearly average of 122,000 cubic meters worth 11.90 million baht in the period 1905–9 (see Table X). During this period of twenty-odd years the industry was brought almost entirely under the control of Western firms in forest operations and milling, as well as in the export of timber.

As late as 1895 most leases were held by Burmese foresters, although a few were in the hands of Thai lessees.[24] The Burmese lessee first obtained his lease by ingratiating himself with the Laos authorities. He then applied to European trading companies in Bangkok for capital to develop his lease. In return he paid a rather high rate of interest and agreed to sell logs to the trading company on the stream banks. The borrowed money was used to buy elephants and to pay wages during the three or four years which elapsed before the first logs were ready to be sold.[25] In 1895 it was estimated that about 42 percent of the timber delivered was taken by British subjects, 48 percent by Thai subjects (mostly Chinese), and 10 percent by one Chinese under French protection. In the same year the total amount of capital invested in the teak industry was estimated at 14,000,000 baht (about £900,000 at the exchange rate for 1895), most of which was British. Ten or fifteen years earlier, little or no European capital had been invested in the teak industry.

In the early 1890's the teak forests were already suffering from hasty and indiscriminate felling of trees. Undersized timber was cut, no planned replacement was undertaken, and (as a writer in 1895 said) "all the western forests in the neighborhood of the streams available for floating timber have become practically exhausted."[26] The result was the establishment in 1895 of tighter government control over forestry operation. The new regulations on leases and the cutting of timber gave an impetus to large firms because

[23] Arnold Wright and Oliver Breakspear (eds.), *Twentieth Century Impressions of Siam* (London, 1908), pp. 170–74.

[24] This paragraph is based largely on *Report on Teak Trade in Siam*, Miscellaneous Series, No. 357, Reports on Subjects of General and Commercial Interest, Great Britain, Foreign Office (London, 1895).

[25] When first cut or ringed, teak logs will sink if placed in water. After three or four years they are dry enough to float.

[26] Smyth, *op. cit.*, I, 104–7.

of the emphasis which was placed on long-term planning and selective cutting over a large area. At the same time, the quality of exports, about which there had long been complaints, was greatly improved as export trade became virtually monopolized by four or five large European firms.

The total quantity of foreign capital invested in the teak industry has probably not increased very much since about 1900, at which time it was around £2,500,000. British capital alone was estimated at £2,000,000 in 1899, and the East Asiatic Co. (Danish) had entered the teak trade and built a large modern sawmill in 1898.[27] In 1924 six firms (four British, one French, and one Danish) were said to have about £3,000,000 invested in the industry.[28]

The Chinese continued to control a part of the industry. In 1924 they owned three of the nine modern sawmills in Bangkok (and nearly all of the small hand mills), and in 1940 they owned two of seven large modern sawmills.[29] European firms dominated the operation of forests and the export trade, however. In 1938, 88 percent of the teak forests were worked by European firms, 7 percent by local lessees (probably Chinese), and 5 percent by the Forest Department.[30] During the 1930's the government began to develop plans to work more of the forests itself, but so far not much has been done.

In the beginning the labor used to work the teak forests was brought in from Burma and from French territory to the east. Eventually, the lessees began to use the native Laos labor, which proved to be satisfactory. Labor in the sawmills has until recently been almost entirely Chinese. According to the 1937 census there were 21,000 workers in "Forestry, Hunting, and Trapping" and 16,000 in "Manufactures of Wood."[31]

The production of teak timber has varied considerably from year to year. One major reason for yearly variations is the dependence on rainfall to raise rivers up to a level high enough to carry the logs. Teak received at the Bangkok mills in any given year is by no means equivalent to the teak cut or put in the water in that year. Demand and price conditions also influence the output, of course, and their effect is complicated by the three- to four-year lag between the time the tree is cut and the time the log reaches Bangkok.

Teak exports have declined both absolutely and relatively since 1900–1910. Teak represented only about 4 percent of total commodity exports from 1920 to 1940, but represented about 10 percent in the earlier decade. In both value and volume the peak of teak exports came in 1905–9.

[27] *Annual Diplomatic and Consular Reports for 1898–1899*, Great Britain.

[28] W. A. Graham, *Siam*, II, 67–68.

[29] Graham, *op. cit.*, II, 89–90; Callis, *op. cit.*, p. 66. Apparently two mills went out of business between these dates.

[30] Thailand, Ministry of Economic Affairs, *Commercial Directory for Siam, 1939* (4th ed.; Bangkok, 1939), pp. 137–45.

[31] *Statistical Year Book of Thailand*, XXI, 80.

Although we have been concerned only with teak, it is worth noting that teak is only a small part of the total *volume* of timber production in Thailand. In 1949, for example, timber production was as follows:[32]

Timber	Volume (*cu. m.*)
Teak	193,000
Other timber	1,087,000
Total	1,280,000

In addition there was a large consumption of wood for charcoal and firewood. Nearly all of the timber is consumed domestically.

The Role of the Government (to 1950)

To increase the total production and export of tin, teak, and rubber has not been a major aim of government policy. Many government actions concerning these commodities were designed to secure for the government a part of the income earned by the foreign firms. Others were designed to control the manner and rate of exploitation. In some of its actions, notably in connection with the tin and rubber cartels, the government has sought to maintain or increase the rate of output of these industries, but in others it has clearly sought to slow the rate at which timber and mineral resources were developed (and exhausted).

The government has long controlled the mining of tin. In Thailand the title to all mineral rights is vested in the king. The small Chinese miner of the nineteenth century had to have a lease, and he paid a royalty to the government. Thailand's treaties with Western powers provided that leases should be granted to their subjects, and by 1891 some thirteen mining leases had been so granted.[33] Little had been done to develop these leases, however, when a new system of leases was introduced under the supervision of Western mining experts. Royalties were calculated on a sliding scale based on the price of tin, and the area of leases was greatly restricted in order to force the lessees to concentrate on mining instead of on hoodwinking the public with prospectuses describing their "exclusive rights to thousands of acres of land in the rich tin-bearing region."

It has long been the policy of the government to allow private firms and individuals to prospect and mine *only* in the region from the province of Chumporn to the south, i.e., in peninsular Thailand. The rest of the country is reserved for the future or for development by the government. In the areas in which mining has been permitted, government policy has been to encourage the production and export of tin. By and large, foreign mining companies

---

[32] *Annual Report for the Year 1950 to the Food and Agriculture Organization of United Nations*, Thailand, Ministry of Agriculture (Bangkok, 1951), p. 13.

[33] Smyth, *op. cit.*, I, 296-300.

have received considerate treatment from the Thai government. It, in turn, has benefited from the royalties paid by the tin producers. The government also received revenue from rentals and fees and, since the war, it has made a profit on the portion of their foreign exchange proceeds which exporters have had to surrender to the Bank of Thailand at the official rate. In 1947, 100 percent of foreign-exchange proceeds of tin sales had to be surrendered, but by 1949 the surrender requirement had been reduced to 40 percent.

During the life of the tin cartel Thailand succeeded in obtaining extremely favorable quotas.[34] The government had a strong bargaining position which it exploited successfully. The cartel sponsors were eager to have all important, or potentially important, producers of tin covered by the cartel agreement. Thailand was a relatively small producer (6 percent of world production in 1929), but she was the fourth largest tin producer and, to add the crucial fact, her tin-producing districts lay just across an unguarded border from Malayan tin-producing districts. The success of the cartel scheme might well have been endangered by tin smuggled into Thailand and sold as Thai tin.

The upshot was that when Thailand joined the cartel in July 1931, a few months after it began operation, she received favorable terms. Her quota was fixed at 10,000 tons, only 5 percent below 1929 production, and she was to be exempted from any production curtailments subsequently imposed on cartel members. "This meant that Thailand's rate of restriction would be far below that of other agreement countries, if not zero at times."[35] This proved to be the case.

In the postwar years 1945–51, there was no restriction on tin production. The government encouraged the rehabilitation of the mines, and it placed no new restrictions on foreign firms. The government would no doubt like to see a larger part of the industry in Thai hands, but it has not yet found a way to accomplish this objective.

Rubber was produced in Thailand for several years without license, tax, or other interference by the government. The growers and tappers were independent entrepreneurs and, unlike tin producers, they needed no license from the government to begin operations. Not until the mid-1930's did the government place an export tax on rubber. The export duty was set at 7 percent ad valorem, and this rate is still in force. The government has encouraged the cultivation of rubber by allowing land to be taken from the state for a nominal fee, and by taxing rubber production lightly. A permit must be obtained to plant new rubber but since the war this has been granted without difficulty. The government has tried to improve the yield of rubber by selling

---

[34] The basic source for the following description of the tin cartel is K. E. Knorr, *Tin Under Control*, Food Research Institute (Stanford University Press, 1945), *passim*. For an account of the political maneuvering in Thailand, see also Virginia M. Thompson, *Thailand, the New Siam*, pp. 459–67.   [35] Knorr, *op. cit.*, p. 112.

good quality seeds and seedlings to the planters, but it has had little success in this effort. Government efforts to standardize and improve the grading of rubber have also had little success.

Thailand was not a member of the Stevenson plan, the cartel scheme of the 1920's. The high prices maintained by this cartel probably induced Thai rubber growers to plant more rubber, although the acreage figures given above are not accurate enough to enable us to compare the acreage increase of the 1920's with that of the 1930's. During the latter decade, however, Thailand was a member of a cartel and new planting was *supposed* to be rigidly controlled.

When the new rubber cartel was formed in 1933, Thailand was given exceptionally favorable terms to induce her to become a member. The reasons were about the same as in the case of tin: a potential for increasing output, good opportunities for smuggling from one of the two largest rubber producers (Malaya), and the desire to bring in one of the largest producing nations even though it accounted for only a tiny fraction of the world total.

Again the result was that the quotas allotted to Thailand did not necessitate much curtailment of output; indeed, in most years she was not able to produce her full quota.[36] Thus, so far as Thailand was concerned, the cartel did little to control or restrict output. For rubber, as for tin, the government succeeded through its negotiations in maintaining and increasing the national output.

Since the war there has been no restriction on rubber production. The government has encouraged production through its land policy and through technical assistance to growers, while at the same time it has derived revenue from the industry by taxing exports and by requiring exporters to surrender a part of their foreign exchange earnings to the Bank of Thailand at the official rate of exchange. At first, 100 percent of the proceeds had to be surrendered, but the surrender requirement was reduced to 20 percent in 1947.

Originally, teak forests were controlled by the princes and chiefs of the semi-independent Laos states. As the Northern states were slowly and steadily brought under the direct rule of the Bangkok government, the latter began to promulgate laws and regulations concerning the teak forests. Generally speaking, forestry laws tended to control the exploitation of the forests and to prevent the wanton and indiscriminate cutting of timber, which became so extreme in the late nineteenth century that the teak companies themselves urged government regulation to stop it because no single company could compete successfully if it alone undertook the proper measures of conservation. The emphasis of the government has therefore been not to secure the largest possible output of timber, but to adjust cutting to the rate of replacement. At

---

[36] K. E. Knorr, *World Rubber and Its Regulation*, Food Research Institute (Stanford University Press, 1945), p. 248; "Restriction Group Increases Siam's Rubber Share," *Far Eastern Survey*, VII (April 20, 1938), 90–91.

the same time the government has collected revenue through a system of leases and royalties. In the last twenty years the government has indicated its intention to work a larger part of the forest area itself.

It was in 1895 that a Forestry Department was organized, under the direction of a British forest officer. The system he established was based on control by the central government (hereafter the Laos chiefs received only a share of the profits), provided for a regular system of forest leases with a twelve-year felling cycle, and established a minimum girth for cutting. The new forest regulations also increased the royalties.

When the original leases expired in 1909 a new and more restrictive system was introduced which provided for a thirty-year felling cycle, reduced the number of leases to forty, increased royalties 20 percent, and increased the minimum girth for felling trees. In 1925 the first half period of the new leases expired, and still more changes were introduced. Minimum exploitable girth was again increased, the Forestry Department was charged with selection and girdling of all trees to be felled, and royalties were raised. In early 1952, the government announced that when leases held by foreign firms expired they would not be renewed. The forests were to be leased to local firms or worked by the government itself.

Summary

The three commodities discussed in this chapter have, with the partial exception of teak, been largely exported. They have been produced for foreign markets and their production has been greatly influenced by world price and demand conditions over which Thailand has no control. Furthermore, in the case of tin, teak, and, to a lesser extent, rubber as well, all stages of production, processing, and trade have been in foreign hands. Tin has been controlled by European and Chinese capital and by Chinese labor; teak forests have been worked by European companies; the milling has been done by European and Chinese mills, using chiefly Chinese labor; and the export has been done by the European companies. Rubber is cultivated by Chinese and Thai planters, but the trade is in Chinese hands. (Many of the Chinese in these three industries are Thai nationals by birth, but Chinese by ancestry and culture.) Generally speaking, Thai participation in the three industries has been limited to rubber planting and labor in teak forests. (Obviously there are many exceptions to such a generalization.)

Historically, the policy of the government has been to obtain a portion of the proceeds of these industries through taxes, royalties, and export duties, and gradually to impose tighter control on the industries. Notably in the case of teak, regulation has steadily moved in the direction of conservation and control rather than maximum production (and revenue). Tin production has also been somewhat restricted because of the limited numbers of mining and prospecting leases issued.

6

Imports and Home-Market Industries 1850–1950

THE GROWTH OF EXPORTS since 1850 has meant increased money incomes to the people and the government of Thailand. Of course a considerable part of the export proceeds went to foreigners who supplied capital, management, and (in the case of the Chinese) labor, but part also reached the rice farmers and enabled them for the first time to buy goods in the market place. Before this source of income appeared, money transactions do not appear to have been very important in Thailand. Some money was required to pay taxes, but until 1855 the land tax could be paid in kind, and the *corvée* obligation was usually discharged by working the required amount of time for the state. No doubt a considerable amount of specialization and exchange took place at the village level—people trading vegetables, or swapping fish for fruit or basketwork for cloth—but this trade was largely within the self-sufficient village economy. Some regional trade took place: in the North and Northeast, itinerant caravans carried goods of high value per unit of weight to remote towns and villages; in the Central Plain, trading boats went out on canals and rivers with goods from Bangkok; and, in the South, coastal trading ships called at the peninsular ports. In addition, goods flowed to Bangkok in payment of taxes. Much of the trade of 1850 was barter, but even barter was a relatively minor part of the total economic life of the people. Most families grew most of their own food, built their own houses, and made their own clothes.

With the growth of production for sale, however, families became less self-sufficient. They began to buy more of their requirements in the market place. Many of the goods purchased were imported, and many domestic (mainly cottage) industries began to decline. This decline in local industries was uneven. Some industries (such as textiles) were affected more than others (such as pottery and basketwork), and the less accessible regions were affected much less than was the Central Plain with its network of navigable canals and rivers. Nevertheless the tendency existed and was strengthened by the low ceiling on import duties provided in the foreign treaties and by the lack of interest in nonagricultural production on the part of the Thai.

Only in the last three or four decades has nonagricultural production shown signs of reviving. The initiative in this revival has come chiefly from foreigners or from the government, which has had to adjust its efforts to the speed with which it could throw off treaty restrictions on its jurisdiction and revenues, develop economic and political independence, in fact as well as in name, and effectively tap new sources of revenue. A fourth limiting factor has been the speed with which the government could develop an efficient administrative organization. Even though progress along this line has been discouraging, in recent years the government has enlarged its role in nonagricultural production.

This chapter will describe the relative decline of certain industries, the growth of imports, and the more recent revival of domestic industries. Because of lack of space as well as lack of data, in discussing the decline of industries we will concentrate on only two industries: textiles and sugar. Textiles have comprised the most important nonfood articles of consumption, while sugar is a good example of the pattern of early decline and later revival which characterizes many industries in Thailand since 1850.

Nonagricultural production appears to have declined both relatively and absolutely as trade began to increase after 1850. The trends varied by region and sometimes the evidence is weak, but such production appears to have first declined and then partly recovered in the last several decades.

THE DECLINE OF DOMESTIC INDUSTRIES

Textiles

Even before Thailand became a free-trade nation in the middle of the nineteenth century, the student of economic history should have been able to predict that textiles would quickly become her major import. When Dutch and English traders established "factories" in the old capital of Ayuthia during the seventeenth century, they found a ready market for cloth of all kinds. Their successors, though greatly restricted, found cloth to be a popular article of import. Chinese junks usually brought cloth, as did the royal junks returning from India, Java, and China.

It was not that Thailand could not produce textile fibers and cloth. Both cotton and silk were produced, and early accounts describe the prevalence of the hand loom in households all over the country. Indeed, silk and cotton cloth was exported in small quantities from the North and Northeast, and Crawfurd (1821), Malloch (1850), and Bowring (1855) all listed *raw* cotton as an export from Bangkok. But the production of cloth was a slow, painful process. Tools and equipment were primitive; the yield of raw cotton and silk was low because of plant diseases, insects, and poor strains; and the finished product was coarse and expensive, though strong and durable. Furthermore, the local dyes were somber and less appealing than the bright colors of the imported cloth. As a result, even though climate and custom required little clothing and people had plenty of time to work up the local materials into cloth, they were eager to buy the cheaper, if less durable, foreign cloth.

The Center.—Of all the Thai regions, the Central Plain has probably been the most anxious to buy imported cloth. In the first place, this region is by nature not as well suited to produce silk and cotton as are the North and Northeast. The yearly floods make it difficult to cultivate cotton and mulberry trees, while in the dry season it is too dry. Irrigation may change all this by controlling the water supply, but in the decades after 1850 there was little control. Second, transportation favored the foreign goods. A large area in the Central region was accessible by boat from Bangkok. Goods from the North and Northeast, on the other hand, took several weeks of difficult travel to reach the Central Plain. From the North goods could come by water when the rivers were high, but from the Northeast the journey was overland and very difficult. In either case there was danger from bandits. Furthermore, such transportation was extremely expensive. The nature of internal transportation was such that no reliable figures of its cost are available, but it is quite likely that it was cheaper to ship a ton of cloth from England to Bangkok than from Chiengmai to Bangkok. The textile-producing regions of Thailand simply could not compete with the textile centers of Europe. Third, the Central Plain could easily expand the cultivation and export of rice, as we have seen. This gave the people a source of money income. Finally, the system of canals and rivers made it possible for the rice to be exported economically.

Transportation thus played a crucial role in fixing the character and regional distribution of Thailand's imports and exports. Transportation facilities made it easy for the Center to import foreign goods as well as to export rice, while the *lack* of transportation facilities connecting the other regions with the Center made it difficult for these regions to compete with foreign textiles in the Central market and at the same time perpetuated their self-sufficiency, since they could neither import foreign goods nor export rice except at great cost.

The introduction of free trade to Bangkok, coupled with technical developments in ocean transportation and manufacturing, thus brought the market of Bangkok and the Central Plain within the orbit of European manufactures. Foreign textiles were not new to this region, but they now came in larger quantities, and people were better able to obtain money incomes with which to buy them.

Yet the foreign-textile imports did not win in a day, even in the Center. The Thai farmer wanted a sturdy cloth, and often he bought foreign yarn to make his own cloth (as he still does). In 1867 it was reported that the cloth imported was not durable enough, and that "there is an extensive manufacture in Siam by hand-looms (which may be seen in every village) of phanungs, or sarongs, woven of . . . cotton twists."[1] Two years later the British consul again noted that textile imports were not increasing. He said that "unless a better wearing material than the cotton goods now sent can be manufactured

---

[1] *Commercial Reports from Her Majesty's Consuls in China, Japan, and Siam, 1867*, Great Britain, Foreign Office (London, 1868), p. 318.

at prices sufficiently low to tempt these people, the bulk of them, particularly the workers in the field, will continue to manufacture their own from the cotton of the country, which is sufficiently abundant for the purpose."[2] By 1883 the consul was saying that "every year Siam becomes more dependent upon the manufactures of Europe and China,"[3] but he noted that coarse silks and cottons were still made for home use. In his annual report for 1885 the consul said: "The manufacture of native hand-woven cotton cloths has of later years decreased considerably, the imported goods, though not so durable, being far cheaper." In 1910 Gerini said that "the local [cotton] industry, which has been languishing for the last 50 years, has been more or less supplanted by the foreign one,"[4] and several other accounts say the same thing. These reports do not always specify what region is referred to, but most of them refer to the Central Plain.

Some weaving continued to exist in the Center, especially in the less commercialized parts of the region as we have defined it. The weavers used mostly imported yarn. But, in general, home weaving declined in this region during the latter part of the nineteenth century, and the people turned to imported cloth.

The North.—The dividing line between the region which was conquered by foreign textiles and those in which the penetration was resisted was never a sharp one. Adventurous traders were often found who were willing to take the risks involved, and some foreign textiles soon reached the towns of the North and Northeast. The penetration of foreign goods steadily expanded, always fighting against the natural barriers, and always offering keen competition to the local industries.

Reports on the North from 1860 to 1920 establish two major facts: (1) most households in the region had their own hand looms on which were woven most of the clothes for the family from locally grown cotton and silk, and (2) markets in the larger towns stocked an increasing quantity of foreign textiles and other goods.

Several observers writing of the 1870's and 1880's have noted that nearly every house had a loom which was used to make clothes for the family,[5] but a few years later Curtis wrote that "in the large cities the homes are giving up their looms and spinning wheels . . . [although] in the towns and vil-

[2] *Commercial Reports from Her Majesty's Consuls in China and Siam, 1869*, Great Britain, Foreign Office (London, 1869), p. 98.

[3] *Commercial Report by Her Majesty's Agent and Consul-General in Siam for the Year 1883*, Great Britain, Foreign Office (London, 1884), p. 4.

[4] G. E. Gerini, *Siam, Its Production, Arts, and Manufactures*, pp. 209–10.

[5] For the North this comment is found in: Mary Backus (ed.), *Siam and Laos as Seen by Our American Missionaries* (Philadelphia, 1884), p. 440; Carl Bock, *Temples and Elephants* (London, 1884), p. 324 A. Cecil Carter, *The Kingdom of Siam*, p. 26; Archibald R. Colquhoun, *Amongst the Shans*, pp. 128–29; Holt S. Hallett, *A Thousand Miles on an Elephant in the Shan States*, p. 87.

lages they are as much used as in former ages."[6] This distinction is also made by Freeman.[7] Locally grown cotton was cheap and plentiful, but silk was more expensive. Cotton was grown in gardens around the houses, and silkworms were collected wild in the forest and bred in the villages. Some raw silk was imported for local manufacture. Primitive spinning and weaving implements were used and are still in use down to the present day.

Although home weaving was widely practiced, foreign piece goods found a market in the North. A report of the Chief Commissioner of British Burma, in 1873, noted that Chiengmai was "the centre of a very large miscellaneous English piece-goods trade," and that from Chiengmai "English piece-goods and hardware permeate through the Siamese feudatory principalities."[8] The British Consular Report for 1874 noted that there were at least one hundred shops in Chiengmai selling imported manufactures. These would have been small shops, but the number indicates a considerable interest in foreign goods. Quantities of cotton cloth brought up from Bangkok were found even as far as Luang Prabang[9] (no longer part of Thailand). In the 1880's caravans went through the Shan states to Moulmein, taking with them on the return journey "every description of cheap cotton goods, bright coloured flannels, and odds and ends of trumpery."[10]

Markups over the Bangkok prices were sometimes surprisingly low, considering the difficulty of transportation. Hallett quotes a Mr. Wilson who had made a study of the markups between Bangkok and Chiengmai and found them to range between 12 and 67 percent (on imports to Chiengmai), depending on value, bulk, and weight.[11] Markups probably varied a good deal from year to year, however. In 1894 they were estimated to be about 30 percent over Bangkok prices,[12] and in 1898 the markup on staple goods was said to be not over 15 percent, this partly because the Chinese traders made most of their profits on the baht-rupee exchange rate.[13] Markups were much greater in outlying towns and villages where people were not familiar with prices and where competition was less keen.

The railway did not cross the mountain barriers and reach Chiengmai until the 1920's, and even then the local production of cloth survived. Railway rates were high; the railway still did not serve such towns as Chiengrai, Nan, Phre, and villages all over the North; and to some extent the people probably

[6] Lillian J. Curtis, *The Laos of North Siam* (Philadelphia, 1903), p. 163.

[7] J. H. Freeman, *An Oriental Land of the Free*, pp. 53–54.

[8] Cited in Archibald R. Colquhoun, *Across Chrysê* (London, 1883), pp. 220–21.

[9] Backus (ed.), *op. cit.*, p. 535.

[10] G. J. Younghusband, *Eighteen Hundred Miles on a Burmese Tat* (London, 1888), p. 75.

[11] Hallett, *op. cit.*, pp. 296–97.

[12] *Diplomatic and Consular Reports on Trade and Finance, Siam, Report for the Year 1894 on the Trade of Chiengmai*, Great Britain, Foreign Office (London, 1895).

[13] *Annual Series, Diplomatic and Consular Reports, Siam, Report for the Year 1898 on the Trade and Commerce of Chiengmai and District*, Great Britain, Foreign Office (London, 1899).

preferred their own designs. The importation of German aniline dyes enabled the local product to match the foreign textiles in color. In any case local production continued to exist alongside the increasing import of foreign goods.

The Northeast.—The Northeast was even less accessible from Bangkok than was the North—at least until the railway was built. Cut off by a band of rugged, mountainous country, the region had no river connection with Bangkok. Its rivers drained to the east toward the Mekong River, and toward Saigon. Navigable streams are rare in the Northeast, and the few that do exist very nearly dry up in the hot, dry months. Except for some caravan trade, this region had very little trade with the outside. The people grew cotton, bred silkworms, and produced their own cloth.

The best account of the trade of the Northeast before the railway was opened to Korat is that given by H. Warington Smyth.[14] He dwelt on the difficulties of travel within the region as well as to places outside it, and asserted that until an outlet for trade was found the people would continue to produce only for their own meager wants. For 1893 Smyth estimated the total value of the external trade of the Korat Plateau at about £120,000 (1,500,000 baht) per year, divided equally between exports and imports. Virtually all of this trade was with Bangkok. Goods were taken from Bangkok to Saraburi by boat, and then transported over the mountain range to Korat by bullock caravan. Of the £60,000 of imports, textiles were put at £50,000. The imports were divided about as follows: one-third sold in Korat, one-third taken east to Ubon, one-third distributed along the Nongkhai trail to the north.

The town of Korat has long been a silk-weaving center, and silk cloth was (and still is) exported at the same time that foreign textiles were imported. After trade increased, and especially after the railway was opened to Korat, the production of silk began to decline in the Northeast. As early as 1902 the Thai government tried to revive and strengthen the silk industry by technical assistance.[15] Japanese experts were brought in to survey the industry and to give instruction to home weavers as well as to teach in a school which was established in Korat. Experiment and demonstration stations were set up, and Japanese experts brought in modern looms on which they gave free weaving lessons to the villagers. Meanwhile, several hundred girls were graduated from the silk school, and new equipment was imported and distributed by the government. After several years, however, it was noticed that silk exports had not increased, and raw-silk imports were no smaller. An investigation revealed that the silk weavers had completely rejected the new methods, that the graduates of the school had promptly dropped all they had been taught when they returned to their villages, and that the new equipment supplied by

14 *Five Years in Siam*, I, 220–54.
15 This account is based on W. A. Graham, *Siam*, II, 87–89. See also J. C. Barnett, *Report of the First Annual Exhibition of Agriculture and Commerce*, pp. 30–31.

the government was stored away in attics and barns. According to Graham:

Efforts made by the authorities to combat this astonishing lethargy only had the effect of decreasing the cultivation of silk wherever they were applied, and the Government, finding itself therefore equally unable either to lead or to drive its people to better things, abandoned the whole undertaking and left the silk-growers to look after themselves. With the weavers the Japanese experts had never had even the shadow of an influence, and thus the silk situation in 1922 was exactly as in 1901, before the King set about improving it.[16]

The production of silk thus remained at a low ebb, but it did not disappear. Home weaving in the Northeast continued to exist. Cotton was also grown and woven at home in this region. Nearly all of the cloth, both cotton and silk, was made for use within the family of the producer.

Although home weaving survived, the railway to Korat increased the exports (especially rice) and imports of the region. In 1910 the total value of exports and imports from the Northeast was estimated at 6,000,000 baht.[17] This trade was almost entirely in the hands of Chinese traders who operated from Bangkok. Cotton piece goods, which were distributed all over the plateau by caravan and river boat, formed the largest item of import. A considerable quantity of imported goods was sold to the French Laos states across the Mekong River.

Recent position (to 1950).—Outside the Central Plain, household weaving thus continued to exist even though village markets stocked a wide selection of foreign textiles. Recent evidence confirms the regional trends suggested above. Indeed, there is some evidence that weaving as a household industry increased both relatively and absolutely from 1930 to 1950, and that the tendency toward decline was therefore reversed.

In his survey in 1931, Zimmerman found that the commercialized districts (especially the Central Plain) purchased most of the clothing used, while "in outlying districts most of the clothing is woven at home."[18] Andrews concurred.[19] He said weaving was the most important handicraft in Thailand in 1934 although it did not yield much *cash* income because most weaving was for home use. His findings by region were: very little household weaving in the Center and almost none in the South. In the Northeast, household weaving was so widespread that little or no clothing had to be bought from necessity, although some was purchased for reasons of fashion and taste. Weaving in the Northeast was not developed commercially except in the towns of Korat and Ubon. In the North, household weaving was also widespread, but less so

---

[16] Graham, *op. cit.*, p. 89.

[17] Aymé Martin, *Siam Mouvement Économique du Laos Siamois (Monthons Isan et Oudon)*, Rapports Commerciaux des Agents Diplomatiques et Consulaires de France, No. 865, Ministry of Commerce and Industry (Paris, 1910).

[18] Carle C. Zimmerman, *Siam, Rural Economic Survey, 1930–31*, pp. 51, 109.

[19] James M. Andrews, *Siam, 2nd Rural Economic Survey, 1934–35*, pp. 122–28.

than in the Northeast. Commercial development had gone further, however. By 1950 the regional pattern was probably about the same. One indication is given by 1948 figures of the area planted in cotton by region: Northeast, 140,000 rai; North, 26,000; Center, 24,000 (mostly in outlying sections); South, 290 rai.[20] Personal observation also confirms the regional pattern suggested. One sees small quantities of raw cotton piled on porches all over the Northeast, while in both the Northeast and the North a great deal of household weaving is to be seen. Such things are rarely seen in the Central and Southern provinces.

Available data on imports of cotton yarn (see below) also indicate an increase in domestic weaving, most of which is done in households, but there is no way to determine the regional pattern of utilization of this yarn.

Although domestic production has increased in recent years, the trend of textile imports has continued upward.* Ever since 1850 textiles have been Thailand's major import. The value of these imports for selected years is given in Table XI. Unfortunately, no measure of the physical volume of imports is available for the earlier years, but the value figures alone are enough to show a remarkable growth over the course of the century. Price changes in recent decades obscure any *trend* which may exist, but cloth imports rose rapidly from the 1850's to the 1920's. During this period domestic weaving probably declined relatively if not absolutely.

Equally striking has been the increase in the import of cotton yarn from 1,380 metric tons in 1920 to 3,795 in 1941 and 5,760 in 1949. The growth of yarn imports indicates the growth of domestic weaving, most of which takes place in households. The value of yarn imports had risen to nearly one-fifth the value of cloth imports in 1941 and to over one-third in 1949, and the value added in weaving would bring the total value of the cloth woven domestically much closer to the value of imports.

An even stronger indication of the expansion of domestic production is found in the estimates of raw cotton produced in Thailand.[21] Small quantities have long been grown, but during the 1910's and 1920's the output was only 650 to 1,000 metric tons. Output began to increase in the mid-1930's and by 1941 it reached 3,000 metric tons. During the war, which gave a strong impetus to cotton production, output hit a peak of 14,000 metric tons in 1943. By 1948 it had fallen to 5,300 tons.

These figures indicate that even before the war the quantity of textiles woven domestically (from both imported yarn and domestic cotton) was perhaps half as large as the quantity of imported cloth, while during and since

[20] Supplied by the Department of Agriculture, Bangkok.

* This statement was written from the perspective of 1951. For more recent developments, see Ch. 12.

[21] *Statistical Year Book of Thailand.* Estimates given here are in *ginned* cotton. Figures in the sources appear to refer to unginned cotton, but we have adjusted these estimates to eliminate the weight of the seed. The 1948 figure was supplied by the Department of Agriculture, Bangkok.

TABLE XI

VALUE OF COTTON TEXTILE IMPORTS IN SELECTED YEARS[a]

(*Thousand Baht*)

Period	Cotton Manu- factures	Cotton Yarns	Physical Quantity of Yarn (*Metric Tons*)[b]
1859	1,500	180	—
1864	1,660	270	—
1870	1,530	320	—
1880	2,760	460	—
1892	3,600	510	—
1900	7,870	900	—
1910/11	10,700	1,090	—
1920/21	32,350	6,000	1,380
1925/26	28,690	7,560	3,360
1930/31	18,760	5,150	4,110
1935/36	18,870	3,610	3,370
1941	24,630	4,770	3,795
1949	440,550	155,320	5,760

[a] For some years the yarn figures include a small quantity of silk and other yarns. The 1949 figures represent the total value of all textile and yarn imports.
[b] Dash indicates that figures are not available.

Sources: Figures for 1859, *Bangkok Calendar for 1861*; 1864–80, *Annual Diplomatic and Consular Reports on Trade and Finance from Her Majesty's Consuls in Siam*, Great Britain, Foreign Office; 1892–1900, *Comparative Statement of the Imports and Exports of Siam, 1892–1901* (Bangkok: American Presbyterian Press); 1910–41, *Statistical Year Book of Thailand*; 1949, figure of yarns (weight), *Economic Survey of Asia and the Far East, 1950* (New York: UN Publications, 1951), p. 405. Others from *Report of the Financial Adviser, 1941–50*, Thailand, Ministry of Finance (Bangkok, 1951), p. 10

the war domestically woven cloth has considerably *exceeded* imports. Available estimates of quantity are as follows (metric tons):[22]

Period	Imports of Cotton Cloth	Imports of Cotton Yarn	Domestic Raw Cotton Production
1937/38	8,900	2,770	2,300
1938/39	14,200	4,212	1,500
1941	14,500	3,795	3,000
1943	800	240	14,000
1948	6,000	4,831	5,300
1949	7,000	5,764	5,000

[22] Figures for 1937–43, *Statistical Year Book*, XXI, 216–50, 466; others from *Economic Survey of Asia and the Far East, 1950* (New York: UN Publications, 1951), pp. 404–5; except cotton

These figures show that domestic weaving and cotton production have expanded considerably in recent years. The domestic industry may have been mildly stimulated by tariffs on imported textiles, but these have remained relatively low. The shift in the terms of trade against rice during the 1930's may also have provided a stimulus, but one which would have been reversed in the years since World War II. The virtual exclusion of imports during the war undoubtedly gave a great boost to domestic production. The drop in acreage and output since the war reflects the removal of that stimulus. The net growth in domestic production suggests, however, that farm households have become increasingly aware of the economic advantages of household weaving. The sharp drop in the price of yarns from 1920 to 1941 would have encouraged their use, but the change can scarcely be explained in terms of changes in relative prices or in technique.

A large-scale textile industry has not developed in Thailand. The reasons for this include the low tariffs on foreign textiles, the relatively small domestic market, the small supply of fiber available locally, and the lack of capital, entrepreneurship, and trained labor. Some weaving establishments have been set up from time to time, but these have rarely employed more than twenty or thirty workers, and they have not used modern machinery.

In the 1920's the army set up a mill to spin and weave cotton textiles for army use. In the 1930's the government effort was somewhat expanded, but it remains quite unimportant and nearly all of the output is taken by the government.

In 1950 a spinning mill was set up by a group of Shanghai and Hong Kong Chinese who brought in some of their machinery from Shanghai. This enterprise, the Bangkok Cotton Mills, had 23,000 spindles in early 1952 and was capable of producing about 3,500 metric tons of cotton yarn per year. No weaving is done by the mill. Most of the raw cotton is grown locally, although some is imported. The plant employs about 1,100 Thai women as full-time workers. Competition from imported yarns is keen, and when textile prices dropped in early 1952 the Bangkok Cotton Mills appealed to the government for increased tariff protection. The duty on cotton-yarn imports, only 0.90 baht per kilogram, was equal to 3–6 percent ad valorem from 1945 to 1952.

Besides the spindles of the Bangkok Cotton Mills, there are 10,000 to 12,000 privately owned spindles, and 10,000 in the government mills. The total number of spindles is thus about 43,000. These are capable of spinning about 5,500 metric tons of yarn per year. In addition to this yarn output, an unknown amount is produced as a household industry and in small workshops. Domestic yarn production in 1950 was about equal to yarn imports.

Weaving is still primarily a household industry, and the relative increase

production for 1948 and 1949, which figures were supplied by the Department of Agriculture, Bangkok. Imports of cloth and yarn for 1948 and 1949 refer to the port of Bangkok only.

indicated by the above figures has occurred almost entirely in households. Equipment and technique have changed very little. Foreign dyes and machine-spun yarn are more widely used, but few other changes have been made. Production for sale increased in the 1930's and 1940's, and a number of small weaving establishments are engaged in commercial production. These rarely employ more than 20 or 30 workers. In 1950 there were 330 such workshops, employing a total of about 3,000 workers, in the Bangkok area alone.[23] The number outside Bangkok is not known, but it is probably smaller. It seems safe to say that the great bulk of the cloth produced in Thailand is woven in households for family use.

Since the war the silk industry has been greatly stimulated through the initiative of Mr. James Thompson and the Thai Silk Company.* Thompson has successfully put Thai silk on the world market, and at the same time he has revived interest in traditional patterns and types of cloth, and induced weavers all over the North and Northeast to use fast dyes and to produce for sale. He has made few changes in the traditional methods and tools of the weavers, however. The major changes in technique introduced by Thompson have been the use of fast dyes and flying shuttles. The latter device enables workers to increase their output considerably.

The equipment of weavers in Thailand is extremely crude. Using traditional methods, a girl may work for two weeks to weave a silk pasin (1.5 meters) of complicated design. The weaving of cotton—and simpler silk designs—goes faster, and a weaver can turn out up to a meter per day. With the new shuttle a single weaver may produce up to six meters per day, although complicated designs go much more slowly.

It may be that the development of a strong money demand for locally woven cottons and silks may gradually induce weavers to improve their methods and tools. At any rate, this promises to be more successful in promoting improvements than was the earlier government effort to improve the silk industry by beginning with production rather than demand. Quick changes cannot be expected, however. Thompson found that it was only with great difficulty that he could persuade weavers in various parts of the country to make cloth in commercial quantities. Frequently they are simply not interested in turning out more than one or two pieces (of conventional length) per month, and to offer them a higher price is fruitless. Production for sale has gradually increased, however, in response to the renewed interest in traditional patterns.

Since 1850 the quantity of clothing worn by the people has increased. This increase, plus the increase in population (from about 6 million to 18 million), has meant an enormous increase in the annual consumption of textiles.

Although domestic production appears to have declined in the Central and

[23] Department of Industrial Works, Ministry of Industries, Bangkok.
* This passage was written from the perspective of 1951. From 1951 to 1970, several other producers of silk entered the market.

Southern regions, the increase in cotton acreage, the increased population, the large import of yarns, the large increase in total consumption, the volume of regional trade in locally produced textiles, and the statistics of production and trade all lead to the conclusion that the absolute volume of textiles woven in Thailand must be considerably greater in 1950 than it was in 1850, and also greater than the volume of 1950 imports. Although the relative position is less clear, it seems likely that domestic production as a percentage of total consumption first declined from 1850 to about 1920, since which time it has gradually increased. In 1949 roughly 60 percent of textiles consumed were woven in Thailand.

Aside from the recovery itself, the most striking thing about textile production in Thailand is that it is carried on as a household industry.* The survival and recovery of the industry has been assisted by mild tariff protection (a minor factor), by the total protection of wartime interruption of imports, and by the shift in the terms of trade against rice in the 1930's. But the survival of the industry as a household craft requires further explanation. Household manufacture for family use is not very vulnerable to price competition when there is no money cost of production and when no alternative employment exists in practice.[24] These conditions are present in the household weaving in Thailand and may explain its survival. Another factor may be that the farm family has become more experienced in monetary calculations and more aware of the savings to be made by household weaving in idle seasons.

Sugar[25]

For a time after the Bowring Treaty it appeared that those who predicted that sugar would become one of the major exports of Thailand were right. Acreage and output increased, and by 1859 exports amounted to 204,000 piculs, a rise from 107,000 piculs in 1849.[26] This was the peak of sugar exports, although few expected it to be.

At that time, the natural advantages of Thailand for the cultivation of sugar were still attracting the attention of entrepreneurs. Steam sugar mills of modern design were built in 1862 and 1870, and the British consul reported in 1866 that "native mills are springing up in all direction." In 1865 there

---

* This paragraph refers to the situation in 1951–52. Factory output has subsequently increased; see Ch. 12.

[24] The increase of imported yarns meant that there was some money-cost of production, but as long as yarn was cheaper than the equivalent amount of cloth (which it was) the differential would serve the same purpose.

[25] Three kinds of sugar are produced in Thailand: coconut, palmyra, and cane sugar. The first two of these are produced chiefly on a small scale as a part-time household industry. In total production they have sometimes been as important as cane sugar, and their production has varied much less. Because we are concerned with *change*, this discussion of the sugar industry will refer mainly to *cane* sugar.

[26] "Monograph on Sugar in Siam," *The Record*, Thailand, Ministry of Commerce, January 1922, pp. 6–17. This article is the basic source for the following discussion.

were 25 mills on the river near Nakon Chaisi, employing an average of 200 workers each.[27] The steam mill put up in 1870 was owned by the Indochinese Sugar Co., a British firm which secured a grant of 7,500 rai of land from the government at a very low rental. The company intended to cultivate sugar cane as well as to manufacture the sugar.

The government helped the industry along by cutting in half the inland-transit duty on sugar and for a time it appeared that the industry might prosper, but in 1871 the crop was ruined by floods in Nakon Chaisi, the largest sugar-growing area, and growers were unable to repay advances.[28] After this it is not clear just what happened to the industry, but production and exports steadily declined. This decline came in spite of the fact that the steam plows brought in by the Indochinese Sugar Co. were technically a success, enabling land to be cultivated much more cheaply than it could be done with hired hand labor.[29]

Two basic reasons may be advanced for the decline in sugar: taxation and low world prices. As early as 1864 the British consul commented on the number of taxes which fell on sugar—taxes on land, on the cane itself, on mills, boilers, and the boats used for transport—and said these were "undoubtedly the main cause of its decrease."[30] Abuses of their powers by tax monopolists also contributed. Furthermore, a piecemeal approach to taxation had resulted in land-tax rates on sugar-cane cultivation which varied from 0.375 baht per rai to 4.50 baht per rai according to the locality concerned.[31] Unequal inland-transit duties were supposed to offset the inequality in tax rates, but when the inland-transit duties were subsequently reduced or eliminated, the unequal land-tax rates remained.

The history of the Ministry of Agriculture, on the other hand, says simply that sugar cultivation on a large scale was stopped because prices were so low.[32] By 1889 the export of sugar had ceased, sugar factories were deserted, and the price of the best white sugar in Bangkok was so low that "the native grower finds it difficult to compete."[33] The decline of the infant sugar industry in Thailand was probably rather closely connected with the subsidized development of beet sugar on the European continent which caused such a remarkable fall in world sugar prices. Using 1900 as the base, sugar prices fell from 264 in

[27] *Bangkok Recorder*, April 15, 1865, p. 64.

[28] *The Siam Repository*, IV (1872), 375–76.

[29] Chao Phya Wongsa Nuprapath, *History of the Ministry of Agriculture*, pp. 305–6. (In Thai language.)

[30] *Commercial Reports from Her Majesty's Consuls in China and Siam, 1864*, Great Britain, Foreign Office (London, 1865), pp. 215–16.

[31] Phya Indra Montri (F. H. Giles), "Memorandum on the System of Taxation" (typewritten, September 4, 1917), in the files of the Financial Adviser, Ministry of Finance, Bangkok.

[32] Chao Phya Wongsa Nuprapath, *op. cit.*, pp. 305–6.

[33] *Annual Series, Diplomatic and Consular Reports on Trade and Finance, Siam, Report for the Year 1889*, Great Britain, Foreign Office (London, 1890).

1873 to 130 in 1886 and to 100 in 1900.[34] Thailand could not protect her sugar industry against this fall (even if she had wished to, which is not known) because her import duties were fixed at 3 percent by treaties with the same European powers whose subsidies to beet sugar were contributing to the sharp drop in the world price of sugar, and because she could not afford subsidies to her domestic producers. Also important is the fact that the *baht* price of rice was increasing from 1850 to 1920. Since rice cultivation was practicable on the sugar lands of Nakon Chaisi, there was a strong inducement to shift from sugar cane to rice.

Actually, the price inducement to turn to rice cannot be firmly established. Baht prices of rice did increase from 1850 to 1920, but sugar prices (in baht) also increased during at least a part of that period. The trouble is that the wide variations in quality of sugar as marketed in Thailand make it difficult to use scattered price data for comparative purposes. For this reason we have not found it possible to make direct comparisons of Bangkok prices for rice and sugar since 1850. All we can say is that rice prices appear to have risen relative to sugar prices over most of the period concerned.

In any case the export of sugar irregularly declined from the peak of 1859 until the 1880's, when export practically ceased. The new steam mills and most of the smaller mills stood idle, while the land went out of cultivation or was planted in rice. Only in Changwat Chonburi did production continue on any scale. This decline in production applied mainly to the commercial production of *cane* sugar. Coconut and palmyra sugar was made as before, so far as we know, while crude cane sugar continued to be produced on a small scale.

By 1921 the production of cane sugar had begun to revive. Area planted in sugar cane rose from a yearly average of 39,000 rai in the period 1907–9 to 53,000 rai in 1918–20.[35] The total production of cane sugar in a "normal year" was estimated in 1921 to be about 155,000 piculs, of which nearly all was brown sugar, plus about 170,000 piculs of jaggery and molasses, making a total of 325,000 piculs. In 1859 sugar exports had reached a peak of 203,000 piculs. After allowing 100,000 to 200,000 piculs for home consumption and assuming that the proportion of jaggery and molasses was about the same in 1859 as in 1921, we arrive at an estimate for total production in 1859 of around 600,000 to 800,000 piculs, compared with the estimate for 1921 of 325,000 piculs. This suggests that the output of cane sugar in 1921 was somewhat less than half the peak output of 1859 and, judging by the area in sugar cane, production in 1907 was about 80 percent of the 1921 figure. This partial revival of the

[34] W. W. Rostow, *The British Economy of the 19th Century* (Oxford University Press, 1948), pp. 98–99. The exchange value of the baht fell sharply from 1886 to 1900, and the price of sugar expressed in baht therefore did not fall as sharply as these figures suggest, and it may even have risen from 1886 to 1900. Indeed, this may be one reason sugar production revived in Thailand (see below).

[35] "Monograph on Sugar in Siam," p. 8. The impetus given by wartime conditions probably was the main reason for this increase.

industry occurred while the duty on sugar was only 3 percent ad valorem. Most of the sugar cane was grown on Chinese plantations in Changwat Chon-buri and milled by small, crude, Chinese-owned mills.

In the meantime the import of sugar from Java and the Philippines rose from almost zero around 1880 to a considerable item in 1925 (see Table XII). The import duty was limited by treaty to 3 percent ad valorem until 1927, when a specific duty was applied. At first the duty was three satang (0.03 baht) per kilogram, but it was raised to five satang in 1931 and to eight satang in 1936. At the first rate the duty amounted to 15–25 percent ad valorem, while the third rate became as much as 100 percent ad valorem when the price of sugar dropped during the middle 1930's.

Since the 1920's the sugar industry has grown considerably. Private pro-

TABLE XII
Import of Manufactured Sugar[a]

Period	Volume (Piculs)[b]	Value (Baht)[b]
1882	—	28,000
1886	17,300	211,000
1890	20,300	302,000
1895	86,000	700,000
1900	177,000	1,714,000
1905	—	3,250,000
1910/11	—	2,800,000
1915/16	320,000	3,200,000
1920/21	—	3,700,000
1925/26	—	8,100,000
1930/31	865,000	6,300,000
1935/36	724,000	3,550,000
1941	541,000	5,133,000
1945	76,000	19,425,000
1950	167,000[c]	34,000,000[c]

[a] For some years the import of molasses may be included, but for most years the figures represent imports of manufactured sugar only.

[b] A part of the fluctuation in value is due to changes in the exchange rate. Dash indicates figures are not available.

[c] Estimated.

Sources: Figures for 1882–1905, *Annual Diplomatic and Consular Reports on Trade and Finance from Her Majesty's Consuls in Siam*, Great Britain, Foreign Office; 1910/11–1945, *Statistical Year Book of Thailand*.

ducers have expanded their production, partly because of the tariff, and in the late 1930's the government built a modern sugar mill in Lampang. World War II gave a further impetus to sugar, and by 1948 the area planted in cane was about 270,000 rai.[36] The government now [1950] has 6 sugar mills and there are some 15 private ones. Most of the mills are small.

In 1950 the domestic production of cane sugar was estimated to be about 1,000,000 piculs, of which about half was white sugar and half, brown.[37] In addition, about 1,000,000 piculs of molasses was produced. Government factories produced in 1950 about a third of the white sugar and molasses, and about one-fifth of the brown sugar. Small Chinese mills produced most of the remainder.

In spite of an import duty of 0.75 baht per kilogram, domestic sugar producers were threatened by strong competition from imported sugar in the postwar years. In 1949 the duty was raised to 1.50 baht per kilogram (about 45 percent ad valorem), but even this added protection was not enough, and to safeguard domestic producers the government prohibited the import of white sugar in early 1952. At that time the annual consumption of *white* sugar was estimated to be about 670,000 piculs, of which 170,000 was imported.[38] Little or no brown sugar or molasses was imported.

Thus the sugar industry, which in 1860 had been capable of supplying domestic requirements of sugar and exporting a considerable amount besides, went into a sharp decline about 1870. The low prices at which Javanese and Philippine sugar was offered in the unprotected market of Thailand, the chaotic tax system, and the organization of the local industry all combined to bring about the decline in domestic production. Another important factor was the *increase* in the baht price of rice which took place while sugar prices were falling. Production never ceased entirely, however, and by the first decades of the twentieth century it was reviving. World War I, tariff protection since the 1920's, government initiative since the 1930's, and World War II all stimulated the local industry. It is probable that by the 1920's the total production of sugar had risen to 35–50 percent of the 1860 level, and by 1950 production was probably twice the 1860 level. In 1950 the domestic industry required a large amount of protection, however, and there was no prospect of exporting sugar from Thailand.

THE GROWTH AND NATURE OF IMPORTS, TO 1950

Not all local industries declined when faced with the competition of foreign goods. Notable examples of those which did not were industries whose products cannot be transported long distances because of low value in relation

---

[36] Supplied by the Department of Agriculture, Bangkok.
[37] This is an estimate made by the Department of Industrial Works, Ministry of Industries, Bangkok.
[38] *The Bangkok Post*, March 27, 1952.

to bulkiness or weight (such as baskets, tile, bricks, and cheap pottery). Other products cannot be imported because of their nature, such as services. Furthermore, there were some products, peculiarly Thai in material, design, and workmanship, to which foreign producers offered no *direct* competition (lacquer ware, niello ware, silverwork, and fishing nets and traps).

Many of these products are important to the economic life of the people. No adequate information exists on national consumption patterns, but if we consider the material belongings of the "average" household—which means the rice farmer and his family—it is clear that baskets, mats, numerous items of pottery ranging from huge water jars to tiny pots, heavy bamboo storage baskets (in the North and Northeast), tile and thatch roofing, wooden sandals, woven hats, boats, bullock carts, and many other items represent a large part of the total material belongings. Although many of these products are made within the household, there is also a considerable amount of specialization and trade in them within and among villages. A familiar feature all over Thailand is the morning market which may serve one village, several villages, or a whole province, and to which the people (usually women) bring their products to sell and exchange.

Broadly then, it can be said (in 1950) that of the three necessities—food, clothing, shelter—clothing imports represent a significant part of total consumption, while of the paraphernalia required to operate the household, imports supply only a small part. Some imported food products are widely consumed, although they form a negligible part of the total diet. For the most part, and certainly for the bulk of the population, imports are luxury goods which can be dispensed with rather easily when money income falls. The economy of Thailand has an extremely broad subsistence base onto which the money economy has been grafted. The nature of her imports and their relation to the economy gives Thailand an extremely high income-elasticity of demand for imports, which in turn is a major reason why she has been able consistently to maintain a strong export balance of trade. When exports fall, thus reducing incomes, imports tend to fall immediately in the same degree. Since Thailand "normally" had an export surplus, 1850 to 1950, this adjustment process acted to preserve that position even when exports declined sharply.

The general nature of Thailand's imports did not change much between 1850 and 1950. Throughout the century virtually all imports consisted of manufactured goods. The proportion of total imports represented by the tariff classification "Fuel and Raw Materials" has exhibited a tendency to rise, but it remains relatively small, as may be seen in the following figures:[39]

[39] Figures for 1859, *Bangkok Calendar for 1861*; 1864, 1870, 1880, *Annual Diplomatic and Consular Reports from Her Majesty's Consuls in Siam*, Great Britain; 1892, 1900, *Comparative Statement of the Imports and Exports of Siam, 1892–1901* (Bangkok, n.d.);1910–41, *Statistical Year Book of Thailand*. Prior to 1920, the percentages refer to imports through the port of Bangkok only.

PERCENTAGE OF "FUEL AND RAW MATERIALS"
IN TOTAL COMMODITY IMPORTS

Year	Percentage
1859	3.4
1864	3.7
1870	2.2
1880	4.1
1892	5.7
1900	11.7
1910	8.7
1925	8.1
1935	14.0
1941	11.2

Another characteristic of Thailand's imports is that most have been "consumption goods" rather than "capital goods." This has been true in spite of the fact that Thailand produces little or no capital goods herself. We will consider the following classes of imports as capital goods:

Fuels and materials
Chemical products
Electrical appliances and machinery
Machinery (excluding electrical)
Metal manufactures (excluding machinery)

Some of the goods falling into these classes are imported for final consumption and do not enter directly into the production of other goods. Probably a large part is so consumed. Nevertheless, these classes include most of the goods which could form a physical part of plant and equipment or of domestically produced goods. These classes of imports have comprised the following proportion of total commodity imports:[40]

PERCENTAGE OF CAPITAL GOODS IN
TOTAL COMMODITY IMPORTS

Year	Percentage	Year	Percentage
1859	7.7	1910	20.0
1864	12.2	1925	18.3
1870	16.7	1930	26.0
1880	10.9	1935	30.0
1892	16.7	1941	30.0
1900	20.7	1949	23.4

[40] Figures for 1859, *Bangkok Calendar for 1861*; 1864, 1870, 1880, *Annual Diplomatic and Consular Reports from Her Majesty's Consuls in Siam*, Great Britain; 1892, 1900, *Comparative Statement of Imports and Exports, 1892–1901*; 1910–41, *Statistical Year Book of Thailand*; 1949, *Report of Financial Adviser Covering the Years 1941 to 1950*, Thailand, Ministry of Finance (Bangkok, 1951), pp. 9–10.

The proportion of capital-goods imports appears to have risen secularly. Tariff policy may account for part of the increase since 1926, while government imports of machinery and equipment for railways and irrigation works help to account for the longer-run increase.

We have little information about the ratio of imports to national income. The discussion in Chapter 2 suggested that in 1850 the ratio was very small (perhaps 4 or 5 percent). According to the only available estimates, the ratio of imports to gross national product was 13 percent in 1938/39 and 11 percent in 1950.[41]

Thailand's imports have included an enormous variety of merchandise. Most items have been imported in relatively small quantities. Examination of the detailed table of "Imports by Tariff Classification" in the *Statistical Year Book* will drive home the point that, with a few exceptions, the volume and value of each separate class of imported goods have been extremely small. This suggests that most articles are consumed by a relatively small part of the total population. To some extent, it is the foreign community, the Chinese, and the higher-income groups, located mainly in Bangkok but also in smaller numbers elsewhere, who are the buyers of imported goods. Many items are probably consumed almost entirely within this small segment of the population. In one study of food imports[42] it was estimated that items of high unit value (canned fruits, confectionery, biscuits) had in 1929 a limited market of possibly 10,000 customers, including Europeans, upper-income Thai, and a few Chinese, while staple food items (canned milk, flour, sardines) might have a market of 2,000,000 people. Both groups would be considerably larger in 1950.

Data on consumption patterns are almost nonexistent, but it is the author's opinion, based on observation of the stock-in-trade of retail stores all over the country, that most imported consumers' goods (and not only foods) are widely but haphazardly consumed. The bulk of the people have no set consumption habits as far as most imported goods are concerned. Instead, their surplus money income is spent more or less capriciously, and the stores carry a wide range of novelties with which to tempt the buyer. Few of these are consumed very widely, nor is consumption concentrated in geographic area or in income class. Several staple articles of import are rather widely consumed, however. These include textiles, yarns, kerosene, and canned milk.

In summary, we have four points to make concerning the market for imported consumers' goods down to 1950.[43]

[41] J. S. Gould, "Thailand's National Income and Its Meaning," National Economic Council, Thailand (Bangkok, January 1953).

[42] Don C. Bliss, *Market for American Foodstuffs in Siam,* Trade Information Bulletin 610, U.S. Bureau of Foreign and Domestic Commerce (Washington, D.C., 1929).

[43] These points are based on study of the detailed breakdown of imports for the last thirty to forty years, on observation of retail stocks all over the country, and on impressions given in a

1. Some items have a very small market which is limited to the foreign community, upper-income Thai, and a few Chinese.

2. Some items (such as kerosene and canned milk) are widely consumed in all parts of the country.

3. Some items are erratically purchased as novelties. The buyers of these goods change from year to year, and the group is composed of people in all income levels and geographic regions. The consumption of this category of imports varies directly with money income.

4. A large number of people purchase no imported goods. This large group includes people at the bottom of the money-income scale, many of whom live in the more remote provinces of the North and Northeast.

There is one final point to be made concerning the general nature of imports. Consumer-goods imports are, with a few exceptions such as medicines and kerosene, not essential to maintain the basic minimum living standard of the people. This is another way of saying that the imports are luxuries rather than basic necessities, but it brings out the advantage Thailand enjoys in having an export economy based largely on a staple food product (rice) in comparison with countries such as Cuba (sugar) or Malaya (rubber). The imports of what we have called "capital goods" have, on the other hand, become increasingly essential to the economy. As the country has come to rely on railway transportation, trucks, buses, electricity, and irrigation works, the import of material and supplies to operate, maintain, and replace this equipment has become more and more necessary. Such dependence on imports will inevitably increase in the future because Thailand does not, nor can she expect to, produce such goods, barring the discovery of minerals which Thailand is not now believed to possess. A future problem of economic policy will be to insure that an adequate proportion of total imports consists of capital goods.

The fact that a large proportion of Thailand's imports are nonessential in the sense that the life of the people could go on relatively undisturbed without them does not mean, however, that the government could expect successfully to replace consumer-goods imports with capital-goods imports. The attempt (e.g., through prohibition of certain "nonessential" imports) would quickly bring about a reduction in exports, particularly of rice, and thus reduce the nation's ability to buy abroad. In other words, consumer-goods imports are important incentives to production for export.

The point made above, that Thailand's imports consist of a large number of separate items but a very small quantity of each, makes it all the more difficult to replace imports with domestic production. The Thai market is so small that large-scale production cannot be undertaken unless a part of the output is exported. Tariff protection can favor a domestic industry in the

---

number of descriptions of the country and its people, but not on any exact analysis of the market, because none exists.

home market but not in the foreign one, and subsidized exports are neither condoned by world opinion nor financially practicable for so small a country, lacking any particular qualifications for undertaking production of the commodities. It follows that Thailand particularly needs to develop industries which can operate efficiently on a small scale. Cost studies of small-scale, perhaps seasonal, industries should be made and publicized.

There are other advantages of small-scale industry.[44] The relative scarcity of capital compared with labor makes it desirable, other things being equal, to use little capital relative to labor.[45] Small-scale industry would require simple buildings, much of which could be constructed in Thailand with little or no *money* cost and with simple machinery and equipment. Economies could also be made on the overhead costs of management and supervision. Small industries could be located in areas in which underemployment and seasonal unemployment exist, and wage rates would be lower than in cities. By adapting the industry to the existing subsistence economy, important social insurance costs could be avoided, since the workers would have farm families and relatives to fall back on in slack periods. Small plants, dispersed throughout the country, would be congenial to the undisciplined, individualistic nature of the people. Nor would workers have to leave their families and villages or break strong cultural ties to them. Finally, a considerable amount of funds for capital investment might be forthcoming from rural hoards which would be completely unavailable to large-scale industries. Requirements of money capital would be smaller also because idle time could be used to make many things which would have to be purchased under other circumstances.

DOMESTIC MANUFACTURING INDUSTRIES, TO 1950

Until recent years factory production has been of very little importance in Thailand. Only in the last two or three decades has an infant "industrial Thailand" emerged. This movement, sponsored in large part by the government, has still [1950] barely begun, but in relative terms the progress has been considerable. (See Ch. 12 for developments since 1950.)

Unfortunately there are no reliable statistics which can be used to present a comprehensive picture of either the growth of manufacturing or the present extent of it. The Factory Control Division, Ministry of Industry, receives reports from some industries in the Bangkok-Thonburi area, but not for the entire country and not for much small-scale production in Bangkok. The Department of Industrial Works, Ministry of Industry, controls most gov-

---

[44] Cf. Henry C. Aubrey, "Small Industry in Economic Development," *Social Research,* XVIII (September 1951), 269–312.

[45] See, however, A. E. Kahn, "Investment Criteria for Development Programs," *Quarterly Journal of Economics,* LXV (February 1951). It may be that advantages of small-scale industry, including the cost of capital, would raise its social marginal product above that of large-scale industry and thereby enable it to qualify under the principal criterion proposed by Professor Kahn.

ernment factories, but accounting records adequate for analysis of the operation of these factories do not exist.

As a result this section must be based on scattered data available for specific industries, on a few figures obtained from the firms themselves, and on the estimates of gross national product made by Dr. Joseph S. Gould, Economic Adviser to the Thai government.

The largest industries in the country, rice milling and lumber milling, are not included in "manufacturing" in the sense used here. The distinction is an arbitrary one, but we shall use "manufacturing" in the lay sense in which it excludes such simple processing of raw materials as rice and lumber milling. We also exclude household industries and simple handicrafts.

In 1919 the British consul reported that there were only seven "factories" in Bangkok.[46] The seven included a cement plant, three aerated-water plants, a soap factory, a cigarette factory, and a leather factory. Of these, only the cement plant and one of the aerated-water plants were the result of Thai capital and entrepreneurship, and the cement plant at that time had foreign management and was partly owned by foreigners. This is a slim list to contain all the factories in the Bangkok area, especially since it is unlikely that there were *any* factories elsewhere.

We may take this estimate of manufacturing industry as a beginning point and assume that before 1919 manufacturing was quite unimportant. This section will therefore be concerned with developments in the last three decades. Before leaving this point we should note that prior to 1919 there were a few industrial ventures besides those mentioned above. The Siam Electric Company had its beginning in 1887 and with European capital and management it brought electricity and tramcars to Bangkok. We have already mentioned the railways, on which construction began about 1890. Except for two small lines these were constructed through government initiative and capital. Shipbuilding (aside from small craft) has been carried on desultorily for decades. During World War I a private Thai citizen built two steamships and sold them to the East Asiatic Company.[47] There were six printing offices in Bangkok in 1872 and twenty-five by about 1910.[48] There were also many small workshops and several larger activities such as manufacture of salt and sugar, spirits, and building materials. To say that there were only seven "factories" in 1919 is an oversimplification, but it seems clear that manufacturing production was very small.

The development of manufacturing was limited in part by the lack of resources, but a number of other factors continued to retard development of

---

[46] *Report of the Commercial Situation in Siam at the Close of the Year 1919,* by J. Crosby, Great Britain, Foreign Office (London, 1920), pp. 19–20. The exact definition used for a "factory" is not clear, but it undoubtedly excluded processing of raw materials (e.g., rice mills) and small workshops.

[47] Ake Wisakul, *Commercial Navigation in Thailand* (Bangkok, 1949).

[48] Gerini, *Siam, Its Production, Arts, and Manufactures,* pp. 163, 259–61.

even those few industries for which raw materials were available.[49] Until 1927 inland-transit duties were levied on internal shipments of certain articles for which no export duty was specified in the Bowring-model treaties. The rates of these duties varied, but the over-all average was about 10 percent ad valorem.[50] The duties did not yield much revenue, but the government was reluctant to abolish them until the revenue could be replaced. Specifically, the government was reluctant to abolish inland-transit duties before it won some degree of customs autonomy from the treaty powers. Since imported articles paid only a 3-percent duty, the inland-transit duties were a distinct discouragement to local entrepreneurs and their abolition was often recommended. When the treaties were revised and import duties increased, in 1926, the inland-transit duties were at last removed. Although no sudden burst of new enterprise followed these two important fiscal changes, both tended to encourage local industries.

The 3-percent limit on import duties may also have hindered the growth of domestic industries.

Another retarding factor was the small size of the Thai market for most commodities. Except for cotton textiles—which form by far the largest import —the quantity of each article imported is much too small to support even one modern plant.[51] Furthermore, most of the raw material would have had to be imported, since cotton production was relatively small before World War II. Development of a factory demand for raw cotton might have stimulated its production, however.

Manufacturing industry was also retarded by the lack of capital, entrepreneurship, and skilled labor. There was no organized source of capital for industrial ventures—no industrial banks and no private market for stocks or bonds. The government was committed to a conservative financial policy which allowed it little scope for such ventures. The Thai who amassed wealth usually preferred to hold it in real estate, jewelry, and sometimes in foreign securities, while Chinese and other foreigners employed their capital in trade and extractive industries. Because information on earnings in Thailand is scattered and inadequate, we can say little or nothing about relative profits in different industries and the rate of return required to attract capital. Needless to say, expected earnings have to be heavily discounted for a risk factor.

[49] The theoretical case for development of such industries in Thailand is based on the wide extent of underemployment, much of which is seasonal, on serious imperfections in the market as an allocator of resources, especially in connection with *knowledge* of demand and cost conditions, and on considerations of internal and external economies.

[50] *The Record,* Thailand, Ministry of Commerce (October 1927), pp. 119-20.

[51] Not even the cotton-textiles market could support many modern plants. In 1941, for example, cotton-textile imports totaled 24,630,000 baht, but there were thirty-six different tariff classifications. The largest single item was "dyed shirting," with a c.i.f. value of 3,774,000 baht, then equal to about U.S. $1,200,000. Of course a cotton mill can turn out several different lines, but these figures should suffice to show that the market is not great enough to support a large industry.

Finally, manufacturing was—and still is—retarded by the lack of power. As late as 1952 Thailand had not a single hydroelectric plant, and most electricity was generated by burning rice husks. Power was expensive and highly unreliable. Furthermore, the supply was not adequate anywhere in the country. Many towns and virtually all rural regions had no electricity at all.

Private Industries

Privately owned factories in Thailand produce light consumers' goods almost exclusively. There is little or no heavy industry. Much private production takes place in homes and small workshops. Here, especially among the Chinese in the larger towns and cities, one can find a bewildering variety of enterprises going on. Family labor is used for work which pays an astonishingly low reward (this applies mainly to Chinese). As in the retail trade, there has been little movement toward concentration and consolidation of the small workshops into larger establishments. Modern productive techniques are also very little used. Unfortunately, statistics of the volume and value of such small-scale production do not exist, nor can estimates be easily made. Because of the lack of data, all we shall try to do in this section is to mention briefly the few larger-scale manfacturing concerns established prior to 1950.

The Siam Cement Company, formed in 1913 with a capital of one million baht, half of which was furnished by King Rama VI from the privy purse, was the first manufacturing enterprise of any importance to be established in Thailand.[52] The establishment of the company was due in large measure to the encouragement and interest of the king. Annual imports of cement were then about 120,000 casks, so the plant was designed for about that capacity. Modern equipment was installed in the plant, which was located near the sources of raw materials (except for fuel and gypsum). The company was very successful, and paid an average annual dividend of 12 percent from 1915 to 1923. During this period output averaged 137,000 casks, all used domestically. In 1923 the company employed about 300 workers, of whom 70 were Chinese (for the heavy labor) and the rest Thai. Management and part of the capital was European. In 1923 the capacity was increased to 300,000 casks and capital to three million baht. The company continued to operate successfully until the war. In 1938/39 output was 92,000 metric tons. After the war, production increased rapidly to 165,000 metric tons in 1950 and 247,000 tons in 1952.[53] The company has supplied cement for both government and private construction. The existence of a steady, even rising demand, the availability of materials locally, and the high transport cost on imported cement have enabled the Siam Cement Company to produce and sell cement successfully

---

[52] "Siam Cement Company," *The Record,* Thailand, Department of Commerce (July 1923), pp. 13–15.

[53] *Economic Bulletin for Asia and the Far East,* UN, ECAFE, IV, No. 1, 39.

without tariff protection—except for the 3-percent duty. A good quality Portland cement has been produced. The company has in recent years been given a concession to work the iron mines in Lopburi. A small quantity of ore is smelted and made into structural iron.

Some industries were established as a result of tariffs levied following the treaty revisions in 1926, although the government apparently did not intend to foster domestic industry when the rates were set. In fact, when domestic production began and imports declined, the principal reaction was one of concern for the lost revenue. An example of this was the match industry. Foreign match firms established plants in Bangkok and began to produce matches with imported materials which escaped the higher duty. When the duty on materials was increased, local sources were developed. To preserve its revenue the government then levied an excise tax on domestic matches, but at a lower rate than the duty on imports. In 1950 there were four match factories, all private, employing a total of about 700 workers.[54] These factories produce nearly all of the matches consumed in Thailand.

The tobacco industry also received an impetus from the tariff. Tobacco had long been grown in various parts of the country, principally the North and Northeast, and a small, scattered household industry existed to make "Siamese" cigarettes. One of the seven factories listed in 1919 by the British consul was a cigarette factory owned by a Greek. Imports of cigarettes were quite large, however, and when the new tariff was drawn up in 1926, a duty of 25 percent ad valorem was placed on "manufactured tobacco." This duty encouraged not only the domestic production of tobacco, but also the domestic manufacture of cigarettes from imported leaf, which was subject to an import duty of only 5 percent.

In 1931 a tariff amendment made all tobacco, manufactured and unmanufactured, subject to an ad valorem duty of 50 percent. In 1934 the rate was raised to 60 percent. Meanwhile, several tobacco factories were established in Thailand. Most of them were small and for the most part they used imported leaf from the United States and China.

As cigarette production increased, following the tariff increases, imports of manufactured tobacco (chiefly cigarettes) decreased and imports of unmanufactured tobacco increased. Manufactured tobacco imports dropped from 9 million baht in 1926 to one million in 1941. Imports of unmanufactured tobacco first increased (until 1937) and then declined as domestic production increased (see Table XIII).

The largest operation was that carried on by the British-American Tobacco Company. This firm tried to lessen the burden of import duties by encouraging the cultivation of Virginia tobacco in Thailand. It also set up stations in the North and Northeast, built curing sheds, supplied the farmers with

[54] Factory Control Division, Ministry of Industry, Bangkok.

TABLE XIII

Tobacco Imports, 1925-50

Period	Manufactured		Unmanufactured	
	Volume (Metric Tons)[a]	Value (Thousand Baht)	Volume (Metric Tons)[a]	Value (Thousand Baht)[a]
1925/26	—	8,886	—	—
1926/27	—	9,024	—	—
1927/28	—	8,797	—	—
1928/29	3,405	8,454	300	195
1929/30	3,475	8,604	312	192
1930/31	2,763	7,070	844	524
1931/32	2,227	4,580	384	252
1932/33	2,105	4,228	255	243
1933/34	1,926	4,249	597	641
1934/35	2,151	4,643	570	547
1935/36	2,127	4,713	739	762
1936/37	1,635	3,802	1,845	1,667
1937/38	1,449	3,236	2,490	2,294
1938/39	1,045	2,583	1,900	1,715
1939/40	494	1,355	748	805
1940	213	903	1,113	1,329
1941	215	990	1,394	1,631
1942	7	156	411	1,230
1943	24	370	633	2,039
1944	48	2,520	178	660
1945	16	485	7	60
1946	—	4,290	600	8,470
1947	—	3,800	1,848	25,070
1948	—	5,200	659	8,690
1949	—	4,390	1,192	17,360
1950	—	8,660	1,648	52,460

[a] Dash indicates figures are not available.

Sources: 1925-45 inclusive, *Statistical Year Book of Thailand*; 1946-50 inclusive, Thailand Tobacco Monopoly.

seeds, and brought in tobacco experts to advise them. Furthermore, it developed local brand names and marketed a fairly standardized product all over the country. The operations of the company were strikingly successful, and in September 1941 the Thai government paid it the compliment of "nationalization" and purchased the entire operation for 5.5 million baht.[55] The contract also provided for royalties to the British-American Tobacco Company.

[55] Supplied by Thailand Tobacco Monopoly. This sum was then equal to about U.S. $2,000,000.

By 1941 the manufacture of cigarettes was one of the largest industries in the country. The output was entirely consumed at home, and the domestic product had substantially replaced imports in the mass market.

Other industries were also encouraged by tariff increases in the 1920's and 1930's. A European firm built a soap factory; a group of Thai entrepreneurs organized the Boon Rawd Brewery (but eventually had to accept a large amount of capital from the government); a number of small sugar factories, largely in the hands of Chinese, began operations and were greatly stimulated by the high specific duties on sugar; and alcohol distilleries increased in number and expanded their output.

In most cases the tariffs were intended for revenue rather than protection. Ever since about 1890 the government had sought to revise the foreign treaties in order to increase its revenues from customs. It gave little thought to the idea of protection to domestic industry. Most goods singled out for special duties were either luxuries or articles which were very widely consumed. When high tariffs were levied on articles with a large market in Thailand, however, local production tended to begin *if the necessary raw materials* were available locally. In the first tariff, for example, the general rate was 5 percent ad valorem except for beer, wine, and spirits (12 percent ad valorem), manufactured tobacco (25 percent ad valorem), motor cars and equipment (10 percent ad valorem), and specific duties on kerosene, benzine, matches, and sugar. Except for motor cars, kerosene, and benzine—products for which the necessary raw materials were *not* available locally—domestic production of all these products was undertaken.

Later amendments enlarged the list of special tariffs, and in 1936 the tariff was changed from a predominantly ad valorem to a predominantly *specific* tariff. Domestic industry continued to respond when high tariffs were combined with locally available materials. The tobacco, soap, match, sugar, and alcohol industries are among those which responded to protection. World War II provided a further stimulus to these and other industries, some of which have declined since the revival of imports at the end of the war.

Other industries have developed without the benefit of high tariff rates, although the protection afforded by the war stimulated some of them to expand. The weaving industry has expanded in the last few decades, as we have seen. During the war several small factories began to produce such rubber goods as shoes, sandals, and tubing, and since the war this production has continued.[56]

Bottled soft drinks are popular all over the country, and a number of aerated-water plants are in operation. In Bangkok-Thonburi alone there are

---

[56] These articles, particularly shoes, are sold in markets all over the country. The merchants frequently stamp them "Made in Hong Kong" or "Made in Singapore," however, because they say people will think the quality is poor if they are made in Thailand.

thirty-one plants, and others are located in the principal provincial towns. Production in 1949 reached about 1.8 million cases (of 12 bottles to the case).[57] Another popular product is ice, which is used the year round. Other manufacturing industries in which private factories are operating include tanning and leather products, glass bottles, vegetable-oil pressing, brick and tile, printing, salt, perfumery and cosmetics, machine shops, furniture, medicine, food processing, pottery, and others. Most of these are quite small. In all of them, most of the entrepreneurship and capital is supplied by Chinese.

Government Industries

The government has long shown an interest in direct ownership and operation of manufacturing industries. So far, the bulk of the government's industrial activities have been in public-service projects such as railways, water works, and electric power, but much planning has been done along other lines. Indeed, if all the plans approved by the government and announced to the public from 1930 to 1950 had been completed, Thailand would have an imposing array of government-operated industries. As it is, the list in 1950 is quite modest.[58]

The Army Survey Department built a paper factory in 1917/18, but it used hand labor and produced very little paper.[59] In 1923/24 the high price of foreign paper induced the government to install machinery which made the plant theoretically capable of producing seven tons of paper per week. In 1938 a second and larger government paper factory began operations in Kanburi. Using modern machinery, the plant produced a good quality paper from bamboo, but its operations were never very successful. Production was erratic and the plant consistently operated at a loss. In 1942 the two factories were transferred to the newly created Ministry of Industries and new capital was invested, but they have continued to show a book loss. In 1950 the combined output was about 2,000 metric tons and 600 workers were employed.[60]

The army also started a textile factory in 1933/34. Output consisted of material for the army such as drill, undershirts, mosquito netting, and absorbent cotton. Throughout the 1930's there were recurring plans to expand the operation with plants in Korat and Pitsanulok, but by the outbreak of

---

[57] Department of Customs.

[58] The government owns shares in, but does not directly control or operate, a number of concerns such as the Thai Cement Co., Boon Rawd Brewery, Thai Rubber Co., etc. In this section we will discuss only fully owned ventures. Estimates of production and employment of government factories vary widely. There is no way to evaluate the divergent estimates, and the figures given in this section are merely one of the many available sets.

[59] *History of the Activities and Functions of the Ministry of Industries from 1942 to 1951,* Ministry of Industries (Bangkok, 1951). (In Thai language.) This is the basic source for this and the following two paragraphs, unless otherwise stated.

[60] Department of Industrial Works, Ministry of Industries, Bangkok. Another estimate from the same source put 1950 paper output at 1,300 tons.

war little had actually been done. In 1942 the Ministry of Industries took over administration of the establishments, and in 1950 there were three factories with an output of 1,400,000 meters of cloth, most of which was taken by the army and police. There were 590 workers employed.[61] These plants survive principally because they have an assured market in the government.

The first government sugar mill was built in Lampang in 1937/38. This mill and the second one, constructed at Utaradit in 1941, produced white sugar. In addition, small mills to produce brown sugar and molasses were put up during the war in four other changwats. The Ministry of Industries took over the operation of all the mills in 1946. In 1950 the labor force was about 3,150 and the output was only 300,000 piculs of sugar, of which about 170,000 piculs was white sugar.[62] Thus, in spite of all the assistance given by the government, the government-operated sugar factories produced less sugar in 1950 than did the small private factories with their crude equipment. Furthermore, government factories cannot compete with imported sugar even though a heavy specific duty (1.50 baht per kilogram, or about 45 percent ad valorem) is levied on sugar imports. Early in 1952 sugar imports were banned in order to protect the domestic industry.

Although the government has long controlled distilleries very closely because of their importance as a source of revenue, the first one owned and operated by the government was acquired in 1929, when a Chinese-owned distillery was taken over and operated by the Excise Department. Since then, the government has constructed or purchased 12 others. In 1950, the 13 government-owned distilleries employed 2,800 workers and produced 25 million liters of liquors.[63]

In the rather poor record of government-operated industry in Thailand, the record of the Tobacco Monopoly provides a striking contrast. This organization, formed in 1941 to operate the properties of the British-American Tobacco Company which were purchased by the government as a going concern, is a semiautonomous body responsible to the Excise Department, Ministry of Finance. It has not been placed under the Ministry of Industries.

The Monopoly has the exclusive right to buy, sell, and manufacture all tobacco products in Thailand. In practice its exclusive rights apply to Virginia-type tobaccos, and not to domestic varieties. The latter may be grown and sold freely, except that restrictions are placed on the manufacture of cigarettes in order to prevent the development of competition with the nationally sold Monopoly brands. "Siamese-type" cigarettes, mostly wrapped in palm and banana leaves, are widely produced as a household industry. In fact the area planted in "Siamese" tobacco is still larger than the area planted in

[61] Department of Industrial Works, Ministry of Industries, Bangkok.
[62] Department of Industrial Works, Ministry of Industries.
[63] Idem.

Virginia-type tobacco. In 1950 the respective areas were 110,000 rai and 75,000 rai.

All Virginia-type tobacco grown in the country must be sold to the Monopoly, and importers of cigarettes, cigars, and unmanufactured tobacco must sell their imports entirely to the Monopoly. Sales are made to the consumer through ordinary marketing channels. Merchants obtain their supplies from the Monopoly.

The Monopoly operates buying stations and curing sheds in the North and Northeast, and provides a number of services to growers.[64] Men skilled in tobacco cultivation are employed in field offices to assist the farmers. Furthermore, partly as an inducement to farmers and partly to maintain quality, the Monopoly furnishes seeds and seedlings at a very low cost. Fertilizer is also supplied at cost. During the harvest season, regular buying days are held at field stations. The buyer examines each farmer's tobacco, grades it, and quotes a price. There is no bargaining, and the farmer invariably accepts the price offered, but the grades are understood by farmers and the prices are fixed for fairly long periods.

Most of the tobacco farmers grow tobacco as a side crop and put the bulk of their land in rice. For example, a man with ten rai may plant nine rai in rice and one in tobacco. In the North, tobacco is sometimes grown as a second crop after the rice season is over. Even though tobacco yields a higher money income than rice, farmers often have to be persuaded to grow it in commercial quantities. For one thing, they consider tobacco a more uncertain crop than rice.

In the Bangkok factories domestic tobacco is mixed with imported leaf tobacco in varying proportions and several brands of cigarettes are manufactured. Output of cigarettes has increased from 700 million in 1946 to 5 billion in 1950, and production is still inadequate. In 1951–52, prices of the largest selling brands were 2 baht and 3 baht for a pack of 20 cigarettes, compared with 5 to 7 baht per 20 cigarettes for imported British and American cigarettes.

Financially, the Monopoly has been remarkably successful. Even though its "costs" include the payment of heavy import duties and other taxes to the government, its profits have been large. For the most part, profits have been left in the business and reinvested. Through 1950, approximately 400 million baht had been reinvested since the end of the war, and the large new factory now under construction will be paid for entirely from profits. Each year, a

---

[64] Not all buying stations and curing sheds are owned and operated by the Monopoly. Some are owned privately, although after the tobacco is cured it must be sold to the Monopoly. Growers who sell to the private buyers are called "outside growers." Each farmer is assigned to a tobacco station according to geographical location but it makes little difference to him whether it is a Monopoly or private station because the price he receives is the same.

portion of the *previous* year's profits is included in the revenue budget of the government, and the balance left in the Monopoly. For recent years, the reported net profit and the amount taken as a "dividend" by the government have been as follows:[65]

Year	Net Profit (Million Baht)	Allocated to Government Revenue (Million Baht)
1946	26.4	
1947	60.0	9.0
1948	104.5	15.0
1949	174.0	40.0
1950	206.0	100.0

Besides the above shares of the net profits, the government also derives revenue from the tobacco industry through duties on tobacco imports, stamp taxes, and a kind of excise tax. These taxes are all included as costs to the Monopoly and have therefore been deducted before the above net-profit figure is obtained. The totals of these taxes for recent years (other than share in profits) follow:

Year	Taxes on Tobacco (Million Baht)
1946	71.1
1947	134.5
1948	103.6
1949	123.9
1950	163.2

The above figures show that the government realizes a handsome revenue from the Tobacco Monopoly, in addition to which a sizable sum is reinvested. The Monopoly is sometimes criticized for the low price it pays to growers, but it is generally considered to be an efficient and well-operated organization, although critics maintain that profits should be even larger. In the postwar years management included personnel from the British-American Tobacco Company, but this staff was withdrawn in March 1949 because of disagreements concerning salary and royalties. Since that time the Monopoly has been administered solely by Thai personnel, as it was during the war. A few foreign experts are still employed, however.

The Monopoly is the largest single industrial organization in the country, and Dr. Gould estimated that in 1948 the value-added through tobacco manufacture surpassed even the value-added through rice milling.[66] Since rice is the staple product of the country and there are numerous large mills in Bangkok and hundreds of small ones in upcountry districts, it is somewhat sur-

[65] Supplied by Government Tobacco Monopoly.
[66] "Estimates of Gross National Product and Net National Income of Thailand, 1938/39, 1946, 1947, and 1948" (mimeo., Bangkok, January 1950).

prising that the manufacture of the product of a mere 75,000 rai could add more value to the raw material than is added to rice through milling. One reason is that the Monopoly has a protected market in which it is the only seller, and a raw-material market in which it is the only buyer. By exploiting both the monopoly and the monopsony positions, it has been able to maximize the differential—i.e., the value-added. Nevertheless, good management and efficient operation have been necessary to develop the market and to maintain output, and especially to produce such a high proportion of profit (and taxes) in the margin between selling and buying prices.

This most successful of government-operated industries has all the characteristics which we mentioned as favorable to the development of a domestic industry: a large domestic market, a relatively simple technique, raw material available locally, and a large measure of protection. Not many industries have these characteristics to such a degree.

In addition to the above industries, the government plans to establish several others. Either directly or as part owner the government in 1952 was engaged in, or had plans to develop, the following industries:

Rice milling	Vegetable-oil pressing
Sugar refining	Tapioca
Weaving	Fish storage
Ore smelting (iron and tin)	Ammonium sulphate
Rubber goods	Chlorine
Paper	Leather tanning
Cement	Electricity
Salt	Alcohol distilling
Glass	Abattoirs
Tobacco	Jute bags
Shipping	Railways

In spite of increased government participation in manufacturing industry, the results actually achieved have been small. For example, in 1950 the net revenue from government-operated commercial services totaled 506,000,000 baht, but all except 30,000,000 baht came from the Tobacco Monopoly and from long-established enterprises such as the railways, opium *régie,* post and telegraph, and electric power.[67] All the new manufacturing ventures put together yielded little or no profit. Indeed, if accurate accounts were kept, most would probably show a loss.

According to Gould's estimates, the proportion of the gross national product generated by the government sector has not increased significantly since before the war.[68] It was 9.4 percent in 1938/39 and 9.7 percent in 1950.

[67] Bank of Thailand. The total figure includes no revenue from the Tobacco Monopoly except the distribution of profits.

[68] J. S. Gould, "Thailand's National Income and Its Meaning" (mimeo.; Bangkok, January 1953).

As the government expands its role in manufacturing industry, it is to be hoped that effective accounting systems will be introduced and other controls imposed. Only in this way will the government and the public be able to evaluate the performance of these industries. So far, with a few exceptions, government enterprises have not kept adequate records of capital investment, cost, receipts, and output.

The Relative Importance of Manufacturing

From its modest position in 1920, manufacturing increased considerably by 1950, although it remained relatively small. The proportion of the labor force engaged in manufacturing is one indication of its size and importance. Available census estimates are as follows:[69]

Year	Category	Number of Persons	Percentage of Total Labor Force
1929	Industrial pursuits	165,000	2.2
1937	Manufacturing industries	111,000	1.6
1947	Manufacturing	196,000	2.2

The decrease from 1929 to 1937 is merely a matter of classification—in 1929 the category "Industrial Pursuits" included "Transportation and Communication." Allowing for this difference, the figures for the two years would be nearly the same. In spite of the possible margin of error in these statistics, it is clear that the proportion of the labor force in manufacturing is quite small. Excluding women engaged in agriculture, the figures rise to 3.7 percent in 1929, 2.9 percent in 1937, and 3.9 percent in 1947. Since employment in rice milling and lumber milling is included in the above figures, manufacturing in Thailand is evidently a relatively minor activity.

Most of the manufacturing which does exist is conducted on a very small scale. To emphasize this point we give below the number of manufacturing plants employing over 50 workers in 1949:[70]

Type of Plant	Number	Type of Plant	Number
Rice mills	19	Water plant	1
Sawmills	18	Ice	1
Smoked rubber sheets	8	Machine shop	1
Sugar	8	Aerated water	1
Shipbuilding	6	Soap	1
Printing and binding	4	Cement	1
Matches	3	Brewery	1
Cigarettes	2	Total	75

[69] Statistical Year Book of Thailand, XIX, 19; XXI, 75. Monthly Bulletin of Statistics, Thailand, Central Statistical Office, No. 1, June 1952, p. 28.

[70] This list is given in Statistics, Memoranda and Documents, pp. 33–34, where it is said that there has been no increase in the number of firms employing over 50 workers since 1948.

This list is not complete, but it helps to emphasize the unimportance of large-scale production in Thailand, especially since 45 of the 75 plants are raw-material processors rather than manufacturing plants in the sense used here. Among the plants which we know to be omitted from the list are the following:

Weaving mills (government).	3
Rubber-goods manufacture ...	6
Shellac and sticklac	4 to 6
Distilleries	10
Paper mills (government) ...	2
Soap	2
Aerated water	4
Total	31 to 33

Manufacturing appears in a somewhat different perspective in Gould's estimate of national income and product.[71] In 1938/39 and 1950 respectively, manufacturing was the source of 9.9 percent and 12.6 percent of gross geographical product. In 1938/39 the value-added through manufacture was 95 million baht, while the total value of the paddy crop (before milling) was approximately 175 million baht. And in 1950, manufactures accounted for 3,239 million baht against approximately 5,200 million baht for paddy production. In other words, the value-added in manufacturing was 54 percent in 1938/39 and 62 percent in 1950 of the value of paddy production. Yet rice is the staple food and major export, and its cultivation the major occupation of 80 to 90 percent of the working population.[72]

Similarly, according to Dr. Gould's estimates the value-added through manufacturing was 75 percent of the total value of commodity imports in 1938/39, and 112 percent in 1950. This is an unexpected result, since shops all over the country are stocked with imported goods, while domestically produced commodities other than food, cigarettes, and various handicraft articles appear relatively unimportant. It does not seem possible for manufacturing to equal or approach imports in value, especially since we are comparing the value-added through manufacture with the total value (c.i.f.) of imports.

One reason why manufacturing appears so important is that Dr. Gould's manufacturing figures (properly) include the value-added in processing certain raw materials and foods for export and domestic use. Nevertheless, the

---

[71] *Op. cit.* According to Dr. Gould these estimates are very rough, with a large probable margin of error. The major excluded items are domestic service, rent of owner-occupied houses, and value-added by household industries and handicrafts. Other items have had to be based on extremely questionable data. Nevertheless, these are the only available estimates of the gross national product of Thailand.

[72] Even more striking is the fact that the value of paddy production is only 44 percent of the value reported for agricultural output alone. Considering the predominance of rice, the statistics seem open to serious question.

comparisons given above suggest that manufacturing is of greater relative importance than has been generally recognized. (The same is true of services, which produced income equal to 180 percent of the value of paddy production in 1938/39 and 110 percent in 1950.) It is an oversimplification to think of Thailand as producing little besides rice, rubber, tin, and teak, exchanging these products for imported articles, and supporting just enough of a trading class to effect the exchange. According to Gould's earlier estimates, the *combined* contribution of rice, rubber, tin, and teak was only 25 percent of gross national product in 1938/39 and 28 percent in 1948.

No amount of manipulation of questionable statistics can transform the Thailand of 1950 into an industrial nation, but, relative to other sources of gross national product, manufacturing is becoming increasingly important. Already it seems larger than is commonly believed, as is indicated by the comparison between imports and domestic manufacturing. A census of manufactures is needed to clarify this picture.

At the same time we should recognize the continuing predominance of agriculture and other extractive industries. Judging by Gould's figures, given below, the relative importance of such industries has increased in the postwar period.[73]

GROSS GEOGRAPHICAL PRODUCT BY INDUSTRIAL ORIGIN

	1938/39		1950	
	Baht (*Million*)	Percentage	Baht (*Million*)	Percentage
Agriculture, forestry, and fishing.	436	45.6	14,650	57.3
Mining and quarrying	31	3.2	395	1.6
Construction			163	0.6
Manufacturing	95	9.9	3,239	12.6
Electricity and water	6	0.6	38	0.2
Commerce	258	26.9	3,865	15.1
Transportation and communication	28	2.8	278	1.1
Government (general)	47	5.0	1,058	4.0
Personal service and other.......	57	6.0	1,909	7.5
Total	958	100.0	25,595	100.0

Conclusions

Most private manufacturing plants have been established by Chinese and other foreigners. Others have been established or assisted by the government. The Thai as private entrepreneurs have played a comparatively small part.

The government has greatly enlarged its role in recent decades, but with

[73] J. S. Gould, "Thailand's National Income and Its Meaning."

mixed success. The Tobacco Monopoly has been outstandingly successful, while other industries such as sugar and paper have a record of poor management, inadequate accounting, and erratic production. Nevertheless, the trend is strongly in the direction of government-operated manufacturing industry. This trend is shown by recent appropriations for a wide variety of manufacturing plants, by frequent announcements of government plans for this or that industry, and by the award of ministry rank to the newly established (1942) Ministry of Industries.

One reason for the expanding role of government in industry is the desire to prevent new industries from coming under the control of Chinese and other foreigners. As long as the Chinese community remains a separate entity in Thailand, full and free encouragement to private initiative will not be given.[74] This attitude finds some justification in the fact that the Chinese have tended in the past to form informal associations which, although composed of many small, fiercely competitive firms, have resisted the entry of outsiders —i.e., Thai or other non-Chinese—to the field.[75]

Experience since tariff autonomy was substantially achieved in 1926 suggests that manufacturing industry responds to certain conditions. When a wide domestic market exists for the product, when raw materials are available locally, and when a considerable degree of protection is provided, industries are established in Thailand. Since 1936 this has happened in the cases of soap, sugar, tobacco, cotton textiles, alcohol, and a number of smaller industries. Even in these cases, however, entrepreneurship has come from Chinese and other foreigners, or from government.

Whether Thailand has gained or lost from her tariffs and government-operated industries is a question of great economic importance. A final answer can of course not be given because the industries are still in their infancy, but some comments may not be premature.

In no case has a tariff been reduced because the protected industry has "grown up" enough to compete. The effective rate of duty has sometimes fallen because prices have increased on articles which paid specific duties, but no deliberate reductions have been made. This is not necessarily an indication of failure to grow up, however, because the government has usually been unwilling to relinquish a source of revenue, and it has simply levied an excise tax on the domestic industry whenever tariffs have encouraged one to emerge. The prime concern of the government's tariff policy has always been revenue.

---

[74] If the assimilation of the Chinese population proceeds, and if rigid immigration controls continue, the habit of considering Chinese as foreigners will probably die out. Already many businessmen of Chinese ancestry are considered to be Thai, culturally as well as legally, and further mixture through intermarriage will gradually eliminate the distinction.

[75] There is little or no documentary evidence on this point, but it was made by a number of persons interviewed in the course of this study.

Where tariffs are intended primarily to produce revenue, it is difficult to speak of the loss suffered by the consumers through payment of higher prices. There are sound arguments for tariffs as a form of tax in a country such as Thailand, and it is difficult to separate the tariff as a tax from the tariff as an influence on the allocation of resources.

The case for the development of industries in Thailand rests on variations of the infant-industry argument, and on the unquestioned facts that under-employment, seasonal unemployment, and imperfect knowledge exist.[76] Without entering into the great debate about free trade, we may observe that neither protection nor government operation, as they have been applied in Thailand, strikes very directly at the problems involved. Until an adequate supply of power and better education facilities are made available, not much progress can be expected. The government could enlarge its role in both of these latter respects to advantage. In addition to electric power and education, the government should disseminate information about products and techniques suitable for small-scale industry. Such a program would be much more likely to develop industries which could utilize underemployed and seasonally unemployed labor than would the duller instruments of tariffs and large-scale, government-operated industries.

The record of government factories is not good. Perhaps corruption can be eliminated and efficient management achieved, but the experience to date is not encouraging. Investment expenditures have not been carefully supervised, schedules have not been met, production has been erratic, poor in quality, and far below capacity, losses have been common, and accounting has been inadequate.

Considering the stage of administrative efficiency reached in Thailand and the capacity of the economy to respond to protection, we may conclude that the development of manufacturing industry would be better served by the provision of basic public services than by tariffs or government factories.

This course of action would tend to encourage those industries in which Thailand has a comparative advantage, or in which a potential comparative advantage is most likely to develop. Lacking efficient government organization, it may be wiser to rely on the dictates of comparative advantage and the response of private entrepreneurs. While their response is not as prompt as in a fully developed market economy, there is evidence that it does exist. If aided by the provision of basic public services such as power and education, the present weak response might become stronger and more effective.

[76] Knowledge of market conditions is imperfect everywhere, but there is a wide difference between the ability of would-be entrepreneurs in (say) the United States to evaluate the prospects of an enterprise and the ability of similar groups in Thailand.

7

Currency and Exchange
1850–1950

THE CURRENCY and exchange system of Thailand has been basically a simple one during most of the period since 1850. Nevertheless, the monetary history of Thailand contains several complicated episodes which will occupy us in this chapter. Since World War II the complexity of multiple exchange rates has been added to the system.

The purposes of this chapter are three: (1) to describe the main outlines of the currency and exchange system, (2) to explain the changes in it, and (3) to examine the events of certain critical periods in detail. For convenience, the one-hundred-year period beginning in 1850 will be divided into three parts: 1850–1902, 1902–41, and 1941–50.

1850–1902

During the whole of the period 1850–1902 Thailand was on a silver standard. The international value of the baht depended on the weight and fineness of the silver in it, and on the world price of silver in terms of gold. Net payments or receipts on international account were settled largely by shipments of silver.

In 1850 the currency of Thailand consisted of bullet-shaped lumps of silver known as baht or ticals. The term "baht" referred to a measurement of weight (15 grams) as well as to a unit of currency, and its exchange value was fixed at 8 baht per pound sterling by the weight of the coin, plus the world price of silver in sterling. This rate varied as the price of silver changed in terms of gold. Various types of subsidiary currency have been used from time to time. Cowrie shells, of which it took several hundred to equal one baht, were once widely used. They have since been replaced by metal coins. The various types of subsidiary currency are of no importance in the present discussion. Suffice it to say that the subsidiary coins were first based on the *att*, with 64 att to the baht, but that later on the decimal system was adopted and is still in use.[1] One hundred *satang* are equal to one baht.

As trade quickened after 1850, a way had to be devised to put imported silver into circulation. Because commodity exports normally exceeded imports there was a net inflow of silver, but trade was hampered because foreign coins

---

[1] For further details on the coins of Thailand see Reginald Le May, *The Coinage of Siam* (Bangkok, 1932), *passim*; and various articles in the *Siam Society Journal*.

did not circulate freely and silver bullion was awkward to use in trade. The treasury operated a small mint, but it was far from adequate to handle the volume of coins desired. Finally, as an emergency solution, the British consul proposed that foreign coins be made legal tender in Thailand. King Mongkut accepted this proposal and issued in 1857 a "Proclamation Concerning the Use of Foreign Coins."[2] This proclamation decreed that foreign coins should be legal tender and fixed the rate of exchange at 5 baht to $3. (The dollar most commonly used was the Mexican, but the Straits dollar was the same weight.) The proclamation also provided for the Treasury to purchase dollars in exchange for baht as desired by the merchants. The basic rate of 5 baht for $3 (allowing for a small commission to the Treasury) remained unchanged throughout the nineteenth century.[3]

During the reign of King Mongkut a modern mint was established to make the flat, round coins which began gradually to replace the bullet-shaped variety. Foreign coins were withdrawn from circulation as the mint became capable of supplying the needs of trade.

Thus it was very soon after 1850 that the monetary system of Thailand developed the characteristics it was to retain until 1902. During most of the period the export balance of the nation required a net inflow of silver which was sold to the mint. The baht coins it paid out in exchange represented an addition to the domestic circulation. Foreign treaties provided that no restriction or tariff should be placed on imports and exports of gold and silver, and the system was allowed to work automatically.

Over most of the period it was private traders and exchange merchants who handled the shipments of silver. When the discount on dollars reached the point that it became profitable to import them at the fixed buying rate of the Treasury, traders would do so. Their actions prevented large fluctuation in the rate of exchange. Toward the end of the nineteenth century banks took over this function. The first bank in Thailand was a branch of the Hong Kong and Shanghai Banking Corporation, established in Bangkok in 1888. It was followed by branches of the Chartered Bank of India, Australia and China in 1894 and the Banque de L'Indochine in 1897.[4] These banks existed primarily to finance foreign trade and to deal in foreign exchange. They were authorized to issue bank notes, but the total circulation of such notes was never very large. It was only 3.3 million baht in December 1902, fourteen

---

[2] Text is to be found in Pramoj and Pramoj, "The King of Siam Speaks," pp. 52–57.

[3] Now and then the baht fell below its official value of $.60 because the mint officers were monkeying around with its weight or fineness. In 1880, for example, the baht was bringing only $.40 in Singapore. *Commercial Report by Her Majesty's Agent and Consul-General in Siam for the Year 1880*, Great Britain, Foreign Office (London, 1881).

[4] W. J. F. Williamson, "Finance," in A. Wright and O. T. Breakspear (eds.), *Twentieth Century Impressions of Siam* (London, 1908), pp. 112–20. The Siam Commercial Bank was founded in 1904 with strong government backing. Other banks followed, but the three foreign banks and the Siam Commercial Bank were the major banks in Thailand for several decades.

years after the notes were introduced.[5] The circulation of bank notes was largely limited to Bangkok.

Outside of Bangkok and vicinity, money was not very widely used in 1850, but since then its use has steadily expanded. In village markets the chief currency was cowrie shells, while in remote regions salt and other commodities were used. The only way money could be moved from one place to another was by shipping heavy bags of silver. This was both expensive and risky. Child, onetime United States minister in Bangkok, described coolies carrying bags of coins through the streets, boats loaded with coins going up the river to pay for rice, and cartloads coming from the interior in payment of taxes.[6] Another problem was that the rupee circulated in the North and the rupee and the Straits dollar in the dependent Malay States. The Bangkok government did not put the baht into effective circulation in these regions until well into the twentieth century.

The monetary mechanism in the period 1850–1902 was thus an extremely simple one, but it worked effectively. The government had neither responsibility for, nor control over, the supply of money, which adjusted itself automatically to the needs of trade. When export trade was flourishing, local banks and merchants imported silver and sold it to the Treasury in exchange for baht. When export trade was slack and money was needed to pay for imports, merchants and banks sold baht to the Treasury in exchange for the silver dollars they needed to send abroad. Ordinarily, however, imports declined with exports, and the "normal" situation was an export balance paid for in part with imports of silver.

When the price of silver in terms of gold began to fall after 1870, the exchange value of the baht in terms of sterling also fell (see Appendix D for the baht/sterling exchange rate year by year). The ratio of exchange with the Straits (and Mexican) dollar was unchanged, however, because both were silver. The depreciation of the baht stimulated exports, but it also increased the cost of imports. Most imports originated in England, while a large part of the exports went to silver-standard countries. The government was particularly disturbed by the rising cost (in baht) of supplies and equipment for railway construction at the turn of the century.

The monetary mechanism continued to work as silver depreciation proceeded. Silver flowed into the country and the mint converted it into the coin of the realm. This probably could have gone on indefinitely as far as the bulk of the population was concerned, although the import trade was disturbed by it. Only the increasing concern of the government with essential imports, foreign loans, and (perhaps) national honor led to a break with silver. Foreign advisers also had a hand in this.

    [5] "The Currency History of Siam, 1902–23," *The Record*, Thailand, Ministry of Commerce, III (October 1923), 3, 14.
    [6] Jacob T. Child, *The Pearl of Asia* (Chicago, 1892), pp. 327–28.

The continued and accelerated fall in silver reduced the exchange value of the baht from 8 baht per pound sterling (1 baht equals 2s. 6d.) to a low of 21 baht per pound sterling (1 baht equals 11d.) in 1902. The government then decided to break the tie to silver, a course strongly recommended by the Financial Adviser, Mr. C. Rivett-Carnac.

We may note at this point that the government began to employ a number of foreign advisers and technical experts in the last decade of the nineteenth century. To prevent undue influence from any single nation, advisers of different nationalities were employed. The General Adviser was American, the Legal Adviser Belgian or French, and the Financial Adviser invariably English. These officials possessed a considerable amount of power and influence, and the Financial Adviser has long figured prominently in Thai financial policy. Other advisers were dispensed with earlier, but a Financial Adviser remained until 1950. The power of the early Financial Advisers appears to have been considerable—more about this later.

1902-41

Establishment of the gold-exchange standard.—The steady fall of silver forced the Thai government to consider the prospect of having trade and finance constantly disturbed by it. Even if the silver price were to rise, a stable relationship with gold, such as that which existed from 1850 to 1870, might never be restored. The government badly needed to fix an exchange rate for the baht which would represent in some sense an equilibrium rate for the conditions of trade and finance of the nation. In spite of a strong balance of trade, the baht was depreciating because of its tie to silver. The desire of the government to borrow foreign capital was also a strong argument in favor of a stable exchange rate. As early as 1899 the Financial Adviser said that if the baht were based on gold, the government would find it easier to borrow money abroad and at the same time private foreign capitalists would be encouraged to invest money in the country.[7]

For a time the price of silver steadied, but when the baht fell to 11d. (21.70 per pound sterling) in November 1902, the mint was finally closed to the free coinage of silver.[8] A new system was introduced under which the Treasury was authorized to pay out baht in Bangkok against sterling drafts on London. Similarly, the Treasury sold sterling in exchange for baht. At first the rate was fixed at 17 baht per pound sterling, but this proved to be too great

---

[7] C. Rivett-Carnac, "Memorandum on Closing the Royal Mint to the Free Coinage of Dollars," September 11, 1899 (typewritten MS). In the files of the Financial Adviser, Ministry of Finance, Bangkok.

[8] For a detailed description of the period 1902-23, see the two-part article, "The Currency History of Siam," *The Record*, III (October 1923), 3-14, and IV (January 1924), 7-20. These articles appear to have been written by Mr. W. J. F. Williamson, Financial Adviser from 1903 to 1924. As far as they go, they give a very full account of events in this trying period of Thailand's finances.

an appreciation (from 21.70 to 17.00) and the rate was changed to 20.00 in December 1902. Aside from a small spread to cover service charges, the Treasury stood ready to sell at 20 baht per pound sterling and to buy at the same rate.

This system of exchange-rate stabilization has been followed, with minor exceptions, ever since. Actually, this system had been used since 1857 to stabilize the baht/Straits-dollar rate, but now the baht was linked to the world system of rates based on gold (or on sterling).

The action of the government was strongly opposed by the three big commercial banks in Bangkok because of losses they suffered.[9] They threatened to go on strike and they did, in fact, refuse to transact business for a few days. The manager of the Chartered Bank went so far as to refuse to honor Treasury drafts drawn in baht against the government balances with that bank. (He soon had to back down, however, and he was later removed at the insistence of the Ministry of Finance.) Apparently the banks had been speculating on the continued fall of silver, but the government (and the Financial Adviser) saw no reason why their losses should be covered. Fortunately, the almost exactly similar experience in India could be used as a precedent and, although some concessions were made, the banks were not compensated for their losses.

The new system did not entirely insulate the currency system of Thailand from the influence of silver. Silver coins still represented the bulk of the money supply of the nation, and if the world price of silver should *rise*, there was a danger that the coins might be exported as bullion. (Foreign treaties still required free trade in gold and silver.) As it happened, the price of silver did begin to rise from the low point reached in 1902. A system was then developed whereby the baht was appreciated in successive stages as the price of silver advanced in terms of gold. Thus the baht/sterling rate was changed no less than sixteen times between December 1902 and December 1907, and every change was an appreciation of the baht. The rate finally attained was 13 baht to the pound. The policy of the government was to increase the value of the baht as required by increases in the price of silver, but not to decrease it if silver should subsequently fall in price. Therefore, since the price of silver decreased after 1906–7, the rate of 13 baht per pound of sterling was stable for several years (see Appendix D). In 1908 a Gold Standard Act was adopted which put Thailand officially on the gold-exchange standard. In practice she had been on it since 1902, but at an appreciating rate.

Had it been possible to convert the money in circulation into a truly token money when the gold-exchange standard was adopted, Thailand would have avoided much future trouble. This could have been done either by reducing the weight and fineness of the baht, or by replacing coins with paper money.

---

[9] This paragraph is based on the Financial Adviser's files re the "Gold Exchange Standard Scheme," Ministry of Finance, Bangkok.

The first alternative was rejected because the government feared that such a move would seriously undermine public confidence in the money.[10] Silver coins could not be replaced by paper money for the same reason. The circulation of paper money increased rapidly after its introduction in 1902, but it was fully convertible and was backed by a strong currency reserve of silver and foreign exchange. Silver coins continued to comprise the bulk of the money in circulation.

The new monetary mechanism worked very satisfactorily until almost the end of World War I. From 1902 to 1907 Thailand successfully appreciated the baht from 21.70 to 13 baht per pound sterling, and stabilized it at the latter rate. Over most of the period 1902–19 the demand for baht was strong, and the government supplied baht in exchange for sterling. For the period as a whole, the net purchases of sterling were considerable. Most were paid for at the rate of 13 baht. The stabilization fund sold out of baht and banks were supplied with baht from the Treasury Reserve, which in turn was credited with the sterling balances abroad. Even the Treasury was hard pressed to supply all the currency demanded by the banks, and it succeeded only by supplying paper money. The circulation of paper currency steadily increased, as shown by the following figures:[11]

As of March 31	Notes in Circulation (Baht)
1903	3,500,000
1907	15,200,000
1911	18,800,000
1915	31,400,000
1919	113,800,000

The note circulation was backed by a 100-percent reserve, part of which could be invested in sterling securities. The reserve requirement was altered from time to time, but in general the currency reserve was very conservatively administered. Until 1906, 75 percent had to be kept in silver coin while the remaining 25 percent could be invested in first-class foreign securities. In 1906 the law was changed to allow 50 percent to be invested. But in fact the amount invested was consistently kept below the permissible ratio, just to be on the safe side. Silver coins continued to circulate, and according to one estimate the quantity of silver in circulation increased from 40 million baht in 1890 to 120 million baht in 1906.[12] Official estimates show a silver circulation of 100 million baht in 1907, 74 million in 1915, and 103 million in 1919.[13] On the

---

[10] Report of the Financial Adviser for 1907/8, Thailand, Ministry of Finance, pp. 11–12.

[11] Statistical Year Book of Siam, 1936/37, Thailand, XIX, 317–27. Over the entire period circulation increased in every year except one.

[12] E. Florio, "Notes on Currency Questions," typewritten memorandum, June 20, 1906. In the files of the Financial Adviser, Ministry of Finance, Bangkok.

[13] Statistical Year Book, XIX, 317–27.

whole, paper money appeared to be growing in popularity during this period, but much of the relative increase in the circulation of notes was attributable to the strong demand for baht which could only be satisfied by issuing paper money. Silver was not readily available because of wartime controls by the Allies.

Movements of the exchange naturally provoked a great deal of discussion about the effect of the changes on the Thai economy. Most of the discussion was limited to bankers, traders, and government—the rice farmer has left no record of his views. The fluctuations of the exchange may have affected the volume of imports more immediately, but the volume of rice exports does not appear to have been much affected. Exports increased when the exchange rate was rising as well as when it was falling or stable. The movement of rice exports was erratic because of the weather and water supply, but the trend was upward throughout the period. The rice farmer does not seem to have adjusted his production in response to changes in the rate of exchange. The rising price of rice at the time the baht rose in value tended to counteract the influence of the exchange rate, however.

The postwar crisis: 1919–22.—Toward the end of World War I a series of events led to a major financial and economic crisis in Thailand. As early as 1916 the price of silver began to rise, and Williamson, the Financial Adviser, began to write memos on the subject.[14] He pointed out that the baht was in danger of being melted down and exported when the silver price reached 39–40 English pence per ounce. Furthermore, the danger point of the baht was the lowest of any of the silver currencies in the Far East. In 1916 the adviser recommended a reduction in the weight or fineness of the baht, but this was not done. Meanwhile, silver prices continued to rise, as shown by the following figures:

LONDON PRICE PER OUNCE OF BRITISH STANDARD SILVER (.925)[15]

(*Pence*)

Year	High	Low	Average
1916	37	27	31
1917	55	36	41
1918	50	43	48
1919	79	48	57
1920	90	39	61
1921	43	31	37

In 1917, after permission was hastily obtained from foreign consuls (because of treaty provisions), the export of silver was prohibited.

---

[14] Several of these are contained in the file marked "Bar Silver, from 1916," in the files of the Financial Adviser, Ministry of Finance, Bangkok.

[15] U.S. Treasury Department, *Annual Report of the Director of the Mint, 1935* (Washington, D.C., 1936), p. 89.

Throughout the war years there was a strong demand for baht because export products were in demand while the supply of imports was curtailed. The Treasury was able to supply baht only by issuing paper money. Silver bullion was not purchased for minting into coins because of the high price and wartime controls by the Allies. Some coins were released from the currency reserve by progressive reductions in the percentage required to be held in coin, but most of the increase in the amount of money came from the issue of notes.

At the end of the war in Europe, the two disturbing forces acting on the monetary system became even stronger. First, an unprecedented demand for rice hit the port of Bangkok and pushed the price up to levels never dreamed of previously. The price of "Number 1 White Garden Rice, including duty and gunnies" had ranged from 5.5 to 7.5 baht per picul in 1914–18.[16] In the first ten months of 1918 it was 9 to 11 baht per picul; in December 1918 the average monthly price was 14 baht; and it continued to rise, hitting 34 baht in June 1919. At such prices there was a frantic scramble for rice to export, while at the same time the Treasury was swamped with demands for baht currency from exporters and banks. To meet these demands, emergency measures had to be taken. The currency-reserve requirement was altered to allow 100 percent of the reserve to be invested in foreign securities, thus releasing the last of the silver coins held in that reserve; the paper currency was declared inconvertible; and when a new shipment of paper currency failed to arrive from Europe, one-baht notes were overprinted as 50-baht notes. Through use of these measures the Treasury acquired a large amount of sterling (all at 13 baht), and the currency in circulation increased sharply. The volume of notes outstanding rose from 60 million baht on March 31, 1918, to 114 million on March 31, 1919, and to a peak of 143 million in July 1919. By this time the craze to export rice was endangering the food supply of the nation, and the high rice prices were hurting the nonfarming segments of the population. Finally, in June 1919, the export of rice was prohibited except under certain conditions.

The second disturbing factor at the end of the war was the rising price of silver. This rise began in earnest in early 1919. The price rose from 48d. to 58d. per ounce between April and May 1919, and the increase continued thereafter. Since the export of silver was profitable at about 39d. per ounce when the exchange rate was 13 baht per pound sterling, the baht was obviously in danger of being melted down and exported, despite the export embargo. The temptation to smuggle was very great, and it is quite probable that a considerable part of the silver circulation was smuggled out between 1917 and 1920. In September 1919, to protect the silver circulation, the government reluctantly raised the exchange rate from 13 to 12 baht per pound sterling. This step imme-

---

[16] "The Rice Control, 1919–21," *The Record*, Thailand, Ministry of Commerce, I (June 1921), 4–10. This is the best available account of the postwar crisis as it concerned rice.

diately reduced the baht value of the Treasury holdings of foreign exchange. For this reason, and also because the prohibition of rice exports was resulting in a demand by the banks for sterling rather than baht, the government was extremely reluctant to take the step. Worse was yet to come. As the silver price continued to rise in late 1919, the exchange rate was increased from 12 to 10.89 baht per pound sterling in October, to 9.90 and finally to 9.54 per pound sterling in November 1919. (This was the selling rate. Buying was 9.14 per pound sterling, but it was purely theoretical!) Silver rose even higher, but the government was unwilling to increase the exchange rate any further.

Now the real tragedy appeared. The rain needed to mature the rice crop planted in June 1919 did not fall. The prospect of a crop failure loomed up in the fall of 1919, and when it became certain that the harvest was to be seriously short the government announced an absolute prohibition on rice exports after December 31, 1919. The consequences of simultaneously banning rice exports and appreciating the baht were perfectly clear to those concerned with the problem. This combination would result in a heavy demand for sterling which would have to be supplied by the Treasury at the rate of 9.54 baht per pound sterling. Most of the Treasury holdings had been purchased for 13 baht. The demand for sterling was further augmented by speculative purchases of sterling and by heavy orders from importers who wanted to take advantage of the favorable rate. In 1920/21 alone the Treasury sold 5 million pounds and for the first time since 1850 there was an import balance of trade. But the cost of this crisis cannot be measured merely by the reduction of exports and the Treasury loss on sterling sales. We would also have to include the direct and indirect loss of revenue to the government, the hardship and trouble caused by indebtedness arising from the crop failure, and perhaps even the cost of foreign loans subsequently obtained to shore up the finances of the country. By any calculation the cost was heavy.

The crisis was so severe because the two forces causing it supplemented rather than offset each other, and because the action necessary to counteract the monetary effects of the rice failure could not be taken because of the silver problem. For example, when exports were so sharply reduced, the import balance and the Treasury sales of sterling could have been greatly reduced or even eliminated by reducing the exchange value of the baht, say to 20 baht per pound sterling. This would have discouraged imports and prevented speculative purchases of sterling by banks and others. But this action would have made it immensely profitable to melt down and export the silver coinage of the country. It was to prevent the export of silver that the government appreciated the baht to 9.54.

Basically, the government had to decide whether to protect its foreign-exchange reserves or the silver currency, and it chose to protect the latter. Presumably the dominant factor determining the decision was its fear that people would lose confidence in the money if silver disappeared from circulation. While we have no basis for disputing the importance of this factor, it nevertheless appears that the government in fact pursued a middle course which did not protect silver although it did entail the loss of a large amount of sterling reserves. Thailand got the disadvantage of both courses but the advantage of neither! The average price of silver during 1920 was 61*d*. (high was 90*d*., low was 39*d*.), but at 9.54 baht per pound sterling it was profitable to export baht coins when the silver price exceeded about 52*d*. Furthermore, ever since 1917 there had been periods during which the export of silver was profitable. It is probable that much silver left the country in spite of the embargo. Since the government was definitely unwilling to raise the exchange value of the baht high enough to protect silver, it might have been wiser to have *lowered* it in order to protect the foreign-exchange reserve.

As it happened, the exchange rate was left at 9.54 until January 1923. The major sales of sterling by the Treasury were in 1919/20 and 1920/21, although sales continued to exceed purchases in 1921/22 and 1922/23. Rice exports were negligible throughout 1920, but the crop harvested in December 1920 was a good one and exports revived in 1921. Both Burma and Indochina had good crops of rice, the price dropped back to prewar levels, and the export ban was removed in January 1921. Meanwhile, heavy purchases of sterling from the Treasury to cover the unfavorable turn in the balance of payments had sharply reduced the currency in circulation, which fell from the peak of 143 million baht in July 1919, to 108 million by March 31, 1920, and to 73 million by March 31, 1921.

Although the situation had in most respects returned to normal by early 1921, the exchange rate was left at 9.54. To understand the reason for this, we must examine the relationship between the government and the commercial banks. During the war and prewar years in which the exchange was stabilized at 13 baht per pound sterling, the banks were controlled by the government in regard to the rate at which they could sell sterling. The purpose of the control was to prevent speculation and to limit the banks to the function of spot dealing in exchange.[17] Other traders were not controlled in this way. Furthermore, to accommodate the Treasury the banks built up an "overbought" position in sterling on which they lost one baht per pound when the rate changed from 13 to 12 per pound sterling. That is, the banks purchased sterling from exporters for 13 baht per pound and they intended to sell it to the Treasury in exchange for baht. But because the Treasury was having trouble supplying the necessary baht, the banks became long in sterling ("oversold" in terms of baht), and they strongly protested against being forced to lose one baht per pound sterling on these holdings. The gov-

---

[17] "Treasury and Exchange Banks—a Communique by the Ministry of Finance," *The Bangkok Times*, December 1, 1922. This was apparently intended to prevent the development of a futures market in baht which might put unexpected pressure on the Treasury.

ernment acknowledged the justice of the protests, and the "Tical 13" contracts were signed to protect the banks against loss.[18] These contracts provided that the Treasury would purchase from the banks, for 13 baht per pound sterling, an amount of sterling equal to the overbought balance of each bank at the time of the appreciation of the baht. An audit was made by the Ministry of Finance to determine the amount involved. When the "Tical 13" contracts were signed (late 1919) it was expected that they would soon be cleared because Thailand's strong balance of trade meant that the banks "normally" had to sell sterling to the Treasury. The first sales were to be made at 13 baht per pound sterling and the contracts would soon be finished. But the silver situation and the crop failure of 1919 intervened and caused the banks to *buy* sterling from the Treasury (at 9.54) throughout 1920, and in 1921 and 1922 as well. During this period the government tried to limit its sterling sales by rationing the banks and as a result the banks built up "oversold" positions—that is, they sold more sterling to the public than they were able to buy from the Treasury. Once again the government entered into agreements with the banks. This time it agreed to maintain the exchange rate at 9.54 per pound sterling until the banks cleared their oversold positions. The banks in turn agreed to try to reduce their oversold positions as rapidly as possible by selling sterling only to bona fide buyers. But in spite of the recovery of rice exports in 1921, the banks continued to buy sterling from the Treasury in 1921 and 1922 and, what was worse, their oversold position did not fall by as much as their purchases from the Treasury.[19] Apparently speculators were buying sterling in anticipation of a devaluation of the baht. Finally the government decided that the strain was too much and that the export trade, on which the recovery of finance depended, was being damaged by the high rate. On January 3, 1923, the rate was changed to 11 baht per pound sterling.

After this, recovery was rapid. Exports improved, the sterling drain stopped, and banks sold a net of over 2 million pounds sterling to the Treasury in the year 1923/24. Apparently there was no further compensation to the banks for their remaining oversold account. The obligation of the government in this case was not a formal one, however, since the agreements were never put in writing.

This episode in the monetary history of Thailand has been described in such detail because it illustrates so well the money mechanism which existed from 1902 to 1941. Basically, the mechanism was an automatic one, driven

---

[18] The rest of this paragraph is based on memoranda and correspondence in the files of the Financial Adviser, Ministry of Finance, Bangkok.

[19] *Report of the Financial Adviser, 1923/24*, Thailand, Ministry of Finance, pp. 9–13. It was during this period that the Treasury was buying sterling from the exchange banks at 13 baht per pound sterling because of the "Tical 13" contracts and selling to them at 9.54 baht per pound sterling—a situation which aroused resentment in some circles.

by the flow of trade, and "managed" only in the sense that certain rules were fixed by the government. Once the exchange rate was set, the government stood ready to buy and sell at that rate, but no other control was exercised. The government's role was a passive one, and the supply of money adjusted itself according to the flow of trade and finance. When the export trade was booming, the internal circulation of money tended to increase because more foreign exchange was earned than was required to pay for imports and remittances. The excess was sold to the Treasury in exchange for baht, which increased the internal circulation. When export trade was slack for any reason, the reverse process was set in motion and the supply of money decreased. "Normally," the supply of foreign exchange at the stabilized rate slightly exceeded the amount demanded, and the Treasury purchased the excess with new issues of currency. The increased note circulation was fully covered by the foreign exchange acquired.

Of course the net position of the Treasury in any year depended on invisibles as well as on commodity trade. Payments probably exceeded receipts on account of such items as travel, interest, dividends, and personal remittances, while inflows of long-term capital probably exceeded outflows in most years. Statistics are not available for any of these items, however. Treasury purchases and sales of sterling represented a "balancing item" in the balance of payments to a large extent. They played the same role as did gold movements in the classical gold-standard case. And, generally speaking, it is clear that exports formed the main source of foreign exchange (augmented by sporadic capital imports), and that imports, travel, interest and dividends, and personal remittances were the main uses, leaving a small balance of foreign exchange which had to be sold to the Treasury. There are many exceptions to this generalization in the period since 1902 (caused by silver prices, crop failures, world-wide booms and depressions, and wars), but it broadly describes the balance of payments position toward which the Thai economy tended to move.

Throughout this chapter we have assumed that the internal money supply increased or decreased in a one-to-one relation to Treasury holdings of foreign exchange. It may seem strange to the modern student of monetary theory that we have so completely ignored the phenomenon of multiple expansion based on a fractional reserve requirement. The reason is simply that deposit money was very little used in Thailand. Most transactions in money were settled by transfers of coin or notes and not by check. Demand deposits were only a small fraction of the coin and currency in circulation, and banks generally kept rather high cash reserves against deposits. Banks did not even exist outside of Bangkok. As a result, when the Treasury purchased foreign exchange from the banks, the funds received by the banks did not form the basis for multiple expansion of the money supply. In fact the tendency of people to hoard money probably made the increase in effective circulation even less than the increase in notes (or coins) issued. The tendency of the government to run a budget surplus had the same effect.

The postwar crisis also illustrates the extent to which foreign treaties hampered effective monetary management in Thailand. Although permission was obtained to prohibit the export of silver, this measure was considerably less satisfactory in alleviating the crisis than tariffs and quotas would have been. The terms of the treaties forbade the use of the latter measures, however, and Thailand was forced to undergo a painful adjustment process without any power to lessen its severity. (The treaties were silent on the question of devaluation but, as we have seen, the government chose not to take this course because of the silver situation.) Imports were unrestricted and the import duty was limited to 3 percent ad valorem. Many importers took advantage of the overvalued baht to stock up on goods, which served to increase the loss of reserves.

The cessation of rice exports was so brief that the postwar crisis does little to explain how the classical "transfer problem" would be solved in Thailand. The incomes of rice growers and middlemen decreased sharply, but the reduction in imports resulting from this cause was offset by additions to inventories made by importers who took advantage of the favorable exchange rate. Neither domestic nor world prices appear to have been affected by the monetary changes accompanying the rice embargo. As a result, the import surplus was quite large. It was covered primarily by changes in the balances of foreign exchange, notably by Treasury sales of sterling. The commodity import surplus was about 60 million baht in 1920/21, and in that one year the Treasury sold 50 million baht worth of sterling (at 9.54 baht per pound sterling). Because rice exports recovered in the following year, we cannot tell what the long-run adjustment process might have been.

The stable period between the wars.—After her recovery in 1923 from the postwar crisis, Thailand enjoyed a long period of relative calm as far as her monetary affairs were concerned. Beginning January 1923 the exchange rate was successfully stabilized at 11 baht per pound sterling, and in 1928 Thailand went on the gold-exchange standard with the baht defined as 0.6627 grams of gold—a weight which confirmed that rate. When Britain devalued in September 1931 the baht at first stayed on a gold basis and fluctuated in terms of sterling, but in May 1932 the link with sterling was reestablished at the former rate. This rate was maintained until quotations came to an end with the Japanese invasion. Thus, except for one six-month period, the exchange rate remained at 11 baht per pound sterling from 1923 to 1941.

The monetary mechanism continued to operate as before. Over most of the period the strong balance of trade meant that banks had to sell sterling to the Treasury in exchange for baht notes. The currency in circulation increased, and a strong reserve of gold and foreign exchange was maintained. Monetary policy was little changed by the constitutional government when it came to power in 1932, and over the entire period 1923-41 the currency was backed by a reserve which frequently amounted to more than 100 percent of the net circulation.

Thailand thus escaped the monetary and balance-of-payments difficulties of the boom-and-bust period of the 'twenties and 'thirties. Of course her economy was affected: export prices fell sharply (rice from 7.40 to 2.90 baht per picul between 1929 and 1934, rubber from 33 to 7 baht, and tin from 100 to 50 baht); import prices fell by a smaller margin and the terms of trade worsened; income was reduced; and the pressure of debt and taxes on the farmers became heavier. Yet the monetary mechanism and the balance of payments quickly adjusted to the new conditions. Throughout the period there was a commodity export surplus, and in all years except one the government had a surplus of ordinary revenues over ordinary expenditures. Indeed, in the three years 1932/33 to 1934/35 it had the largest budget surpluses on record up to that time. The ability of the economy to adjust so rapidly and with apparent ease may be attributed to several factors: (1) the absence of a thoroughgoing exchange economy in which commitments, plans, and operations are largely based on monetary calculations, (2) the relation of imports to living standards (i.e., they are largely luxuries which can be readily dispensed with), (3) inelasticity of supply in a falling market (this applies especially to rice), and (4) the willingness of the government to allow the automatic adjustment to take place without offsetting it in any way. Indeed, through its budget surpluses the government increased the severity of the adjustment.

Money in circulation did not increase in every single year, but from 1923 to December 1941 notes in private circulation rose from 77 million to 287 million baht.[20] In several years the government surplus and appropriations for various reserves caused notes in circulation to decrease even though the Treasury was buying foreign exchange. Ironically enough, silver coins became unpopular during this period and were gradually withdrawn. The amount of coins in circulation dropped from 68 million baht in 1923 to 26 million in 1941, as people came to prefer the convenience of paper money.

Deposit money increased during the period, but it was still small in comparison to the note circulation, and the use of checks was largely limited to the Bangkok area. As of December 1941, demand deposits of commercial banks were 77 million baht (compared to notes in circulation of 287 million baht).[21]

When the Japanese invasion came, the trade balance was strong, currency in circulation was increasing, the cover for the currency consisted of a reserve of over 100 percent in cash and securities, and the exchange rate was steady at the Treasury buying rate.

---

[20] *Statistical Year Book of Thailand.*

[21] *International Financial Statistics,* International Monetary Fund (October 1950), pp. 122-23.

1941–50: War and Postwar[22]

The outbreak of war put an end to the operation of the monetary mechanism which had been developed in Thailand. Trade was also sharply curtailed. The sterling portion of the currency reserve, held in London, was lost, and the note circulation was left without adequate cover. This situation was met in January 1942 by reducing the gold value of the baht and making government securities eligible to be held in the currency reserve. Later in 1942 the baht was devalued another 36 percent when Thailand went on a yen-exchange standard at the rate of one baht to one yen. This relationship lasted until the Japanese surrender.

During the war the currency circulation was enormously inflated from three sources. First, an export surplus vis-à-vis Japan was financed by issuing baht notes against yen credits. Second, budget deficits were financed by turning over noninterest-bearing Treasury bonds to the Bank of Thailand, a process which entailed the following issues of notes:

Year	Baht
1943	147,900,000
1944	20,000,000
1945	132,600,000
Total	300,500,000

The third and by far the largest source of currency inflation was the expenditure made by Japanese occupation forces. Thailand was required to supply the Japanese with baht notes in exchange for yen credits, which could of course not be used. Under this system the following enormous sums were delivered to the Japanese and added to the note circulation of Thailand:

Year	Baht
1942	24,000,000
1943	192,700,000
1944	514,000,000
1945	799,400,000
Total	1,530,100,000

Such huge expenditures, made in a country whose "ordinary" government expenditures had rarely exceeded 100 million baht per year, whose money

22 The basic source for this section is the *Report of the Financial Adviser Covering the Years 1941 to 1950*, Thailand, Ministry of Finance (Bangkok, 1951). See also B. R. Shenoy, "The Currency, Banking and Exchange System of Thailand," International Monetary Fund, *Staff Papers, I* (September 1950), 289–314; United Nations, ECAFE, "Financial Institutions and the Mobilization of Domestic Capital in Thailand" (Research and Statistics Series, Trade and Finance Paper No. 3) (Bangkok: mimeo., March 1950); and *Annual Reports*, Bank of Thailand, 1942–51.

supply formerly could be increased (in practice) only through an export surplus covered by sales of sterling to the Treasury, and whose imports of consumption goods had suddenly been cut off, could only lead to drastic increases
in prices and the money supply. These are shown in Table XIV. The prices

TABLE XIV

MONEY SUPPLY AND PRICES, 1941–51

(*Millions of Baht*)

As of December 31	Currency[a]	Demand Deposits[b]	Total Supply of Money	Cost of Living Index[c]
1941	287	77	364	131
1942	365	109	474	177
1943				265
1944	1,125	249	1,374	470
1945	1,725	432	2,157	902
1946	1,866	967	2,833	1,070
1947	1,890	846	2,736	1,250
1948	2,205	853	3,058	1,250
1949	2,365	938	3,303	1,200
1950	3,043	1,142	4,185	1,240
1951	3,757	1,413	5,170	1,370

[a] Less amounts held in government treasuries.
[b] Demand deposits with the Bank of Thailand and other banks.
[c] 1938 equals 100. Index is based on family budget of white-collar workers and wage earners
in Bangkok.
    Source: *International Financial Statistics*, International Monetary Fund, October 1950 and
April 1954.

of some goods rose to fantastic levels and, where resources were available,
this was a strong incentive to increased domestic production. Thus—to give
some notable examples—in 1945 the price of white sugar was 39 times its
1937–40 average, iron and steel bars 69 times, white cotton shirting 43 times,
and grey cotton yarn 29 times their 1937–40 averages.[23] Little wonder that
attempts were made to expand the production of these commodities! Output
was not easily increased, however, and the principal result of the increased
expenditure and money supply was increased prices.
    The government could do little to alleviate the situation. In February
1945 the Bank of Thailand withdrew thousand-baht notes from circulation
and gave one-percent Savings Bonds in exchange. This reduced the note
circulation by 371 million baht, but the relief was temporary because the

[23] *Statistical Year Book*, XXI, 547–48.

bonds were redeemable in twelve months. No real solution was possible as long as Japanese expenditures continued at such a rate.

When Japan surrendered in September 1945, Thailand's yen balance became worthless, and the currency was left with no cover except a small amount of gold and silver in Thailand and 257,000 ounces of gold in the Federal Reserve Bank of New York. (In 1949, a small quantity of gold held by the Bank of Japan was returned to Thailand.) Britain released one million pounds of the prewar sterling reserve in 1946, but the remainder was frozen and applied to the arrears of interest and principal on Thai government loans held in England, arrears of pensions to former British officials in the Thai government, and Allied war claims. The balance in the reserve in December 1941 had been about 13 million pounds sterling.[24]

Thus when Thailand faced the task of restoring her currency to a sound basis at the end of the war, she had practically no foreign assets with which to work. At the same time there was an enormous pent-up demand for foreign consumption goods and huge sums of money in circulation. All the elements of a severe and persistent crisis seemed to be present.

Obviously, the best solution lay in a quick revival of the export trade, but while the demand for imports was immediate, the recovery of exports took time. Tin dredges were not in operating condition, teak production took time to start moving again, and in the early postwar period there was an attempt to require Thailand to export rice for nothing, as a sort of penalty for her part in the war. When rice exports were not forthcoming, the punitive aspects were modified to provide for payment of a fixed price (well below market price). The effect of these measures was to hamper the revival of the rice exports, although it is now generally accepted that the amount of rice smuggled out of Thailand in 1946 and 1947 was at least equal to, and possibly larger than, official deliveries under the rice agreements. The smuggled rice served to ease the foreign-exchange shortage, even though it did so outside the established system. Toward the end of 1947 the punitive aspects of rice procurement were completely dropped, and exports recovered in 1948 and 1949.

At the end of the war the government was faced with the problem of fixing an exchange rate for the baht. This problem was especially difficult because of the drastic changes in price levels at home and abroad, the absence of trade in the period immediately after the war, the lack of reserves, and the accumulated demand for imports of consumption goods. After a first tentative try at 60, the baht was officially fixed at 40 baht per pound sterling (9.925 per U.S. dollar) in May 1946. At the same time the government imposed full control on all exchange transactions. The entire proceeds of all exports had to be turned over to the Bank of Thailand at the official rate, and

---

[24] The blocked sterling reserve was not a complete loss to Thailand. The greater part of the confiscated funds was used to redeem Thai bonds and to pay off pension arrears. The remainder presumably will be returned to Thailand.

exchange was sold only for approved imports. While this full-scale exchange control remained in force, all transactions outside it were illegal. Nevertheless, a flourishing black market existed, in which the baht was worth about half its official value.

Over-all exchange control was considered necessary at the end of the war because Thailand had practically no foreign-exchange reserves and because the currency in circulation had vastly increased during the war. Without control, the government could not build up the exchange reserves necessary to stabilize the exchange rate. Furthermore, control of inflation would have been more difficult because the full impact of the drastic price increases resulting from postwar shortages would have struck Thailand. The essential problem was to revive the export trade and restrain imports enough to restore the export surplus on which Thailand's international solvency depended. As Mr. Doll has written, "In May 1946 Siam was starting from scratch; the till was completely empty and the only asset she possessed was her potential power to acquire stocks of foreign exchange."[25]

When it became apparent that over-all exchange control could not be enforced, the government developed a modified and much more workable system. After January 1947 exporters were required to surrender all or a part of the foreign-exchange proceeds of the four major exports—rice, rubber, tin, and teak—to the Bank of Thailand at the *official* rate of exchange. The surrender requirement was 100 percent for rice and 50 percent for the others. Later, the surrender requirement was reduced to 20 percent for rubber, 40 percent for tin, and eliminated in the case of teak. Rice remained at 100 percent. Part of the foreign exchange accumulated by the Bank of Thailand in this way was sold at the official rate to importers of certain "essential" goods such as fuel oils and to the government for its remittances. Beginning in March 1948, some foreign exchange was sold by the Bank of Thailand at rates slightly below the open-market rates. The remainder was placed in the currency reserve, which increased rapidly. All other transactions were uncontrolled, and the open-market rate was legalized in late 1947.

This in effect gave Thailand a system of multiple exchange rates. Specific provisions have been changed from time to time, but the general outlines of the system remained the same from 1947 to 1952.

The principal advantage of this system was that it provided a maximum of control with a minimum of administrative red tape. Except for a few transactions, the foreign-exchange market was free. The system also enabled the government to accumulate a stock of foreign exchange, to influence the composition of imports, and to earn a book profit on the exchange purchased at the official rate and sold at the free rate. Considerable stability has also been achieved. The official rate has changed only once—in September 1949,

[25] *Report of the Financial Adviser, 1941-50*, p. 60.

when sterling was devalued. Thailand followed only part of the way, raising the value of the baht in terms of sterling (from 40 to 35 baht per pound) and lowering it in terms of U.S. dollars (from 9.925 to 12.50 baht per dollar). The free rate has varied as follows:[26]

AVERAGE MONTHLY SELLING RATES OF COMMERCIAL BANKS

Year	Baht per Pound Sterling	Baht per U.S. Dollar
1947	75.8	24.1
1948	60.2	20.0
1949	60.0	21.7
1950	57.0	22.3
1951	54.0	21.6

It is a remarkable fact that in spite of the abnormal demand for imports, the disorganized state of export industries, and the political turmoil of the early postwar period, Thailand quickly re-established her traditional export balance of trade and restored her currency to a sound position. Official figures show an import balance in 1946 and 1947, but exports were considerably understated as a result of smuggling during the period of full exchange control and punitive rice procurement. The export balance came back strongly in 1948–50, and the baht was made freely convertible at the free rate except for the controlled transactions mentioned above.

Several factors contributed to the restoration of the export balance of trade and the recovery of the baht.[27] First of all, the heavy world demand for Thailand's exports, coupled with reduced supplies from other sources, greatly increased the value of her trade. Second, her rapid recovery of production enabled her to cash in on the high prices. Internal stability facilitated the recovery of production. Third, a simple but effective system of exchange control drained off a portion of the export proceeds and simultaneously strengthened the national finances and prevented the possible dissipation of this income by those who would have received it. Fourth, nonessential imports were discouraged by tariffs and by the fact that they had to be purchased at the open-market rate of exchange, a rate which undervalued the baht. This factor led to the accumulation of large sums of currency by farmers and others in the interior.[28] Fifth, domestic investment programs requiring large imports of capital goods were of limited importance. Such programs did exist, as in railway reconstruction and in irrigation, but they were not large enough to create an import surplus. Finally, the flexibility of the Thai econ-

[26] Source: Bank of Thailand.

[27] Commodity trade statistics are presented in Appendix C. Rough estimates of the balance of payments are found in *Annual Reports*, Bank of Thailand, and in the *Balance of Payments Yearbooks* and *International Financial Statistics* of the International Monetary Fund.

[28] *Annual Report, 1948*, Bank of Thailand, p. 9.

omy, caused in part by its subsistence base, made it possible for consumption to be restrained enough to restore the "normal" export balance.

While the money supply continued to increase (see Table XIV), nearly all new issues after the war were made in exchange for foreign currency, and the currency reserve showed an impressive recovery. The reserve was further strengthened by the release of Thailand's gold deposits in Japan. The reserve of gold and free foreign exchange rose from its low point of 8.1 percent of notes in circulation in December 1945 to 87.2 percent in December 1951. This extraordinary improvement was achieved while the currency in circulation doubled. Postwar increases have come about chiefly through the traditional mechanism, under which the currency department (now administered by the Bank of Thailand) pays for foreign exchange with issues of baht notes. Note circulation has been reduced (compared to what it would otherwise have been), and the reserve ratio increased, through sales of foreign exchange made by the Bank of Thailand at the open-market rate. Exchange purchased at official rates is sold at the higher market rates. The effect of this transaction is to reduce note circulation by the amount of the profit made. The following figures depict the steady recovery in the currency reserves:[29]

GOLD AND FOREIGN EXCHANGE RESERVE AS PERCENTAGE OF NOTES IN CIRCULATION

As at End of Year	Percentage
1945	8.1
1946	16.1
1947	19.8
1948	29.4
1949	48.8
1950	78.3
1951	87.2

It should be noted that the reserve is valued at the *official* rate of exchange in the above figures. If it were valued at the open-market rates, the reserve ratio would be considerably higher—e.g., it would be 119 percent in 1951, instead of 87 percent.

The Bank of Thailand handled currency and exchange problems with great skill from 1945 to 1951. The continuity of policy was remarkable in view of changes on the political front. After severe price inflation during and just after the war, and after losing virtually all foreign exchange reserves, Thailand stopped the rise of prices (until the Korean war began), accumulated a currency reserve of gold and dollars almost equal to the greatly expanded

[29] Source: *Annual Reports*, Bank of Thailand, 1945–51.

note circulation, and devised a modified system of exchange control which worked and was administratively enforceable. In 1951 the baht was convertible at the free rate and it was one of the strongest currencies in the world.

The multiple exchange-rate system raises a question about the proper rate to use in converting baht values into other currencies. No exact answer is possible, if only because the very existence of the various rates has altered the course of events, but we may get some idea by considering the proportion of international transactions effected at each rate. Since 1947, as we have seen, all or part of the export proceeds of rice, tin, and rubber have been surrendered to the Bank of Thailand at the official rate. The amounts surrendered have been equal to approximately 70 percent of total export proceeds. The remaining 30 percent has been convertible into baht at the open-market rate. This means that approximately 70 percent of the foreign exchange earned by Thai exports was not sold in the open market. The effect of this reduction in supply was to increase the price of the remainder—i.e., to reduce the exchange value of the baht in the open market below what it would have been without exchange control.

The Bank of Thailand sold a part of the foreign exchange it purchased. It sold some at the official rate and some at a shade below the open-market rate. The amounts of such sales have not been disclosed but, judging by announcements of the kinds of commodities involved, the amount of exchange sold at the *official* rate probably has not covered more than 20 percent of total imports.

Since only 30 percent of the exchange earned by exports is available in the open market [1951] while about 80 percent of imports must be purchased with exchange bought there, it follows that the open-market exchange value of the baht is lower than it would be if all transactions were free.[30] On the other hand, since only 20 percent of imports are purchased at the official rate while 70 percent of export proceeds must be sold at that rate, it follows that the official rate overvalues the baht. If all transactions were free, the exchange rate would settle somewhere between the two rates.

Comparison of domestic and foreign prices is not much help in determining a proper par. Some prices are comparable if converted at the official rate, others at the open-market rate. Generalization is not possible, but it is interesting to note that prices of the three commodities for which surrender requirements still exist have risen far more than prices in general. The price of rice, for example, rose from about 60 baht per metric ton in 1935–39 to about 1,200 baht in 1950. This is the internal price of rice, based on the foreign price converted at the *official* rate. If figured at the open-market rate, the price of rice would have risen fortyfold instead of twentyfold. Yet available price

[30] The excess of demand for exchange (to pay for imports) over the supply (from uncontrolled exports) in the free market is made up by sales at the open-market rate by the Bank of Thailand, and perhaps also by a net addition to supply from invisibles and capital inflow.

indexes in 1950 were only 12 times the 1938 level. Rice (and also tin and rubber) has been in great demand since 1945, and the price reflects it.

Exchange control has shielded the domestic economy from part of the shock of such enormous price increases, and it has enabled the government to strengthen its financial position by skimming off and mobilizing a sizable portion of the export income which otherwise might have been dissipated. At the same time the low value of the baht on the open market has discouraged imports of consumer goods.

In a free market the exchange rate would probably settle somewhere between the official and open-market rates, but we cannot estimate precisely where. It would depend in part on the action taken by the Bank of Thailand, which is in a position to exert considerable influence on the exchange rate. In 1951 and 1952 it influenced the open-market rate by reducing the rate at which it sold sterling for approved imports.[31] Eventually the Bank may bring the two rates together by progressively increasing the value of the baht in the open market and perhaps by reducing the official value to meet it. This would eliminate the exchange profit of the Bank, but exchange control has already served the purposes of easing the transition to postwar economic conditions and enabling Thailand to build up her financial reserves. The baht probably could be stabilized at about 14 or 15 to the U.S. dollar, or 37–40 to the pound.

The Conservative Monetary Policy

A notable feature of Thai monetary policy has been its consistent conservatism. Conservative policies were initiated by the monarchy and they have been continued by the constitutional regime in spite of many changes in the government. The chief aim of monetary policy has been to safeguard the international position of the baht, and the government seems to have put this aim above such national interests as economic development and stability of prices and incomes.

The principal reason for the desire of the government to place the baht in a sound international position has doubtless been the very real fear of foreign intervention. The experience of other nations in this respect was not lost on Thailand, and ever since 1850 there is ample evidence that the government has deliberately pursued an ultraconservative policy in order to make certain that no nation would ever have an excuse to intervene in Thailand on the grounds of financial irresponsibility. Because it tied up national reserves of liquid funds and necessitated the postponement of productive investments, this policy entailed a certain cost to the nation. On the other hand, it may have been the means of preserving the independence of the nation.

---

[31] This refers not to the official rate allowed for a few favored imports, but to the rate slightly below the open-market rate. By reducing this rate (i.e., selling sterling for fewer baht per pound) the Bank has caused the open-market value of the baht to rise.

Aspects of conservatism in monetary policy have already been brought out in the preceding account of monetary history, but we will summarize them here. The policy concerning reserves provides a prime example. Not only has the currency reserve itself consistently equaled or exceeded the value of notes outstanding but, in addition, several other reserves, whose chief purpose was to support the exchange, have been established from time to time. In the beginning a large part of the currency reserve was kept in silver because notes were convertible upon demand, and because the public had not proved its willingness to accept the paper money. Later the law was changed to allow first 25 percent and then 50 percent of the currency reserve to be invested in first-class foreign securities, but in most years the percentage invested remained well below the permissible amount. A highly liquid reserve was desired, and domestic securities were not eligible because there were only a few such securities and no ready market for them. Direct investment of reserve funds in public works was not allowed because it would tie up funds and prevent their use in case of emergency.[32]

The practice of maintaining a currency reserve of cash and liquid foreign securities has, with the exception of the period during and immediately after World War II, been followed ever since notes were first issued in 1902. Thus one of the largest accumulations of liquid funds in Thailand has been rendered unavailable for productive investment. Sometimes the size of the reserve has seemed to exceed the amount needed for protection—e.g., in 1930/31 the reserve was 130 percent of the net circulation—but the Financial Adviser defended the position by warning of possible crop failures.[33] Since the end of World War II, the currency reserve has been steadily increased, and in 1951 it was over 100 percent of the notes in circulation, if valued at open-market rates.

In addition to the currency reserve, a gold-standard reserve fund was sometimes maintained to act as a stabilization fund. When the second sterling loan was raised in 1907, £932,500 of the total proceeds of £2,767,000 was allocated to the stabilization fund. Later an additional £500,000 of the loan proceeds was transferred to this fund, so that over 50 percent of the 1907 loan was used for exchange stabilization.[34] The stabilization fund was later increased, but the main point of interest here is that this fund represented an *addition* to the currency reserve, which was itself conservative.

Conservatism in monetary policy also appears in other forms. The reluctance to reduce the weight or fineness of the silver coins between 1902 and 1918

---

[32] As early as 1917 there was criticism of this aspect of policy, and the Financial Adviser explained that because of the need for liquidity the reserve could not be invested "in such a manner as to aid, directly, the commerce and industries of the country." *Report of the Financial Adviser, 1917/18*, pp. 7–8.

[33] *Report of the Financial Adviser, 1930/31*, p. 17.

[34] The £500,000 was later used for railway construction when the price of silver rose and the stabilization fund found itself buying instead of selling sterling.

was largely a question of judgment, but it is no surprise that the government decided not to make any change. The question of a central bank came up as early as 1890 and frequently thereafter, especially in 1915 when W. B. Hunter was brought to Bangkok to study the problem; but in the late 1930's the Financial Adviser was still opposing such a bank and the Bank of Thailand was in fact not established until 1942. The government was excessively dependent on foreign banks for decades. In the provinces the absence of banking facilities and the circulation of foreign coins were serious hindrances to trade, but the government was reluctant to tackle these problems. Banking facilities are still not adequate, although a few commercial banks have opened branches in the major provincial towns. The rupee continued to circulate in the North and the dollar in the South until well into the twentieth century because the government was afraid its reserves were inadequate to replace them successfully. In 1903 a provincial official reported that the baht would oust the rupee in the North if the government would only make it legal tender and accept it in payment of taxes and royalties,[35] but as late as 1917 the Financial Adviser was advising caution in pressing the baht into circulation because of the rising price of silver and the limited resources of the government.

The Currency Act of 1928 was drafted by Sir Edward Cook, one of the best of the advisers, who later wrote that he was "fully conscious that the law was on particularly conservative lines," but that there were "obvious reasons" for that.[36] This law, though modified by emergency amendments, is still the basic currency law of Thailand. The advisers continued to exert influence until well into the constitutional regime. In 1933 the Financial Adviser (James Baxter) wrote to the Bank of England for advice about a proposed sale of silver coins held in the currency reserve. He was told that it would be all right to sell the silver, but not all right to use the proceeds for capital investment as he had suggested. There was a coup d'état about that time and Baxter became fearful that the new government might be financially irresponsible, whereupon he dropped the silver sale and wrote the Bank of England that he intended to "stand sentinel over the Currency Reserve" and prevent any attempts to meddle with it.[37]

Such examples could be multiplied, but it is clear from the evidence in the files as well as from the statements of former government officials interviewed in the course of this study, that the conservative policy was not forced on an unwilling government. The government itself desired the policy, although the

[35] Letter to H.R.H., the Minister of Finance from Luang Upanick, Commissioner of Finance from Monthon Bayab, dated March 21, 1903. In the files of the Financial Adviser, Ministry of Finance, Bangkok.

[36] Letter from Sir Edward Cook to James Baxter, then Financial Adviser, May 13, 1933. In the files of the Financial Adviser, Ministry of Finance, Bangkok.

[37] Correspondence between James Baxter, Financial Adviser, and C. F. Cobbold and H. A. Siepman of the Bank of England, dated 1933. In the files of the Financial Adviser, Ministry of Finance, Bangkok.

particular forms it sometimes took may have been inspired by the Financial Adviser or, through him, the British government.

British interest arose from the following circumstances. Approximately 70 percent of Thailand's imports originated in Britain, and a large part of her exports went to British territories. British firms located in Bangkok were prominent in this trade, two or three principal banks were British, and British firms dominated the tin and teak industries. Beginning in 1905 sterling loans were sold, chiefly in Britain. Finally, after the political crisis of the 1890's, it was informally recognized that Britain had a paramount interest in Thailand. Some have said that Thailand was a colony in all but name. The principal aim of British policy was to maintain order and stability, and to prevent anything from disturbing or endangering her trade or investments. Maintenance of the status quo in Thailand also meant that she would remain a buffer between French and British possessions in Southeast Asia, thus eliminating the need for military expenditures to protect Burma on the east and Malaya on the north. A conservative financial policy in Thailand was a safe, simple, and unimaginative means to this end.

The importance of the conservative monetary policy followed by the Thai government lies in the fact that to stabilize the exchange rate and keep the baht fully convertible, the government had to tie up virtually all the liquid capital resources of the nation. The interests of foreign banks and foreign bondholders were thus placed above national interests such as development and utilization of resources. The consistent policy of maintaining high liquid reserves reflects the determination of the government to meet international obligations and to maintain the international position of the currency in spite of domestic economic needs. To this end the wealth of the nation was devoted.

Presumably the currency reserve was maintained for use in case of need, but it is difficult to imagine a combination of circumstances in which the *entire* currency of the country would be presented for exchange into foreign currency. Not even the crisis of 1919–21, with all the factors aggravating its severity, required the use of more than 50 percent of the then existing reserves of foreign exchange. Yet from 1902 to 1941 a reserve of nearly 100 percent (often more) was maintained. During this period irrigation projects were postponed and power projects and other desirable developmental projects were neglected because of lack of funds. Between 1905 and 1924, £13.6 million (equal to about 170 million baht at the appropriate rates of exchange) was borrowed abroad, requiring long-term repayment of principal and interest. At the same time, foreign-exchange reserves of 100–200 million baht were maintained unused—this in addition to Treasury and other reserves. In 1951 the reserve of gold and foreign exchange totaled U.S. $262 million, and no plans for its use were in prospect. Compared to this reserve, the World Bank loan of U.S. $25.4 million and U.S. economic aid of $6–7 million per year appear somewhat insignificant.

In view of the scarcity of investment funds in Thailand, it seems that the Thai government has been overcautious in immobilizing such a large portion of its liquid assets. But until the government develops an administrative efficiency which will insure that the funds will not be misused and squandered away, many able officials in the government would prefer to continue to leave the reserve as it is.

We may conclude that, after Thailand broke with silver in 1902, she fully accepted the consequences of linking the Thai economy to the world economic system, and that the government accepted its responsibilities in connection with the maintenance of that system. Not only did Thailand faithfully obey the rules of the game in regard to stabilization and monetary management, but she also accepted the implicit dictum of the system that internal adjustments should be automatic. In fact, under both the silver standard (1850–1902) and the gold (or sterling) exchange standard (1902–41) Thailand trusted to the automatic mechanism for any adjustments which became necessary. In this respect she was merely keeping abreast of the times, for the world economic system based on sterling, convertibility, and noninterference demanded just such a policy. But while we could hardly expect Thailand to rebel against the system, we may nevertheless question the effect of that system upon her development.

8

Sources of Government Revenue
1850–1950

FROM 1850 TO 1950, Thailand changed from a predominantly subsistence, barter economy to a predominantly money economy. During this period of transition, the ordinary importance of government receipts and expenditures was enhanced by the fact that there were virtually no liquid funds for capital investment, no banking system to provide such funds or to facilitate the transfer of money within the country, and little or no entrepreneurship except that supplied by foreigners and the government. In other words, government receipts and expenditures, though small by Western standards, were the only large aggregation of liquid funds being spent and received within the economy, and were therefore a major generating force in the Thai economy. The amount of revenue accumulated by the government, and the uses to which these funds were put, were therefore of great significance to the economic development of the nation.

Enormous changes have taken place in both the volume and nature of government revenues since 1850.[1] Over much of this period the fiscal system has been restricted by foreign treaties but, even before these treaties were revised, the manner of collection was changed and the fiscal system generally modernized. The purpose of this chapter is to describe the major changes in the volume and sources of revenue during the century since 1850.

The central government now budgets for almost all revenues and expenditures in Thailand. Formerly, provincial governments had more autonomy in finances than they now have, but the trend in administrative and fiscal organization has been toward greater, rather than less, centralization. Since 1890, from which date we have figures on revenues, the central government has collected and expended nearly 100 percent of government revenue.

The Prebudget Period, 1850–91

As we have seen, the revenue estimates for about 1850 given by Pallegoix and Malloch were 27 million baht and 32 million baht, respectively. We sug-

---

[1] The basic sources for the statistics of revenue given in this chapter are two: *Statistical Year Books of Thailand* and *Reports of the Financial Advisers.* For any given year these two sources may differ because of subsequent revisions or different classifications. In the figures quoted in this and the following chapters, an attempt has been made to select the best figures available according to a consistent classification. See also Appendix B.

gested that these estimates were gross exaggerations because even in 1892—after considerable expansion of rice cultivation and increase in trade, after the conversion of taxes into money had gone further, and after considerable improvement in the administrative system—the revenue was only 15 million baht. Pallegoix estimated that money payments in lieu of *corvée* brought in 12 million baht, but forty years later, after the *corvée* had been increasingly converted into a money tax, the yield was only one million baht. It was similarly true of the land tax.

Apparently the observers were dazzled by the magnificence of the court, and perhaps also misled by assuming that taxes were uniformly collected at the declared rates, while in fact most taxes were not collected at all in some regions, such as the Northeast. It seems probable that the estimates of Malloch and Pallegoix were much too high, although we have no other estimates for the same period.

Between 1850 and 1892 we have only one estimate of revenue. For 1868, the last year of the reign of King Rama IV, an estimate of 8 million baht has been made.[2] There is no way to evaluate this estimate, however.

Because of the lack of data, not much can be said about the changes in taxation from 1850 to 1891. The little information we have deals with the tax system, rather than with quantitative estimates. State trading, which was declining before the Bowring Treaty, was eliminated by that treaty. There was a greater use of taxation after the treaty, although collection was often "farmed" to tax monopolists, most of whom were Chinese. Gradually the farm system was replaced with direct collection. Taxes were also increasingly collected in money, rather than in kind, after 1850.

During this period the central government also began to administer the provinces more directly. Control was tightened in a number of ways, but as late as 1900 the central government received no revenue from the North, part of the Northeast, or the Malay States of the South.[3] Oddly enough, the tighter control over the Northern provinces was partly the result of British pressure on the Thai government to protect Burmese foresters and British traders.[4] Through provincial commissioners appointed by the king, visits of the king himself, establishment of provincial police forces responsible to Bangkok, dispositions of the army, and the superior administrative ability of H.H. Prince Damrong, Minister of Interior, the political unity of the country was improved. Economic unity had to await the development of transportation, however.

---

[2] *Siam, General and Medical Features,* sponsored by 8th Congress, Far Eastern Association of Tropical Medicine (Bangkok, 1930), p. 41. This estimate is found in other places, but no original source, and no breakdown of the figure, is ever given.

[3] *Report of the Financial Adviser, 1901/02.* Three of these Malay states were later ceded to Britain. They had long sent token "tribute" to Bangkok in the form of gold and silver trees, but no regular part of their revenues.

[4] Great Britain, India Office, *East India (Treaty with the King of Siam)* (London, 1874).

From Fiscal Reform to Fiscal Autonomy, 1892–1926

Until 1892 the administration of Thailand's finances was confused and badly organized. There was no budget, little or no audit, and no separation of the king's personal finances from the general revenues of the country. In 1892 the financial system was renovated as part of a general reorganization of government initiated by King Chulalongkorn. A budget system with a regular audit was introduced; the king's personal expenditures were separated from the ordinary state expenditures; and improvements were made in the collection of taxes. No doubt Campbell was right when he scoffed at the statement that the king had given up control over his personal finances;[5] no such surrender was intended in 1892. The king was still an absolute monarch. Nevertheless, the reforms represented a vast improvement. From 1892 to 1902 revenue increased from 15 million to 40 million baht without the imposition of any new taxes. In fact, some old taxes were abolished. Improved administration was the principal reason for the increase in revenue, but the decline of silver and the consequent rise in baht prices also contributed.

The reorganization in 1892 and subsequent years was a sweeping one which affected virtually the entire administrative system.[6] In 1894/95 the provinces, or changwats, were grouped into eighteen monthons, each under a lord lieutenant who was responsible to the Ministry of Interior. New ministries were formed and legal and other reforms were introduced throughout the 1890's. While many changes have since been made in the number and function of the ministries, the structure of government adopted in 1892 has been in use ever since.

Because it is a useful beginning point, we will briefly examine the major sources of revenue in the early 1890's. The two direct taxes, land tax and capitation tax, accounted for only 8–12 percent of total revenue. The opium monopoly and gambling farms accounted for about 40 percent, while commercial services and the royalties on mining and forestry yielded only about 5 percent of total revenue. The other major sources were excise taxes (15 percent), inland-transit duties (5 percent), and customs duties (12–15 percent). Of the customs revenue, export duties made up about two-thirds, import duties one-third. The rates of both export and import duties were fixed by treaty, as were the rates of land tax and inland-transit duties. Furthermore, virtually all *new* taxes were forbidden by the treaties.[7] Since the

---

[5] J. G. D. Campbell, *Siam in the Twentieth Century* (London, 1902), p. 91 n.

[6] *Siam, General and Medical Features*, pp. 9–11; W. A. Graham, *Siam* (3d ed.; London, 1924), I, 219–40. The reforms introduced in the 1890's are the more impressive when we realize that they took place while the French threat to Thailand was greatest.

[7] Strictly speaking, the treaties did not forbid the imposition of *all* new taxes, but they accomplished this result in practice by: (1) forbidding any levy on imported articles except for a 3-percent duty, (2) fixing the export duties and inland-transit duties on nearly every important article of domestic production, and (3) forbidding any other levies on these articles. Considering the structure of the economy and the nature of the administration machinery, these provisions

treaties had been in force since 1856, the general composition of government revenues probably changed very little between 1856 and 1892.

The result of the rigidity thus introduced into the fiscal system was that Thailand could neither increase her revenues as she chose, nor could she eliminate undesirable or inefficient taxes by replacing them with others. The administrative reforms of 1892 and later years, plus the general increase in trade and production, led to a large increase in government revenues in the years following 1892, but this increase took place while the revenue system remained virtually unchanged. In the meantime the achievement of fiscal autonomy was the major objective of Thai diplomacy.

Some changes were made in the sources of revenue between 1892 and 1926, however. Great Britain amended the Bowring Treaty in 1900 to allow Thailand to increase her land tax to the rate charged in Lower Burma. Following this concession a new land tax was put into effect in 1905, which yielded twice the revenue of the old one. The revenue from the capitation tax also increased after 1899, when the *corvée* obligation was converted into a money tax. It increased again in 1910 when the Chinese were required to pay the regular yearly tax instead of the triennial tax they had formerly paid. These two direct taxes (land and capitation) increased relatively as well as absolutely, and from 1910 to 1926 they accounted for 20–25 percent of total revenue.

Royalties charged on the output of mines and forests increased as the government improved its administration of these activities. Eventually the royalty charged on tin exports was determined by a sliding scale based on the price. The revenues from mines and forests varied a good deal from 1892 to 1926, but in general the trend was upward and by 1926 the yield was about 8 percent of total revenue.

One increasingly important source of revenue was commercial services, the largest of which was the net revenue of the state railways. This item steadily increased as railway construction proceeded. Other commercial services, minor in comparison with the railways, were the postal service, telephone, telegraph, and the Bangkok water works. Altogether, the revenue from commercial services rose from almost nothing in 1892 to 13 percent of total revenue in 1926. The import and sale of opium continued to be an important source of revenue. The Thai have never been greatly addicted to opium, partly because of strict laws against their use of it, and the opium sold in Thailand is largely consumed by the Chinese. This may be one reason why the periodic government announcements of the imminent curtailment of opium smoking never came to much. Even so, opium smoking has been somewhat restricted and controlled through the licensing of smokers, reduction in the number of

blocked any new taxes except *direct* taxes, and the government thought the capitation tax was already high enough. An income tax was obviously out of the question. For the terms of the various treaties, see *State Papers of the Kingdom of Siam, 1664/1886* (London, 1886), *passim.*

houses, and the very high prices charged by the opium *régie*. Profits on opium formed the largest single source of revenue from 1905 to 1926, averaging around 20 percent of the total. Prior to 1905 gambling was the largest single revenue producer, but the policy of suppressing gambling put opium in first place.

Thailand's efforts to reform her fiscal system centered around the campaign to revise the import duties. The government was convinced by foreign advisers and critics that a modern state should not receive 30 to 40 percent of its revenue from gambling and opium, and it was aware that the many export and inland-transit duties were harmful as well as inefficient. Yet if these taxes were to be abolished, something had to replace them. And not only replacement was needed—the increasing demands for expenditure meant that more and more revenue was required. Increased duties on imports seemed to be the ideal solution. Such duties were easy to collect, their yield would rise as trade increased, and the duties would tend to fall on those who purchased the imported goods. Furthermore, in view of the importance of subsistence agriculture in Thailand, and the small amount of domestic production for sale locally, no satisfactory alternative form of tax existed. Direct taxation (land and capitation taxes) was as high as was practicable, and other taxes were precluded because they would violate some treaty provision, discourage domestic production, or prove impossible to collect.

For all of these reasons, Thailand desired to revise the treaties to allow for increases in import duties. (It is interesting to note that increased tariffs were desired for revenue only. There was no thought of protection for domestic industries.) In 1883 the treaties had been amended to raise the duty on liquor imports to 10 percent, but the general rate of duty remained 3 percent. As a percentage of total revenue, import duties amounted to less than 3 percent in 1898/99, 5 percent in 1908/9, and 4 percent in 1918/19. Even in free-trade Britain, customs revenue was over 20 percent of the total.

In spite of all the arguments in favor of it, revision of the treaties proved to be difficult. The crucial negotiations were with Britain because of her influence as a world power and her importance in the trade of Thailand. The Thai government tried to link tariff revision with the abolition of gambling and other fiscal reforms which were being urged upon Thailand by her many official and unofficial foreign advisers. Thailand stated her willingness to eliminate gambling if the revenue so lost could be replaced by increased tariffs. Actually, King Chulalongkorn was convinced that state-licensed gambling was an evil, and he was determined to eliminate it as soon as possible even without tariff revision. The campaign against gambling was started as early as 1890, but progress was very slow at first. The plan was to gradually eliminate it in the provinces before attempting to do so in Bangkok.

In the meantime negotiations were opened with the treaty powers, and proposals for tariff revision were drawn up. The Financial Adviser reported in 1905/6 that gambling in the provinces was being abolished, and that the government "confidently" looked to the treaty powers to assist in the abolition of the evil in Bangkok by allowing treaty revision to replace the revenue lost. The adviser expressed the hope that he would be able to report some progress within a year, but in his report for 1907/8 he said merely that the elimination of gambling in Bangkok awaited the outcome of negotiations for tariff revision. In 1908 the Financial Adviser wanted to eliminate the inland-transit duties at once because he thought they hampered trade and production, and to abolish gambling slowly, but both Prince Damrong and Edward Strobel, the General Adviser, urged that the case for treaty revision would be stronger if immediate elimination of gambling were offered as a *quid pro quo*.[8]

Apparently the treaty powers were not willing to accept the elimination of gambling as a *quid pro quo*. For several years the adviser was silent on this question, but in his 1916/17 report he announced that the government had decided to go ahead with the abolition of gambling even though "for various reasons, no progress has been made in the negotiations for the revision of the Customs Tariff." The government did go ahead, and by 1917/18 the revenue from gambling dropped almost to zero. Thus was eliminated a source which had formerly accounted for some 20 percent of total revenue.

Thailand did not ask for full fiscal autonomy in the treaty negotiations. At first she merely wanted to increase the general tariff rate from 3 percent to 5 percent. Later, in 1908, the proposal was to make the general rate 10 percent and to eliminate all export duties except on rice and cattle.[9] We do not know what Britain asked as a *quid pro quo*, but we do know that she refused to allow the changes in the tariff. This meant that Thailand was denied fresh sources of revenue, that undesirable sources had to be retained, and that certain projects could not be undertaken because of the lack of funds.

The first break in the impasse came in 1920 when the United States and Thailand signed a new treaty which recognized the complete fiscal autonomy of Thailand, subject to the conditions of equality of treatment with other nations.[10] Not much additional progress was made for a few years, but in 1925/26 a Thai delegation, accompanied by the Foreign Adviser, Mr. Francis B. Sayre, toured Europe and successfully negotiated new treaties with all the major powers. The most difficult task was to get a treaty with Britain, and the result was a compromise. The British treaty provided that the tariff on

---

[8] File on "Proposals for Revision of Customs Tariff," in the files of the Financial Adviser, Ministry of Finance, Bangkok.

[9] *Idem.*

[10] Phya Kalyan Maitri (Francis B. Sayre, ed.); *Siam: Treaties with Foreign Powers, 1920–1927*, published by order of the Royal Siamese Government (Norwood, Mass., 1928), pp. 262–70. Subsequent negotiation with other nations was facilitated by an article in the United States treaty which provided that her recognition of fiscal autonomy was also subject to the condition that other nations, when assenting to tariff changes, must do so without receiving any *quid pro quo*. This provision was a great help to the Thai delegation in its negotiations with other powers. (The writer is indebted to H.H. Prince Vivadhanajai for this point.)

cotton goods, iron and steel manufactures, and machinery was to be limited to 5 percent ad valorem for ten years. These commodities comprised the major imports from Britain. Furthermore, notes were exchanged in which Thailand stated that she had no present intention to increase the export duties on rice, tin, or teak. Some minor limitations were found in other treaties, but for the most part they conferred fiscal autonomy.

The successful completion of these treaties meant that Thailand regained control over her financial structure for the first time since the Bowring Treaty, signed seventy years before. As might be expected, changes in the tax structure were not long in coming.

Before we examine the changes since 1926, we will briefly describe the foreign loans raised by the Thai government. Before 1905 Thailand had no internal or external debt. The government met all of its expenditures from revenue, and from 1892 to 1905 it built up a treasury reserve in addition to providing for railway construction and all ordinary expenditures. But the difficulty of increasing revenue sufficiently to cover the increasing expenditures, plus the obligations imposed by the gold standard, led the government to seek foreign capital for investment expenditures. The following is a list of the sums it borrowed:

Year	Principal (Pounds Sterling)	Interest Rate (Percent)	Sale Price	Net Proceeds (After Commissions, etc.)
1905	1,000,000	4.5	95.50	90.50
1907	3,000,000	4.5	98.00	93.75
1909	4,630,000	4.0		100.00
1922	2,000,000	7.0	100.00	93.50
1924	3,000,000	6.0	95.50	90.50

Proceeds of the 1905 and 1907 loans were used for railway construction, except for some £900,000 of the latter which was put into the exchange stabilization fund. The 1909 loan was provided for in the treaty with Great Britain in which Thailand gave up her rights over three Malay states in exchange for concessions with regard to extraterritoriality. The loan was to be used exclusively for the construction of a railway from Bangkok to the Malay border.

The 1922 and 1924 loans were ostensibly raised to reimburse the treasury reserve for expenditures made on irrigation and railways during the war, when a foreign loan was not obtainable, and for losses suffered during the 1920–21 crisis. These loans were secured at high interest rates, and when the government began to enjoy a revenue surplus, it soon began to build up a reserve for their redemption.

As a matter of fact, the primary purpose of the 1922 and 1924 loans, and of one-third of the 1907 loan, was to ensure the international solvency of

Thailand and to bolster the exchange position. Thus some £5,900,000 of the total of £13,630,000 was devoted to reinforcing the credit of Thailand rather than to productive investments. Nor can it be said that these loans were necessitated by domestic investment activity. The portion of the 1907 loan allocated to the stabilization fund was intended merely to increase that fund against unforeseen contingencies. No domestic investment was under way except railway construction, and that was being fully financed from loan funds. The 1922 and 1924 loans were needed partly to finance railway construction and irrigation, but primarily to recoup the Treasury for exchange losses and to increase confidence in the baht.

Of course the sums used in this way may have forestalled complications arising from a flight from the baht. On the other hand, considering the price Thailand had to pay for those loans which were used for productive purposes, a price which should include the full amount of the loans used for stabilization as well as interest charges, she might have been better off if she had relied entirely on revenue. This is a judgment made with the aid of hindsight, however, and in the uncertainty of the moment the government may have been justified in taking the course it did.

Considered by themselves, the productive loans were soundly used. They financed a large part of railway construction, and operating profits alone were sufficient to cover the interest cost. Many indirect benefits also accrued to the nation.

In the beginning, Thailand's loans were a hot political issue, for nations realized that Thailand would be linked closer to the nation which held her bonds. When the 1905 loan was made, Franco-British competition for influence in Thailand was still keen, and the loan had to be handled jointly by French and British bankers. Half of it was floated in Paris and half in London. By 1907 German influence was growing in Southeast Asia, and Germany insisted on having a part in the 1907 loan. At the last minute, the plan to issue the bonds only in London and Paris was changed, and 25 percent of the loan was sold in Berlin through a German bank. Both of these loans were the subjects of much discussion in the embassies and foreign offices of the nations concerned, but by the 1920's the political situation was more stable, and the Financial Adviser saw to it that loans were handled by British banks and floated in London.

Fiscal Autonomy, 1926–50

Thailand lost no time in altering her tax structure when the treaty revisions were complete. The major changes were in customs duties, although a number of inefficient taxes were abolished.

A new tariff became effective in March 1927, and the yield of import duties jumped in one year from 7 million to 16 million baht. The new duties were still quite low, for the most part. The general rate was increased to 5 percent.

In addition, certain specific articles were subject to higher rates. Special ad valorem duties were put on beer and wine (12 percent), manufactured tobacco (25 percent), and motor cars and equipment (10 percent); and specific duties were levied on kerosene, benzine, matches, and sugar—all articles which were widely consumed. The new tariff was clearly designed for revenue rather than for protection. The percentage of total import duties to the value of commodity imports rose from 3.7 percent in 1926/27 to 8.5 percent in 1927/28, and import duties increased from 7.0 percent to 13.7 percent of total government revenue.

Upon the adoption of the new tariff, the government abolished the inefficient inland-transit duties which had long hampered domestic production and trade. A large number of petty export duties were also abolished, although the duty on rice exports was retained. Royalties on tin and teak also remained unchanged.

During the next several years the tendency was to rely on import duties for an ever larger part of total revenues. The tariff was changed frequently from 1927 to 1941, and nearly every change was an increase. The following figures illustrate the increasing importance of import duties in the budget:

Period	Percentage of Total Revenue	Percentage of Total Commodity Imports
1926/27	7.0	3.7
1927/28	13.7	8.5
1930/31	14.5	9.4
1935/36	25.0	22.0
1941	21.0	21.8
1950	27.0	20.6

The steady increases in the tariff obviously changed it from a minor revenue producer, representing 8.5 percent of total commodity imports in 1927/28, to a major source of revenue and a stiff levy on imports which reached 28 percent of total commodity imports at its peak in 1936/37. When other sources of revenue dropped during the depression, the government turned in desperation to tariffs for the revenue it needed, and duties on some articles reached extremely high levels. To avoid valuation problems and to simplify collection procedures, specific duties increasingly replaced ad valorem duties during this period, and by 1936 the tariff consisted mainly of specific duties.

As the tariff was increased, imports of some articles dropped off and local production began. The government had to learn to adjust tariffs and excise taxes so as to obtain the maximum revenue without alternately killing off and reviving the local industry. Tariffs encouraged local production of sugar, soap, cigarettes, and matches, and during the 1930's the government got some experience in the use of taxation to influence the structure of business. For example, the tariff on matches led to the establishment of match factories in Thailand. At first these factories used imported splints and box materials, assembling them locally in order to escape the tariff. When a tariff was put on materials, local supplies were used. In the meantime the import of matches decreased sharply and the government, to replace the revenue lost, levied an excise tax on locally produced matches. The excise tax and the import duty had to be fixed in such a relation to one another that local production would not be discontinued. Meanwhile, these taxes on matches were encouraging the use of mechanical lighters, and a stiff duty had to be put on them also. Similar experience was gained with sugar, tobacco, and other products. Therefore, although the tariff was still used primarily for revenue purposes, the government began to see the possibilities of using it as an instrument to influence the allocation of resources.

Aside from tariff changes, not many new experiments in taxation were made in the 1920's and 1930's. During the depression, land and capitation taxes were reduced because the government feared that farmers would be unable to pay and that the enforcement machinery would break down if faced with mass delinquency. The constitutional government announced its intention to reform the tax structure, but few real changes were made. An income tax was introduced, but it yielded little revenue because of widespread evasion and the relatively small number of people with taxable money incomes. The principal sources of revenue remained about the same, except that import duties increased in importance (see Table XV).

In 1938 the long-awaited revenue code of the constitutional government was enacted into law. The new code was supposed to shift the burden of taxation from the rice farmer onto business and high-income groups. Land and capitation taxes, two long-established sources of revenue, were completely abolished. New taxes were placed on businesses and the income tax was revised. These proved to be disappointingly small revenue producers, however, and as late as 1941 the income tax yielded only two percent of total revenue, while all direct taxes on business yielded only one percent. Except for the land and capitation taxes, the principal sources of revenue were not much affected by the new code. Most revenue continued to come from the opium *régie*, customs duties, excise taxes, commercial services, and fees, fines, and licenses (see Table XV).

The war put heavy new demands on the revenue system at the same time that customs duties were sharply reduced. Total revenue doubled from 1941 to 1945, but the inflation of prices was far greater than that, and revenue lagged behind expenditure throughout the war. No important new sources of revenue were developed in the war years. Except for customs and the royalties from mines and forests, the usual sources yielded increased revenues as prices went up. A surtax was levied on incomes and in 1945 the yield from this tax, together with the regular income tax, amounted to almost 9 percent of total revenue.

TABLE XV

Sources of Revenue Compared for Different Years

(Millions of Baht)

Source	1892	1905	1906	1915	1917	1926	1927	1938	1941	1944	1950
Direct Taxes											
Land tax	1.02	3.86	7.58	8.22	8.68	11.62	12.83	7.42			
Capitation	0.45	4.14	4.93	7.69	8.34	10.06	10.05	7.74			
Income and salary tax								1.85	3.30	22.87	111.98
Indirect Taxes											
Import duties	1.74	2.69	3.01	3.49	4.18	7.16	16.03	30.58	33.76	11.75	577.75
Export duties		2.79	2.86	3.67	3.70	4.05	5.00	5.46	11.17	3.38	170.56
Excise taxes	2.30	4.16	3.95	6.22	8.62	10.87	12.15	6.98	19.68	57.70	356.62
Inland transit	0.28	1.56	1.67	1.89	2.09	2.10	0.88				
Gambling farms	4.28	8.64	6.65	7.46	0.33						
State Domains											
Forest revenue	0.15	2.05	1.47	1.61	2.65	3.82	4.55	3.78	4.05	5.54	27.30
Mining revenue	0.53	1.21	1.54	2.43	4.94	4.34	4.01	5.27	11.13	4.37	65.36
State Enterprises											
Opium *régie*	2.48	10.26	8.87	16.56	21.18	18.01	18.18	10.39	14.27	61.33	110.15
Commercial services		2.34	2.98	4.84	5.18	13.64	15.42	21.11	33.83	63.18	395.55
Rice sales											140.00
Fees, Fines, and Licenses	0.26	3.54	3.89	5.56	7.60	7.17	8.20	12.64	16.68	20.01	118.09
Other	1.89	3.22	6.11	4.72	4.97	7.75	10.14	5.01	13.13	35.88	65.93
Total revenue	15.38	50.46	55.51	74.36	82.46	100.59	117.44	118.23	161.00	286.01	2,139.29

Sources: *Statistical Year Books of Thailand* and *Reports of the Financial Advisers.* Some of the 1950 estimates were obtained from the Bank of Thailand.

The yield from excise taxes, commercial services, and the opium *régie* also increased sharply during the war.

Revenue increased rapidly in the postwar years from 315 million baht in 1945 to 2.14 billion baht in 1950.[11] This huge increase was partly the result of inflation and partly the result of a speedy revival of trade.

The major sources of revenue varied little from the prewar pattern. Customs duties made a strong comeback, aided by high specific duties which were partly intended to discourage consumption because of the shortage of foreign exchange. By 1950 the duties on imports reached 578 million baht, or 27 percent of total revenues, and export duties added another 170 million baht.[12] Profits of the opium *régie* did not increase much from the wartime level, but revenue from other commercial services did.[13] Excise taxes also increased enormously—from 60 million baht in 1945 to 356 million in 1950. The yield of income taxes increased some, but in 1949 and 1950 still amounted to only 4 or 5 percent of total revenues. Since rates were fairly high, it is obvious that tax evasion was widespread. If the 1950 income tax had been collected in full, it probably would have yielded many times its actual yield of 112 million baht, but when the tax begins to take 50 percent of the higher incomes, the inducement to bribe tax officials becomes enormous. Furthermore, the difficulties of getting accurate accounting statements from family enterprises are great. Many of them are said to keep three sets of books—one for tax purposes, one for their own use, and one to produce when the tax collector demands to see the "real" accounts.

Government profit on rice trading is one large new source of revenue. It accounted for 329 million baht in 1949 and 140 million baht in 1950. These figures represent merely the profits transferred to the Ministry of Finance in these years. They do not represent the *total* profit of the Rice Bureau. The complete records of this agency are not available to the public. It is frequently alleged that part of the rice profits are being siphoned off by high officials, and for this reason it is unfortunate that the government does not render a full accounting.

The major sources of government revenue in 1950 were thus about the same as the prewar sources, with the exception of the profits from rice trading. Virtually the only direct tax of any importance was the income tax, and in 1950 it accounted for only 5 percent of revenue. Nearly 95 percent of revenue came from indirect sources. It is interesting to note that government enter-

---

[11] Comptroller-General's Department, Ministry of Finance. Both figures are provisional, as are all statistics of revenue and expenditures since 1944.

[12] Exports also pay an indirect tax through the exchange control system, but this tax does not appear in government revenues.

[13] Revenue of commercial services is ambiguous as it is handled in the accounts. In some cases, notably the railways, the total income of the enterprise is included in the government revenues, and expenditures are budgeted. In other cases, e.g., the tobacco monopoly, only the *net profit* is included in revenues, and expenditures do not appear at all.

prises of all kinds—opium *régie*, rice trading, and other commercial services—yielded about 650 million baht, or 30 percent of total revenues.

The heavy dependence on indirect taxes is not unwise in a country such as Thailand. Such taxes are relatively easy to collect. Because they tend to reduce consumption and are regressive, they encourage savings, which can be used for productive investment. Because they can be levied on articles which are widely consumed, the tax burden can be spread over a large part of the population. There is, however, one major reason why direct taxes on incomes would be desirable. A large part of the money income of the nation is received by Chinese and other foreigners. A substantial portion of the savings of this group leaves the country as dividends and personal remittances. Income taxes would be desirable because they would fall most heavily on this group which is now lightly taxed in comparison with the Thai. It is difficult to enforce income taxes, however, because of inability to enforce proper accounting methods. This is particularly true of Chinese partnerships and proprietorships.[14]

In view of the necessity to encourage enterprise, it might be better for the government to keep income-tax rates low and to rely on other measures for discouraging remittances. The question is a difficult one, however, because of the equity argument for taxes on income. If the problem were merely to finance ordinary expenditures, progressive income taxes might be indicated on the grounds of equity. But since the problem is to encourage capital formation, excise taxes and import duties are indicated because they discourage consumption and at the same time leave large incomes more intact.

In the postwar period the Thai government borrowed abroad for the first time since 1924. All of the loans were obtained from other governments, not the private capital market. In 1946 Thailand received a credit of $10,000,000 at 2⅜-percent interest from the United States, and one from India of *Rs.* 50,000,000 at 3 percent. Only $6,200,000 of the U.S. credit was drawn, and the Indian credit was repaid in full in 1949. These loans were used to finance essential imports at the end of the war, when Thailand had no foreign-exchange reserve to draw upon.

In the latter part of 1950 the World Bank lent Thailand $25,400,000 to cover the foreign-exchange costs of developmental projects. Of the total, $18,000,000 was provided for the great Chainat irrigation project to harness the Chao Phya River in the Central Plain; $3,000,000 for railway reconstruction; and $4,400,000 for development of the port of Bangkok.

One great advantage of these loans is that advice and technical assistance is provided by the World Bank and co-operating UN agencies. In addition,

---

14 This may be one reason why the government increased the alien registration fee from 20 to 400 baht per person per year in 1952. Aliens between the ages of 16 and 60 are liable. Opposition from the Chinese has been bitter. (The tax applies only to immigrants. All persons born in Thailand are Thai nationals.)

the Bank exercises some control over the operations of the projects and requires a careful accounting of the funds expended. Such safeguards are important in view of the nature of administration in Thailand.

These projects are all vital to the economy. Irrigation we have discussed already. The railways suffered from bombing and lack of maintenance during the war, and their reduced capacity has been a distinct handicap to postwar recovery. The port project involves dredging the bar at the mouth of the Chao Phya River to enable larger ships to come up the river to Bangkok (about 30 miles inland). In the past, large ships have had to anchor at Koh-si-chang, an island in the Gulf of Thailand, and expensive lighterage charges have had to be paid. The project also includes improvement of facilities at the port itself. Increases in port revenues are expected to repay the cost of the project. In addition, there will be indirect benefits in the form of lower cost of imports and increased tourist trade.

It seems likely that the government will rely on foreign capital for at least a part of the foreign-exchange costs of future developmental projects. In early 1952 it announced that an application would be made for another World Bank loan to finance hydroelectric projects. Apparently the government prefers to borrow at low interest rates rather than to utilize its own reserves of foreign exchange. In this way, valuable technical assistance is secured, and there is less danger of loss of confidence in the baht—a result which could follow a change in the traditional policy of maintaining 100-percent reserves against notes in circulation.

Greater use has been made of internal loans in recent years, but government institutions continue to hold most of the bonds and treasury bills issued. The securities are not purchased by individuals and private firms to any great extent.

9

Government Expenditures
1850–1950

In view of the scarcity of private capital for investment purposes and the importance of the Thai government as an entrepreneur, the capital expenditures of government take on a critical significance. Limitations on the ability of the government to direct funds into productive purposes greatly restrict its ability to aid and encourage economic development. In this chapter we shall describe the size of expenditures, their relation to revenue, and some determinants of the share allocated to capital investment. Fortunately, "ordinary" and "capital" expenditures have been budgeted separately for the most part, and it is possible to distinguish between them (see Appendix B).

The Size of Expenditures

Generally speaking, expenditures have been limited by the amount of revenue available. We saw in Chapter 8 how the government had to struggle for many years to get rid of limitations on its fiscal autonomy. These limitations slowed the growth of revenue and thereby also slowed the growth of expenditures. Some expenditures were made from the proceeds of foreign loans (and, more recently, internal loans as well), but the sums borrowed were relatively small in relation to total expenditures.

In other words, revenues have been the autonomous or independent variable, expenditures the dependent. But revenues in turn have been limited by noneconomic circumstances outside the control of the government itself—that is, by treaty provisions. The result has been that expenditures on worthwhile projects have frequently had to be postponed because the government was unable to increase revenue, unwilling or unable to borrow abroad, unable to borrow internally, and unwilling to finance projects simply by creating money.

In short, Thailand has been extremely faithful to the principle of finance which asserts that expenditures should be covered by revenues in each fiscal year. Until the outbreak of World War II, expenditures from foreign loans were virtually the only exception made to this rule.

From 1850 to 1892, the accounts of receipts and expenditures were not published, if indeed any were kept. No foreign or domestic loans were sought in this period, however, and no fiat money issued. The government budget therefore had to be balanced, although a surplus may have been accumulated in some years and spent in others.

From 1892 to 1950, ordinary revenue exceeded ordinary expenditures in nearly every year except in the early 1920's and during World War II (for yearly figures see Appendix B). The policy of the government was to balance the budget on ordinary account, and this policy was faithfully adhered to. As revenues increased, there was pressure to increase expenditures also, but in most years ordinary expenditures were sufficiently restricted to yield a surplus. Exceptional circumstances existed in the two periods in which the ordinary budget ran a deficit. In the 1920's the aftereffects of the postwar crisis and the extravagance of the royal court were chiefly responsible for the deficits. In World War II large defense expenditures and inflationary pressures arising from Japanese expenditures were responsible. Only in such extreme circumstances did the government break its rule.

Until 1904/5, capital expenditures on railway construction were also met from ordinary revenue, and in many years a surplus still remained to be added to the treasury reserve. Beginning in 1905, foreign loans were secured to finance capital expenditures, and from 1905 through 1926 a large part of such expenditures was made from loan proceeds. Not all was, however. During World War I a foreign loan could not be arranged, and capital expenditures on railways and irrigation were made from revenue and from the accumulated treasury reserve. These expenditures were largely covered by the increased revenues of the war period, but the crop failure and silver crisis at the end of the war resulted in heavy exchange losses which had to be charged against the treasury reserve. Because of these losses and the series of budget deficits from 1920 to 1925, two foreign loans were floated in 1922 and 1924 to bolster the exchange position of the nation. The alleged purpose of these loans was to replenish the treasury reserve for capital expenditures made from it during the war. Actually, ordinary revenue sufficed to cover wartime capital expenditures, and the loan became necessary only after the postwar crisis appeared.

When King Rama VII came to the throne in 1925, he launched an economy drive designed to reduce expenditures and to put the government's finances on a sound basis. His Majesty's civil list was cut from 9 million baht to 6 million baht as a first step, salaries were cut, and various other economy measures were adopted. The successful revision of foreign treaties helped by providing sources of increased revenues. As a result of these measures, the budget was balanced, capital expenditures were financed from revenue, and a reserve for debt redemption was accumulated.[1]

From 1924 to 1941, no more foreign loans were secured. Both ordinary and capital expenditures were made from revenue, or from the treasury

---

[1] This reserve was in addition to regular appropriations for amortization of the loans.

reserve, except for internal loans made in 1933 and 1940. All through the depression, except in fiscal 1931/32, the government maintained a surplus on ordinary account even though revenues fell drastically. Some capital expenditures in this period (1926–41) were made from reserves, bringing protests from the Financial Adviser, but most capital expenditures were covered by revenues (see Appendix B).[2]

During World War II, the government incurred deficits on ordinary account because of heavy defense expenditures and because inflation pushed expenditures up faster than revenues.[3] Since the war, revenue has more than covered ordinary expenditure, leaving a surplus on ordinary account. But capital expenditures have been large enough to convert these surpluses into deficits. The deficits have been financed partly from internal loans, partly from foreign loans, and partly from United States economic aid (since 1950). Because no private bond market exists in Thailand, when treasury bonds are issued they are usually sold to the Bank of Thailand. This is tantamount to direct creation of money, and it has been avoided as much as possible.

Expenditures have increased vastly in terms of baht. From 168 million baht in 1941, ordinary expenditures increased to 967 million in 1947, and to 2,169 million in 1951. Much, but not all, of this increase is accounted for by inflation. Part is attributable to a growth in the services and functions of government. Capital expenditures have also increased as the government has enlarged its role. From a prewar peak of 37 million baht in 1941, capital expenditures rose to 611 million in 1951.

Modern notions of fiscal policy as an instrument for controlling economic activity have played little or no part in Thai finance. One reason is that the level of agricultural employment has not fallen in depressed years, while most nonagricultural labor was Chinese and the government was not greatly concerned about them. Also important is the fact that a balanced budget has been dictated both by external factors and domestic resources. In recent years increasing pressure on the government to finance developmental projects has resulted in capital deficits. These may be expected to continue, and the government will doubtless continue its efforts to cover such deficits by foreign loans and economic aid.

The Nature of Expenditures

The bulk of ordinary expenditures have of course been used for routine administration of the government. We shall not attempt a critical discussion

---

[2] "Capital expenditures" as used here does not include many capital items which were charged to revenue. Thus the government's "capital" account contained no provision for buildings, city streets, much road building, the telegraph system, etc.

[3] The large sums of money turned over to the Japanese have not been treated as government expenditures in the Thai accounts. If these sums were counted, the wartime deficits would be enormous.

of all the various items of expenditure; instead, we wish merely to show the relative importance of certain significant items.

An interesting comparison can be made of the amounts spent on education and on defense. Because of Thailand's highly centralized administration, virtually all expenditures for education are made by the central government. Furthermore, there are few privately financed schools. Formerly, schools conducted by priests in the numerous temples throughout Thailand were an important part of the educational system. These temple schools, which were operated with little or no financial aid from the central government, have been declining in relative importance in recent years.

"Defense" expenditures as used here include all expenditures for army, navy, and air force, but *not* police forces. Certain defense appropriations which were charged to "capital account" have been included here along with the ordinary appropriations.

TABLE XVI

SELECTED GOVERNMENT EXPENDITURES

Year	Amount (Million Baht)			Percentage of Total Ordinary Expenditures		
	Defense	Education	Royal	Defense	Education	Royal
1892	3.36	0.30	3.75	26	2	29
1900	4.08	1.01	6.15	14	4	22
1910	13.69	1.25	10.37	24	2	18
1920	21.52	2.34	9.79	27	3	12
1930	18.41	6.68	6.94	20	7	8
1935	23.16	9.38	1.30	27	11	2
1941	59.66	17.13	0.96	36	10	0.6
1945	211.11	21.15	1.67	51	5	0.4
1949[a]	450.00	170.00	10.00	28	11	0.6

[a] Figures for 1949 have been adjusted to include an estimated portion of the salary supplements paid to government employees.

Sources: *Statistical Year Books of Thailand; Reports of the Financial Advisers* for the years concerned.

Table XVI shows that defense expenditures have consistently exceeded those for education. The former have averaged about 25 percent of the total in the constitutional regime as well as in the period of the absolute monarchy, although the percentage has varied from year to year. The percentage spent for education, on the other hand, has slowly but steadily increased ever since 1892, except for the years after World War II. Even when revenues and expenditures dropped during the depression, the appropriation for education increased. The increase was slow, however, and public education remains extremely inadequate. While improvement in public education cannot take place overnight because teachers must be trained and facilities provided, the lack of funds has undoubtedly hampered education in Thailand. The rate of growth has been limited by available funds rather than by physical limits of personnel or facilities.

The amount of defense expenditures has also increased steadily since 1900. Only in the depression years of the 1930's did it drop appreciably, and even then the *ratio* to total ordinary expenditures did not drop much. That defense expenditures have stayed around 20–25 percent of the total for so long suggests that the military were quite powerful under the monarchy, as under the constitutional regime. The ratio did not drop even in the relatively peaceful decade of the 1920's, during the first part of which treasury reserves were quite low because of exchange losses and budget deficits. Appropriations for irrigation and road building were held to around 2 million baht each, but defense expenditures did not drop below 20 million baht during this decade.

Since World War II, large appropriations for defense purposes have continued. The percentage of these to total ordinary expenditures has remained above 25 percent, and the preliminary budget for 1952 allotted 40 percent for defense.

Another interesting item is "Royal" expenditures. This includes His Majesty's civil list, private drawing account, travel expenses, upkeep of palaces, and expenses of the royal household. As Table XVI shows, royal expenditure continued to represent a considerable part of the total until 1932, when the advent of a constitutional government sharply reduced the privileges of the Crown.

Even before 1932, royal expenditures had formed a steadily decreasing percentage of total expenditures. The percentage declined because other expenditures were increasing rather than because the kings reduced theirs. For example, King Rama VI has the reputation of an extravagant monarch. He increased the civil list, increased his own allowances, and ran up debts of several million baht by the time he died; but he still spent a smaller *percentage* of total expenditures than did his father. When King Rama VII came to the throne, he made sharp cuts in the civil list and in his personal expenditures. Royal expenditures dropped from an average of about 10 million baht per year under King Rama VI to about 7 million under King Rama VII. By 1935 royal expenditures were reduced to around one million baht. Since then they have been a small item in the total budget.

The greater part of governmental machinery is located in Bangkok, and most government employees work there. Salaries of such employees form the largest single item of expenditure. Since 1941 salaries have lagged behind the cost of living. To alleviate this condition, which was encouraging graft and undermining the civil service, salary supplements were paid, beginning in 1946. These soon exceeded the basic salaries and it became clear that a revision of the scale was necessary. This was done in 1952.

Capital Expenditures

The capital expenditures of government are of such great importance that we will devote a separate section to a discussion of their size, the type of projects chosen, the method of financing, and the major factors limiting the amount of capital invested.

During the fifty-year period 1892–1941, capital expenditures averaged about 7.6 million baht per year, equal to 11 percent of ordinary expenditures. This statement refers to the capital expenditures which can be separated from ordinary expenditures. Many capital items cannot be separated because the accounts are not available. The yearly figures varied a great deal from the over-all average for the period (see Appendix B for yearly data). Generally speaking, capital expenditures were highest just before and just after World War I, when work on both the northern and southern railway lines was pushed, and irrigation work was started. They then declined until the late 1930's, when a new peak was reached.

Since 1941 the value of the baht has changed so drastically that comparison with previous periods is difficult. Capital expenditures rose from 21 million baht in 1942 to 611 million baht in 1951. That this probably represents a substantial real increase would seem to be indicated by the fact that the latter amount represented 28 percent of ordinary expenditures.

During most of the period since 1892, the government's capital expenditures were made for public-works projects, the largest and most important of which were railways and irrigation. These two projects, plus the Bangkok water works and the government power station, were the only ones financed by the government until the constitutional regime began to expand the role of the government in the 1930's.[4] Except for the irrigation works, all these projects were expected to pay for themselves in time. Thus, it was no accident that highway construction was retarded, and that those highways constructed did not compete with the railway. Highways could not be made to pay for themselves directly, but railways could. The government definitely seems to have used the *direct* return as one criterion for allocating capital—at least before 1932. One reason for the delay in authorizing irrigation works was the lack of a direct return.

Since the advent of the constitutional regime, many proposals have been made for government capital investment in a number of different industries and projects. Small amounts have been used for a wide range of purposes, but the major items are still railways, irrigation, and roads. The government

---

[4] The relatively small amounts spent on the paper factory, the telegraph system, roads, on developing the silk industry, etc., were charged to ordinary expenditures during the monarchy.

has taken the initiative in developing several domestic industries, but the results have so far been small. For the last twenty years, however, the trend has been distinctly in the direction of larger participation by the government in trade and production, and this trend seems likely to continue. The issue of public vs. private ownership of industry has never been very keenly debated in Thailand. For one thing, everybody was aware that if the government remained neutral, business and industry would remain in the hands of Chinese and other foreigners. Nevertheless, under the monarchy the government tended to follow a laissez faire policy. Such a policy was in part imposed by foreign treaties. But when the government saw that it had to act, as in the case of railways, no allegiance to laissez faire doctrine hindered government ownership and operation.

Some ideological discussion took place in the 1930's, most of which centered around the allegedly socialistic schemes of Nai Pridi Phanomyong, one of the leaders of the revolution in 1932. Not even Pridi's strongest opponents appear to have wanted to exclude government from ownership of industry, however. Most criticism of government efforts centers on its inefficiency. Thus the Tobacco Monopoly is praised while the government-operated sugar and paper mills are condemned.

Until 1932, the capital account of government listed only railway construction, irrigation, water works, and electric power, but since then it has included appropriations for such things as distilleries, paper mills, cotton mills, sugar factories, promotion of cotton cultivation, co-operatives, cottage industries, vocational education, slaughterhouses, and port facilities. The amounts appropriated for such purposes are still quite small in comparison to those for railways, irrigation, and highways, but limits are fixed by trained personnel and funds rather than by doctrinal objections to government in business.

Of the total capital expenditures in the period 1892–1941, about 25 percent was financed by foreign loans, the rest from domestic sources (principally ordinary revenues). Thailand has a spotless record as a debtor; all of the loans were repaid in full. No serious transfer problem appears to have arisen in either direction. The yearly transfers were quite small, however.

Capital expenditures were limited, as we have seen, by revenue, by unwillingness (or inability) to borrow additional sums at home or abroad, by a conservative monetary and fiscal policy which required substantial reserves to be maintained by the government, and by failure to reduce nonessential ordinary expenditures.

In many ways the government's policy appears to have been shortsighted. Through the provision of additional public services such as transportation, power, and irrigation, the national income and the revenues of government could have been increased more rapidly, thus making further investment possible. A risk factor was involved, however, and it must have been heavily weighted. That is, the government was careful not to endanger its political independence by borrowing heavily or letting reserves get low enough to threaten international solvency in case of a crop failure or other catastrophe.

Another factor which acted to retard capital expenditure was foreign economic and diplomatic pressure. Thailand's monetary policy was largely designed to maintain the exchange value of the baht, and the nation's reserves were mobilized for this purpose. The revenues of government were also restricted by foreign treaties. These factors influenced expenditures, and in addition there was the restraining influence of the Financial Adviser, who was one of the most powerful figures in the government until about 1930. Without his approval a foreign loan could probably not have been marketed successfully, and the government could scarcely have carried out any financial measures to which he had strong objections. On the whole, the entire line of Financial Advisers (1896–1950) favored conservative monetary and fiscal policies.

W. D. Reeve, in his interesting essay on administration in Thailand, wrote that some foreign advisers, either from the force of their personalities or the diffidence of the ministers, became the *de facto* heads of their ministries.[5] Apparently this was not true of the Ministry of Finance, which has had a number of able ministers, but the Financial Adviser was nevertheless a powerful figure whose advice could not conveniently be ignored. And, as a matter of fact, Thailand has been so determined to preserve her independence that any advice which would contribute to the attainment of that goal would have been gladly accepted.

Nevertheless, any unnecessary postponement or curtailment of developmental projects which took place because of such direct or indirect pressures represents a cost to the nation.

The history of irrigation in Thailand provides an example of the postponement of developmental works to the ultimate detriment of the nation. We saw in Chapter 4 that unsatisfactory conditions in the Central Plain in 1898–99 led to an investigation by the Minister of Agriculture and the creation of a Department of Irrigation. In 1902 J. H. Van der Heide was brought in to study the irrigation needs of the country, but neither his original plan, published in 1903, nor any of his subsequent, reduced schemes was ever sanctioned. Finally, after a last scheme was rejected in 1909, he resigned and the Department of Irrigation was abolished until several years of poor water supply forced the government to revive it.

When Van der Heide's first scheme came before the government in 1903, the baht had just been linked to gold at a fixed exchange rate. Revenue was just enough to cover ordinary expenditures and the cost of railway construction. Since 1892 a treasury reserve had been accumulated from revenue sur-

---

[5] *Public Administration in Siam* (Oxford University Press, 1951), pp. 33–35.

pluses, but after 1901/2 no surplus had been earned. In 1903 the financial situation was as follows:

Item	Million Baht
Revenue	43.5
Ordinary expenditures	40.8
Capital expenditures	3.1
Treasury reserve	20–21
Foreign debt	0
Internal debt	0

A new Financial Adviser, W. J. F. Williamson, had just assumed his duties. In one of his first reports he urged a cautious policy to correct the "danger of such a situation" as existed in 1903.[6] He recommended that part of the proceeds of a proposed sterling loan be put in the treasury reserve to bring it up to 22 million baht, that one million baht be budgeted to an "emergency reserve fund," and that the budget should be framed so as to make certain that a surplus would be achieved. Furthermore, he said that although more money could usefully be expended, expenditures might even have to be *reduced* in order to avoid "financial embarrassment."

With that program, the adviser naturally opposed the irrigation scheme, which was to cost 4 million baht per year. He wrote as follows:

It is, in my opinion, impossible to think of embarking . . . upon the gigantic Irrigation project lately submitted by the Ministry of Agriculture: I do not think that project can be thought of for very many years to come. It will be as much as we can do to go on cleaning out some of the old Canals every year and that can very well be done with the supervision of a single European Engineer. Before we can think of a great Irrigation scheme we must provide funds for the strategic Railways which are essential if the outlying Provinces are to be properly governed. Those Railways must be constructed out of borrowed capital and *I am altogether averse to borrowing money for Irrigation* at present in addition to money for Railway Construction. Such a course would be rash in the extreme.[7]

The full scheme was rejected by the government in 1903, as was a smaller-scale plan submitted at the same time. The government authorized the Irrigation Department to go on cleaning and dredging old canals, and gave it a small appropriation for the purpose..

In 1906 the whole question of irrigation came before the government again. Van der Heide submitted a plan for "irrigation at reduced capacity," calling for a total expenditure of 24 million baht and designed to pay for itself

---

[6] "Memorandum by the Financial Adviser upon the Cash Balances of the Government," unpublished report submitted to the Minister of Finance in 1903 (10 pp.). In the files of the Financial Adviser, Ministry of Finance, Bangkok.

[7] *Loc. cit.* (Italics added.)

from lock fees and land taxes in nineteen years.[8] The council of ministers concerned itself with two questions: how to populate the irrigated area, and where to get the money for the scheme. The council finally decided to postpone the scheme for at least two years.

We have no record of Williamson's position, but the chances are that he opposed the plan. When the Irrigation Department tried once again in 1908 to obtain permission to go ahead with two much smaller projects, Williamson still disapproved. The combined cost of these two projects was only 6 million baht, but, after expressing his disagreement with Van der Heide as to which of the two should be undertaken first, Williamson wrote:

> To my mind it has not yet been satisfactorily shown that new irrigation works are required in Siam, except as feeders to already existing systems, owing to the want of sufficiently dense population, and *I have consequently always been opposed* to the Government committing itself to any of Mr. Van der Heide's ambitious projects. The policy hitherto followed, of confining the energies of the Irrigation Department to the improvement of canals already in existence, has, therefore, commended itself to me, and I see no reason for any departure therefrom in the present circumstances of the country.[9]

Turning to the question of financing the proposed projects, Williamson observed that the funds would have to come from the recent sterling loan, but that the available balance was not adequate. Of the net proceeds of £2,797,500, £932,500 was earmarked for the exchange-stabilization fund, and another £500,000 was temporarily pledged to that fund. This left only £1,365,000 for capital investment, and £930,000 had already been used for railway construction. The remainder was also allocated to the railways. In short, irrigation could not be financed because over half of the 1907 loan was used to support the exchange. The irrigation schemes were rejected.

A few months later, when he was working on the budget for the next fiscal year (1909/10), Williamson recommended a reduction in the *regular* appropriation for the Irrigation Department, which had been running about one million baht per year. He was concerned about a possible deficit on current account, and he said:

> The Irrigation Department, despite its name, is at present, and has been from the time of its inception, engaged almost entirely in improving the system of water communication, as represented by the klongs of the country. To a certain extent the dredging of the klongs improves the drainage of the cultivable areas, but the main benefit which the operations of the Irrigation Department bestow upon the

---

[8] *Project Estimate for Works of Irrigation, Drainage and Navigation to Develop the Plain of Central Siam*, Thailand, Royal Irrigation Department (Bangkok, 1915), III, 16–19.

[9] W. J. F. Williamson, "Further Proposed Schemes of Irrigation Department," a memorandum to H.R.H., the Minister of Finance, dated August 14, 1908 (typewritten, 6 pp.). In the files of the Financial Adviser, Ministry of Finance, Bangkok. (Italics added.)

people is to make it easier for them to move about by water and bring their produce to market.[10]

In view of the fact that Williamson was largely responsible for limiting the department to this role, his criticism of it on that ground hardly seems justified.

The appropriation was cut and it stayed at a reduced level until work began in 1916 on the projects designed by Sir Thomas Ward. By that time the war prevented the use of foreign capital, and irrigation works were financed from revenue.

Williamson does not seem to have resisted Ward's schemes. He remained Financial Adviser until 1924, and from 1916 to 1924 the work went on. Irrigation has never been pushed very rapidly, however. The total capital expenditure for irrigation works in the twenty-five years ending in 1940 was only 47 million baht, an average of slightly less than 2 million baht per year.

Considering the compelling case for irrigation in Thailand, the reluctance of the government and its advisers to undertake the major projects is strange. As late as 1950 only 4 million rai out of a total cultivated area of about 36 million rai were irrigated, and for fifty years appropriations for the Department of Irrigation had limited it to a modest scale of operations, which meant that the full advantages of irrigation could not be secured.

There are several possible reasons for the delay. First, irrigation could not easily be made to pay for itself directly. Farmers were not accustomed to paying for the water which came to their fields from the distribution canals, and they would not have understood why they should pay for water supplied to them in years of low rainfall. Such water would come through the same canals. At any rate, the government was of the opinion that it was not practicable to charge fees for irrigation services rendered to farmers in the Central Plain.[11] In the North, where co-operative schemes had long involved a money cost to individual farmers, fees were considered practicable, but the Central Plain was always first in the minds of irrigation planners.[12] The fact that irrigation could not be made to pay for itself directly made it less attractive

[10] W. J. F. Williamson, "Memorandum on the Financial Position Created by the Present and Prospective Public Indebtedness of the Government," dated February 27, 1909 (typewritten, 9 pp.). In the files of the Financial Adviser, Ministry of Finance, Bangkok.

[11] Van der Heide's original scheme provided for sale of both water and land, and in this way he tried to make irrigation pay for itself. When irrigation projects were eventually undertaken after the Ward report, these features were removed because they were contrary to tradition. The FAO Mission to Thailand in 1948 again recommended that a charge be made for irrigation services, and plans are being made to do so when the Chainat project is completed.

[12] In 1932, when top government officials turned down a proposed project in Chiengmai province, the gist of their objections was that the Central Plain should have priority because after all Chiengmai "was very far from Bangkok." From minutes of the 20th (Special) Meeting of the Board of Commercial Development, January 5, 1932. In the files of the Financial Adviser, Ministry of Finance, Bangkok.

to the government than projects such as railways, electricity, and water works, which did promise a direct return.

Second, the benefits of irrigation were not as striking as in countries such as Egypt. Here was no desert, suddenly to be converted into fertile land. Instead, most of the land which it was proposed to irrigate was already under cultivation. Furthermore, in good years the land yielded as much as it would yield with irrigation. The argument for irrigation was that the risk of crop failure resulting from seasonal and yearly variation in rainfall would be lessened by achieving more control over the water supply. This was a powerful argument, but it suffered from the fact that an estimate could not be made of the increased production which would result. In good years, perhaps no increase would result.

Third, when projects were designed to irrigate uncultivated land, opponents said that the population of Thailand was not large enough to cultivate the newly opened land. Proponents replied that the population was fast increasing, and that irrigation would enlarge the area a single farmer could cultivate, and thus increase the average income.

Finally, the resources of revenue and foreign capital available to the government were limited. Having decided how much it could spend, and presumably being unable to reduce ordinary expenditures, the government had to exclude some of the proposed projects. Because there were pressing political as well as economic arguments for railway construction, irrigation was consistently postponed. It was in this context that the influence of the Financial Adviser was important. But in view of the facts that revenue was limited partly by foreign treaties, that British Financial Advisers largely decided whether additional foreign loans were wise or not, and that Williamson obviously did not approve of irrigation in Thailand, a large measure of responsibility for the delay must be borne by him and by Britain, the dominant power in Thailand both politically and economically. Since World War II the government has not wished to move faster because of technical limits and because additional expenditures would increase inflationary pressures, already severe.

In spite of the above reasons, a sound economic case can be made for investment in irrigation works. A record of the river level at Ayuthia since 1827 indicated only 32 years of "ideal" water supply in 99 years. Of the remaining years, in 22 the water supply was fairly good, in 30 years it was low enough to damage crops considerably, and in 15 years it was too high. Furthermore, about once every 30 years a severe crop failure occurred because of an unusually bad drought or flood. While irrigation could not completely eliminate the influence of rainfall variation, engineers and agriculturists generally agree that it could reduce the harmful effect of the worst years and virtually eliminate the effect of the milder variations.

Obviously, the net gain from irrigation would vary a great deal from year to year. This fact makes it difficult both to compute the gain and to make a convincing case. One approach to the problem is through the "area damaged" statistics collected by the Ministry of Agriculture.[13] The following figures indicate the importance of the damaged area:[14]

Period	Percentage of Damaged to Planted Area
1910–14	3
1915–19	16
1920–24	8
1925–29	13
1930–34	10
1935–39	15
1940–44	15
1948–50	3

If we assume that the damaged area will average only 10 percent, and that the loss on this area is only 50 percent of the normal yield, it follows that some 5 percent of the yearly crop is lost because of damage. At the 1950 rate of production, this amounts to 3,800,000 piculs. If proper irrigation works were provided for the entire area planted in rice, a substantial part of this loss could be avoided.[15] Unfortunately, data are not available to enable us to compare the investment required for such full-scale works with the value of the probable average gain in rice production.

Such a computation would in any case omit many valuable direct and indirect benefits of irrigation. Yields would probably be increased and stabilized even on the area which is officially undamaged. The greater stability of harvests would reduce one of the major causes of rural indebtedness. Farmers would be able to cultivate more land because they would not have to wait for the rains to come before they begin plowing and planting. Second crops would become practicable in many areas, thus enabling the farmers to utilize the idle months after the rice harvest and perhaps also to improve the soil with legumes. Proper drainage could encourage animal husbandry in the cattle-deficient Central Plain. Finally, the revenues of the government would be increased in a number of ways.

[13] These statistics are not entirely satisfactory for the purpose, because they do not include all areas which would have benefited from a better water supply. Actually, they principally include the area which had to be replanted at the beginning of the season, and the area which was damaged before harvest to such an extent that over half the paddy was ruined. Much of the replanted area is harvested, and the loss consists merely of seed and labor. On the other hand, much minor damage is not reflected in the statistics.

[14] *Statistical Year Books of Thailand.* Figures for 1948–50 were supplied by the Department of Agriculture, Bangkok. The five-year averages conceal great variations in individual years.

[15] We do not assert that it would be wise to attempt to provide a system of controlled water supply for the entire rice area. Obviously, detailed studies of each region must be made to determine which can be handled economically and which cannot. Costs of irrigation per rai will vary greatly from region to region.

In spite of our inability to make exact calculations of cost and profit on a nation-wide basis, it seems clear that the social marginal productivity of irrigation in Thailand is quite high. For individual projects it is probably even higher. We have already mentioned the fact that the crop failure of 1919–20 alone reduced the rice exports in a single year by more than the estimated cost of Van der Heide's entire project for the Central Plain—and at that time nearly all exports came from the Central Plain.[16] The yearly average crop loss is not so dramatic, but it is a strong argument for irrigation.

We cannot put the blame for the postponement of irrigation works from 1903 to 1916 on Williamson alone. No doubt there were many other officials who disapproved of the scheme. Furthermore, Williamson may have had good noneconomic reasons for opposing additional foreign loans and for recommending the allocation of expenditures he did. All we wish to assert here is that the Financial Adviser did exert a conservative influence in the determination of capital expenditures. However, because of his position, the influence was probably a powerful one.

Other Financial Advisers continued the conservative tradition, although Williamson's successors seem to have encouraged productive investments such as irrigation, roads, and railways. Sir Edward Cook (1924–30) drafted a very conservative currency act, floated a loan at a high rate of interest to replenish the treasury reserves, and in the late 1920's built up a large debt-redemption reserve. James Baxter (1933–35) and W. M. A. Doll (1936–50) constantly urged the government to follow a cautious policy and to maintain high liquid reserves. On the whole, the government did continue to follow conservative monetary and fiscal policies, even though the power of the Financial Adviser has been waning. Since about 1930 the government has of its own volition followed rather conservative policies. Probably it has preferred such policies.

In recent years the government has been strongly inclined to increase developmental expenditures, but it has retained many aspects of the long tradition of conservative finance. Since World War II, a surplus on ordinary account has been maintained, capital deficits have been covered largely by foreign rather than internal loans, and the currency reserve has been steadily augmented and guarded against the raids of various ministries.*

The finances of the nation are sound and revenue is capable of being greatly increased through honest and efficient administration. If administration could be improved on both the collection and expenditure sides, the government should have sufficient funds to carry out a respectable number of the developmental projects which Thailand sorely needs.

---

[16] Van der Heide's estimate for irrigating the Central Plain was 47 million baht (Ward's in 1915 was 100–120 million baht). Rice exports were valued at 123 million baht in 1919/20, 29 million in 1920/21, and 141 million in 1921/22. However, the drought in 1919/20 was so severe that much damage would have occurred even if the projects had been completed.

* This passage is written from the perspective of 1951. See Ch. 12 for an account of financial policy since 1951.

10

The Development of an Exchange Economy
1850–1950

No empirical study can explain all: the semblance of this noble end is attained only by the use of imagination little restrained by specific data and unchanneled by the compulsion to formulate findings in terms that assure correspondence with empirically observed phenomena.[1]

IF THIS STATEMENT, which might well be taken as a motto for this chapter, applies to the study of Western nations, how much more valid it is for a study of Thailand, where statistics have never been taken seriously! In the preceding chapters an effort has been made to describe in a factual way the major economic changes of the last century. This description has been anchored to statistical evidence as securely as possible, although much of the evidence itself must be regarded with suspicion. In the following pages, an attempt will be made to analyze and explain some of the major economic developments. For this purpose statistics are often of little help or they are unavailable. Nevertheless, these are important matters, and we will venture to explore them in the hope that long immersion in the experience and problems of a nation may enable us to suggest relationships which are reasonable and explanatory even though they cannot always be established by empirical evidence.

The Balance of Payments and Its Adjustment, 1850–1950

As we saw in Chapter 7, Thailand has had an export surplus in commodity trade from 1850 to 1950. Between 1850 and 1941 she had an import surplus in only one year. That was in 1920/21, when very unusual circumstances interfered with the normal operation of the system. During and after World War II there were import surpluses, but by 1948 the export surplus was restored. Yearly trade figures are presented in Appendix C.

Commodity trade statistics refer to visible trade only. Little or no data on Thailand's invisible transactions exist, but it seems clear that invisible payments exceeded receipts on current account in this period, and perhaps on capital account as well in some years. Thailand had little income in the form of interest, dividends, travel and tourist expenditures, or personal remittances

---

[1] Simon Kuznets, "The State as a Unit in Economic Growth," *Journal of Economic History,* XI (Winter 1951), 26.

from abroad.[2] Expenditures for these items are much larger. Imports are valued c.i.f., and exports are sold f.o.b., so payments made for shipping and insurance are included in commodity trade figures.

One reason for Thailand's persistent export surplus is that foreigners receive a considerable portion of the export proceeds and choose to dispose of a good share of it by remittances in the form of interest, dividends, and personal remittances. Figures are not available, but the role of foreigners (including Chinese) in the tin and teak industries, in the marketing system, in banking, and in the entire commercial system makes it obvious that a large share of the money income of the nation must accrue to them.

One form of remittances has received much publicity in Thailand: namely, those sent by Chinese immigrants to their families in China. Various estimates—largely guesses—have been made of the magnitude of this item.[3] If these estimates are approximately correct, remittances have comprised a significant drain on the Thai economy. For example, if remittances averaged 25 million baht from 1890 to 1941, the total would have been about 1,250 million baht, compared to an aggregate investment in railways and irrigation through 1941 of about 250 million baht. The total amount of government capital expenditures from 1892 to 1941, including those financed from foreign loans, was only about 380 million baht. Had the remittances been invested in Thailand the addition to the national capital would obviously have been of considerable importance.

A different view is expressed by Landon, who has stated that the remittances probably amounted to not more than 2 percent of the "wealth" created by the Chinese, and not more than 10 percent of their net profits. He deprecates the significance of the remittances, lauds the Chinese for their energy and industriousness (which is not being questioned here), and says that "there would have been no progress without the Chinese."[4]

Remittances were also made by other foreigners. The amounts involved were probably smaller, however. Callis roughly estimated entrepreneur investments other than Chinese at U.S. $25 million in 1914, $75 million in 1930, and $90 million in 1938.[5] If profits remitted equaled 10 percent of investment, remittances were about 7 million baht in 1914, 17 million in 1930, and 20 million in 1938.

[2] Tourist expenditures have been larger since World War II, and the living expenditures of the expanding Western community now constitutes a substantial invisible receipt. In addition, remittances to China have been smaller since 1949. The statements in the text refer in a general way to the period 1850–1950.

[3] In 1912 and 1915 Chinese remittances were estimated at 26 and 30 million baht (£2 and £2.3 million) per year. From a letter to H.M. the King from Chao Phya Yomaraj, dated March 1, 1916, in the files of the Financial Adviser, Bangkok. In the 1930's they were estimated at 30–40 million baht (then £2.7–£3.6 million). From *Report of the Financial Adviser, 1936/7.*

[4] *The Chinese in Thailand* (New York, 1941), pp. 43–45.

[5] H. G. Callis, *Foreign Capital in Southeast Asia* (New York, 1942), p. 70. "Rentier" investments have consisted solely of Thai government bonds.

Judging from trade figures and scanty information about invisibles, Thailand's trade surplus has thus been required to pay for a deficit of invisible current items, the largest of which has been the remittances of individuals and firms. Capital imports have been small and sporadic, and never large enough to turn the trade balance passive. There have been some capital exports, chiefly purchases of foreign securities by the wealthy class.

Sometimes the remittances of Chinese are referred to as capital items and, if this definition were adopted, Thailand would probably have been a net capital exporter over most of the century we are examining![6] It is in this sense that these remittances may be considered a drain on the Thai economy. Obviously a borrowing nation must expect to service its borrowed capital through payments of interest and dividends, and presumably the marginal value product of the capital equals or exceeds the service costs. But as a rule the Chinese did not import capital; they came as penniless immigrants, and from their wages and trading profits they accumulated money savings to remit to China. It may be argued that the marginal value product of the inflowing labor and entrepreneurship exceeded the remittances, and that these are comparable to the service of imported capital. Yet the division of functions between Thai and Chinese, plus the tendency of the latter to remit their savings to China, meant that a substantial part of the money savings of the population of Thailand was transferred abroad. This is of the nature of a capital export, though it may not be classified as such in the balance of payments. And, while no clear-cut logical distinction can be drawn between payments of interest and dividends to service foreign capital imports and personal remittances made by imported labor, a practical difference exists: that is, a significant part of the population did not consider Thailand as their permanent abode for the purpose of saving-investment decisions. Had they done so (as many did), their savings would have contributed to capital formation in Thailand. Those who planned eventually to return to China also tended to avoid long-term investments. (Suppose immigrants to the United States had remitted most of their savings to Europe and returned there to retire. Surely the economic development of the United States would have been slower than it was if this had been the usual pattern instead of the exceptional case.)

Thailand apparently has not followed the pattern of "stages" of development suggested by various writers. In most of these theoretical schemes, the underdeveloped country is supposed to run a deficit in its balance of payments in the first stage of development, and to import capital on balance.[7]

---

[6] The International Monetary Fund defines capital items as "those representing changes in the international creditor-debtor position of the reporting country and in its monetary gold holdings." *Balance of Payments Yearbook*, 1948–49, p. 7. Even under this definition Chinese remittances are not as easy to classify as (say) those made by Italians in the United States. In many cases the Chinese remitter is investing for his future, in a sense.

[7] For example, see C. P. Kindleberger, *The Dollar Shortage* (New York, 1950), Ch. 6.

We cannot offer much explanation for the small amount of foreign capital to enter Thailand. In Chapter 6 we mentioned several factors which retarded the development of manufacturing industry. These factors—lack of power, inadequate transportation, small size of the Thai market, inland-transit duties on domestically-produced goods, lack of reliable supplies of raw materials, virtually free import of foreign goods—may also have deterred the inflow of foreign capital.

It may be interesting to examine the reasons why Thailand has been able so consistently to maintain a commodity export surplus even though her major export has been a crop subject to variable harvests. Even when large decreases in exports have occurred, in nearly every case imports have fallen enough to leave an export surplus. We shall try to describe the mechanism of adjustment which has operated to reduce imports so promptly.

In the first place, decreases in exports have been caused almost entirely by natural events or by external factors such as a slump in world markets for those exports. Such decreases may therefore be considered as autonomous as far as the Thai economy is concerned. Since exports comprise one of the largest sources of money income, when exports decrease the money income of the nation is immediately decreased by the same amount (or more). Compared to exports, both private domestic investment and government expenditures are relatively small.[8]

Imports, on the other hand, are highly dependent on income. We saw in Chapter 6 that they consist largely of goods which can be dispensed with when income falls. The broad subsistence base of the economy enables the bulk of the population quickly to reduce purchases of imported goods when income falls without as painful a reduction in the standard of living as would occur in a country such as Britain. The climate and traditional consumption habits of the people, as well as the small margin of liquid savings among the bulk of the population, also facilitate the reduction of imports. Because the rice harvest at the end of a calendar year is the source of exports for the *next* year, importers can easily adjust their orders to suit the expected volume of exports. The fact that most imports are supplied through Hong Kong and Singapore means that importers can quickly adjust the size of their orders to the demand.

The mechanism of adjustment appears to be simple and direct, and most of the work is done through the income effect. Exports fall, reducing money income. When money income falls, imports fall. The multiplier effect through an induced fall in private domestic investment is probably negligible because investment itself is insignificant, but in any case it would tend in the same direction, i.e., toward a reduction in income and imports. Some multiplier effect through induced falls in domestic consumption and government ex-

[8] Compare Appendixes B and C for the relative size of exports and government expenditures. No estimates of private domestic investment are available, but from the nature of the economy it is presumed to be insignificant.

penditures may appear, but the chief influence is through the direct effect of exports on income.

The price effect also appears to be negligible. World prices would not be affected noticeably by changes occurring in Thailand, and there are few industries in Thailand offering direct competition to imports. The fall in income might tend to depress domestic prices and augment the reduction of imports, but this probably constitutes a minor part of the entire adjustment.

The process has not been hindered or delayed by actions taken by the government. When payments exceed receipts on international account, the Treasury sells foreign exchange for baht and the money in circulation is reduced in the same amount. No offsetting is attempted. Indeed, on several occasions (e.g., 1930–33) when exports fell sharply, the government reduced its expenditures enough to show a surplus and thereby accentuated the reduction in the money supply. In not trying to offset deflationary forces, the government has been obedient to the "rules of the game" of the gold-exchange standard.

Another reason for the flexibility of the adjustment process is the fact that fixed contractual obligations payable in money are not of much importance in Thailand. Such items as wages, salaries, rent, and insurance, which are fixed in terms of money in Western nations and perhaps protected by contract or union activity, are quite unimportant in Thailand. The bulk of the people do not have fixed money incomes of any kind, nor do they have many fixed obligations. With 85 percent of the labor force engaged in rice cultivation as individual proprietors, when the crop fails or prices fall, the reduction in income is direct. The service trades and crafts which have developed in the villages (e.g., food vendors and sampan coffee shops) lose many of their customers, and the operators are reabsorbed into the subsistence economy of the rice village which most had never left except to follow a part-time occupation. The incomes of middlemen and trades also depend directly on exports. The absence of fixed monetary obligations and rigid prices accounts for much of the flexibility and ease of adjustment in the balance of trade.

Finally, the adjustment process is flexible because of the lack of fixed, invisible payment items in the balance of payments. Remittances in particular are very responsive to income charges.

This discussion of the mechanism of adjustment in the balance of payments suggests that the Thai marginal propensity to import is relatively high, and that a tendency toward an adverse balance of trade resulting from a fall in exports will be corrected rapidly through a reduction in income and imports. Government action or inaction has encouraged this adjustment in the past. (A rise in exports would start the reverse sequence.)

Thailand has so far had little or no experience with tendencies toward an adverse trade balance resulting from domestic investment programs. Because of her high marginal propensity to import, an expansion of domestic investment would quickly result in an increase in imports. Besides direct imports of equipment and supplies, part of the increased incomes resulting from domestic expenditure would be spent for imports. The ratio of investment to foreign exchange requirements[9] would thus be relatively low for two reasons: high marginal propensity to import and the necessity to import capital equipment. If Thailand undertakes large investment programs in the future, she may begin to experience balance-of-payments difficulties.

In the past such difficulties have not arisen because of the very low level of domestic investment, both public and private. Perhaps Thailand has not yet entered the first stage in the "cycle" of development referred to above.

Resource Allocation

Between 1850 and 1950 the economy of Thailand became increasingly commercialized. From a basically barter and subsistence economy it has steadily turned toward greater use of trade and money exchange. We suggested in previous chapters that a major reason for this was the existence of a strong money demand in the world market for rice and other products. At the same time, the opening of Thailand to the free import of foreign merchandise served to encourage production to earn a money income.

During the century commercialization did not penetrate into all parts of the country in the same degree. In some villages and provinces the people still have little contact with world or national markets. Instead, they satisfy most of their wants themselves and eke out a meager subsistence from their farms and the forests around them. Even in such villages, however, there is some trade. Textiles, kerosene, and other luxuries are brought in by traders, and a few local agricultural or forest products are sold in exchange.

Even in the more commercialized sections, most of the population continued to specialize in rice cultivation throughout the whole of the century. This made them less dependent on the money economy than they might have been. Many features of the self-sufficient, pre-1850 economy continued to exist. Farmers supplied most of their own food in the form of rice and fish, and produced a large part of their requirements of fuel, furniture, housing, and household implements. Many of these items required no money payment, although some exchange and part-time specialization of production existed at the village level.

The trend has been for the money economy to spread over the country and embrace a larger and larger portion of the total population. The degree of penetration has been greatest in the Central Plain and, next to that, along the railways, the seacoasts, and wherever transportation facilities are good.

As households began to sell a larger part of their production to get money

---

[9] This is called the "expansion ratio" by J. J. Polak, in "Balance of Payments Problems of Countries Reconstructing with the Help of Foreign Loans," *Quarterly Journal of Economics*, LVII (February 1943), 208–40.

with which to buy a larger part of their requirements, people became more familiar with—and more dependent on—money and monetary calculations. This knowledge and experience may make the population more responsive to monetary incentives as time goes on.

The above summary refers to the role of the great bulk of the Thai population. Other roles, such as those of merchants, middlemen, wage labor in industry and trade, management and entrepreneurship in commerce and industry, and banking, were left largely to foreigners, chiefly Chinese.[10]

In this section we will endeavor to explain why this division of labor arose, and why no more economic development took place. We use the term "economic development" to mean an increase in the use of capital and land relative to labor, and/or improvement in technique of production. Such development should lead to economic progress in the sense of an increase in per capita income.

In attempting to explain the lack of development, we will concentrate on the reasons why the Thai did not either improve rice cultivation in order to increase output per unit of labor or develop other industries offering opportunities for such increases.

Economic development could have occurred without a shift from rice cultivation, although past experience suggests that development is accompanied by a fall in the proportion of the labor force engaged in agriculture and an increase in the proportion in secondary and tertiary industries.[11] The *Thai* population largely remained in agriculture, and from 1850 to 1950 it neither improved techniques nor increased the proportion of capital to labor. Moreover, in this period most changes in the economy as a whole were in volume rather than in kind. New methods were not used, new products were not developed. No product of any importance (except rubber) was exported in 1950 which was not exported in 1850. In the following pages we will offer a tentative explanation for this lack of change.

One reason is that the price of rice increased sharply after 1850.[12] This rise must have encouraged existing farmers to concentrate on rice and their sons to become rice farmers, rather than to embark on other occupations. By selling surplus rice for money they were able to buy a widening variety of consumer goods, some of which they had formerly made for themselves. Such specialization is the chief basis for whatever increase in average real income has occurred since 1850.

The importance of the increase in rice prices must be modified, however, by the fact that many other prices also increased, some of them prob-

---

10 The classifications were of course not as clean-cut as indicated here, but such a division of labor along racial and national lines did arise.

11 Colin Clark, *The Conditions of Economic Progress* (2d ed.; London, 1951), Ch. 9.

12 For two centuries prior to 1850, the price of rice was about 0.30–0.50 baht per picul. From Dilock, *op. cit.*, p. 145. After 1855 the average price quickly rose to 2.00–2.50 baht, and by 1900 it was 5.00 baht.

ably as much or more than rice. Data on this point are inadequate. We know that some prices (e.g., sugar) first declined relative to rice, and that many (e.g., cattle, wages) increased substantially, but we cannot make very exact comparisons. In any case, the increase in rice prices may be given as one factor which encouraged specialization in its production.[13]

The extension of rice cultivation was also encouraged by the facts that suitable land was available and that the laws and customs of the country made it easy for individuals to acquire the land. Tax laws also provided an incentive to plant more land in rice. Aside from a small fee, unclaimed land was free to those who would clear and cultivate it. Land laws also served to prevent the growth of large estates and this, indirectly, may have helped to delay improvements in techniques and the use of more capital relative to labor. On the other hand, the continued use of old techniques tended to keep farms small. It is possible that the laws and customs which encouraged an independent peasantry may have delayed economic development.

The growth of trade and commerce after 1850 led to an increase in demand for wage labor. Since rice cultivation was becoming more attractive, and since few Thai people were very willing to become wage laborers, wages tended to rise. Scarcity of labor and a persistent tendency for wages to rise were features of the Thai economy from 1850 until the 1920's.[14]

Had the scarcity of labor been allowed to continue, it is possible that wages might have risen enough to attract labor from agriculture. The high wages and the loss of manpower in agriculture might, in turn, have induced farmers to use more capital and to improve their techniques. Similarly, the employers of labor in trade and industry might have been induced to develop methods of using labor sparingly. In this way technical and organizational change might have been initiated in Thailand. And the Thai might have been drawn into other activities in which they could have achieved proficiency. A cumulative process might have been set in motion.

As it happened, however, the scarcity of labor had other consequences. Immigration of Chinese was permitted and encouraged from 1850 until the

[13] Why the immigrating Chinese did not respond to this encouragement and enter rice cultivation is not known. Many came from farming families, and apparently Thai laws and customs would have allowed them to take unclaimed land. In 1935–37, less than one percent of incoming male Chinese aliens declared their profession to be agriculture. From *Statistical Year Book*, XIX, 70. Some say the Chinese wanted higher incomes or a better chance to expand than they could get in rice farming. Yet they became vegetable farmers around Bangkok or worked for a lifetime as coolies in rice mills. Others say the Chinese wanted to stick together in larger communities, yet they became merchants and middlemen and lived in the most isolated and remote villages. The fact is that they did not become rice farmers, but we do not know why.

[14] For example, on October 4, 1890, *The Bangkok Times* had a long editorial describing the scarcity of labor and urging encouragement of immigration instead of *allowing the farming classes to be disturbed*. Another account for 1904 states that "still the demand for coolie labour exceeds the supply and appears likely to do so for a considerable time to come." From J. Antonio, *Guide to Bangkok and Siam* (Bangkok, 1904), p. 33.

1930's. Other nationalities came, too, but the Chinese were the most numerous. They came with no possessions to speak of, and often they had to borrow the small sum charged for deck passage from Canton, Swatow, and Hainan. They crowded the decks of incoming junks and steamers and upon arrival they spread over the country and filled the bulk of the jobs in commerce and industry. They became entrepreneurs as well as laborers and craftsmen.

The number of immigrants is not known, but it must have been substantial.[15] Immigrants were favorably treated. Until 1910 they paid somewhat less than a third the capitation tax paid by the Thai, and not until the 1930's were any restrictions placed on their economic activities.

The demand for labor was thus filled largely with Chinese immigrants. The rise of wages did not go far enough to attract the Thai away from agriculture and to induce the other changes which might have occurred in consequence of that. Instead, the division of labor between Chinese and Thai was encouraged. Another factor strengthening that division and preventing the entry of Thai into commerce and wage labor was the clannishness of the Chinese immigrants. Not only did they form secret societies which fought among themselves, but they effectively combined to prevent the entry of an outsider into a trade, craft, line of business, or even a particular rice mill.[16] Even where formal societies were not organized, the dominance of the Chinese in retail and wholesale trade, rice milling, middleman activities, and labor made it difficult for an outsider to break in. The Chinese were more skillful in these activities than were the inexperienced Thai, and the situation could not change because the Thai had no opportunity to obtain experience, nor were the prospective rewards adequate to draw them out of agriculture. Chinese employers would favor Chinese workers, and Chinese wholesalers would almost automatically quote better prices to Chinese retailers than to Thai.

Tariffs were another significant factor in the picture. The 3-percent ceiling on import duties (1856–1926) was not much of a hindrance to imports. Even if Chinese immigration had been prevented and wages had risen enough to attract labor from agriculture, it is possible that new industries would not have developed because of competition from imports. On the other hand,

---

[15] Chinese immigration actually started long before 1850. By that time immigrants totaled about 15,000 per year. Victor Purcell, *The Chinese in Southeast Asia*, p. 145, states that by 1900 they were arriving in Bangkok at the rate of 18,000 per year and in even larger numbers in the peninsula. Yet at that time the great flood of immigration had not begun. In the 1920's Chinese arrivals at the port of Bangkok ranged from 70,000 to 140,000 per year, but this was not *net* immigration because considerable numbers returned to China. From *Statistical Year Book of Siam*, XIX, 66. Immigration dropped off sharply in the 1930's because of the depression and restrictions imposed by the Thai government.

[16] H.H. Prince Damrong Rajanubhab, *True Stories of Past Events* (5th ed.; Bangkok, 1951), pp. 313–64 (in Thai language). H. W. Smyth, *Five Years in Siam*, I, 285–86, wrote that in the 1890's these societies "are nearly as powerful as the King himself. By judicious use of their business faculties and their powers of combination, they hold the Siamese in the palm of their hands."

immigration restrictions plus selective protection might have attracted labor from agriculture and encouraged entrepreneurs to undertake new lines of production. And, since knowledge and experience accumulate in these activities, the new industries might have advanced enough to require less protection as time went on.

The foregoing discussion is highly conjectural. Even if immigration restrictions and selective protection had been in effect, it is possible that wage and price incentives would not have brought much change. The barriers of culture and tradition certainly were formidable. Nevertheless, we can safely say that unrestricted immigration and virtually free imports would tend to bring about just the result which did occur, and that the reversal of these factors would *tend* toward other results. Whether the tendency would have been strong enough or not is of course unknown.

Other factors also contributed to the result. The government did not provide essential public works. Bangkok was not connected by rail with the North until the 1920's, nor with the Northeast (other than Korat) until the 1930's. Even now feeder-type transportation is inadequate. The power situation is worse. Only Bangkok and a few provincial cities have electricity, and their supply is both expensive and unreliable. Education facilities are seriously inadequate to equip the nation with a trained labor force. Irrigation facilities have been developed very slowly.

It is in this context that the conservative monetary and fiscal policies become significant. By employing its resources to full advantage, the government could have provided the nation with additional public-works facilities which would themselves have represented an inducement to numerous private undertakings. But if the government had attempted to do this, or perhaps had engaged in deficit financing on occasion, there would probably have been serious repercussions from the British government. For this reason, Britain and the Financial Advisers must bear part of the responsibility for the course actually followed.

Of all the factors discussed above, the single most important one probably was the unwillingness of the Thai to engage in business or to leave the farm. The cultural resistance was very strong.

Yet as the money economy spread over the nation, people did begin to allow monetary calculations to influence their actions. This change came slowly, but the influx of foreign labor, capital, and entrepreneurship was rapid. The inflowing factors of production went into trade and extractive industries, for the most part. The low tariffs and lack of public works also discouraged them from undertaking new industries competitive with imports. Not until the 1920's and 1930's did the government begin to take measures to replace them with Thai. These have had little success.

The foregoing discussion suggests that the allocation of resources which has taken place in Thailand has not developed as it might have under certain other conceivable conditions. In view of the drastically different conceptions of economic and social organization which came into contact in Thailand in 1850, such an argument must be inconclusive because it depends on unpredictable responses. The essential question is whether monetary incentives arising from the expansion of foreign trade (initially based on or adapted to the traditional social organization) would have been sufficiently powerful to draw resources of land, labor, and capital into other pursuits. This question cannot be answered with certainty, but we have suggested a number of ways in which the monetary attractions might have been increased. In view of the extent to which the Thai have adapted to a money economy, it seems likely that they would have responded to price and wage differentials between agriculture and other industries such as might have arisen with selective limitations on imports and immigration.

The extent of the response is also important in determining whether the result would justify the cost or not. But the probable result is too uncertain for us to be able to say much about that. The bulk of the Thai might still be engaged in agriculture, but the percentage in other activities would probably be greater. The economy of Thailand might be more diversified and, since the savings of the commercial classes would have been more largely available for domestic investment, capital formation would have proceeded faster.

This and other cumulative advantages of economic development could have accrued to Thailand. For example, people could have acquired experience in business management and technical skills, and the growth of a trained labor force might have facilitated the development of additional industries. Significant internal and external economies might have appeared.

This is a form of the familiar infant-industry argument. In 1850 all Thailand's industries were infants (except possibly rice production) and, in the absence of special encouragements to their development, production was bound to be limited to traditional activities such as rice growing or to the simple extractive industries such as teak, tin, and sticklac. The infant-industry argument is particularly compelling in a country like Thailand, where it cannot be assumed that the expectations of would-be entrepreneurs will approximate the actual results. Far less than in Western nations can it be assumed that knowledge of cost and demand conditions will be adequate to cause resources to move into industries offering relatively greater rewards. Furthermore, even where knowledge and expectations indicate the advantage of a move, cultural resistance and age-old conservatism may be overcome only when the expected margin of profit is quite large.

On the other hand, these considerations mean that the cost of starting an industry might have been relatively greater because a larger incentive (e.g., a crushingly heavy tariff) would be required to move resources. This also suggests a need for greater reliance on government initiative in developing new industries. Or, as in Japan, the government might get the industries started and then sell them to private interests.

Beyond the *infant-industry* case, there is the argument that, in an economy like Thailand's in 1850, changes in one sector might set off a series of reactions in that and other sectors which would lead to technical and organizational change. We have suggested that the attraction of labor from agriculture might have induced farmers to change their techniques and to use more capital and land relative to labor. The high wages in industry might have induced entrepreneurs to adopt new methods in order to increase productivity per man-hour. Such mutual interactions might have been cumulative. Induced changes in techniques and organization probably could have been more readily adopted than in Western economic development because the vast stock of technical and scientific knowledge of the West existed to be drawn upon. It did not need to be discovered. But some stimulus, capable of setting off the reactions, had first to arise.

If the above thesis is plausible—namely, that in Thailand exceptionally wide profit margins and price differentials would have had to emerge before a shift of resources into new industries would have taken place—then it partially explains the pattern of resource allocation which actually developed. Price and wage differentials were first removed or satisfied by the inflow of foreign labor and goods because these moved at smaller margins than did the Thai people. The expanding Thai population remained in rice farming because new land was available, prices were favorable, and opportunities elsewhere were limited by large-scale immigration and unrestricted import of foreign goods. Thus the existing situation perpetuated itself.

Whether the actual course of events has resulted in a smaller increase in per capita income than would have occurred under our hypothetical alternative (an "incentive program" involving restraints on immigration, selective protection, and other encouragements to industry) is of course impossible to determine. As it happened, very little change occurred in per capita income, although even here no firm conclusions are possible.[17] The amount of cultivated land per capita increased enough to more than offset the apparent decline in yields observed in the last fifty years, and a part of the rice crop (and other products) was sold for a money income. With this money income the average household bought some articles which were formerly made within the village or family, perhaps at great cost in labor, and some which had not formed a part of the standard of living in 1850. In 1950 the average family was probably as well fed and housed as in 1850, and it was probably better provided with clothing and with supplements to the necessities of life.

---

[17] Our chief interest is in the change in *Thai* per capita income, for we are considering the import of foreign labor and entrepreneurship as a variable whose effect on Thai incomes and allocation of resources we are trying to evaluate.

Money income was many times the 1850 level, but such a comparison is not very helpful. Money was used very little in 1850.

Had an "incentive program" been followed, we cannot even guess what the effect on real income would have been. But certainly the stimulus to change would have been greater.

The processes through which a subsistence economy becomes "dynamic" in some sense are very little known, but as it was the Thai remained almost as deeply entrenched in traditional agricultural pursuits as they were before 1850. Nothing in the economic situation encouraged them to break out of that pattern. Such precipitating factors might have been present in the "incentive program," although the experience of other nations yields conflicting lessons in this respect.

One of the most telling arguments against the "incentive program" is that there is no assurance that the government would have been competent to administer it. The record in similar activities is not encouraging. Furthermore, the demands of officials ("squeeze") on private entrepreneurs could have so discouraged them, or influenced their already cautious expectations, that few new ventures would have been undertaken. A second argument is that there is no criterion to use in balancing costs in one period against rewards in another. Western economic theory commonly assumes that knowledge of present and future costs and demands is adequate to enable the "effective expectants" (i.e.—by analogy to effective demand—those individuals and firms who can back up their expectations with purchasing power) to allocate resources in such a way that current and future rewards are balanced to the maximum welfare of the total population. Such an assumption is far less justified in an underdeveloped subsistence economy. Therefore, if the "incentive program" involved an initial cost in the form of reduced real income to rice producers (e.g., because of higher prices for imports or lower net prices for rice on account of high-cost middlemen and millers), but also a later increase (e.g., when some agriculturists were drawn into other occupations with higher income and technical improvements were induced), we cannot compare this course of events with the actual one in welfare terms.

Further discussion would not take us very far. The principal point of this section is that the allocation of resources which developed in Thailand in the past century was greatly influenced by unrestricted immigration, treaty restrictions on revenues and tariffs, the consequent inflow of imports and delay in provision of public utilities, and the hampering influence of conservative monetary and fiscal policies.

From the perspective of the entire population, or perhaps of the Far East, resources probably moved in accordance with the law of comparative advantage. That is, in comparison with Chinese labor, Thai labor probably was relatively more productive in rice cultivation than in trade. Especially was this true if we consider the skills and capabilities that each possessed at the time the movement started, and at any point in time thereafter.

From the perspective of the Thai population, however, the law of comparative advantage, working in an open system in which both goods and factors of production were mobile, meant that the Thai as a group were limited by competition to agriculture until they could acquire the skill and experience needed to compete in other fields. But they had no chance to acquire such skill and experience. In other words, the allocation of resources dictated by comparative advantage tended to perpetuate itself because there were no forces acting to change the basic conditions (the functions and parameters of the system). Under an "incentive program," economic pressures would have existed to cause such changes. No one can say what the outcome would have been.

The above argument does not bring us into the controversy regarding the presumption in favor of free trade on the part of classical economic theory (qualified in a number of ways) for two reasons. First, the classical problem has been to find the optimum position for a country or a set of countries under the assumption that tastes, techniques, demand and supply functions, etc., were given. Here our entire case is based upon the likelihood of bringing about *changes* in such functions and parameters. Second, classical theory has commonly assumed that factors of production, particularly labor, are not mobile between nations. Here we have been faced with a high degree of mobility.

Contemporary writers in the period 1870–1900 frequently drew comparisons between Thailand and Japan, the only two Asian nations to retain their independence. Many expected "progressive Siam" to surpass Japan in economic development. Instead, Thailand remained virtually static except for quantitative changes in traditional lines of production, while Japan entered a period of rapid technological and economic change. The actions Japan took were just the ones Thailand could not take. This of course does not mean that Thailand could have matched the Japanese record, but a sharp contrast nevertheless appears when we observe that in Thailand, unlike Japan, virtually no new products and no new methods emerged in the last century. Economic changes were in volume rather than in kind.

Conclusions*

In the course of this study we have seen many changes in the economy of Thailand in the last hundred years, but not much "progress" in the sense of an increase in the per capita income, and not much "development" in the sense of the utilization of more capital, relative to labor, and of new techniques. The principal changes have been the spread of the use of money,

* This section was written from the perspective of 1951–52, as were all of Chs. 1–10.

increased specialization and exchange based chiefly on world markets, and the growth of a racial division of labor. The rapidly growing population has been chiefly absorbed in the cultivation of more land in rice. The time may not be far off when the supply of cultivable land will run out, especially for cultivation with existing techniques, and other employments will have to be found to prevent a fall in real incomes.

For the most part economic changes have occurred in response to external stimuli. Thailand has been a sort of passive entity, adapting to changes and market influences originating in the world economy. Few innovations have originated within, and most of the adaptive response to external influence has taken place along traditional lines.

Nevertheless, it is noteworthy that some response to economic inducements has occurred. Increases in demand have increased prices and led to increases in output. In response to money incentives subsistence farmers have not only produced rice for sale but have also shifted from glutinous to ordinary rice. On the other hand we have observed that in many instances wage and price differentials did not evoke much response from the Thai. However, as people become more familiar with money and monetary calculations, it is reasonable to expect their responses to quicken.

This may be our most significant conclusion, that a weak response to economic inducements has existed in Thailand. If, in view of the formidable obstacles in their way, market forces have worked (however crudely) in the past century, the elimination of some of the greatest obstacles offers at least a hope for quicker and more efficient operation of such forces in the future.

In other words, the wisest policy for the government may be to facilitate the operation of market forces through provision of basic public services, education, technical assistance, and the like. With such assistance, it is possible that a modest flowering of individual enterprise may yet occur. Such enterprise is likely to appear in small-scale activities, for the highly individualistic character of the Thai remains a barrier to large-scale private undertakings. The routine and discipline of large organizations is not congenial to them. Nor are they willing to invest their savings in fractional shares of organizations over which they have no effective control. Where technical factors dictate large-scale undertakings, government initiative may therefore be necessary.

As long as the Chinese minority continues to form a separate body in the nation, *Thai* entrepreneurship will be hampered. In this connection a kind of "infant entrepreneurship" argument can be advanced. Because of the strangle hold the Chinese have on business activities, the Thai have little chance to acquire experience and develop know-how in them. The fledgling Thai firm has to deal with Chinese suppliers and customers who allegedly discriminate against it. It must also be admitted, however, that the Thai have not shown much enthusiasm for business enterprise. The Chinese are better trained, more energetic, and quicker to seize opportunities. They also compete vigorously with each other in retail and wholesale trade, services, and other activities. So far the government has tried merely to exclude Chinese from certain occupations, but this has had little success in stimulating Thai enterprise. Restrictions on immigration have now almost stopped the (legal) inflow of Chinese. In time, the Chinese may become fully assimilated and the problem will disappear. At present it is a difficult one for which the government has found no solution. We concluded that the inflow of Chinese in the past century has been an influence tending to prevent the development of a dynamic economy, in some sense. The present minority has the same influence today, but only because it remains a separate, unassimilated body.

The trend in recent decades has been toward increased government ownership and operation of industry. In part, the government has stepped in to fill a vacuum, since neither the Thai nor the Chinese have shown any intention of developing large-scale industries. Actually, however, the government is continuing a long tradition of leadership from the top. Most of the economic and social changes that originated within Thailand from 1850 to 1932 were introduced and urged upon the people by the kings. Since 1932 the constitutional government (or the ruling clique of the day) has taken over this function. The difficulty of accumulating large amounts of capital and of operating large impersonal organizations on a private basis may force the government to undertake industries which have to be operated on a large scale.

The outlook for such industries is not clear because the past record is uneven. Some government enterprises have operated with a fair degree of success, while others have a record of mismanagement, wasteful use of capital funds, inefficient production, and inadequate accounting. Perhaps the greatest hindrance to—and danger of—government operation is corruption. Most government employees are honest. Others have no opportunities to be dishonest. But in a great many transactions between the government and private sectors, one or both of the parties in the transaction has to deal with the problems of pay-offs, additions to a bid for "services," underquality deliveries, or others of the infinitely varied forms of corruption. For this reason alone, there is a presumption in favor of private enterprise. The provision of utilities can only be undertaken by the government, however, and we may conclude that it might best concentrate on such activities.

Development has of course been limited by the scarcity of capital. Assuming competent and honest administration, the government could have expanded (and can now expand) the use of credit based on currency reserves. Since World War II loans have been obtained from the World Bank while foreign-exchange reserves have been left unused. Except for the fear of improper management, there is not much justification for this course.

No methods have been devised for mobilizing small savings in Thailand. People prefer to keep their savings in the form of gold or cash, and they have not made much use of banks, postal savings, or co-operatives for this purpose.

Nor are they willing to invest in the stock of a corporation which they do not understand or trust.

Because of the scarcity of capital and the nature of rural savings, as well as for other reasons we have discussed above, small-scale industries are particularly suitable for Thailand.

For her economic development Thailand needs to have a widely based enterprise and initiative which can utilize to the full the small savings of the people and the potential of real capital formation which exists in underemployed and seasonally unemployed labor. The government might well devote its energies and limited resources to the creation of conditions favorable to the development of such enterprise. Attention to power, transportation, and education is especially indicated by this criterion.

11

Economic Change Since 1950: I

THE PURPOSE of the remaining two chapters is to provide a broad, impressionistic survey of economic changes in Thailand from 1950 to about 1970. These two decades have been eventful ones for Thailand, marked by dramatic economic changes in some areas, but by continuity and evolutionary change in others.

Description and analysis of economic changes since 1950 are at once easier than for the earlier period, because of the high rate of growth in the output of economic statistics, and more difficult, because of the increasing size and complexity of the Thai economy. Thailand has received much attention in recent years from economists both in and out of government, and greater use can be made of secondary sources. That Thai economists have begun to write about their own economy is a hopeful sign, although most such writing is still done in theses and dissertations, or in government reports and documents. Thailand now has a group of able, articulate young economists scattered through the government, and it seems likely that they will play an increasingly influential role in national economic development.

The proliferation of economic statistics, although welcome because of the areas opened up for investigation and analysis, is nevertheless a mixed blessing because of the uncertain reliability of data. One finds anomalies and unaccountable discrepancies in almost every series, and official estimates of the same series, published at different times, may vary greatly. Frequently, these variations result from changes in the method of estimation, but the revisions cover only a few years, leaving one with a discontinuous time series. These problems of course exist in every country in some degree; in Thailand they exist in an extreme form.

Myrdal has emphasized the "extreme frailty" of economic statistics for all countries in South and Southeast Asia.[1] In the end, however, after discussing the conceptual and statistical weaknesses in the data, he decided to "hazard" the publication of numerous economic statistics. The economist who wishes to study the economy of Thailand is faced with the same dilemma—he can proceed to use questionable statistics to draw questionable conclusions, or he

---

[1] G. Myrdal, *Asian Drama*, I, Ch. II, and *passim*. See also the comment by J. Edward Ely in *Journal of Economic Literature*, March 1970, and Myrdal's reply.

can do nothing, except possibly to rely on impressions gained from personal observations. The latter alternative seems even less attractive than the former.

Furthermore, the study of a single nation's economy places less strain upon the data than does a comparative study of several nations. Thai economic statistics vary in reliability—monetary and trade figures are perhaps the best, labor force figures among the worst. Longer-term trends appear to be safer than short-term changes, and the margin of error probably rises with disaggregation.

In contrast to the earlier period (1850–1950), changes in the economy of Thailand since 1950 can be described through the use of national income and product accounts. The first rudimentary national income estimates were made by Dr. Joseph Gould for 1938/39 and 1950,[2] but the preparation of national income estimates soon became a regular function, first of the National Economic Council, and later of the National Economic Development Board (NEDB). Serious problems have been encountered in the compilation of these estimates, and the basis of estimation has changed several times in the course of the period we wish to examine. Although these changes make the use of a continuous series somewhat hazardous, one can still use the national income data to obtain a general view of growth and change in the economy of Thailand since 1950.[3]

From 1951 to 1969 the gross national product in constant (1962) prices rose from 35.2 billion baht to 112.4 billion baht, for a remarkably high cumulative growth rate of 6.6 percent per year. In current prices, GNP rose from 29.8 billion baht to 130.8 billion baht, yielding a cumulative growth rate of 8.5 percent. These calculations imply an annual average price rise of 1.9 percent, which is probably one of the lowest rates in the world in this inflationary period. Table XVII contains the annual figures.[4]

[2] Joseph S. Gould, "Preliminary Estimates of the Gross Geographical Product and Domestic National Income of Thailand, 1938/39, 1946–50" (mimeo., Bangkok: National Economic Council, July 1952). See also *supra*, pp. 145–46.

[3] After discussing some of the questions and problems involved in Thai national income data, Robert J. Muscat writes: "One is forced to conclude that the accounts raise more questions than they answer and do not provide reliable information for close economic analysis." (*Development Strategy in Thailand*, New York: 1966, pp. 65–66.) However, Muscat himself uses these data as the basis for a very interesting analysis of Thai economic policy in the postwar period.

[4] These figures represent the most recent estimates for each of the years included in the period, but they still involve three different bases of estimation, for the three subperiods 1951–56, 1957–59, and 1960–68. The most recent revision of estimates for 1951–56 appeared in the 1964 edition of *National Income Statistics of Thailand* (Thailand National Economic Development Board), while the most recent revision of the estimates for 1957–59 appeared in the 1965 edition of that volume. In 1969 still another revision was made of accounting and estimating procedures, but the resulting revisions extended back only to 1960.

Professor Paul B. Trescott has carefully examined the various estimates of income and product and subjected them to a number of analytical tests in his "Measurement of Thailand's Economic Growth, 1946–1965," *Warasan Sethasat* (Thai Economic Journal), IV, No. 1 (1968/69), 16–106. He concluded that the official estimates for 1951–56 understate the actual levels of income and

TABLE XVII

Gross National Product and Population

| | Gross National Product (Billions of Baht) | | | | | | |
| | In Current Prices | | In Constant Prices (1962) | | | | |
Year	(1) Official Estimates	(2) Adjusted Estimate	(3) Official Estimates	(4) Adjusted Estimate	(5) Population (Millions)	(6) GNP per Capita 1962 Prices (Baht)	(7) GNP per Capita Current Prices (Baht)
1951	28.2	29.8	33.5	35.2	20.2	1,743	1,475
1952	29.5	31.1	35.4	37.1	20.8	1,784	1,495
1953	32.2	34.0	39.5	41.5	21.5	1,930	1,581
1954	32.0	33.7	39.2	41.0	22.1	1,855	1,525
1955	39.3	41.6	43.2	45.6	22.8	2,000	1,825
1956	40.9	42.9	44.4	46.5	23.4	1,987	1,833
1957	45.2	45.2	48.2	48.2	24.1	2,000	1,876
1958	47.0	47.0	48.6	48.6	24.9	1,952	1,888
1959	50.3	50.3	53.6	53.6	25.6	2,094	1,965
1960	53.9	53.9	56.0	56.0	26.4	2,121	2,042
1961	58.9	58.9	58.9	58.9	27.2	2,165	2,165
1962	63.7	63.7	63.7	63.7	28.1	2,267	2,267
1963	68.0	68.0	69.1	69.1	28.9	2,391	2,353
1964	74.6	74.6	73.6	73.6	29.8	2,470	2,503
1965	84.3	84.3	79.5	79.5	30.7	2,590	2,746
1966	101.3	101.3	89.1	89.1	31.7	2,811	3,196
1967	108.4	108.4	94.2	94.2	32.7	2,881	3,315
1968	117.6	117.6	102.7	102.7	33.7	3,047	3,490
1969	130.8	130.8	112.4	112.4	34.7	3,239	3,769

Sources: GNP, 1960–69, National Income of Thailand, Revised Estimates 1960–69, NEDB, mimeo. (Bangkok, Aug. 1970); 1957–59, National Income of Thailand, 1965 ed., NEDB; 1951–56, cols. (1) and (3), National Income Statistics of Thailand, 1964 ed., NEDB; cols. (2) and (4), Paul B. Trescott, "Measurement of Thailand's Economic Growth, 1946–1965," Warasan Sethasat (Thai Economic Journal), IV, No. 1 (1968/69), 16–106. Population, 1951–69, National Statistical Office, Quarterly Bulletin of Statistics.

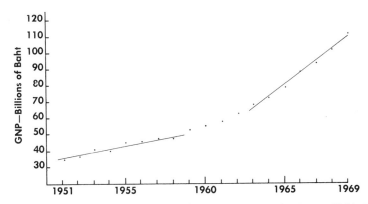

Chart II. Gross national product in constant (1962) prices, 1951–69. Source: Table XVII, col. 4.

The growth in GNP was modest in the first part of this period, as may be seen in Chart II. From 1951 to 1958, GNP in constant prices rose from 35.2 billion baht to 48.6 billion baht—an annual growth rate of 4.7 percent. Beginning in 1959, the rate of growth sharply increased, and for the whole period 1959 to 1969, GNP in constant prices rose at the rate of 8.6 percent per year. Despite all the (very real) questions about accuracy and reliability of the basic data, it seems clear that the rate of growth increased significantly between these two periods. The change can be seen in Chart II. It is interesting to observe at this point that the rise in the rate of growth preceded the American military presence in Thailand by several years, although the very high rates in 1966–68 were certainly affected by this build-up.

According to official estimates, population has grown since 1950 at the rate of about 3.1 percent per year, rising from 20.2 million in 1951 to 34.7 million in 1969. On the basis of these estimates, GNP per capita in constant (1962) prices rose from 1,743 baht in 1951 to 3,239 baht in 1969, with most of the increase occurring in the second part of the period, 1959 to 1969. Annual figures for population and per capita GNP are also presented in Table XVII. These data show that increases in income have exceeded population growth by a sufficient margin to permit a substantial rise in real income per capita.

To place population growth in historical perspective, we may note that the absolute increase in the 20-year period 1950–70 is somewhat larger than the

product, and he produced his own "best guess" estimates for these years. We have used these estimates in our "adjusted estimates" in Table XVII (cols. 2 and 4). The official estimates for 1957–59 were accepted as his "best guess" by Professor Trescott, and we have also used those. The recent revisions of 1960–69 data were not available to Professor Trescott; we have used them instead of his "best guess" estimates.

Therefore, the "adjusted estimate" column in Table XVII uses the most recent official estimate except for 1951–56. For those years we have used Professor Trescott's estimates, except that we have converted them (in col. 4) to 1962 constant prices (his were in 1956 prices).

absolute increase in the preceding one hundred years. The figures are 5.5 million for 1850, 19.6 million for 1950, and 35.7 million for 1970.[5] Such dramatic comparisons can be made for many countries, but the rapid population growth in Thailand has aroused concern in recent years and has led to much discussion in and out of government. There is a growing recognition of the relationships between population growth and economic development. No religious or cultural barriers prevent the use of family planning techniques, and a few experimental family planning centers have found a lively demand for their services. The population problem has been discussed within the government, but in early 1970 it was reported that the Cabinet had declined to adopt an official policy. However, a subsequent report stated that the Cabinet formally reached the following decision: "The Government of Thailand accepts it as a policy to support family planning on a voluntary basis in order to overcome various problems in connection with the high rate of population growth which would become obstacles to economic and social development of the nation." How much "support" will be given remains to be seen. Economic development, urbanization, and related factors may begin to affect the birth rate, but it is difficult to be optimistic about the prospects for reducing the rate of population growth in the immediate future.

The composition of GNP is presented in Table XVIII. These figures are in current prices because we cannot link the three separate estimates (for 1952–56, 1957–59, and 1960–69) and obtain a consistent series in terms of constant prices for the several components, and because we will be primarily interested in examining relative shares.

The share of gross domestic fixed investment (including government investment) rose from around 13 percent of GNP in the early part of this period to 24 percent in 1969. These are high investment ratios, and they will be further discussed below.

Comparable expenditures for consumption are not available for 1952–56, but both private and government consumption expenditures rose steadily from 1957 to 1969 (see Table XVIII). Over this eleven-year period, the private marginal propensity to consume ($\Delta C_p \div \Delta GNP$) was about 0.65, and the governmental marginal propensity to consume ($\Delta C_g \div \Delta GNP$) was about 0.12. These data are presented in a scatter diagram in Chart III. The constant-slope regression line fits fairly well except for 1966, but it is provided only as a description of experience in this period, not as a basis for any prediction of the future. In terms of constant (1962) prices, the private marginal propensity to consume for the period 1960–68 was about 0.63, which is very close to our estimate in current prices for the longer period (0.65).[6]

Consumption expenditures can also be divided into domestic (C_d) and

---

[5] For the 1850 estimate, see above, pp. 7–8. The 1950 figure is an official estimate, whereas the 1970 figure is obtained by assuming a continued rate of growth of 3 percent in 1969 and 1970.

[6] "National Income of Thailand, Revised Estimates, 1960–69," p. 30. Thai data divide government expenditures into consumption and investment, a useful distinction.

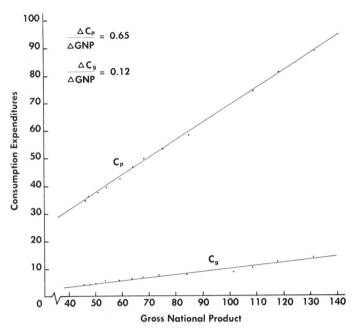

Chart III. Private consumption (C_p) and government consumption (C_g) related to GNP, 1957–69. Source: Table XVIII.

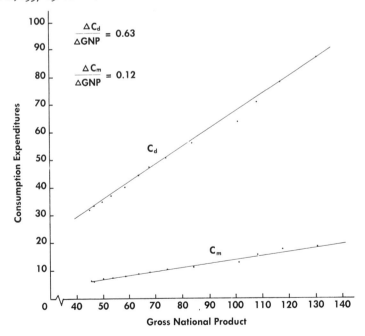

Chart IV. Consumption of domestic goods (C_d) and imported goods (C_m) related to GNP, 1957–69. Source: Table XVIII.

TABLE XVIII

EXPENDITURE FOR GROSS NATIONAL PRODUCT AT CURRENT PRICES

(Billions of Baht)

Year	(1) Private Consumption C_p	(2) Government Consumption C_v	(3) Gross Domestic Fixed Investment I	(4) Exports of Goods & Services X	(5) Imports of Goods & Services M	(6) GNP[a]	(7) I/GNP (Col. 3 ÷ Col. 6)	(8) X/GNP (Col. 4 ÷ Col. 6)
1952			3.7			28.2	13.1%	
1953			4.6			29.5	15.6	
1954			4.7			32.0	14.7	
1955			4.7			39.3	12.0	
1956			5.1			40.9	12.5	
1957	34.5	4.2	6.3	8.6	9.0	45.2	13.9	19.0%
1958	35.8	4.2	6.2	7.1	8.4	47.0	13.2	15.1
1959	37.8	4.2	7.0	8.1	9.3	50.3	13.9	16.1
1960	39.3	5.3	7.5	9.4	10.2	53.9	13.9	17.4
1961	42.5	5.6	8.3	11.1	10.9	58.9	14.1	18.8
1962	46.8	6.3	10.1	10.8	12.2	63.7	15.9	17.0
1963	49.9	6.9	12.1	11.2	13.6	68.0	17.8	16.5
1964	53.6	7.5	14.5	14.0	15.2	74.6	19.4	18.8
1965	58.6	8.3	16.0	15.4	16.5	84.3	19.0	18.3
1966	66.7	9.3	20.4	19.3	19.7	101.3	20.1	19.1
1967	75.0	10.7	24.8	21.4	23.8	108.4	22.9	19.7
1968	81.7	13.1	27.8	21.6	26.4	117.6	23.6	18.4
1969	89.5	14.7	30.9	22.2	27.9	130.8	23.6	17.0

[a] Cols. 1 to 5 do not sum to GNP because of a statistical discrepancy, and because inventory change is omitted from col. 3, which includes only gross *fixed* domestic investment.

Sources: 1951–56, *National Income Statistics of Thailand*, 1964 ed.; 1957–59, *National Income of Thailand*, 1965 ed.; 1960–69, "National Income of Thailand, Revised Estimates, 1960–69," Mimeo.

imported (C_m) components. These data refer to the combined total of private and government consumption, however, because "imports for consumption" cannot be divided between the private and government sectors. (It seems likely that the private sector accounts for the great majority of imports for consumption, perhaps as much as 90 percent.) For the period 1957–69, the marginal propensity to consume *domestic* goods and services $(\Delta C_d \div \Delta GNP)$ was about 0.63, while the marginal propensity to *import* consumer goods and services $(\Delta C_m \div \Delta GNP)$ was about 0.12. As may be seen in Chart IV, a constant slope regression line fits quite well except for 1966. In the case of imports, the values for 1967 and 1968 seem to be slightly above the "normal" relationship for this period. This may reflect the increasing number of foreign residents in these years, and the extraordinary import demand associated with the American military presence in Thailand.

Modern economic theory usually treats investment and exports as autonomous expenditures, with consumption playing a passive role. Historically, exports have been the dominant form of autonomous expenditure in Thailand. Prior to 1950, exports substantially exceeded the sum of private and government investment,[7] but this relationship changed in the period under review. Gross fixed domestic investment first exceeded exports of goods and services in 1963, an excess that continued (and grew) through 1969 (see Table XVIII). This shift away from an export-dominated economy has profound implications for the future of the Thai economy. Among other things, it means that the smooth, rapid, and relatively painless adjustment of the domestic economy in response to swings in the external balance may no longer exist. As described in Chapter 10, above, a fall in exports formerly was promptly matched by a fall in imports, because the initial fall in exports set in motion a process of income reduction, magnified through the multiplier process. Therefore, an automatic adjustment occurred in the balance of payments. Now that investment expenditures comprise the largest element of autonomous expenditure, however, this equilibrating process will be weakened. Only if investment expenditures vary directly with exports—without offsetting measures being taken— would the traditional mechanism remain unimpaired. This argument implies that Thailand may begin to experience more balance-of-payments difficulties in the future, especially if exports decline.

As may be seen in Table XVIII, the ratio of exports of goods and services to GNP has fluctuated between 15 and 19 percent from 1957 to 1969; it stood at 17 percent in 1969. This figure is somewhat misleading, however, because the export figure includes a large item for military expenditures in Thailand. If we consider *merchandise* exports alone, the ratio of exports to GNP fell from 17 percent in 1957 to 11 percent in 1969. As military expenditures decline, ways must be found to expand exports and conventional service items to replace these receipts of foreign exchange.

7 See above, pp. 206–7.

In the theory of economic development, great emphasis is placed on the size of investment and its share in the GNP. The ratio of gross fixed domestic investment to GNP hovered around 13 percent from 1952 to 1960, but it then rose steadily from 1960 to 1968, reaching 24 percent in 1968.[8] These high ratios of investment to GNP, especially for a relatively poor country like Thailand, have been challenged by several economists. In his analysis of Thai national income estimates, Prot Panitpakdi concluded that fixed investment is over-valued and GNP undervalued.[9] A former national income adviser, William Abraham, also thought the investment figures were exaggerated; he stated that the official estimates "strain the credulity of observers who are in a position to make comparisons with other countries."[10] On the other hand, economists have argued that investment in the agricultural sector tends to be overlooked in official estimates, and that investment is therefore understated. In the case of Thailand, Usher has argued that both investment and output in the agricultural sector have been understated, but it is uncertain whether or not he thinks inclusion of the omitted activities would raise the *ratio* of investment to GNP.[11]

Although we cannot settle this question, it is worth noting that the rapid growth of GNP during this period implies a rather high investment ratio. This follows from the definitional relationships among the capital-output ratio, the investment ratio, and the rate of growth in GNP. If one assumes a given (and constant) incremental capital-output ratio (ICOR), or $I \div \Delta GNP$, one can calculate the rate of growth in GNP that is consistent with a given rate of investment. For example, if ICOR = 3.0, and investment were 15 percent of GNP, the annual increase in GNP would be 5 percent.[12] Using the figures in Table XVIII for the two periods 1952–59 and 1960–68, we can calculate the ICOR's as, respectively, 1.65 and 1.82. These values are already rather low, especially in view of the fact that much investment in Thailand has been in roads, dams, and other capital-intensive projects. If the estimates for GNP were increased and those for investment reduced, as suggested by Prot Panitpakdi, the result would be to reduce the already low values for

---

[8] In using gross domestic *fixed* investment, we are omitting the change in inventories. For some purposes, this omission is undesirable, but the official estimates of inventory change vary greatly and appear to be subject to a large margin of error.

[9] "National Accounts Estimates of Thailand," in T. H. Silcock (ed.), *Thailand: Social and Economic Studies in Development* (Canberra, Australia, 1967), pp. 120–21.

[10] William I. Abraham, "Report to the Government of Thailand by the National Income Adviser" (mimeo., Bangkok, August 1963). A subsequent revision reduced the specific estimates that Abraham was criticizing.

[11] Dan Usher, "Income as a Measure of Productivity: Alternative Comparisons of Agricultural and Non-Agricultural Productivity in Thailand," *Economica*, XXXIII (1966).

[12] In other words: $I / \Delta GNP = 3.0$
$$I = .15GNP$$
$$\therefore \Delta GNP / GNP = 0.15 \div 3 = 0.05$$

ICOR, a result that would place other strains upon credulity. This argument suggests that the investment estimates are plausible if the GNP estimates are reasonably accurate.

From 1951 to 1969, the share of government investment in gross domestic fixed investment first declined, especially in 1957 and 1958, and then rose—to about 33 percent in the last seven years of the period. Annual figures are presented in Table XIX. These changes appear to reflect changes in official policy, but may in part reflect accounting changes or inconsistencies. In the early 1950's, the government expanded its role in the manufacturing sector by establishing government enterprises in several industries—textiles, paper, glass, sugar, gunny-bags, and many others.[13] These enterprises were initiated and operated by several different ministries, and in 1954 the National Economic Development Corporation Limited (NEDCOL) was established, ostensibly as a private corporation but actually, in control and function, as a government agency, to expand the government's role in industry. Both Silcock and Muscat provide lists of government enterprises.[14] These industrial investments were in addition to government investment in social overhead facilities, such as power, irrigation, highways, schools, and railways. Since social overhead facilities were being expanded in the early 1950's, partly financed by World Bank loans and United States economic aid, at the same time that the government undertook industrial investments, the share of government in gross fixed investment rose in this period.

The reasons for the government initiative were practical, not ideological. It seemed clear that Thailand badly needed to expand its tiny industrial sector, and equally clear that private *Thai* entrepreneurs were not likely to emerge. However, the government believed that if it simply encouraged private industry, the result would be that Chinese and foreign entrepreneurs would control the new enterprises. As Muscat has said, "the real driving force behind the government's industrial program was the desire to prevent the Chinese community in Thailand from dominating industry."[15] Three additional points need to be made. First, Thailand has had a long tradition of initiative and leadership from the top, and government initiatives in industrial development were consistent with that tradition. Second, it appears that government officials were motivated in part by opportunities for private gain in the establishment and operation of these government enterprises. Third, the question of government *vs.* private ownership of industry has not been an ideological one. Muscat states this point very clearly:

The development of state enterprise in Thailand has always been totally divorced from issues of ideology. The class conflicts and the passionately held and subtly

---

[13] See above, pp. 140–44, 194–95, for a brief account of the role of government before 1952.
[14] Silcock, *Thailand, op. cit.*, pp. 308–16; Muscat, *op. cit.*, pp. 295–300.
[15] Muscat, *op. cit.*, p. 193.

TABLE XIX

Gross Domestic Fixed Investment (Current Prices)

(Billions of Baht)

Year	Sector: Private or Public				Origin of Investment Good			Physical Form		
	Total I_t	Private I_p	Government I_g	Share of Government (Percentage) I_g/I_t	Domestic I_d	Imported I_m	Share of Imports (Percentage) I_m/I_t	Construction	Machinery & Equipment	Share of Construction (Percentage)
1952	3.7	2.5	1.2	32%	2.0	1.7	46%	1.3	2.4	.35%
1953	4.6	2.8	1.8	39	3.0	1.6	35	2.0	2.6	.43
1954	4.7	2.9	1.8	38	3.0	1.7	36	2.0	2.7	.43
1955	4.7	2.9	1.8	38	3.0	1.7	36	2.0	2.7	.43
1956	5.1	3.5	1.6	31	3.3	1.8	35	2.1	3.0	.41
1957	6.3	5.2	1.2	19	3.9	2.4	35	3.2	3.1	.51
1958	6.2	5.1	1.2	19	3.9	2.3	33	3.2	3.0	.52
1959	7.0	5.2	1.7	24	4.7	2.3	30	3.9	3.1	.56
1960	7.5	5.4	2.1	28	4.9	2.6	35	4.5	3.0	.60
1961	8.3	5.9	2.5	30	5.4	2.9	35	5.0	3.3	.60
1962	10.1	6.8	3.3	33	6.6	3.5	35	6.1	4.0	.60
1963	12.1	8.0	4.1	34	7.8	4.3	36	7.0	5.1	.58
1964	14.5	9.9	4.6	32	9.5	5.0	34	7.9	6.6	.54
1965	16.0	10.5	5.4	34	10.5	5.5	34	8.8	7.2	.55
1966	20.4	13.6	6.7	33	13.3	7.1	35	11.1	9.3	.54
1967	24.8	16.6	8.2	33	16.1	8.7	35	13.0	11.8	.52
1968	27.8	18.5	9.3	33	18.5	9.3	33	14.5	13.3	.52
1969	30.9	21.3	9.7	31	20.9	10.0	32	16.7	14.2	.54

Sources: 1952–56, *National Income Statistics of Thailand*, 1964 ed.; 1957–59, *National Income of Thailand*, 1965 ed.; 1960–69, *National Income of Thailand, Revised Estimates 1960–69*, Mimeo.

adumbrated intellectual arguments that formed the background for the develop-ment of various forms and degrees of state capitalism, government intervention or regulation, and socialism in the West, were almost completely absent from the Thai scene during those years when the growth of state enterprise was most rapid."[16]

Nevertheless, government industrial enterprises fell into disfavor in the late 1950's, largely for pragmatic reasons. First of all, they were inefficient. Instead of generating revenues for the government, they became a drain upon the treasury. These enterprises were sharply criticized by many observers, espe-cially by the Bank of Thailand and by the World Bank Mission, which found them with few exceptions to be poorly planned, badly managed, and unprofit-able.[17] The Mission strongly recommended that the government rely upon and encourage private enterprise for industrial development, and that it devote its own energies to provision of power, transportation, and other necessary social overhead facilities. Second, the government perceived that foreign in-vestment was being inhibited by the presence (or threat) of competition from government-owned plants, and that Thailand's prospects for foreign loans and aid would be enhanced if the government restricted its role. Third, an ingenious *modus vivendi* emerged and helped to achieve two important ob-jectives—namely, to reduce the fears of Chinese (and foreign) domination of industry, and to provide a way for certain government officials to share in the profits of new enterprises. This method simply involved the appointment of influential government officials to the boards of directors of the new firms.[18] As members of the boards, these officials could be well paid for their services, and they also comprised a Thai element in the control and operation of the firms. Such a system is obviously subject to abuses, but it may facilitate the process of assimilation and could lead, in time, to the emergence of a group of Thai entrepreneurs. In fact, Thai managers have already emerged in many foreign and joint-venture firms.

For these and other reasons (including political changes), government policy since the late 1950's has been to encourage industrial investment by private firms, and to reduce the active involvement of government in owner-ship and management. This policy accords closely with the recommendations of the World Bank Mission. The Mission urged the government to focus its energies on the development of social overhead facilities—power, transporta-tion, and communication—and further recommended that "the Government should not only refrain from seeking to increase its industrial participation, but should try to disengage itself from its present commitments."[19] Although

---

[16] Muscat, *op. cit.*, p. 192. The same point can be made for the earlier period—see above, p. 195.

[17] *A Public Development Program for Thailand*, International Bank for Reconstruction and Development (Baltimore, Md.: 1959), pp. 90–94. See also Bank of Thailand, *Annual Report*, 1954, 1958.

[18] This *modus vivendi* is described by G. W. Skinner, *Leadership and Power in the Chinese Community in Thailand* (Ithaca, N.Y., 1958), and it appears to have flourished in the past decade.

[19] *A Public Development Program for Thailand, op. cit.*, p. 96.

the government has not disposed of many of the enterprises it had accumulated by 1958, it has, with some exceptions, largely limited its role in industry in recent years to promotion, encouragement, and some minority financing. It has also enunciated a policy of noncompetition. For example, in the first six-year plan the statement is made that "the state is not to engage in new enterprises in competition with private business," and in the second plan the policy is said to be "to restrict the establishment of new state enterprises except where public interest dictates, as in the field of public utilities, of social welfare, and of national security. The policy will be to avoid competition with the private sector and where such competition currently exists consideration will be given to the transfer by sale or lease of the state enterprise to the private sector."[20]

The share of government investment in gross fixed domestic investment has been stable in recent years at about one-third, and nearly all of this share has been invested in social overhead facilities. Private investment has responded vigorously to the opportunities opened to it, and to the positive government encouragement through investment promotion and other measures. The rate of growth in gross domestic fixed investment was an impressive 13.5 percent over the whole period (1952 to 1968), and almost *18* percent from 1960 to 1968. Since 1950, therefore, domestic investment has become a major driving force in the Thai economy.[21]

This rapid increase in investment has also been an important cause of the rise in imports and the swing from surplus to deficit on both current account (total trade in goods and services) and merchandise account. Because of its small, poorly developed industrial sector, Thailand does not have much capacity to produce capital goods. Therefore, when investment takes place, a large part of the machinery and equipment, and some of the building materials as well, must be imported. The share of imported capital goods in gross fixed capital formation has stayed fairly constant at about 35 percent during the period under review (see Table XIX).[22]

This heavy dependence upon imported capital goods has both favorable and unfavorable implications for the Thai economy. On the one hand, it seems clear that Thailand has a comparative disadvantage in the production of many

[20] "National Economic Development Plan," *Royal Thai Government Gazette*, II, No. 208 (as cited in Muscat, *op. cit.,* p. 196); *The Second National Economic and Social Development Plan, 1967–71* (National Economic Development Board, Bangkok, n.d.), p. 115.

[21] U.S. military construction in Thailand is not included in these figures. That is, the construction of air bases and other purely military facilities is not included. Some corollary construction, such as roads and port facilities, *is* included, however. This distinction has created difficult problems for social accounting in Thailand, especially in 1966 and 1967.

[22] The definition of "imports of capital goods" poses some difficult problems. In the NEDB reports, imported capital goods include machinery and equipment, building materials, and certain industrial raw materials. The last category presumably includes only those materials that are used in locally produced capital goods, not raw materials used as inputs in consumer goods industries. Some items of machinery and equipment (e.g., automobiles and boat engines) require an arbitrary division between capital and consumer goods.

All these imports are valued c.i.f. The substantial "local costs" (import duties, transporta-

types of capital goods. It is a simple, straightforward application of trade theory to show that the country can obtain its capital goods more efficiently by exporting rice and other primary products in exchange for machinery and equipment than by producing these goods at home. Furthermore, although the rapid increase in investment in recent years has been accompanied by an upsurge in imports precisely because the import content of investment is so high, it also follows that a reduction in investment (or a slackening in the rate of growth) would quickly be reflected in a reduction in imports (or a lower rate of increase). Therefore, adjustment in the balance of payments may not be so difficult as is sometimes believed. Finally, to the extent that investment is financed by foreign capital, either private or official, the foreign exchange cost of imported machinery and equipment will pose no immediate problem (repayment and servicing of foreign capital are another matter, however).

On the other hand, the commitment to international specialization does require Thailand to expand its capacity to export if it is to sustain its momentum of growth. A reduction in foreign exchange receipts, e.g., because of a fall in rice exports or a reduction in U.S. military activities, could force a contraction in domestic investment in order to bring imports down. Similarly, plans for continued growth in investment expenditures may have to be scaled down unless exports grow. It is for this reason that a policy of promoting industries solely to supply the domestic market may create difficulties in the future. Thailand has developed some new export products since 1950, as we shall see below, but its exports are still composed almost entirely of primary products. Most of the firms in the small but growing manufacturing sector are producing only for the domestic market. Their production may replace imports, of course, but the scope for such import substitution is clearly limited.[23]

The last characteristic of investment that we shall examine is the share of construction in gross domestic fixed investment. It has been observed that construction often represents 50 percent or more of total investment in developed as well as underdeveloped countries. Thailand conforms to this pattern, as may be seen in Table XIX. The share of construction rose from 35 percent in 1952 to 51 percent in 1957, and it has remained between 50 and 60 percent from 1957 to 1969. Some major projects have been constructed by foreign contractors (especially roads, dams, and power projects), but the domestic construction industry has been one of the fastest growing sectors of the economy, and it has developed an impressive capability. Although construction uses relatively more labor than in high-wage countries, a variety of techniques are utilized. Some capital-intensive machinery is used, especially in roads and other heavy construction, while in buildings more labor is used along with

---

tion, fees, middleman's mark-up, etc.) are not included in import value. If these costs were included, "imports of capital goods" would comprise almost 50 percent of gross domestic fixed investment.

[23] See *International Development, 1966* (Dobbs Ferry, N.Y., 1967).

TABLE XX

Gross Domestic Product by Industrial Origin

A. Value—Billions of Baht at Current Prices

Industrial Origin	1951	1955	1960	1965	1968	1969
Agriculture	14.1	12.9	21.5	29.4	37.0	41.7
Mining and quarrying	0.5	0.6	0.6	1.8	2.1	2.5
Manufacturing	2.9	4.6	6.8	12.0	17.6	19.2
Construction	0.8	1.6	2.5	4.7	8.2	8.6
Electricity & water supply		0.1	0.2	0.7	1.3	1.6
Transportation and communication	0.9	2.0	4.0	6.0	7.3	8.0
Wholesale & retail trade	5.1	7.7	8.2	13.9	20.3	22.9
Banking, insurance & real estate	0.1	0.5	1.0	2.2	4.1	4.8
Ownership of dwellings	1.0	1.2	1.5	2.1	2.4	2.6
Public administration & defense	0.8	1.9	2.5	3.6	5.0	5.6
Services	1.9	2.6	5.2	8.0	12.1	13.3
Gross domestic product	28.2	39.4	54.0	84.3	117.3	130.6

B. Percentage

Industrial Origin	1951	1955	1960	1965	1968	1969
Agriculture	50.1	42.0	39.8	34.9	31.5	31.9
Mining and quarrying	1.9	1.6	1.1	2.1	1.8	1.9
Manufacturing	10.3	11.8	12.6	14.2	15.0	14.7
Construction	2.9	4.0	4.6	5.6	7.0	6.6
Electricity & water supply	0.1	0.2	0.4	0.8	1.1	1.2
Transportation and communication	3.1	5.1	7.5	7.1	6.2	6.1
Wholesale & retail trade	18.0	19.6	15.2	16.5	17.3	17.5
Banking, insurance & real estate	0.4	1.4	1.9	2.6	3.5	3.6
Ownership of dwellings	3.7	3.0	2.8	2.5	2.0	2.0
Public administration & defense	2.8	4.8	4.6	4.3	4.3	4.3
Services	6.7	6.5	9.6	9.5	10.3	10.2
Gross domestic product	100.0	100.0	100.0	100.0	100.0	100.0

many ingenious devices which use capital sparingly. Casual observation suggests that many adaptive innovations have been made to enable methods to be used which lie in between the traditional, labor-intensive methods and modern, capital-intensive methods.[24]

One might expect construction to comprise an even higher percentage of investment than it does in Thailand. In comparison to developed countries, construction costs appear to be lower per square foot of floor space in buildings, and per mile of roads, while machinery and equipment, being largely imported, are valued at world prices plus shipping costs. It may be that, valued at developed countries' prices, the ratio of construction to total fixed investment is higher than it appears to be in the official figures.

The data on gross domestic product originating in the various industries indicate that substantial structural changes have occurred since 1950. The figures for selected years are presented in Table XX. The sectors that have grown most rapidly are construction, transportation and communication, manufacturing, electricity, services, and finance (banking, insurance, and real estate). Lower rates of growth have prevailed in agriculture, mining, and trade. In terms of percentage shares, the most striking change has been a decline in the share of agriculture and a rise in the share of "industry." This structural shift is emphasized in the following figures:

SHARE OF GROSS DOMESTIC PRODUCT[25] (*Percentage*)

Sector	1951	1968	Change
Agriculture	50.1	31.5	−18.6
Industry	18.3	31.1	+12.8
Services	31.6	37.4	+ 5.8
Total	100.0	100.0	0

The decline in agriculture is particularly striking because Thailand still appears to be primarily an agricultural country. Exports are almost entirely agricultural, and about 80 percent of the labor force is employed in agriculture. However, we must remember that the decline in agriculture is only a relative one. The money value of agriculture's contribution to gross product has steadily increased; it has simply grown less fast than other sectors. Nevertheless, the above figures, showing "industry" to equal agriculture in its contribution to gross domestic product, seem almost incredible. One student of the Thai economy, Dan Usher, has expressed doubts about these figures, especially about the values of output per worker in agriculture and in nonagricultural

[24] No thorough study of the construction industry has yet been made. It would be a very interesting and useful topic for a thesis.

[25] Derived from Table XX. "Industry" includes mining, manufacturing, construction, power, and transportation. "Services" include trade, finance, ownership of dwellings, public administration, and other services. These sectoral shares are based on value added at *market* prices. If valued at factor cost, the share of agriculture would be higher, that of manufacturing lower. Conceptually, valuation at factor cost is preferable, but data on that basis are unavailable prior to 1960.

industry that are implied. According to official estimates, about 80 percent of the employed population was in agriculture in 1968. If we assume that the ratio of total population in the agricultural sector was also 80 percent, we can calculate money income per capita in agriculture and nonagriculture, as follows:

	Population	GNP Originating	GNP Per Capita
Agriculture	27,000,000	Bt. 37.0 billion	Bt. 1,370
Nonagriculture	6,700,000	Bt. 80.3 billion	Bt. 11,980
Total	33,700,000	Bt. 117.3 billion	Bt. 3,480

This calculation indicates that income per capita in nonagricultural activities is 8.7 times as large as income per capita in agriculture. While differentials in favor of the nonagricultural sector have commonly been observed in other countries, they usually range from 4 : 3 to 2 : 1. A differential of 8.7 : 1 can scarcely be believed. Usher made a number of adjustments and concluded that the ratio in Thailand should be about 3 : 1.[26]

Professor Silcock has an interesting and useful discussion of the conceptual and statistical problems involved in measuring the relative size of the agricultural sector in Thailand.[27] He concludes that official statistics understate the size of agriculture's contribution to GNP, but he sees no clear-cut way to correct official figures. In one calculation, he estimates that correction for the undervaluation of rice alone (caused by the rice premium) would increase agriculture's share in GNP by 4 to 6 percentage points in 1961–65.[28] It does seem clear that the effect of the rice premium, tariffs, industrial promotion, and other policies is to undervalue the agricultural share and overvalue the industrial share of GNP. Agriculture has no doubt declined in relative importance, but not to the extent indicated by the above tabulation. The rising share of industry in GNP of course reflects the great emphasis that has been placed on social overhead facilities, involving heavy investment outlays and an expanding construction industry, and on promotion of manufacturing industry. Although agriculture derives benefits from investments in roads, dams, and other public works, it has been a neglected sector in recent years. Investment at the farm level has largely been left up to the individual farmer, typically a smallholder.

THE AGRICULTURAL SECTOR

Although the share of agriculture in GNP has fallen, according to official statistics, from 50 percent in 1950 to 31 percent in 1969, agriculture still remains the principal occupation of the great majority of the people. Approxi-

[26] D. Usher, *The Price Mechanism and the Meaning of National Income Statistics* (New York, 1968), Ch. 13. Also in *Bulletin of Oxford University Institute of Statistics*, 1963. He was using 1963 data, and the nonadjusted ratio was then 10 : 1.

[27] T. H. Silcock, *The Economic Development of Thai Agriculture* (Canberra, Australia, 1970), Ch. 2.

[28] *Ibid.*, pp. 20–24.

mately 80 percent of the labor force is engaged in agriculture, a proportion that has declined very slowly in recent decades.[29] This figure probably exaggerates agriculture's share in the labor force, in that farmers and their families also carry on other activities such as weaving, sewing, canning, carpentry, and various forms of capital formation. Family members may also take part-time or seasonal jobs outside agriculture. Since these activities are not reflected in labor force statistics, the share of agricultural employment in the total tends to be biased upward. Nevertheless, it is a commonplace to speak of Thailand as a predominantly agricultural country. Outside Bangkok, the country is largely rural—the second largest city, Chiengmai, had a population in 1967 of only 82,000.

Traditionally, the agricultural economy of Thailand has been dominated by a single crop—rice. The expansion of rice cultivation has been described above (especially Chapter 3). For almost a century after King Mongkut opened the country to external trade, the trend was toward greater specialization in rice. Since 1950, however, this trend has been broken. From 1950–52 to 1965–67, the area planted in rice rose only 15 percent, while the area in all other crops quadrupled—a 400 percent increase. Table XXI contains annual-average figures for area planted in paddy (rice) and all other crops. In absolute numbers, the area in other crops rose from 5.0 million rai in 1950–52 to 20.5 million rai in 1965–67; the area in paddy rose only from 35.1 million rai to 42.2 million rai. In the latter period, paddy accounted for only 67 percent of the total area planted in crops.[30] We will discuss below some aspects of this new trend toward diversification of agriculture. At this point we should note that crop diversification has occurred in all regions of the country, but it has been most pronounced in the Central and Northeastern regions. Table XXI also contains the regional data.[31] Of the total *increase* of 15.5 million rai in other crops between 1950–52 and 1965–67, the Central region accounted for

[29] Here "agriculture" includes forestry, fishing, and hunting. The labor force refers to the economically active population 15 years of age and over. The percentage of labor in agriculture was estimated to be 88.0 percent in 1954, 81.5 percent in 1960, and 79.9 percent in 1966. (NEDB, *The Second National Economic and Social Development Plan, 1967–71*, p. 52, and *Statistical Yearbook*, No. 24.)

[30] Actually, this figure overstates the relative size of paddy area because many small crops are omitted from the official statistics. For example, chili pepper is omitted from "other crops" even though the area planted is estimated to be 338,000 rai.

[31] Geographic regions in Thailand are defined in Appendix A. This definition was used in the first edition of this book and is retained here to provide comparability. It is identical with the regional definition used by the Ministry of Agriculture in its annual document, *Agricultural Statistics of Thailand*. However, other regional definitions do exist and are used by other government agencies. The principal difference concerns the distinction between the "Center" and the "North," since the regional boundaries for the South and Northeast are clearly fixed by geographic features.

Some economists include a larger number of changwats in the North than we have included in Appendix A. Specifically, the following changwats are often shifted from Center to North: Uttaradit, Sukhothai, Tak, Phitsanulok, Kamphaeng Phet, Phichit, Phetchabun, Nakhon Sawan, and Uthai Thani.

TABLE XXI
Area in Crops, Annual Average[a]
(Million Rai)

Period	Region	Paddy	All Other Crops	Total
1950–52	Center	16.9	1.3	18.2
	North	2.3	.4	2.7
	Northeast	13.1	.7	13.8
	South	2.8	2.6	5.4
	Total	35.1	5.0	40.1
1958–60	Center	17.1	3.5	20.6
	North	2.5	.6	3.1
	Northeast	14.5	2.2	16.7
	South	2.9	3.7	6.6
	Total	37.0	10.1	47.1
1965–67	Center	19.9	8.7	28.6
	North	2.7	1.5	4.2
	Northeast	16.3	4.8	21.0
	South	3.7	5.5	9.3
	Total	42.2	20.5	62.7

[a] Detail may not add because of rounding error and because of discrepancies in the original regional data.

Source: *Agricultural Statistics of Thailand, 1967*, Ministry of Agriculture (Bangkok, 1970).

7.4 million rai and the Northeast for 4.1 million rai. Most of the remaining increase is accounted for by rubber in the South.

During the 1950's, the total area planted in paddy grew very slowly, the long-run trend toward a decline in yield per rai continued, and therefore total output rose only a little. In the 1960's the yield trend also appears to have been reversed, and a significant increase in yield per rai was achieved. Table XXII contains the summary data. From 1950–52 to 1958–60, output rose less (4 percent) than population (27 percent), thus reducing the amount of rice available for export.[32] Paddy yield per rai in 1958–60 (195 kg.) was well below the average fifty years earlier (293 kg.).

After 1960 the yield of paddy per rai ended its long decline and began at last to rise. By 1965–67 the national average was up to 243 kg. per rai, and preliminary estimates show a further rise to 280 kg. per rai in 1968 and 1969.[33]

[32] Output may vary greatly from one year to another because of variation in rainfall and other climatic factors. We try to counteract the influence of such variations by using three-year averages as much as possible.

[33] The apparent rise in yields in 1968–69 may be exaggerated. Through 1967, we have used area and output estimates of the Rice Department, Ministry of Agriculture. For 1968 and 1969,

TABLE XXII
ANNUAL AVERAGE YIELD AND OUTPUT OF PADDY

Region	1950–52	1958–60	1965–67	1968–69
A. Yield (Kilograms per Rai)				
Center	222	217	279	n.a.
North	237	306	426	
Northeast	152	145	169	
South	212	220	220	
Total	197	195	243	280
B. Output (Millions of Tons)				
Center	3.76	3.72	5.55	n.a.
North	.55	.77	1.16	
Northeast	1.99	2.10	2.74	
South	.60	.64	.82	
Total	6.90	7.23	10.27	12.90

Sources: *Agricultural Statistics of Thailand, 1967*; National Statistical Office (1968 and 1969 estimates).

The two principal reasons for the rise in yield per rai are (1) the increase in the area being served by irrigation, or at least by flood control, and (2) wider use of improved seeds. However, these improvements have been modest ones, as the so-called "new generation" varieties have not yet been planted enough to have had much effect upon yields. Chemical fertilizer is also beginning to be used, though still in small amounts in comparison with other countries, and machines are being introduced in certain areas, notably tractors (for plowing and harrowing) and water pumps (for water control). Thus, for the first time since 1850, a significant change in technique has occurred in rice cultivation. This change involves several factors, and it is far from complete in 1970. Another decade or two may be required before Thai agriculture can fully absorb the changes that have been set in motion in recent years.

Paddy yields have increased in all regions, as may be seen in Table XXII. The North continues to produce the highest yields, though area planted is small. The Central region still dominates the rice economy, accounting for almost one-half of area planted and slightly over half of total output of paddy, and its yield, already above the national average, has increased. Many large water control projects have been located in the Central region, and these have

we have used estimates of the National Statistical Office, which are higher than Rice Department figures. This matter is further discussed, below, in the "Note on Reliability of Statistical Data." We should also note that a serious drought occurred in 1967, and output was severely reduced.

contributed to the rise in yields. In the Northeast, the area in paddy has continued to grow despite low yields. Only a small percentage of the paddy area is irrigated, and water supply is poor and uncertain, but yield per rai appears to have risen since 1960. Many agriculturalists have pointed out the unsuitability for rice cultivation of soil and climate in the Northeast, and have urged a shift into other crops and activities, but farmers have continued to expand the area in paddy. In recent years, the area planted in other crops has grown rapidly, but this expansion has been in *addition* to paddy cultivation, not a net shift away from it.

A Note on the Reliability of Statistical Data

In the above discussion, and throughout this study, we have necessarily relied upon official statistics. We should emphasize the fact that Thai agricultural statistics have been seriously questioned in recent years, and doubts expressed about their reliability.

The Census of Agriculture, conducted by the National Statistical Office in 1963 (crop year April 1962–April 1963), yielded results that differed substantially from data the Ministry of Agriculture assembled and published in 1962, as shown by the following comparisons of output estimates (metric tons) :[34]

Crop	Census	Ministry of Agriculture	Crop	Census	Ministry of Agriculture
Cotton	16,970	41,580	Castor beans	17,000	44,000
Kenaf	60,000	134,000	Chili	10,000	73,000
Tobacco	14,000	48,000	Groundnuts	38,000	67,000
Soy beans	15,000	30,000	Cassava	945,000	2,076,000

Such large discrepancies cast grave doubts on the statistical base of economic policy, and have led to much discussion of data-collection techniques. The Ministry of Agriculture has long relied upon reports of village headmen. These are assembled and tabulated at amphur and changwat levels and then forwarded to the Ministry in Bangkok. Supervision is inadequate, and many headmen allegedly turn in the same figures every year, or increase them arbitrarily without really checking with farmers. Aside from that, numerous opportunities for error exist, and internal consistency checks are lacking.

On the other hand, the Census results are also suspect. For some crops, Professor Silcock found that Ministry of Agriculture figures were in closer accord with export statistics than were Census figures.[35] Most observers consider foreign trade statistics to be among the most reliable in Thailand. Silcock was reluctant to state a preference, and he emphasized the need to study each crop individually, but he finally concluded that Ministry figures seem better on the whole than Census figures for "other crops."

[34] See Peter Gajewski, "The 1963 Census of Agriculture and the National Income Accounts" (mimeo., Bangkok, 1965), for a discussion of these two sets of data.

[35] Silcock, *Economic Development*, pp. 25–30.

Paddy output was almost the same in the two sources for the 1962/63 crop year, but NSO and the Department of Rice in the Ministry of Agriculture worked closely together and agreed in advance on the final figures. The post-enumeration survey conducted by NSO indicated that paddy output should be increased 6 percent above the Census figure. For other years, NSO estimates differ substantially from those of the Rice Department.

In the 1965 edition of its *National Income of Thailand*, the National Economic Development Board published the results of its calculation of a "Rice Balance Sheet." Starting with the volume of exports (believed to be accurate because of the careful control of the rice trade), NEDB estimated domestic consumption and other uses (seed, feed, storage losses). For the period 1951–61, the total demand for (or use of) rice was 16.3 percent *higher* than the cumulative total of Ministry production figures. NEDB accordingly revised paddy production figures prior to 1963 by that percentage for national income purposes. The 1963 Census figure, increased 6 percent in line with the post-enumeration survey, was accepted by NEDB. For subsequent years, NEDB has adjusted Rice Department figures upward for national income purposes.

Beginning in 1966, NSO conducted "crop cutting surveys" on a sample basis. These surveys have yielded results that are sharply different from Rice Department figures.[36] NSO figures for output of paddy in 1966 were 13.5 million tons and Rice Department figures were 12.0 million tons; in 1967 the figures were 11.2 million tons and 9.6 million tons, respectively. Rice Department figures are consistently lower than those of the National Statistical Office, and the prevailing view seems to be that NSO estimates are the more accurate of the two. Officials in the Rice Department have stated that the old series based on village headman reports would not be published after 1967. Therefore, we have only NSO estimates for 1968 and 1969. These were used to calculate yields, above, and the shift from one basis to another probably exaggerates the increase in yield per rai.

It is clear that agricultural statistics are subject to large margins of error. Not even for the staple product of the country, rice, are area and output figures reliable. For other crops, and for individual changwats, the margins of error are probably greater than for rice.

For the period 1958–68 we have estimated a rice balance sheet, using approximately the same method and assumptions used in the 1965 NEDB estimate (see Table XXIII). For the subperiod 1958 to 1965 inclusive, the calculated volume of cumulative paddy consumption and export (72.9 million tons) is very close to the cumulative production estimate used by NEDB (73.0 million tons), but 8.6 million tons (13.4 percent) above the Rice Department estimates.

However, for the three years 1966–68 the calculated volume of consumption plus export (30.6 million tons) is about equal to the Rice Department pro-

---

[36] *Agricultural Statistics of Thailand, 1967, op. cit.; Report of Crop Cutting Survey, 1968,* National Statistical Office (Bangkok, 1970?).

TABLE XXIII
Estimated Rice Balance Sheet, 1958–68
(Thousand Metric Tons)

Year	(1) Export of Rice	(2) Human Consumption 150 kg./cap.	(3) Total Rice (1) + (2)	(4) Paddy Equiv. (3) ÷ 0.66	(5) Seed[a] 9.6 kg./rai
1958	1,133	3,731	4,864	7,370	346
1959	1,092	3,843	4,935	7,477	364
1960	1,203	3,958	5,161	7,820	355
1961	1,576	4,077	5,653	8,565	371
1962	1,271	4,199	5,470	8,288	400
1963	1,418	4,325	5,743	8,702	396
1964	1,896	4,455	6,351	9,623	392
1965	1,895	4,589	6,484	9,824	389
1966	1,507	4,726	6,233	9,444	443
1967	1,482	4,902	6,384	9,673	385
1968	1,068	5,055	6,123	9,277	425

Year	(6) Animal Feed[b]	(7) Storage Loss[b]	(8) Apparent Consumption & Use[c]	Production Estimate[d] Min. of Agric.	Production Estimate[d] NEDB
1958	168	84	7,968	5,570	6,478
1959	170	85	8,096	7,053	8,285
1960	174	87	8,436	6,770	7,873
1961	178	89	9,203	7,834	9,058
1962	180	90	8,958	8,177	9,591
1963	183	91	9,372	9,279	9,856
1964	199	99	10,313	10,029	10,800
1965	202	101	10,516	9,558	11,070
1966	206	103	10,196	9,218	11,070
1967	206	103	10,367	11,975	12,900
1968	206	103	10,011	9,595	10,700

Period	Cumulative Apparent Consumption	Cumulative Production Est. Min. of Agric.	Cumulative Production Est. NEDB
1958–65			
1958	7,968	5,570	6,478
1959	16,064	12,623	14,763
1960	24,500	19,393	22,636
1961	33,703	27,227	31,694
1962	42,661	35,404	41,285
1963	52,033	44,683	51,141
1964	62,346	54,712	61,941
1965	72,862	64,270	73,011
1966–68			
1966	10,196	9,218	11,070
1967	20,563	21,193	23,970
1968	30,574	30,788	34,670

[a] Estimated on a basis similar to that of the NEDB 1965 calculation.
[b] Estimate. [c] Col. 8 = Cols. 4 + 5 + 6 + 7.
[d] For previous crop year; i.e. the crop planted in 1960 is exported and consumed in 1961.

duction estimate (30.8 million tons). The NEDB estimate was 4.1 million tons *above* the calculated usage. NSO figures are 5.0 million tons above the calculated usage.

This result casts doubt on NSO's production estimates. It is unlikely that rice consumption per capita has risen in recent years, nor has any other use of paddy developed that could account for 1.4 to 1.7 million tons per year. One possibility is that rice held in stocks rose in the period 1966–68. Our calculation has implicitly assumed that rice stocks have remained constant. However, it seems unlikely that farmers would increase their stocks of paddy so much, nor would millers or other middlemen have much incentive to hold such large stocks. Indeed, it is doubtful that off-farm storage capacity is large enough to accommodate 4 to 5 million tons of paddy. Finally, the 1967/68 crop year was a poor one, with output sharply reduced by a severe drought, and one would expect stocks to be quite low in 1968.

No firm conclusion can be drawn, but this calculation does at least raise doubts about the NSO crop cutting surveys. Perhaps the Ministry of Agriculture has been too hasty in abandoning its traditional system of data collection.

The Rice Premium

A single issue has dominated Thai agricultural policy discussion for two decades—namely, the taxation of rice exports, usually referred to as the "rice premium." We saw in Chapter 4 that Thai farmers had a light burden of taxation in the 1930's. By that time, both of the two historic forms of direct taxation—the head tax and the land tax—had been abolished. However, we also saw how the multiple-exchange rate system and the rice export tax resulted in a heavy tax burden on the rice farmer in the years following World War II (see pp. 87–92, above). In 1955 this multiple-exchange rate system was itself abolished and a unitary exchange rate adopted. At the same time, the government established the "rice premium" system, under which rice exporters were required to pay a specific tax for each ton of rice exported. Premium rates were fixed for the several different grades and types of rice. Since the rice premium (and the export duty)[37] must be paid on rice that is exported but not on rice that is sold and consumed domestically, the domestic price tends to differ from the world price by the amount of the premium.

Although rice premium rates have been changed from time to time, the basic system has remained the same from 1955 to 1970. During this period the rice premium has been the subject of vigorous and sometimes heated discussion and debate, both inside and outside government. It has been discussed in the popular press, in government reports, in political debate, in several theses

---

[37] The economic effect of the export duty (which is 4.2 percent ad valorem for white rice) is exactly the same as that of the rice premium. In this discussion, when we refer to the rice premium we shall mean the sum of the two, unless otherwise stated.

and dissertations by Thai economists, and in many articles and books. One could say that for Thailand the rice premium controversy has been comparable in importance and scope to the Corn Law controversy for England in the first half of the nineteenth century.[38] Although no Ricardo has yet emerged, the rice premium has stimulated more writing by Thai economists than any other issue in the past century.[39]

The intensive analysis and discussion of the rice premium has made it clear that the issue is an extremely complex one, that it can be discussed at several different levels, and that fundamental issues of equity, social policy, and development strategy are involved.[40] One reason the debate has been so protracted and lively may be that certain key points remain obscure because of the lack of reliable and decisive evidence, while others involve values and imponderables not amenable to logical proof.

A full discussion of this issue would require an entire book. Here we shall merely attempt a brief summary of the main points, drawing on the work of the authors cited above.

Premium rates for selected grades of rice are presented in Table XXIV. Private exporters must pay these amounts per ton of rice exported.[41] Although premium rates for specific grades have been changed from time to time, the average level did not vary greatly during the twelve-year period 1955–66. Rate changes were infrequent. For some important grades of rice, such as 100 percent, the premium per ton was changed only twice in twelve years. For other grades, such as broken rice (A1 super), changes were more frequent, but it is

---

[38] Both these cases involved an adjustable set of duties on the major grain staple, but of course the corn laws were *import* duties designed to protect English farmers and keep the domestic price of wheat higher than it would otherwise have been. The Thai rice premium is an *export* duty and a tax on the Thai farmer. It causes the domestic price of rice to be lower than it would otherwise be. In both cases, the effect on income distribution is a central issue in the controversy.

[39] A partial list of significant publications includes Chaiyong Chuchart and Sopin Tongpan, *The Determination and Analysis of Policies to Support and Stabilize Agricultural Prices and Incomes of Thai Farmers* (Bangkok, 1965); Phairach Krisanamis, *Paddy Price Movements and Their Effect on the Economic Situation of Farmers in the Central Plain of Thailand* (Bangkok, 1967); M. C. Sithiporn Kridakara, *Some Aspects of Rice Farming in Siam* (Bangkok, 1970); Sura Sanittanont, *Thailand's Rice Expert Tax: Its Effects on the Rice Economy* (Bangkok, 1967); T. H. Silcock (ed.), *Thailand: Social and Economic Studies in Development* (Canberra, 1967), esp. Chs. 9 and 10; T. H. Silcock, *The Economic Development of Thai Agriculture* (Canberra, 1970); D. Usher, "The Economics of the Rice Premium" (mimeo., Bangkok, 1965?); Edward Van Roy, "The Pursuit of Growth and Stability Through Taxation of Agricultural Exports: Thailand's Experience," *Public Finance*, XXIII, No. 3, 294–317; Melvin Wagner and Sopin Tongpan, "Structure of Thai Rice Prices" (mimeo., Bangkok, 1965).

[40] Two researchers confessed that "prior to starting this research we thought the premium was good. At the time this research was begun, we thought perhaps it should be abolished altogether. After a year of serious and more or less continuous research on the subject, we feel very strongly that more research is needed." Wagner and Tongpan, *op. cit.*, p. 2.

[41] Some rice is exported under government-to-government contracts. In this case, the government's selling price exceeds its buying price, thus generating a profit that is analogous to the rice premium. The rate of such profit appears to be lower than the rice premium rate on commercial exports.

TABLE XXIV
Rice Premium Rates, Selected Grades[a]
(Baht per Metric Ton)

Date of Change[b]	White Rice 100%	White Rice 5%	White Rice 15%	Broken Rice A1 Super	Glutinous Rice (Whole)
Jan. 1, 1956	935	935	935	470	600
April 23, 1958				590	
June 18, 1959				470	
Nov. 4, 1959					840
Dec. 30, 1959	890	890	840	450	800
Aug. 2, 1960				540	
Dec. 30, 1960				500	600
April 17, 1961				540	
June 6, 1961			890		
April 3, 1962	950	950	950	600	
May 15, 1962					800
Oct. 3, 1962					700
July 16, 1963					800
Jan. 16, 1967	1,010	980	940	680	
March 1967	1,090	1,050	1,000	700	840
April 1967	1,240	1,190	1,080	790	
May 1967	1,300	1,230	1,130	810	
June 1967	1,320	1,260	1,150		850
July 1967	1,470	1,400	1,290	840	
Aug. 1967	1,640	1,570	1,460	930	860
Sept. 1967	1,520	1,450	1,350	890	850
Oct.–Nov. 1967	1,640	1,570	1,460	930	980
Dec. 1967					850
Jan. 1968					840
Feb. 1968					900
March 1968	2,070	1,970	1,890	1,270	1,470
April–May 1968	1,960	1,810	1,670	1,090	1,420
June–Oct. 1968	1,830	1,680	1,540	960	1,530
Nov. 1, 1968	1,450	1,450	1,300	800	1,250
Sept. 15, 1969	1,100	1,100	1,100	500	
Dec. 3, 1969	1,000	1,000	900		800

[a] From time to time, special incentive offers were made; e.g., in August 1969, any exporter who sold 2,000 tons was charged only 1,100 baht (for 5 percent rice) instead of the official rate of 1,450 baht.

[b] Rates remained unchanged between dates; e.g., the premium for 100 percent rice was 935 baht per ton from Jan. 1, 1956, to Dec. 30, 1959, then 890 baht until April 3, 1962.

Sources: Bank of Thailand, *Monthly Report*; Bank of Thailand, *IMF Consultations*, 1968, 1969, 1970; Usher, *Economics of the Rice Premium*, p. 2.

TABLE XXV
RICE EXPORTS AND THE RICE PREMIUM

Year	Rice Exports			Rice Premium			
	(1) Volume (Thousand Metric Tons)	(2) Value (Million Baht)	(3) Average Price (Baht/ton)	(4) Total Premium (Million Baht)	(5)a Average Premium (Baht/ton)	(6)b Value of Exports (Percent)	(7)c Total Govt. Revenue (Percent)
						Ratio of Premium to	
1950	1,418	1,672	1,179				
1951	1,474	1,824	1,237				
1952	1,549	2,629	1,697				
1953	1,359	3,747	2,757				
1954	1,001	3,087	3,084				
1955	1,236	3,133	2,535				
1956	1,265	2,861	2,262	842	666	29%	17%
1957	1,570	3,622	2,307	840	535	23	16
1958	1,133	2,968	2,620	812	717	27	15
1959	1,092	2,576	2,359	756	692	29	13
1960	1,203	2,570	2,136	745	619	29	11
1961	1,576	3,598	2,283	872	553	24	12
1962	1,271	3,240	2,534	753	592	23	9
1963	1,418	3,424	2,416	819	578	24	9
1964	1,896	4,389	2,315	1,238	653	28	12
1965	1,895	4,334	2,281	1,192	629	28	11
1966	1,507	4,001	2,650	995	660	25	8
1967	1,482	4,653	3,144	995	671	21	7
1968	1,068	3,775	3,534	1,268	1,187	34	8
1969	1,023	2,945	2,879	1,037	1,014	35	6

a Col. 4 ÷ col. 1.　　b Col. 4 ÷ col. 2.　　c Col. 4 ÷ total government revenue.

Sources: Bank of Thailand, *Monthly Report*; Bank of Thailand, *IMF Consultations*, 1960, 1970; Department of Customs, *Annual Statement of Foreign*

clear that rice premium rates were not used systematically to counteract or otherwise respond to changes in world rice prices.[42] The purposes of specific rate changes, such as those for glutinous rice, are not fully explained, but one purpose is to influence the quantity of exports and the domestic price. For example, if a strong export demand for glutinous rice began to reduce the amount remaining for domestic use, and thus to raise its price in the domestic market, the premium rate could be increased in order to check exports and widen the spread between the world price and domestic price. Even though the over-all rate structure has not shown a sensitive response (or relationship) to world prices, the premium for a specific grade of rice may be changed in response to export demand.

During the three years 1967–69, premium rates were changed much more frequently than in the preceding twelve years. A serious drought occurred in 1967, and it became clear that the rice crop would be a poor one. At the same time, world rice prices began to rise. The government became alarmed about the prospect of a domestic rice shortage and a sharp rise in the domestic price of rice. Early in 1967 the rice premium was placed on an *ad valorem* basis, linked to the export price. For example, the premium for "white rice 5 percent broken" was 30 percent *ad valorem*. "Official" export prices were fixed each month as a basis for premium calculation. (The results of this calculation are shown in Table XXIV for the period January 1967 to December 1969.) The *ad valorem* rate was later raised to 40 percent and 60 percent. Export quotas were also applied to ensure a sufficient domestic supply of rice. Rice exports in 1968 were only 1,068,000 tons, the lowest level since 1954.

As a result of these vigorous measures, the domestic wholesale price of rice was actually driven *down* during the period of most acute shortage. An example will be given, below, for a specific grade of rice.

Long after the crisis was past, in September 1969, premium rates were made specific again. By December 1969 they were back to about the levels existing in 1966.

Since 1955 the rice premium has accounted for 25–35 percent of the total value of rice exports. Annual figures are given in Table XXV. These figures understate the size of the tax on commercial exports, however, because they include the profit on government-to-government contracts, which is often lower than the premium paid by private exporters.[43] They also omit the straight export duty.

[42] For the period 1956–63, one study showed a slight tendency for the average premium rate and average export price to move in the same direction, though the premium changes were quite small in comparison with export price changes. See Chaiyong Chuchart and Sopin Tongpan, *op. cit.*, pp. 39–41.

[43] Usher, "The Economics of the Rice Premium," *op. cit.*, presents some figures comparing the premiums for private and government-to-government exports. However, these figures may not correctly indicate the comparative premium rates because we do not know the composition, by grade, of the two types of exports. It is likely that exports under government contract contain

Despite some problems with the numbers, the rice premium clearly represents a heavy export levy. Such a tax on the staple agricultural product of the country, whose cultivation is the chief occupation of most of the people, inevitably has had important effects upon the economy.

Among other things, the rice premium has been a major source of tax revenue, though its share of total government revenue has declined from 16.5 percent in 1956 to 5.7 percent in 1969 (see Table XXV for annual data).

At one level, economic analysis of the rice premium focuses on its effect on a chain of prices: export price, domestic wholesale and retail prices of rice, and domestic paddy prices (wholesale and ex-farm). Most economists agree that the rice premium has little, if any, effect on the world price of rice.[44] They argue that even though Thailand is one of the major rice exporters, its exports represent only a tiny fraction of total world supply. Thus, Thailand faces a highly elastic world demand curve for rice and has no power to raise its export price above the world price as determined by total supply and demand conditions at any given time. Changes in rice premium rates will have negligible effects on the world price. The most detailed study of rice prices showed that Thai export prices have indeed followed world prices very closely. The authors concluded that "the Thai export price of rice is obviously bound to the world price; therefore, the rice premium has largely been ineffective for stabilizing the export price."[45]

This point is an important one because government spokesmen have sometimes argued that the rice premium causes the export price to be higher than it would otherwise be, and that the burden of the tax is therefore passed on to the foreign consumer. Although such oligopoly power may exist in a small degree in certain instances, as in sales to a market area where people have a marked preference for Thai rice, most economists accept the conclusion reached above, namely, that the rice premium has only negligible effects upon the world price. However, we should note that the statistical evidence is inconclusive: close correlation between Thai export prices and world prices does not prove that premium changes have no effect upon world prices.

---

a higher proportion of the cheaper grades, with lower premiums per ton, than private exports. Usher's figures are as follows:

Period	Quantity of Exports (Thousand Metric Tons)		Premium per Ton (Baht)	
	Private	Government-to-Government	Private	Government-to-Government
Oct. 1959–Sept. 1960	930	308	638	420
Oct. 1960–Sept. 1961	919	585	657	416
Oct. 1961–Sept. 1962	954	465	703	237
Oct. 1962–Sept. 1963	793	448	742	436
Oct. 1963–Sept. 1964	951	803	736	546

[44] Usher, "The Economics of the Rice Premium," op. cit., estimated that elimination of the premium when it averaged 30 percent would cause world price to decline by 2.7 percent.

[45] Churchart and Tongpan, op. cit., p. 36. These and other authors have recognized, however, that rice is not homogeneous and that buyer preference for a particular variety will require a degree of qualification to the above remarks.

The domestic wholesale price of rice tends to be equal to the export price less the rice premium, and less the exporter's margin to cover costs. For example, if white rice 5 percent were selling in the export market at 3,000 baht per ton, if the rice premium were 1,100 baht per ton, and if the costs of export were 50 baht per ton, a commercial exporter would not pay *more* than 1,850 baht per ton in the Bangkok wholesale market (3,000 — 1,100 — 50 = 1,850). On the other hand, he could not obtain this rice for much less than 1,850 baht per ton because of competition from other exporters. This point, a simple one, is generally supported by empirical studies of rice prices, which show the expected relationship between export and wholesale price.[46]

At the next link in the marketing chain, the wholesale price of *paddy* will tend to be equal to the wholesale price of rice in Bangkok, minus a relatively constant package which includes the milling fee, transport cost, and middleman margins. This link is more difficult to establish statistically, because paddy prices vary in different regions as local supply-demand balance shifts. because reliable regional price series do not exist, and because transport costs and middleman margins are difficult to establish. However, studies of the marketing structure have reached the conclusion that it is highly competitive. No doubt oligopsony and monopsony power exist, but the relatively large numbers of millers, traders, and other middlemen, plus the freedom of entry into these occupations, imply that marketing margins will be close to the cost of services performed.[47]

We have, therefore, the following equation:[48]

Paddy price at farm = export price of rice — (rice premium + exporter's margin) — (milling fee + transport cost + middleman's margin)

If we assume that the export price is fixed in the world market and that the several marketing costs are determined competitively, then it follows that a change in the rice premium will be transmitted directly to the paddy price, though probably with some lag. In particular, if the premium were abolished entirely, the paddy price would rise sharply. Usher calculated that it would rise about 85 percent.[49]

[46] Discrepancies may arise because of imperfections in the data, but also because of other barriers and restrictions on rice exports, such as quotas, licensing requirements, and administrative procedures that increase the exporter's cost. There has been increasing manipulation of such invisible barriers in recent years to regulate rice exports.

[47] Farmers receive about 72 percent of the domestic retail value of rice, according to a study made by Dr. Udhis Narkswasdi, *Farmers' Indebtedness and Paddy Marketing in Central Thailand* (Bangkok, 1958), cited in Sura Sanittanont, *op. cit.*, p. 66. In a subsequent study, Usher concluded that the rice trade was highly competitive. He estimated that the farm price of paddy was 79 percent of the *retail* price of rice (for comparable quantities). See D. Usher, "The Thai Rice Trade," in Silcock (ed.), *Thailand, op. cit.* These are much higher percentages of retail prices than farmers receive in most countries.

[48] One ton of paddy yields about 0.66 tons of rice. Therefore, in this equation the "paddy price" refers to the quantity of paddy required to produce a ton of rice, or about 1.51 tons.

[49] Usher, in Silcock, ed., *Thailand, op. cit.*, p. 7. In his calculation, Usher allowed for a fall of 3 percent in the world price.

This analysis of course implies that the burden of the rice premium is borne largely by the rice farmer. The government has denied this conclusion, and has argued that abolition of the rice premium would simply increase the profits of middlemen. It is difficult to put much credence in this argument. As mentioned above, all studies of the rice trade indicate that vigorous competition exists in these activities.

Another piece of evidence can also be adduced. It can be seen in the above equation that a spontaneous *increase* in the export price, with the rice premium left unchanged, has the same effect on the right-hand-side of the equation as does an equal *reduction* in the rice premium with a constant export price. If the government argument were valid, an increase in the export price would have little or no effect upon the paddy price. (Presumably the monopsonistic middleman would be just as eager to take advantage of an increase in his profit margin arising from a rise in the export price as he would one arising from a reduction in the rice premium.) This hypothesis can be tested because, though premium rates have been changed rather infrequently, the world price is constantly changing. Analysis of export prices and paddy prices shows that the two series are positively correlated, and that increases (decreases) in the export price are quickly followed by increases (decreases) in paddy prices. This result is inconsistent with the hypothesis based on the government's argument.[50]

To explain these price relationships during the past fifteen years, it may be helpful to examine the experience with one particular grade of rice. Chart V contains the pertinent price series for white rice, 5 percent broken.[51]

In Chart V we can see that the rice premium rate remained almost constant from 1956 to 1966, even though the export price varied considerably in this period. While the rice premium remained unchanged, fluctuations in the export price were transmitted directly to the domestic wholesale price. In fact, the existence of the constant rice premium made the *percentage* changes in domestic prices larger than those of the export price.

Paddy prices, in turn, closely followed domestic wholesale rice prices, and were therefore also responsive to world price changes. For the period 1956 to 1970, the simple correlation coefficient between the export price (adjusted for premium) and the paddy price was 0.85. See Chart VI for a scatter diagram.

When world rice prices began to rise in 1966, domestic prices immediately followed. To protect the domestic supply of rice and to restrain domestic price rises, export quotas were imposed in the latter part of 1966. When the price rise continued in 1967, rice premium rates were increased sharply—for

[50] M. C. Sithiporn Kridakara, *op. cit.*, has forcefully stated the logical argument summarized above and has challenged various government officials to explain the contradiction. To my knowledge, none of them has yet responded to this specific point.

[51] This term means milled white rice with about 5 percent broken grains. The export price is f.o.b. Bangkok, including duty and premium. The wholesale price is for Bangkok.

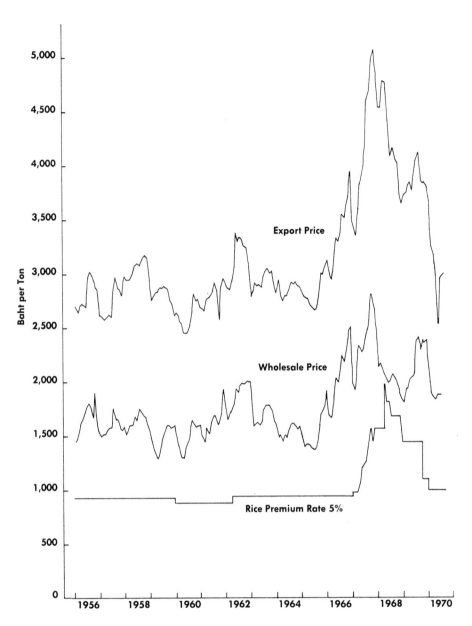

Chart V. White rice, 5% broken. Monthly averages of export price and wholesale price, and premium rate. For sources, see Chart VI and Table XXIV.

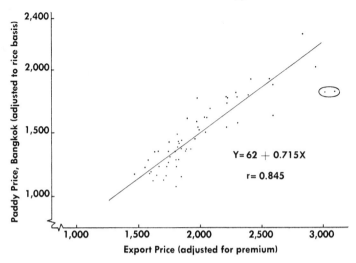

Chart VI. White rice, 5% broken (export rice), related to No. 2 paddy (wholesale price). Monthly averages for February, May, August, and November, 1956–70. The two circled points, for November 1967 and February 1968, deviate from the usual pattern because of quotas and other nonprice restrictions and are omitted from the regression calculations. Sources: Paddy price, 1956–59, Department of Internal Trade; 1960–69, Bank of Thailand, *Monthly Report*. Export rice price, 1956–63, Chuchart and Tongpen, *The Determination and Analysis of Policies to Support and Stabilize Agricultural Prices and Incomes of Thai Farmers* (Bangkok, May 1965); 1964–70, Board of Trade.

5 percent rice, from 950 baht per ton in January 1967 to 1,570 baht per ton by year-end. Export quotas continued in force.

By the third quarter of 1967 it became clear that a severe drought throughout Thailand would badly damage the standing rice crop. Prices soared; the domestic wholesale price of 5 percent rice reached a peak of 2,820 baht per ton (monthly average) in September 1967 (see Chart V). The rice premium was changed frequently during this crisis, reaching a high of 1,970 baht per ton in March 1968,[52] and quotas were also employed. These measures succeeded in reducing domestic prices of rice and paddy; they fell sharply in the last quarter of 1967 and continued to fall throughout 1968 during the period of most acute rice shortage. Rice exports in 1968 were only 1,068,000 tons, down a third from 1967.

The 1968 crop was a good one, but not until late 1969 was the rice premium rate brought back down to pre-crisis levels.

This episode illustrates very well the government's determination to safeguard the domestic supply of rice. (Incidentally, this is a policy that has deep

[52] Actually, the rice premium was shifted from a specific to an ad valorem tax in January 1967. However, in practice an official export price was designated each month to which the ad valorem rate was then applied. At the peak, the rate was 60 percent ad valorem, with a 1,000 baht deduction.

roots in Thai history. From the seventeenth to the nineteenth century, the king could and did prohibit the export of rice whenever the domestic stock ran low. The episode also shows that the rice premium could be used as a device to stabilize the domestic price, even though it was not used for that purpose from 1956 to 1966 to any great extent.

It is interesting to note that government revenue from the rice premium increased from 1967 to 1968, despite the sharp fall in export volume.

The argument thus far can be summarized briefly, if simplistically, with the aid of Chart VII.[53] The world demand curve for Thai rice exports (PZ) is assumed to be perfectly elastic at the prevailing world price (OP). The domestic demand (DD) and supply (SS) curves are both perfectly inelastic in the relevant price range. Under these assumptions, OQ of rice will be consumed domestically, and QX will be exported. The government collects the average rice premium, PR, on each ton exported, thus generating tax revenue amounting to LMNT (the shaded area in Chart VII). Domestic consumers benefit because they can satisfy their demand for rice at the domestic price (OR), which is equal to the world price minus the rice premium, or a total gain amounting to PLTR.

As Chart VII is constructed, if the rice premium were abolished, both world price and quantity exported would remain unchanged. The chief issue concerns the distribution of the two components of the differential between rice output valued at world price and rice output valued at domestic price—namely PLTR and LMNT. The government has argued that both components would be appropriated by monopsonistic middlemen, leaving the farmers' income unchanged. Most economists believe that the prices of middleman services are fixed competitively, and that they would remain substantially unchanged. Thus abolition of the premium would cause the income of rice farmers to rise by PMNR; i.e., both components of the differential would accrue to rice farmers.

In Chart VII, the supply of exports is perfectly inelastic in the relevant range. However, it seems likely that higher paddy prices would encourage greater output, in which case the situation would be as depicted in Chart VIII. Initially, at the world price OP, a rice premium PR is levied, with the result that QX of rice is exported, OQ consumed domestically. Tax revenue is LMNT, as before. But now when the rice premium is abolished and the domestic price rises from OR to OP, total output increases to OW, and the quantity of exports rises from QX to QW. Farm income rises not only because the farmer receives the higher world price for existing output, but also because total output rises.[54]

[53] See Sura Sanittanont, *op. cit.*, Ch. 1, for an excellent diagrammatic analysis of the effects of the rice premium.

[54] This is of course a partial equilibrium analysis and does not allow for the effect on output of other crops, replacement of tax revenue, effect on other sectors, and other complications.

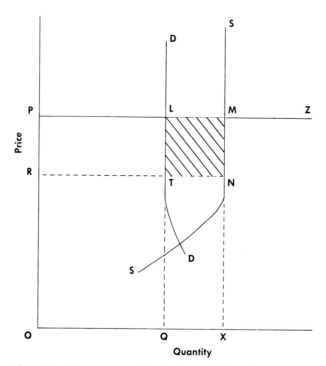

Chart VII. Rice premium, inelastic domestic demand and supply.

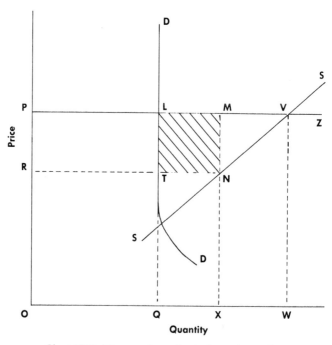

Chart VIII. Rice premium, elastic domestic supply.

The foregoing partial equilibrium analysis provides some insights, but it is not adequate to deal with many issues involved in the rice premium controversy. Everyone seems to agree that the rice premium depresses the domestic price of rice below what it would otherwise be.[55] The government view is that this price effect is desirable because it holds down the cost of living in urban areas and thus prevents the development of pressure for higher wages (and higher salaries for civil servants). Low money wages encourage exports and enable the infant industrial sector to compete with imports. If domestic rice prices were to rise sharply, the real income of nonfarm workers would fall (since rice is a staple foodstuff) and pressure would develop for increases in wages and salaries. Government expenditures would rise and new tax revenues would have to be found, not only to replace the lost rice premium revenue but also to cover the increase in expenditures. It is even possible, so the argument goes, that rice farmers may end up with no rise in their real incomes because industrial (and service sector) prices would rise and restore the real terms of trade between the agricultural and nonagricultural sectors, and because some of the new taxes would fall on rice farmers.

At this level the argument becomes extremely complex because there is no single alternative situation to be compared with the present one. Consideration of the effects of a change in the rice premium on other sectors, other segments of the population, government revenue and expenditure, the balance of payments, incentives to work, etc., introduces many additional variables. Space does not permit an examination of all the interactions, and all the possible combinations of these variables. Therefore, we shall simply summarize the major issues in the discussion.

Opponents of the rice premium argue that it comprises a heavy tax burden on a large part of the population, most of whom have relatively low incomes anyway. Not only is this tax burden excessive and unfair; it also discourages productive effort and hinders improvements in farm technology. Because the rice premium reduces the paddy price received by the farmer, his incentive to expand output is less strong. Therefore, he will not plant as much land as he might otherwise plant; he will not cultivate as intensively; he will not use fertilizer; and he will not be so eager to adopt new seed varieties, especially if they are more expensive and more risky than traditional varieties. For all of these reasons, the rice premium tends to reduce the output of paddy.[56]

The negative influence on fertilizer use has attracted particular attention. Traditionally, Thai rice farmers have not used fertilizers, but the effect of chemical fertilizers on yields has been publicized in recent years, and the ad-

[55] Government spokesmen accept this point even though it contradicts their argument that the premium increases the world price and is borne by the foreign buyer.

[56] In his exhaustive study of supply response, Jere Behrman concluded that a significant response to price existed in Thailand, and that reduction of the premium would induce an increase in the marketed supply of rice (*Supply Response in Underdeveloped Agriculture*, Amsterdam, 1968, pp. 314, 336–37).

vantages seem apparent. However, the price of fertilizer relative to the price of paddy is artificially high in Thailand because of the rice premium. The relevant comparison is the *ratio* of fertilizer price to paddy price. Behrman cites a comparison between Thailand, where one kilogram of nitrogen was equal in value to 6.70 kg. of paddy, and Japan, where 1 kg. of nitrogen was equal in value to only 1.44 kg. of paddy.[57] These figures suggest that the Thai farmer is behaving rationally when he declines to buy fertilizer to apply to his paddy fields. The value of the additional output would scarcely cover the cost of the fertilizer, leaving him no return for his investment and his labor.

This point has particular force in Thailand now, because most of the land best suited for rice-growing has already been brought under cultivation, and future increases in output largely depend upon increases in the yield per rai. Furthermore, some evidence suggests that the agricultural labor force is underemployed, at least seasonally, and opportunity probably exists to utilize that labor in activities that would contribute to an increase in yields if it were economically attractive to the farmer and his family.[58]

Opponents further argue that the rice premium has hampered the growth of exports, prevented Thailand from taking full advantage of its comparative advantage in rice in a period when the export market was favorable, and therefore reduced the gains from trade and contributed to the adverse balance of trade on current account. The disincentive effect upon the farming population has deprived the nation of increases in real output that lay within its capability. By depriving the most populous sector of substantial increases in real income, the rice premium has also hampered the development of domestic nonfarm industries, which need a large domestic market to flourish.

Proponents of the rice premium dispute these several arguments.[59] Some proponents argue that the premium does not reduce the domestic price but raises the world price; therefore the tax burden falls on the foreign buyer. As we have seen, few people take this argument seriously. At the next level, the effect of the premium on the domestic price is admitted, but it is argued that reduction of the premium would not benefit rice farmers because millers and middlemen would appropriate all the benefits for themselves. Government spokesmen have presented no evidence to support their case, and, as we have

---

[57] Behrman, *op. cit.*, p. 88.

[58] This point is controversial. Some economists assert that no surplus labor exists at the peaks of planting and harvesting. Even if they are correct, the agricultural sector might be able to utilize off-season labor to reduce the labor requirements in these peak seasons and thus achieve an increase in output. Obvious possibilities include double-cropping, use of labor to construct capital equipment, investment in labor-saving equipment (pumps, mini-tractors), and increased use of fertilizer.

[59] Systematic statements of the case *for* the rice premium are rare. Nearly all economists who have studied the matter have ended up as opponents. The high government officials who decide the matter do not publish scholarly papers. However, a few officials have made statements or written letters and short papers. Some of these are available in M. C. Sithiporn Kridakara, *op. cit.*, but many arguments must be supplied by imputation, as it were.

seen, all studies of the marketing mechanism point in the other direction.[60] In a brief comment on this matter, the World Bank Mission gave its support to the government view. Although granting that "the tax definitely tends to reduce rice prices within the country," the Report stated that "it seems likely that the tax does not act as a serious disincentive and that, if it were removed or reduced little benefit would accrue to the farmer."[61] No evidence is cited, and one wonders what could have been the basis of this statement.

A related argument is that the rice premium serves to stabilize the domestic price of rice and paddy. While it is true that a variable export duty *could* be used, within limits, to shield the domestic economy from fluctuation in world prices, the fact is that the rice premium has not been managed in this way. Rates have been changed infrequently, and domestic prices have moved in close correspondence with world prices. (The 1967–69 episode is of course an exception to these last statements.) In recognition of this connection, the government has stated its intention to stabilize farm income by placing a floor price on paddy and supporting it at that level by government purchases. Such a program has been initiated, but its practical effect has been small. Government has neither money nor storage facilities for large quantities of paddy, so the program exists mainly on paper. When the rice premium is held constant, as it has been during most of the period 1955 to 1970, it of course does nothing to stabilize either farm prices or incomes. Changes in world prices are transmitted directly to the farmer.

At a deeper level the argument becomes more complex, as emphasis is placed on various intersectoral effects and on alternative uses of agricultural resources. No clear statement exists of the entire case, but we shall attempt to give a brief summary. Thai farmers have specialized in rice, and rice cultivation has been a way of life, not just an occupation. Thailand now needs to develop a diversified agriculture, partly to avoid the risk of excessive dependence on a single crop but also to provide a variety of raw materials for a growing economy. By depressing the domestic price of rice, the premium increases the relative attraction of other crops and thus promotes a diversified agriculture. Some proponents also assert that the supply of rice is inelastic, and that the premium therefore does not reduce rice output. (The alleged inelastic supply may be attributed to cultural factors, or to the lack of additional land suited for rice cultivation.) This point requires the assumption that farmers will *not* respond to higher prices of rice but that they *will* respond to price incentives in other crops. Alternatively, it may be argued that the proceeds of the rice premium are being returned to the agricultural sector, and to rice farmers in particular, in the form of investments in irrigation, transporta-

---

[60] It is true, however, that middlemen holding *stocks* of rice and paddy at the moment a premium reduction was announced would enjoy a windfall profit on those stocks. This windfall gain could be minimized by announcing a premium reduction just before harvest.

[61] *A Public Development Program for Thailand* (IBRD, Baltimore, Md., 1959), pp. 68–69.

tion facilities, and agricultural extension activities. These investments will increase productivity, so it is argued, even more effectively than would an increase in price. Consequently, the depressive effect on output is offset by these social overhead investments.[62]

Low domestic rice prices not only encourage agricultural diversification, but also stimulate nonagricultural industries. Because rice is a staple food and an important component of the standard of living, low rice prices permit firms to pay lower money wages and thus to compete with imported goods. Low wages also encourage foreign capital inflows. The rice premium stimulates import substitution and the growth of new exports, and thus contributes to the modernization of the Thai economy.

Thus, the issue becomes one of developmental strategy, with the rice premium assigned the role of an instrument of modernization. A link may even be made to theories of economic development which assert that it is necessary to force savings in the traditional agricultural sector and transfer them to the nonagricultural (modern) sector. On the assumptions that the supply of rice is inelastic and that surplus labor exists in the agricultural sector, one could apply a dual-economy model deriving from Lewis's celebrated article[63] and conclude that the rice premium would promote economic development.

A related point, one that no doubt carries much weight in top governmental circles, is that low rice prices permit salary levels of government workers to be lower than they would otherwise be. Without the premium, the cost of living would rise, civil service salaries would have to be increased, and government expenditures increased accordingly. Tax revenues would have to rise. It has been argued that the political constituency most vital to the ruling government is the civil service, whose welfare is a paramount concern in setting policy. On the other hand, the rice premium has *not* been used as a price stabilization device—except in the emergency following the 1967 crop failure. Fluctuations in world price have been transmitted directly to domestic prices of rice and paddy because premium rates have been held constant. From 1965 to 1967, for example, the domestic price of rice rose about 56 percent. In the same period, the Bangkok-Thonburi consumer price index rose 8 percent, and the food component of this index rose only 14 percent. This suggests that some estimates of the effect of rice price increases on the cost of living have been too high.

Sometimes, proponents even assert that rice farmers would not benefit from a reduction in the rice premium because they would have to pay higher taxes

[62] In another context, Professor T. H. Silcock observed that "the Thai rice premium . . . can be partly interpreted as a successful capture, for the public purse, of most of the profit resulting from improved transport of Thai rice during the twentieth century." *Economic Development of Thai Agriculture, op. cit.,* p. 5.

[63] W. A. Lewis, "Economic Development with Unlimited Supplies of Labour," *Manchester School,* May 1954.

in some other way, and because the prices of goods they buy would rise.[64] In short, it is argued that the real terms of trade between rice farmers and the rest of the economy would not be improved by a reduced premium.

The actual outcome would depend on the choice of new taxes. This argument has at least the virtue of bringing into sharp focus the question of *equity*, which plays a central role in the entire controversy. Opponents of the rice premium believe that the rice farmer now bears a disproportionate burden of taxation. Usher estimated that the rice farmer paid 22 percent of his income in taxes, compared with about 10 percent for nonfarm sectors.[65] Since farm incomes are much lower than nonfarm incomes, the tax system is severely regressive. On the basis of equity, it is difficult to argue that the Thai farmer should subsidize the higher living standard of the urban, nonfarm population. However, even if political reality required him to do so, forms of taxation could be chosen that would not blunt incentive, reduce output, and distort the allocation of resources as much as the rice premium does.

We may note here that the burden of the rice premium seems heaviest on the larger rice farmers, and on farmers in the Central Plain. Farmers who do not grow rice, or who grow it only for their own subsistence, are not harmed by the premium. Indeed, they are beneficiaries of it because it reduces the prices of goods they buy. Average size of farm is larger in the Central Plain, and the bulk of the rice surplus is produced there; therefore, the principal burden is borne by rice farmers in that region. This point is interesting because it has long been alleged that the Bangkok government is primarily concerned with the Central Plain, and that this region has received favorable treatment. It has done so in some respects, such as provision of transportation and irrigation. Perhaps the government has not fully perceived that its rice premium policy has imposed an especially heavy burden on rice farmers in this region. In any case, since irrigation and other public works have been concentrated in the Central region, a rough kind of social justice may have been achieved, at least *within* the agricultural sector.

Although the weight of informed opinion by Thai economists has been against the rice premium on all three of the serious issues in the controversy—equity, allocative and incentive effects, and developmental strategy—the premium system has been retained. Indeed, premium rates reached new peaks in 1968, after a rash of publications in 1964–67.

Now it is possible that the rice premium will be eliminated by economic

[64] In his translated summary, M. C. Sithiporn Kridakara (*op. cit.*, pp. 148–49) attributes to Mr. Nam Pumwathu, Director General of the Department of Foreign Trade, the "astonishing" statement that "the premium is of great benefit to the rice farmers, because if it were to be abolished government would have to make up for the loss in revenue by taxation in other fields. . . . Since farmers form 80% of the population they . . . would have to bear the burden of this increased taxation, and since the premium relieves the farmers of these higher taxes it is actually of benefit to them rather than the reverse."

[65] Usher, "The Economics of the Rice Premium," *op. cit.*, p. 14.

TABLE XXVI

AVERAGE ANNUAL AREA PLANTED IN CROPS OTHER THAN RICE

(Thousand Rai)

Product	Whole Kingdom 1950–52	1958–60	1965–67	Center 1950–52	1958–60	1965–67	North 1950–52	1958–60	1965–67	Northeast 1950–52	1958–60	1965–67	South 1950–52	1958–60	1965–67
Upland food crops:															
Maize	255	1,275	4,113	102	699	3,453	15	65	160	125	424	419	12	87	81
Mung beans	221	289	808	187	230	737	4	6	29	27	52	26	2	1	16
Cassava	—	371	777	—	327	597	—	2	14	—	21	77	—	21	90
Sugar cane	412	911	865	247	513	603	41	77	52	113	266	187	11	56	22
Oil seeds:															
Castor	76	172	265	52	113	161	1	8	15	22	51	88	—	1	1
Groundnuts	448	661	759	227	359	269	108	94	289	94	187	173	19	18	27
Sesame	107	135	188	87	85	121	3	5	34	17	46	33	—	—	1
Soybeans	136	139	267	68	77	201	66	54	62	2	8	4	—	—	—
Coconuts	560	903	1,598	147	324	639	5	8	81	45	95	197	367	476	682
Fiber crops:															
Cotton	242	302	565	73	119	361	25	15	56	144	168	149	—	—	—
Kapok	—	341	333	—	201	128	—	35	48	—	95	130	—	9	27
Kenaf	62	427	2,631	2	9	44	2	2	4	59	416	2,583	—	—	—
Jute and ramie	30	23	57	15	15	43	—	—	1	14	7	14	—	—	—
Garden crops	n.a.	317	1,021	—	159	419	—	31	207	—	93	252	34	133
Fruits	n.a.	528	1,646	—	244	853	—	32	149	—	156	347	—	97	298
Rubber	2,204	2,930	4,167	—	—	—	—	—	—	—	—	—	2,204	2,930	4,167
Tobacco	243	379	458	70	73	69	89	164	273	79	135	102	5	7	14
Total	4,996	10,103	20,518	1,277	3,547	8,698	357	598	1,474	741	2,220	4,781	2,620	3,737	5,559

Source: *Agricultural Statistics of Thailand, 1967*, Ministry of Agriculture (Bangkok, 1970).

and social forces. The combination of slowly rising domestic output and rapidly rising population may tend to reduce Thailand's exportable rice surplus. At the same time, productivity increases in other countries may reduce world demand for imports of rice. Falling prices of Thai rice exports would force reductions in the premium. There is some paddy price below which Thai farmers will not produce paddy for the market. When the premium reaches zero, foreign and domestic prices come together, and government might then have to devise ways to subsidize rice exports! If that time ever comes, opponents of the rice premium will doubtless say "I told you so," while proponents will congratulate themselves for having so effectively promoted the diversification of agriculture.

THE EXPANSION OF OTHER CROPS

The rapid and substantial growth of crops other than rice has already been mentioned. Further details about area planted in specific crops are provided in Table XXVI. This large increase in other cash crops—to about a third of area planted in crops by 1965–67—has been an important development in Thailand since 1950. The extent of the change is indicated by the fact that rice accounted for only 33 percent of "income originating in agriculture" in 1968.[66] It is a striking fact that rice, the staple food and principal export for generations, is now equaled in the value of its contribution to GNP by the livestock industry plus fruits and vegetables.

Space does not permit a detailed discussion of the movement toward crop diversification; we shall simply stress a few salient points.[67]

First, a small number of crops has accounted for most of the growth in area planted. A few of these crops—notably hard maize, cassava, and kenaf—are for all practical purposes *new* crops to Thailand, whereas others have long been cultivated—cotton, coconuts, rubber, sugar cane, fruits and vegetables—but have recently grown sharply. These eight crops account for 88 percent of the expansion in area from 1950–52 to 1965–67. See Table XXVI for details.

Second, a considerable degree of regional specialization has developed, as may also be seen in Table XXVI. Kenaf is concentrated in the Northeast, maize in the Central region (though government had hoped it would catch on in the Northeast), rubber in the South, cassava in the Southeast (Chonburi). Silcock emphasizes the degree of geographical specialization; he notes that the usual regional categories do not reveal the specialization that exists at the changwat or amphur level. For crop years 1964 and 1965, changwat data show that 75 percent of maize was produced in four changwats in the upper Central region; 75 percent of kenaf in five changwats in the Northeast; 75 percent of cassava in four changwats, three in the Southeast and one in the Northeast; and 75 percent of sugar cane in five changwats in the Central and

[66] "National Income of Thailand, Revised Estimates, 1960–69," *op. cit.*, p. 16.

[67] See Silcock, *Economic Development of Thai Agriculture*, for a crop-by-crop account.

Northeastern regions.[68] Other crops such as groundnuts, fruits, and vegetables are more widely dispersed.

Third, some of the fastest-growing cash crops have been planted in response to *external* demand, and virtually all of the output is exported. Maize and kenaf are the most important examples. Small amounts of sweet maize have long been grown in Thailand for human consumption, but the external demand is for a hard maize that is used for animal feed. Farmers adopted this new crop, they have planted newly cultivated land with it, and they have switched to it from other crops, including sweet maize. Silcock cites one example, Changwat Nakhon Sawan, in which area planted in maize in 1959 is reported as 52,800 rai (82 percent in sweet maize), and in 1964 976,500 rai (100 percent in hard maize). He observes, "The extent of the change must be very great, though it is hardly credible that it can really be as great as this."[69]

The stimulus of external demand was also important in the case of kenaf. High prices resulting from failure of the jute crop in Pakistan stimulated efforts to produce that and similar fibers in Thailand. Jute has not done well, but kenaf has expanded greatly. Part of the output is absorbed by domestic gunny-bag factories, but the market for kenaf has been extremely volatile.

In some other crops, production has been undertaken largely in response to demand in the home market. These crops include cotton, coconuts, sugar cane, fruits and vegetables, and tobacco. The contrast, in source of demand, between this group and the export-oriented crops can be seen in Table XXVII, which shows the percentage of output that is exported. Thai farmers have thus responded to market and price incentives originating both at home and abroad.

Fourth, the expansion of acreage in nonrice crops has been accomplished by the small farmer. He has had some help from government and perhaps more from merchants, but the traditional, smallholding farmer has somehow heard about a new crop, learned something about its cultivation, obtained seed, and taken the necessary risk. He has shown a vigorous and impressive response to the prospect of a higher return in new crops.

Prospective returns in the new crops appear to have been substantially higher than in rice. One bit of evidence on this point is the value at wholesale prices of the average output per rai in various crops, as shown in Table XXVIII for selected years. These figures reflect the Bangkok price, not the farm price, and they tell us nothing about cost and *net* return, but they still imply a strong incentive to the farmer to put some of his land into crops other than rice.

When one examines the figures in Table XXVIII, the real puzzle is why agricultural diversification has not gone even further than it has. The economic incentive to plant other crops seems very strong indeed. For example,

---

[68] *Planted Area, Harvested Area, Production and Yield by Changwats, 1937–65*, Thailand Ministry of Agriculture and Kasetsart University.

[69] Silcock, *Economic Development of Thai Agriculture*, p. 85.

TABLE XXVII

SHARE OF EXPORTS IN THE OUTPUT OF CERTAIN CROPS

(*Thousand Tons*)

Product	Average Annual Output 1965–67	Average Annual Export 1965–67	Percentage Exported
Maize	1,118	1,045	94%
Cassava	709	730	100[a]
Rubber	218	208	95
Kenaf and jute	537	369	69
Cotton	77	—[b]	—
Coconuts	1,127	—	—
Sugar cane	4,278	—[b]	—
Tobacco	81	7[b]	9

[a] The indication in the first two columns that exports *exceeded* output may be accounted for by timing lags, or by statistical discrepancies.

[b] Thailand is a net *importer* of cotton, sugar, and tobacco.

Sources: *Agricultural Statistics of Thailand, 1967*; Department of Customs, *Annual Statement of Foreign Trade.*

the wholesale value of average output per rai in 1965–67 was 850 baht in garden crops, 1,300 baht in local tobacco, 1,634 baht in chili peppers, and 500 baht in groundnuts, compared with only 290 baht in rice. Why didn't farmers put enough land into these higher-earning crops to bring these values down closer to rice? Partial answers are easy to supply: some land now in rice is unsuitable for these or other crops; the values in Table XXVIII do not represent prices received by farmers and tend to exaggerate the value of other crops; costs of cultivation must also be considered; farmers lack knowledge and capital required to cultivate new crops; farmers prefer to grow rice partly for cultural reasons and partly because of the security involved in producing their own staple food. This last point would account for subsistence production, but not for rice production as a cash crop.

In any case, farmers *have* responded to the price incentives, as shown in the statistics of area cultivated given above. Their response occurs through time, with constantly changing circumstances, and perhaps the returns per rai in different crops will tend to be brought closer to equality as time goes on.

Several observers have noted the vigorous economic response of the Thai farmer, and emphasized the point that it is in accord with a model of rational economic behavior.[70] In his exhaustive empirical analysis of Thai production

[70] The major study is Jere Behrman, *Supply Response in Underdeveloped Agriculture* (Amsterdam, 1968), but see also Muscat, *op. cit.*, Ch. 3; G. Sitton, "The Role of the Farmer in the Economic Development of Thailand," Council of Economic and Cultural Affairs, New York, 1962.

TABLE XXVIII
Value of Output per Rai in Selected Crops
(Baht)

	Average Value per Rai[a]	
Product	1958–60	1965–67
Upland food crops:		
Maize	269	325
Mung beans	370	414
Cassava	713	611
Sugar cane	596	606
Oil seeds:		
Castor beans	ʾ523	321
Groundnuts	437	507
Sesame	618	533
Soybeans	350	363
Coconuts	1,249	757
Fiber crops:		
Cotton	486	501
Kapok	1,663	1,452
Kenaf	1,531	569
Garden crops (vegetables)	n.a.	852
Fruits	n.a.	921
Rubber	637	377
Chili	1,183	1,634
Tobacco:		
Local varieties	1,702	1,309
Virginia	976	917
Rice (paddy)	169	291

[a] Average yield per rai times Bangkok wholesale price.
Source: *Agricultural Statistics of Thailand, 1967.*

of kenaf, maize, and cassava during the period 1937–63, Behrman found evidence that Thai farmers responded to both price and yield incentives. His final conclusion deserves to be quoted in full:[71]

The study has provided new and compelling evidence . . . that, in the short run, farmers in underdeveloped countries respond rationally and substantially to economic incentives. No significant evidence, in contrast, has been found for the

---

[71] Behrman, *op. cit.*, p. 337. Peter Bell and Janet Tai have argued that these supply response studies contain serious methodological weaknesses, and that the results obtained are incorrect. They do not present any positive evidence, but express their belief that farmers in Southeast Asia do not respond to economic incentives as assumed in orthodox economic analysis. See their "Markets, Middlemen, and Technology: Agricultural Supply Response in the Dualistic Economies of Southeast Asia," *Malayan Economic Review*, April 1969.

hypothesis that institutional constraints preclude significant responses to economic incentives in underdeveloped agriculture. The burden of proof, thus, now lies with those who maintain that the supply behavior of farmers in underdeveloped agriculture cannot be understood predominantly within the framework of traditional economic analysis.

Fifth, farmers have planted the new cash crops on *part* of their total landholding, but they have continued to grow rice as well. This practice reflects the cultural role of rice, but it also has an economic purpose and interpretation. By planting enough rice for his family, the farmer reduces the risk of venturing into a new cash crop with its uncertain market price. If the bottom drops out of the kenaf market, or if his crop fails, he will be able to get along on a subsistence basis. As Behrman put it, "the hypothesis has been proposed that subsistence farmers always attempt to produce enough grain for on-farm consumption in order to lessen risk by assuring a basic food supply, independent of fluctuations in relative market prices. The estimates [made in this study] for rice provide support for this hypothesis."[72]

Sixth, these new crops have become important new sources of foreign exchange. This point will be further discussed below; here we will note only that the traditional "big four" exports—rice, rubber, tin, and teak—have declined substantially in relative importance. In 1968, for example, these four products accounted for only 52 percent of total merchandise exports, compared with 80–90 percent prior to 1950. Exports of "new" agricultural crops have risen sharply in recent years. In 1968, six of these crops (maize, cassava, kenaf, kapok, oilseeds, and tobacco) accounted for 3.9 billion baht of export proceeds, slightly *more* than total rice exports in that year. In view of the trends in output and price, it is quite possible that maize exports alone may soon exceed rice exports in value.

The vigorous growth in these new export crops has imparted a stimulus to the Thai economy in recent years. Professors Corden and Richter have called attention to this stimulus:[73] "Thailand is one of the few less developed countries other than oil exporters of which one can say that in recent years foreign trade, through growing markets it has provided, has been an 'engine of growth.'"

TENANCY AND DEBT

We saw in Chapter 3 that Thailand has traditionally been a nation of smallholding owner-farmers. Its relatively sparse population meant that ample land was available for the expansion of cultivation as population grew and new families were formed. Unclaimed land was the property of the state, but custom and law permitted individuals to occupy, clear, and cultivate such land. Laws also prevented the growth of large estates. Consequently, tenancy

---

[72] Behrman, *op. cit.*, p. 335.

[73] W. M. Corden and H. V. Richter, "Trade and the Balance of Payments," Ch. 6 in Silcock (ed.), *Thailand: Social and Economic Studies in Development*, p. 149.

has not been a serious problem, although high rates of tenancy have existed in certain localities.

This traditional view is still generally valid, but recent studies and surveys suggest that the situation has begun to change. Population growth and the extension of cultivation have proceeded so far that most of the good land has now been claimed. Settlers must go further afield to find unclaimed land, and disputes over land ownership are more numerous. At the same time, other agricultural developments have increased the farmers' need for credit, and have therefore led to greater emphasis upon registration of land and its use as collateral for loans. Laws concerning land acquisition and registration have been enacted, but farmers are not familiar with them, and old customs persist. Farmers who have *de facto* occupancy of land, but who have taken no formal legal steps to acquire *de jure* rights to it, may be in jeopardy as land pressure increases.

A brief explanation may help to clarify the problem. The Land Code of Thailand provides for three classes of landholders:[74] (1) "Reserve license" (*bai chong*) authorizes the holder to occupy unclaimed land, usually for three years. (2) "Exploitation testimonial" (*nor sor*) is issued to the holder of a "reserve license" when he has brought at least 75 percent of the land under cultivation. He then has a permanent right to the land, but transfer is cumbersome. (3) "Title deed" (*chanod tidin*) is evidence of full ownership and carries full right of transfer. It is comparable to a fee simple deed.

Exact amounts of land held in these three ways are unknown, but a recent estimate was reserve license, 2,500,000 rai; exploitation testimonial, 11,200,000 rai; title deed, 7,500,000 rai; and no document at all, 40,000,000 rai; totaling 61,200,000 rai. Thus, only about 12 percent of total farm landholdings are under a full title deed, and most of this acreage is in the Central region. Farmers holding two-thirds of the area in farms have no legal claim to it at all.[75] They do have a claim based on custom, but the problem is that someone else might obtain a reserve license for the same piece of land, thus creating a conflict. Of the three documents, only the title deed is fully acceptable to lenders as mortgage collateral. Therefore, most farmers cannot use their principal asset, land, as security for a loan. (This may be viewed as a desirable state of affairs, however, because it means that such farmers cannot lose their land through foreclosure.)

---

[74] Actually, the Code is more complicated, but this classification will suffice as an illustration. This paragraph is based on A. N. Seth, "Report on Land Reforms in Thailand" (mimeo., Bangkok, FAO Regional Office, 1968); Toru Yano, "Land Tenure in Thailand," *Asian Survey*, October 1968; and Webster Johnson, *Agricultural Development of Thailand with Special Reference to Rural Institutions*, Land Policy Division, Dept. of Land Development, Thailand (Bangkok, Jan. 1969).

[75] They may have a document used in connection with land tax collection. Yano (*op. cit.*, p. 854) states that this certificate (*soo khoo* I) has nothing to do with land title, but that people often regard it as if it were a true title deed.

Traditionally, a person could take only as much land as he and his family could cultivate, up to a maximum limit of 50 rai (formerly 25 rai). This customary limit was incorporated in legislation in the nineteenth century, and it helped to prevent the emergence of large landed estates in Thailand. Although it was still in the Land Code of 1954, it has since been removed.[76]

It is widely believed in Thailand that tenancy has increased substantially in recent years. The statistical evidence is far from satisfactory, but available data indicate a *declining* trend in tenancy from 1937 to 1963, with some indication from survey data of a sharp rise since 1963.

The principal evidence comes from three agricultural censuses conducted in 1937, 1950, and 1963. Although these censuses differed in scope, method, and definition, in all of them estimates were made of the number (or area) of "pure tenants"; i.e., farmers who rented *all* of the land they cultivated. The percentage of pure tenants declined from 15.7 percent in 1937 to 6.6 percent in 1950, and to 4.1 percent in 1963 (see Table XXIX).[77] As expected, the highest rate of tenancy is found in the Central region, where it was 25.6 percent in 1937, 14.0 percent in 1950, and 10.7 percent in 1963. In other regions pure tenancy is insignificant. However, the declining trend appears in all regions.

Despite these generally encouraging results, the belief persists that tenancy is increasing. Because of this concern, and perhaps because of a suspicion that the census results are incorrect, several surveys have been attempted, mostly in selected changwats in the Central region. The largest of these, conducted in 1967/68, resulted in alarmist headlines proclaiming that tenancy had risen sharply to an average rate of 40 percent in the entire Central region. The factual results were less dramatic, though they do suggest a rise in tenancy. The survey covered riceland in 26 changwats and provided three categories:[78] pure owners (farm *own* land entirely), part owners (farm *some* rented land), and pure tenants (farm rented land entirely). Of the 524,000 families surveyed, 22.5 percent were *pure* tenants and another 15.8 percent were part owners. These two categories were combined to get a tenancy rate of 38.3 percent. However, even the "pure tenant" figure of 22.5 percent is substantially above that found in the 1963 census (10.7 percent). In one changwat (Pathum Thani) the pure tenant ratio was 61 percent, and in several others it was 50 percent or more.

The area included in the 1967 survey of 26 changwats differed somewhat from the Central region, as defined above. Therefore, to make a more exact comparison with census data, we calculated tenancy rates for the three census years for the 26 changwats included in the 1967 survey. The results are shown

[76] Seth, *op. cit.*, p. 13; Muscat, *op. cit.*, p. 138.

[77] I am indebted to Professor Ammar Siamwalla for these data. He kindly made available his worksheets containing the changwat detail for these three censuses.

[78] Thailand Dept. of Land Development, Land Policy Div., *Land Tenure Situation in 26 Changwats in the Central Plain Region* (Bangkok, 1969).

TABLE XXIX
Tenancy in Thailand, 1937–67

Region	Farms		Pure Tenants		Ratio of Tenants
	Area in Rai	Number	Area in Rai	Number	
Regional Pattern[a]					
1937					
Central	15,871,000		4,074,000		25.6%
North	1,719,000		320,000		18.6
Northeast	7,010,000		127,000		1.8
South	4,779,000		114,000		2.4
Total	29,379,000		4,635,000		15.7%
1950					
Central		878,000		123,000	14.0%
North		239,000		15,000	6.2
Northeast		774,000		4,000	0.5
South		315,000		4,000	1.3
Total		2,206,000		146,000	6.6%
1963					
Central		1,086,000		116,000	10.7%
North		379,000		4,000	1.1
Northeast		1,221,000		6,000	0.5
South		493,000		5,000	0.9
Total		3,179,000		131,000	4.1%
Twenty-six Changwats in the Central Plain					
1937	13,739,000		3,671,000		26.7%
1950		733,000		107,000	14.6%
1963		885,000		87,000	9.9%
1967		524,000		118,000	22.5%

[a] Regional groupings are the same as those used in Appendix A. They differ from the regional classification used in the 1963 *Census of Agriculture*.

Sources: *Census of Agriculture*, 1937, 1950, and 1963; *Land Tenure Situation in 26 Changwats in the Central Plain Region*, Land Policy Division, Department of Land Development, Thailand (Bangkok, 1969).

in the lower part of Table XXIX. The percentage of pure tenants declined from 26.7 in 1937 to 9.9 in 1963, then rose to 22.5. The 1967 survey thus provides support for the popular belief that tenancy is increasing in the Central region.

A related matter is the increasing fragmentation of holdings. All children share in inheritance, though perhaps not equally, and this custom tends to cause fragmentation when population is rising. Such fragmentation is detrimental to agricultural productivity. It is possible that some *partial* tenancy results from efforts farmers make to obtain contiguous pieces of land and thus offset the harmful effects of fragmentation, but we have no statistical evidence on this point.

The conditions of agricultural credit in Thailand vary greatly between regions, and even within the same village, but they seem in the main to run counter to the stereotyped view of agricultural credit in underdeveloped countries.[79] First, the main sources of loans are relatives and friends, not landlords, moneylenders, and middlemen. Outside the Central region, about two-thirds of the loans are obtained from relatives and friends. Table XXX contains a detailed breakdown by region. Second, in nearly all cases, repayment of principal and interest is made in cash, not in kind. Third, although the range of interest rates is great, with some loans at very high annual rates, the general conclusion is that interest rates reflect scarcity of capital and degree of risk, and that they are not exploitive. Furthermore, loans from relatives often carry zero or very low rates. The mean monthly interest rate in the survey was 2.4 percent; Rozental states that the *modal* rate, leaving out loans of relatives, was 3-4 percent per month.[80]

Agricultural credit functions almost entirely outside the scope of regulatory agencies, and organized financial institutions play only a small part in it. Commercial banks scarcely touch this market,[81] except indirectly, and the government-sponsored credit cooperatives have not amounted to much. They account for about 10 percent of the loans in the North and Northeast, but only 1.4 percent in the Central region (see Table XXX). Credit cooperatives lend funds provided to them by the central government; they have not mobilized local savings to any great extent.

Commercial agriculture has long been more highly developed in the Central region than elsewhere in Thailand. It is therefore not surprising to find that commercial lenders play a larger role there than in other regions (66 percent of loans, compared with 21 and 31 percent in the North and Northeast), the average loan is larger, interest rates are lower, and loans are more frequently used for productive purposes.

As agricultural development proceeds in other regions, the demand for credit will rise. Rozental argues convincingly that increased availability of agricultural finance would increase farm production and, through its effect on income, also increase the level of saving in the agricultural sector. If farmers had access to credit, especially for terms longer than the present 3-12 months, they could acquire fertilizer, tools, and equipment (pumps, tractors,

[79] The primary source of information about agricultural credit is from a survey made in 1962/63: Pantum Thisjamondol, Virach Arromdee, and Millard Long, *Agricultural Credit in Thailand* (Bangkok, 1965). An excellent derivative source is Alek Rozental, *Finance and Development in Thailand* (New York, 1970).

[80] Rozental, *op. cit.*, p. 68.

[81] The Bangkok Bank has had a pioneering program of agricultural credit, but it has been squeezed by high administrative costs for small loans and legal ceilings on interest rates.

TABLE XXX
Sources of Credit by Region
(Percentages)

Type of Lender	Central Plain Number of Loans	Central Plain Value	North Number of Loans	North Value	Northeast Number of Loans	Northeast Value	South Number of Loans	South Value	Total Number of Loans	Total Value
Relative	17.8	22.6	44.8	47.0	50.0	58.5	40.2	43.0	39.9	32.
Neighbor	14.0	16.7	24.1	19.9	12.1	4.3	15.1	12.9	15.7	15.
Commercial lender	65.9	57.8	20.6	23.3	30.5	26.4	31.8	30.6	36.5	46.
Local store	39.2	13.9	4.1	3.0	12.1	4.6	12.1	10.9	16.5	
Crop buyer	8.2	7.9	5.2	10.1	9.1	6.5	13.7	13.8	8.6	
Landlord	6.6	10.7	0.0	0.0	1.5	5.2	0.0	0.0	2.1	
Moneylender	8.0	14.3	7.8	8.9	3.3	7.5	3.0	1.5	5.4	
Other	3.9	11.0	3.5	1.3	4.5	2.6	3.0	4.4	3.9	
Institutional lender	2.5	3.0	10.3	9.8	7.6	10.8	12.9	13.7	7.9	5.
Credit cooperative	1.4	2.0	10.3	9.8	7.6	10.8	12.1	12.9	7.5	
Other government agency	0.9	1.0	0.0	0.0	0.0	0.0	0.8	0.8	0.4	
Commercial bank	0.0	0.0	0.0	0.0	0.0	0.0	0.0	0.0	0.0	
Total	100.0	100.0	100.0	100.0	100.0	100.0	100.0	100.0	100.0	100.

Source: Pantum *et al.*, *Agricultural Credit in Thailand* (Bangkok, 1965), p. 37.

etc.) that would increase their productivity. They *could* do so, and the high proportion of loans used for productive purposes is encouraging, but many farmers might yield to temptation and borrow to buy consumer goods. Professor Motooka observed that Thai farmers, faced with an array of attractive durable consumer goods (radios, motorbikes, TV sets, etc.) were "living in a certain state of frustration," and that they sometimes bought these goods with borrowed money and thus ran the risk of losing their land because of inability to repay.[82] As commercialization proceeds, as credit become more abundant, and as land titles become more widely used as collateral, a "selection process" may begin to operate in which the shrewd and prudent farmers become more prosperous while the improvident ones lose their land and either become tenants or migrate to an urban area. (Such a process could account for the apparent increase in tenancy rates in the Central region, but this can be only a surmise.) Whether Thailand would accept this outcome, with its implication for change in the traditional pattern of smallholding owner-farmers, remains to be seen.

AGRICULTURAL TECHNOLOGY

For a century after the Thai economy was fully opened to world trade, the principal response in the agricultural sector was a large expansion of rice cultivation in which a growing farm population, using traditional methods and techniques, brought under cultivation an increasing area of land. Certain social overhead investments (railways to the north and northeast, small irrigation systems in the Central Plain) had some influence upon agriculture, but technology remained essentially unchanged from 1850 to 1950 (see Chapter 3).

During the last twenty years, however, a number of new methods, techniques, and facilities have begun to take root and spread. These developments are by no means complete, and they have so far affected only a fraction of the farmers, but it seems possible to say, in 1970, that a modest technological revolution has begun in Thai agriculture.

At the level of the individual farmer, technological change chiefly involves his use of fertilizer and machinery, and his acceptance and use of services, information, and assistance supplied to him from outside—namely, irrigation facilities, improved seed varieties, new cash crops, information about price, demonstrations of improved farming methods, and other extension services.

Until recently, chemical fertilizer was scarcely used at all in Thailand, but imports have grown rapidly in the last fifteen years, as may be seen in Table XXXI. Traditionally, rice farmers have relied on the enriching silt deposited in their paddy fields by the annual flood waters, and on animal manure. More recently, rice farmers have been inhibited by the unfavorable fertilizer–rice price ratio, already mentioned. Although exact data are not available, it ap-

[82] Takeshi Motooka, "The Conditions Governing Agricultural Development in Southeast Asia," *The Developing Economics* V (1967), No. 3, 427–31.

TABLE XXXI
IMPORTS OF FERTILIZER AND TRACTORS IN SELECTED YEARS

Year	Fertilizer Imports[a] (Metric Tons)	Wheeled Tractor Imports[b] (Number)	Year	Fertilizer Imports[a] (Metric Tons)	Wheeled Tractor Imports[b] (Number)
1950	9,400	228	1962		1,353
1955	24,300	262	1963		1,922
			1964		3,446
1957		267	1965	88,900	3,047
1958		384	1966	141,400	3,872
1959		445	1967	218,000	4,305
1960	52,200	855	1968	265,500	3,610
1961		1,487	1969	265,300	2,614

[a] For 1950–64, B. Bond et al., "A Report on the Thailand Fertilizer Situation and Potential," AID (Bangkok, May 1966), p. 134. For 1965–68, Annual Statement of Foreign Trade, Department of Customs, Thailand.
[b] For 1957–67, Thailand Farm Mechanization, op. cit., p. 34. For other years, Annual Statement of Foreign Trade.

pears that most of the chemical fertilizer is used in the rapidly expanding cash crops, such as maize, kenaf, cassava, fruits, and vegetables. The response of various crops to fertilizer has been studied, and it seems clear that increased yields justify the use of larger amounts of fertilizer. To achieve a greater usage rate, farmers must be convinced of the advantages to them, they must be taught proper methods and rates of application, and they need improved sources of credit. One danger is that the government, anxious to promote domestic industry, will protect domestic fertilizer producers and thus create an artificially high fertilizer price in Thailand. Traditionally, fertilizer imports have been free of duty, but in recent years certain types of fertilizer have been placed under "import control," i.e., under quota. In particular, imports of ammonium sulphate and urea fertilizers have been controlled in order to protect a government-owned domestic plant. Such a policy increases price, discourages the use of fertilizer, and reduces output and export of agricultural products.

It was estimated in 1965 that, given prices and the areas of various crops, Thailand could economically utilize about 550,000 metric tons of chemical fertilizer.[83] By 1968, imports had reached 265,500 tons, or 48 percent of that potential. This calculation seems to exaggerate the role of fertilizer in Thai agriculture, however. The absolute amount being used in 1968 was still only

[83] Billy Bond et al., "A Report on the Thailand Fertilizer Situation and Potential" (mimeo., AID (Bangkok, May 1966), p. 29. This calculation evidently allows for the low farm price of paddy, which makes fertilizer use uneconomical in rice cultivation.

4 kg. per rai of cultivated area, compared with about 30 kg. in Taiwan, or 40 kg. in Japan. Chemical fertilizer is scarcely used at all in rice cultivation.[83a] Nevertheless, total utilization of fertilizer has clearly increased greatly since 1950.

Prior to 1950, the use of machinery in Thai agriculture was virtually nil. Farmers relied upon human labor, animal power, and a few simple tools. In recent years, however, the internal combustion engine has penetrated into the countryside and is now quite widely used in a variety of ways. The most important item of equipment is the tractor. Starting from near-zero in 1950, the number of four-wheeled farm tractors rose to 17,500 in 1967, and to 25,000 in 1969.[84] Some import data are presented in Table XXXI. The survey team estimated the potential tractor population at one tractor per 100–150 hectares of culivated land, or 80,000–120,000 tractors, and concluded that by 1967 Thailand had already reached 15–22 percent of its potential.

Tractors are most widely used for land tilling. In 1967 about 60 percent of paddy land in the Central region was tilled by tractor, and even higher rates were reported for upland crops: maize 96 percent, cotton 64 percent, sugar cane 72 percent, and sorghum 75 percent.[85] Tractors are much used for transportation and shelling (maize), but not as yet for threshing. They seem especially valuable in plowing because they overcome the seasonal labor shortage in the plowing season, they extend the period during which plowing can be done, and they permit deeper plowing than is feasible with draft animals. The survey estimated that one tractor and driver could plow in one hour 24–36 times as large an area as one draft animal and one man.

Tractors are largely owned by "custom service" operators, who can be hired by farmers to till specific tracts of land. This system permits intensive use of the capital equipment. When hired labor is used, tractor plowing is cheaper than animal-drawn plowing. An estimate for paddy fields in the Northeast put the comparative costs at 25 baht per rai for tractor, 46 baht per rai for buffalo.[86] Even when the farmer is using his own labor, he may have alternative uses for the time spent in the arduous work of plowing. Most of the custom service operators own only one tractor, and they usually have farms of their own. Since plowing is the principal use made of tractors, all tractor

[83a] This has been the prevailing view among agriculturalists in Thailand, but a recent FAO report states that by 1968 about 53 percent of all fertilizer was used on rice and that this use had developed since 1958 (Wolf Donner and Banlu Puthigorn, *The Marketing of Fertilizer in Thailand*, FAO, Preliminary Economic Report, Bangkok, 1970).

[84] *Thailand Farm Mechanization and Farm Machinery Market,* Royal Government of Thailand (Bangkok, 1969). This document, which reports the results of a survey in 1967/68, is the basic source for this and the following two paragraphs.

[85] *Ibid.*, pp. 100–103.

[86] *Ibid.*, p. 125. Tractor plowing is cheaper in the Central Plain—only 13 baht per rai. I. Inukai, "Farm Mechanization, Output, and Labor Input," *International Labour Review,* May 1970.

owners have a plow, and many have harrows, but other accessory implements are much less common. The average number of accessories per plow is only 1.5.

Other items of mechanical equipment are also being used by farmers, especially water pumps, boat engines, and other transport equipment.

Even though our data are spotty and merely suggestive, it seems clear that in the last two decades motor-driven machinery has begun to play a significantly larger role in Thai agriculture than it did before 1950. As farmers become familiar with such machinery, and as they learn about additional functions it can perform, the volume of machinery in use will probably increase rapidly. Dr. Inukai points out that acceptance of the tractor has a psychological effect on the farmers—the first accepted departure from tradition overcomes a barrier and makes farmers more willing to accept other innovations. Local assembly, repair, and manufacture of parts and components have developed as mechanization has spread. Adaptation of equipment to suit local needs has already begun on a modest scale.

A more recent report on tractors in Thailand stated that 55 percent of the area planted to annual crops in the whole country was now tilled by tractor, and that this use had developed almost entirely in the last ten years.[87] This report further states that tractor use is especially widespread in upland crops and broadcast rice (as opposed to transplanted rice), that four-wheeled tractors can till fields as small as one-fourth of one rai, and that once farmers start using tractors they rarely revert to animal plowing. Farmers are eager to use tractors for harvesting and water pumping, and it seems likely that attachments will soon be devised to permit such use. Tractors have already sharply reduced the seasonal peak in labor demand at the planting season. That increases the pressure for removal of the other seasonal peak—in the harvest season.

The introduction and dissemination of tractors and tractor services have been accomplished by the private sector, in the face of unfavorable factors and circumstances. Plows, corn-shellers, parts, and other accessories are now being produced locally in small shops, and repair shops can be found in every town.

Thai farmers appear to be receptive to new crops and new techniques when they clearly understand the benefits they can expect to derive. However, they are not themselves innovative in basic technology. As Professor Motooka has written, "we cannot find ... anything analogous to the technology of the 'conscious and earnest agriculturalists' which contributed to the early development of Japanese agricultural technology. ... Agricultural technology which has been improved by the peasants themselves is practically non-existent."[88] He concludes that new technology must be developed by outside research

[87] William J. Chancellor, *Survey of Tractor Contractor Operations in Thailand and Malaya.* University of California at Davis, August 1970.
[88] Motooka, *op. cit.*, p. 439.

facilities and then somehow transmitted to the individual farmer. The Thai Government has recognized this responsibility and it has developed a substantial program of agricultural research and extension. This effort has been hampered by the usual difficulties: scarcity of well-trained scientists and technicians, inadequate equipment, and bureaucratic conflicts and delays. In addition, the centralization of control in Bangkok has left the provincial experiment stations with no autonomy and not much chance to display either initiative or imagination. Nevertheless, agricultural research is under way at experiment stations throughout the country.

Once research results have been obtained and verified, the problem is to transmit the new technology to the farmer and persuade him to utilize it. One difficulty at this vital point is the supercilious attitude that many civil servants have toward the farmer. All too often the extension agent is urban-born and educated, with little real interest in village people and their problems.

The "new generation" rice varieties, IR8 and IR5, have scarcely been used in Thailand because of certain disadvantages they possess. In particular, grain quality and taste were unsatisfactory, and Thailand wanted to preserve the reputation of its rice exports. Consequently, instead of permitting the introduction of IR8, an extensive breeding effort was undertaken, in cooperation with the International Rice Research Institute, to cross IR8 with Thai varieties and achieve higher yields while preserving the desirable qualities of Thai rice.[89] This effort appears to have had some success, and three "Thai-style" new generation varieties have been released for planting. Their effect upon Thai rice production remains to be seen. In other crops, some improvements in seeds and techniques have already been developed in the research and experiment program, and others are under way and appear promising for the future.

Since 1950 the agricultural sector has also benefited from substantial government investment in social overhead facilities such as irrigation, transportation, and education. Before 1950 a few irrigation projects had been undertaken, as described in Chapter 4, but by 1947 only 3.8 million rai were irrigated. The area irrigated has since increased rapidly, reaching 14.0 million rai in 1969 (see Table XXXII).[90] Most of the irrigated area is in the Central region, where an extensive system of distribution canals has long existed. Upstream multipurpose dams on the rivers entering this broad delta have increased water storage capacity from zero in 1950 to 16 billion cubic meters in 1969, thus providing partial control over water supply. So far, most of the invest-

[89] Asian Development Bank, *Regional Seminar on Agriculture*, 1969, pp. 212–13.

[90] The exact meaning of area "irrigated" is unclear. It can range all the way from an area that receives flood waters through a canal system to an area in which the water supply is controlled throughout the year. For this and other reasons, estimates of area irrigated vary widely. See Behrman, *op. cit.*, pp. 47–51, for a comparison of Census and Royal Irrigation Department figures.

TABLE XXXII

IRRIGATED AREA

(Millions of Rai)

Year	Whole Kingdom	Region			
		Central	North	Northeast	South
1947	3.8	3.7[a]	.1	—	—
1952	5.2				
1954	5.5	4.9	.2	.4	—
1960	9.6	8.1	.4	.9	.2
1965	11.0	8.6	1.1	1.0	.3
1967	11.4	8.8	1.2	1.1	.3
1969	14.0	—	—	—	—

[a] Estimated.

Sources: 1947, 1952, Royal Irrigation Department; 1954–67, Thailand Department of Commerce and Statistics, *Statistical Yearbook of Thailand*, and Ministry of Agriculture, *Agricultural Statistics of Thailand*; 1969, Bank of Thailand, *IMF Consultation Papers*, 1970.

ment outlay has been in dams and power-generating facilities. Feeder canals, dikes, drainage, and other apparatus needed to deliver water to the individual farm have not kept pace with dam construction. As these are installed, the benefits to agriculture should rise dramatically.

In the Northeast, the river system and topography are not well suited to large-scale irrigation projects,[91] but the need for water is acute. An attempt has been made to supply this need through "tank" irrigation projects—small basins to catch water in the rainy season and store it for later use. These tank projects serve only a small fraction of the area. In the North, irrigation projects have been small-scale and cooperative, whereas in the South irrigation scarcely exists.

The full potential of the increased irrigation capability has not yet been realized, nor can it be until other elements necessary for agricultural transformation are provided, but the facilities already finished—and others now under construction—represent a major change in the resource base of the agricultural sector.

Prior to 1950, no national road system existed in Thailand. Such roads as did exist were feeder roads for the railway, unpaved provincial roads largely used by bullock carts, and short stretches of road around Bangkok. Inter-regional transport of goods and people by road scarcely existed. Such transport took place by rail and water, and was therefore limited to the areas served by these means.

[91] This statement should be qualified to take account of the giant Pa Mong project to harness the Mekong River. The planning for that project is proceeding, but we can do no more than mention it here. This project would have profound effects upon the Northeast, but its prospects are uncertain.

TABLE XXXIII
HIGHWAYS
(Kilometers)

Year	National Highways Paved	National Highways Gravel & Laterite	Provincial Highways Paved	Provincial Highways Gravel & Laterite	Total Paved	Total Gravel & Laterite
1949	760	—	—	—	760	5,030
1957	2,129	5,797	—	—	—	—
1960	2,972	5,387	151	1,967	3,123	7,354
1965	5,046	4,314	405	2,203	5,451	6,517
1967	5,506	4,010	581	3,312	6,087	7,322
1969	7,822	2,146	—	—	—	—

Sources: 1949, Robert Pendleton, *Thailand, Aspects of Landscape and Life* (New York, 1962), p. 295; 1960–67, Thailand Department of Commerce and Statistics, *Statistical Yearbook of Thailand*; 1957, 1969, Bank of Thailand, *IMF Consultation Papers*, 1960, 1970.

Since 1950 a vigorous road-construction program has been carried out, and now most populated areas can be reached by road. Truck and bus transport has increased sharply. By 1969, all but six of the seventy-one changwat capitals were accessible by paved roads.[92] Table XXXIII contains some figures showing the growth in highway mileage since 1950.

Although many connecting roads have yet to be constructed, especially to permit interregional traffic, this expansion of the road system has brought large numbers of people into contact with external markets and has led to a quickening of trade. We should emphasize that these roads pass through, or connect, areas *already* populated. Villages and towns are already there, but the people are largely subsistence farmers with little previous contact with the rest of the economy.

In Hirschman's terms,[93] road construction in Thailand has not been so much a matter of leading with (or building up an excess supply of) social overhead capital as of redressing the balance—making up a relative shortage of social overhead capital. Perhaps it is for this reason that economic response to the new roads has been so vigorous. The people and productive capacity were already there; they needed only to be brought into effective contact with the outside market.

The roads have provided that contact. They have brought trucks, buses,

[92] Roads to the remaining changwat capitals are under construction. Although they connect populated areas, these roads pass through remote areas whose only occupants have been the "hill tribes." Sometimes these people do not welcome the road—it threatens their isolation, independence, and livelihood. On the road from Mae Sot to Umphang, tribesmen attacked and killed members of the construction crew. This opposition to roads is one aspect of the insurgency problem in Thailand.

[93] Albert O. Hirschman, *A Strategy for Economic Development* (New Haven, 1958).

Grade	Public	Private
12	8,000	11,000
11	15,000	17,000
10	45,000	43,000
9	49,000	51,000
8	55,000	65,000
7	86,000	79,000
6	107,000	89,000
5	142,000	101,000
4	792,000	77,000
3	911,000	86,000
2	1,009,000	93,000
1	1,224,000	189,000

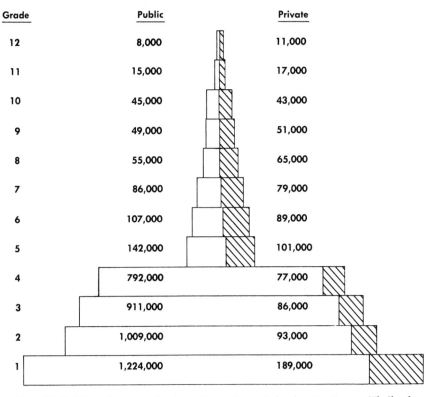

Chart IX. Public and private school enrollment by grade level, 1967. Source: Thailand National Statistical Office, *Statistical Yearbook of Thailand*, XXVIII, 1967–69.

and traders, and they have greatly reduced the cost of transport. Studies of particular roads show large increases in agricultural output in the areas served by the new roads.[94]

Literacy statistics are of doubtful value in Thailand. For what it is worth, the 1960 census reported a national literacy rate of 71 percent; the 10–35 age group showed a rate of 84 percent, the over-50 group only 30 percent. The extension of public education can be demonstrated with more confidence. Schools have been constructed and a large percentage of the eligible age group now attends elementary school, i.e., the first four grades. How much they learn is another question, but at least they learn simple arithmetic and how to read a little. Beyond the fourth grade, the school population drops drastically; only 20,000 students finished secondary school in 1967. See Chart IX for

[94] George W. Wilson, ed., *The Impact of Highway Investment on Development* (Washington, D.C., 1966), Ch. V.

the educational pyramid in 1967. Elementary schools are now found in all regions, but the majority of secondary schools, especially the better ones, are in the Central region.

Each of these several aspects of agricultural technology—fertilizer, machinery, research and extension, irrigation, transportation, and education—is in the early stage of development, and each suffers from growing pains. But putting them all together and considering the difference between 1950 and 1970, it seems fair to say that a significant degree of technological change has occurred in Thai agriculture. Without certain policy barriers, the transformation of traditional agriculture would no doubt have proceeded at a faster rate.

12

Economic Change Since 1950: II

SINCE 1950 Thailand has continued to rely on imports for a substantial part of its requirements of manufactures, both consumer goods and capital goods. Thailand has, on the whole, maintained its traditional posture as an "open" economy, closely connected through trade to the outside world, and largely relying upon competition and market prices (as influenced by tariffs) to regulate the size and composition of imports.

This general observation needs some qualification, of course. First, in the postwar period (1946–53), multiple-exchange rates, import quotas, and other forms of exchange control were used.[1] After 1954, when a single exchange rate was restored, other aspects of exchange control were gradually eliminated, though a few still remained in 1970. Thailand has not yet accepted the obligations of Article VIII in the International Monetary Fund Charter. Second, as already mentioned in the previous chapter, the government established and operated a number of factories in the 1950's. Most of these enterprises were competitive with imports, and they required import quotas and other protective measures in order to survive. Third, ever since Thailand regained tariff autonomy in 1926, it has used tariff rates to influence the size and composition of imports. Tariffs have not been prohibitive, however. They have allowed a wide variety of imported merchandise to enter the country, and have remained the most important source of tax revenues. Imported goods are widely distributed; they are found in every village and town, while in Bangkok almost anything can be purchased (at a price).

Imports and the Tariff Structure

Total merchandise imports have risen dramatically—from 2.5 billion baht in 1950 to 26.9 billion in 1969. As a proportion of GNP, imports rose from 8 percent in 1950 to 20 percent in 1969. During this period imports began to exceed exports, and by 1969 the merchandise trade deficit was 12 billion baht, or 80 percent more than exports.

The composition of imports has continued to change in the directions observed for the pre-1950 period (see Chapter 6, above)—namely, toward a larger proportion of capital goods, particularly machinery, and a smaller pro-

---

[1] The best single account of this episode is S. C. Yang, *A Multiple Exchange Rate System* (Madison, Wis., 1957).

portion of consumer goods. Table XXXIV contains the pertinent data. The Economic Commission for Asia and the Far East (ECAFE) classifies imports into consumer goods, capital goods, and materials, with materials further divided into those "chiefly" for consumer goods and those "chiefly" for capital goods. According to this classification (Table XXXIV-A), the share of consumer goods declined from 59 percent in 1951 to 26 percent in 1969, while capital goods rose from 25 percent to 47 percent in the same period.[2] Materials rose from 16 to 28 percent, with materials chiefly for *consumer* goods accounting for most of the increase. The large proportion of materials for consumer goods reflects the structure of the Thai manufacturing sector, which is oriented toward consumer goods. There is little capacity to produce capital goods.

In Table XXXIV-B, imports are classified according to the Standard International Trade Classification (SITC) for selected years. One can readily see the dominant role of chemicals, machinery, and other manufactures in recent years. The share of machinery and transport equipment alone rose from 14 percent in 1950 to 35 percent in 1969. The food and beverage share fell from 13 to 7 percent, and textile imports fell from 27 percent to 5 percent in this period. (Most of the textile imports remaining in 1969 were accounted for by man-made fibers.)

A division of imports between "primary products" and "manufactured goods," included in Table XXXIV-C, shows that the traditional preponderance of manufactured goods has continued and even increased, reaching a high of 83 percent in 1969. We should note, however, that this classification conceals some of the changes it is supposed to reveal. For example, Thailand installed oil refineries in the 1960's and shifted from imports of refined petroleum products to imports of crude oil, but all petroleum products (crude and refined) are included in SITC 3 and are counted as "primary products." Similar examples of a shift of imports from higher to lower stages of processing can be found in chemicals (SITC 5) and manufactures (SITC 6).

No detailed study of the Thai tariff structure has yet been made, but its broad outlines seem clear. As we saw in Chapter 8, when fiscal autonomy was regained in 1926, tariff rates were increased and import duties soon became the largest source of government revenue. The primary objective of the tariff was revenue, not protection, and most rates were modest. However, as tariff rates steadily increased after 1926, the protective effect began to be felt. During the past two decades, 1950 to 1970, protection of domestic industry has become a more important objective of tariff policy, though import duties still comprise the largest source of government revenue. Actually, the ratios of

---

[2] This classification involves some difficult definitional and conceptual problems, but it is suggestive. The Bank of Thailand publishes an alternative breakdown of consumer and capital goods imports based on World Bank definitions. It shows the ratio of capital goods imports rising from 25 percent in 1960 to 36 percent in 1969, but many items are put in "other imports" (including all road vehicles, even buses and trucks!).

TABLE XXXIV
MERCHANDISE IMPORTS: THREE CLASSIFICATIONS

Category	Value (Million Baht)					Percentage				
	1950[a]	1955	1960	1965	1969	1950[a]	1955	1960	1965	1969
A. Classified by Use										
Consumer goods	2,151	3,554	3,746	5,029	6,908	59.0	48.8	39.2	31.3	25.8
Materials chiefly for consumer goods	341	822	1,152	2,915	5,490	9.4	11.3	12.1	18.2	20.5
Materials chiefly for capital goods	235	670	1,065	1,191	1,937	6.5	9.2	11.1	7.4	7.2
Capital goods	916	2,233	3,597	6,914	12,414	25.1	30.7	37.6	43.1	46.5
Total	3,643	7,279	9,560	16,049	26,749	100.0	100.0	100.0	100.0	100.0
B. Classified by Type of Commodity, According to the Standard International Trade Classification (SITC)										
0 Food	273	662	784	891	1,345	11.1	8.8	8.2	5.5	5.0
1 Beverages and tobacco	54	158	108	201	495	2.2	2.1	1.1	1.2	1.8
2 Crude materials	32	76	143	471	828	1.3	1.0	1.5	2.9	3.1
3 Fuel and lubricants	150	692	1,025	1,364	1,829	6.1	9.2	10.7	8.4	6.8
4 Animal and vegetable oils	8	28	20	33	59	0.3	0.4	0.2	0.2	0.2
5 Chemicals	170	581	974	1,667	3,319	6.9	7.7	10.1	10.3	12.3
6 Manufactures	1,138	2,761	3,289	5,016	6,314	46.2	36.8	34.2	31.0	23.5
7 Machinery and transport	351	1,383	2,390	4,924	9,426	14.3	18.4	24.5	30.5	35.1
8 Miscellaneous manufactures	271	916	522	923	2,609	11.0	12.2	5.4	5.7	9.7
9 Miscellaneous	14	246	367	682	668	0.6	3.3	3.8	4.2	2.5
Total	2,461	7,503	9,622	16,172	26,892	100.0	100.0	100.0	100.0	100.0
C. Classified by Stage of Production										
Primary products (SITC 0–4)	517	1,616	2,080	2,960	4,556	21.0	21.5	21.6	18.3	16.9
Manufactures (SITC 5–9)	1,944	5,887	7,542	13,212	22,336	79.0	78.5	78.4	81.7	83.1
Total	2,461	7,503	9,622	16,172	26,892	100.0	100.0	100.0	100.0	100.0

[a] Figures for Section A are for 1951.

Sources: A. United Nations, Economic Commission for Asia and the Far East, *Statistical Yearbook*. B and C. Thailand Department of Customs, *Annual Statement of Foreign Trade of Thailand*.

import duties to government revenue and to total imports have remained fairly stable, as the following figures show:

	Import Duties as Percentage of	
Year	Government Revenue	Total Imports
1950	27.0	20.6
1955	29.7	17.3
1960	30.4	21.4
1965	24.9	18.3
1969	29.7	20.2

This stability was achieved by increasing tariffs on consumer goods, especially luxuries, as tariffs were reduced on capital goods and intermediate products. The more successful the efforts to promote domestic production to replace imports, and the more tariff concessions given on imported inputs, the higher tariffs had to be on the remaining imports (especially consumer goods) in order to generate desired amounts of government revenue. In some cases, such as petroleum, the loss in import duties was offset by new excise taxes levied on domestic production. Even so, to keep a constant ratio of import duties to total value of imports, other tariff rates had to be increased.

This process has been accelerated by the industrial promotion policy, which allows materials and capital equipment to be imported at reduced rates, with the result that Thailand's tariff structure has assumed a familiar pattern: high tariff rates on consumer goods, lower rates on intermediate products and capital goods. One calculation based on the Customs Tariff Code of 1960 produced the following results: average tariff rate for nondurable consumer goods, 34.3 percent; for durable consumer goods, 42.0 percent; for intermediate goods, 32.6 percent; and for capital goods, 19.3 percent.[3] Tariff changes since 1960 and concessional rates given to promoted firms would tend to increase average tariffs on consumer goods and to reduce them on capital goods and intermediate products, thus widening the spread shown above.

Consequently, the "effective" rates of protection to domestic producers are presumably quite high, though actual effective rates cannot be calculated because no input-output table exists for Thailand. However, Trairong Suwankiri has used a standardized input-output table (based on Belgian and Netherlands data) along with Thai tariff rates to calculate effective rates, with the following results: average effective tariff rate for nondurable consumer goods, 86 percent; for durable consumer goods, 109 percent; for intermediate goods, 74 percent; and for capital goods, 42 percent.[4] These results are based on 1960

[3] Trairong Suwankiri, *The Structure of Protection and Import Substitution in Thailand*, M.A. thesis, University of the Philippines, 1970, p. 11. In this calculation tariff rates are weighted by value of imports.

[4] *Op. cit.*, pp. 11–16. The "effective tariff" seeks to measure the degree of protection afforded to a productive process. It indicates the proportion by which value-added in the protecting nation

tariff rates. If changes since 1960 and tariff reductions allowed promoted firms were taken into consideration, the effective rates would be substantially higher. Even though based on standardized input-output coefficients, these estimates suggest the extent to which the Thai tariff structure is designed to protect manufacturing processes.

For fiscal year 1966/67 the Department of Customs analyzed receipts from import duties by type of commodity and level of duty (ad valorem equivalent). About 55 percent of total duties were collected at rates higher than 30 percent ad valorem, but three-fourths of this high-tariff revenue came from a handful of commodities—man-made fibers, vehicles, refined petroleum products, and tobacco.[5]

Domestic Manufacturing

Prior to World War II, Thailand had developed a small manufacturing capacity, but it had not gone very far by 1941 (see Chapter 6). The dominant manufacturing industries were rice-milling, saw-milling, and other simple processing industries, plus cement, textiles, beverages, and a number of small-scale activities, largely producing for final consumption. Electricity was scarce and unreliable, transportation inadequate (except for areas served by the railway).

During the war some industrial production was undertaken, but most of these ventures failed to survive the resumption of trade. Thus in the early 1950's the industrial sector was still at about the same stage of development it had reached in the immediate prewar period.

Against this background, the development of the industrial sector since 1950 looks impressive even though small in absolute terms. In terms of its share in the gross national product, value-added in the industrial sector (including construction, electric power, transportation, mining, and manufacturing) rose from 18 percent in 1951 to 26 percent in 1960 and to 30 percent in 1969 (see Table XX). Since GNP was itself rising rapidly in this period, this rising sectoral share implies a high rate of industrial growth—namely, 12.1 percent per year.

The expansion of electric power production, pitifully inadequate in 1950, was undertaken by the government. Multipurpose dams were constructed with financial assistance from foreign loans and grants. Although electricity is not yet available to most villages, by the 1960's supply had become adequate to meet industrial demands, and individual firms no longer had to provide their own generating capacity (though some still did). Production grew as follows: energy generated (in 10^6 kwh) for the year 1951, 105; for 1955, 289; for 1960,

---

can exceed value-added at free-trade prices. See W. M. Corden, "The Structure of a Tariff System and the Effective Protective Rate," *Journal of Political Economy*, June 1966.

[5] Data supplied by the Department of Customs. Official figures for imports of alcoholic beverages are absurdly low (20 million baht in 1969) and are belied by the conspicuous consumption in Bangkok and elsewhere.

516; for 1965, 1,339; and for 1969, 3,736.[6] Government investment in roads was a powerful enabling factor in the expansion of the transportation sector, but most of the value-added in transportation was in fact a result of private enterprise.

The share of value-added in manufacturing alone rose from 10 percent in 1951 to 13 percent in 1960, and reached 15 percent in 1968. Table XXXV contains estimates of value-added in manufacturing, by industry. These figures are very rough, based as they are upon fragmentary data. It seems likely that much small-scale and handicraft production is omitted from these estimates, but they nevertheless indicate a vigorous expansion of manufacturing production.

Inspection of Table XXXV indicates where expansion in manufacturing capacity has occurred. The largest increase has been in food processing. Rice-milling is still the largest manufacturing industry, but processing of new products (maize, cassava) has also contributed to growth in food processing. Large increases have occurred in other consumer goods industries, notably beverages, tobacco, textiles, and apparel. More recently, petroleum refining, transport equipment (largely assembly plus construction of truck and bus bodies), and chemicals have been added. Some of the new enterprises have used domestic raw materials, but most of them have relied heavily upon imported materials.

Although manufacturing grew rapidly from 1951 to 1969, it still accounts for only a small part of the employed labor force—at least as far as one can tell. Employment statistics are among the least reliable in Thailand, and it is difficult to find comparable estimates for different years. The following estimates of employment in manufacturing have been made:[7]

	Number	Age Group	Percentage of Labor Force
1947	196,000	14[+]	2.2
1960	456,000	15[+]	3.6
1964	481,000		
1969	710,000	11[+]	4.0

These figures imply a high rate of growth in manufacturing employment, though the absolute increase does not go far to shift the structure of employment and provide nonagricultural outlets for Thailand's rapidly growing labor force. When one attempts to examine the composition of employment, the data appear to be quite unreliable and inadequate. Although little can be

[6] Figures for 1951–65, *Thailand Electric Power Study, December 1966* (Royal Government of Thailand and USOM), p. 147; for 1969, Bank of Thailand, *IMF Consultation Papers*, 1970.

[7] Figures for 1947 and 1960 are census results from the Thailand Department of Commerce and Statistics, *Statistical Yearbook*, No. 22, and the Central Statistical Office, *Thailand Population Census, 1960*; for 1964 from the National Statistical Office, *Report of the 1964 Industrial Census* (1968); and for 1969 from a Department of Labor manpower survey.

TABLE XXXV

VALUE ADDED IN MANUFACTURING BY INDUSTRY

(Million Baht)

Industry	1951	1955	1960	1965	1968	1969
Food	688	1,669	2,309	3,516	4,525	4,646
Beverages	206	403	583	1,041	1,543	1,739
Tobacco	569	721	981	1,194	1,648	1,698
Textiles	31	58	319	817	1,111	1,262
Wearing apparel, including footwear	121	242	536	666	1,082	1,205
Wood and cork, excluding furniture	235	282	257	524	645	679
Furniture and fixtures	37	116	92	161	368	459
Paper and paper products	—	6	18	47	54	68
Printing and publishing	167	110	266	413	529	588
Leather and leather products	46	92	32	32	52	52
Rubber products	138	169	56	122	182	212
Chemicals and chemical products	267	321	491	752	1,070	1,218
Petroleum refining and coal	—	—	3	752	1,376	1,468
Nonmetallic mineral products	78	159	269	624	1,121	1,273
Basic metal industries	4	12	27	52	130	157
Metal products, excluding machinery and transportation	93[a]	43[b]	51	146	247	302
Repairing nonelectrical machinery			36	137	272	341
Electrical machinery and supplies		13	41	99	183	222
Transport equipment	201	229	329	743	1,178	1,250
Miscellaneous			65	138	272	348
Total	2,901	4,647	6,759	11,978	17,586	19,185
Percentage of GNP	10%	12%	13%	14%	15%	15%

[a] The figure for 1951 applies to metal products, nonelectrical and electrical machinery, and miscellaneous.

[b] The figure for 1955 applies to metal products, nonelectrical machinery, and miscellaneous.

Sources: 1951, 1955, Thailand, National Economic Development Board, *National Income Statistics of Thailand*, 1964 edition; 1960–69, "National Income Statistics, Revised Estimates, 1960–69" (August 1970).

said about structure, small enterprises account for much manufacturing employment. The 1964 census of industry shows that firms with fewer than ten employees accounted for two-thirds of the employment (326,000), but for only 10 percent of the output (by value). Firms with over 100 employees accounted for only 71,000 workers, but for 55 percent of output by value.

Unfortunately, the statistics necessary for a detailed analysis of the development of manufacturing in Thailand do not exist. One cannot obtain data, by industry, on employment, investment, output, wages, number and size of firms, profit margins, and the like. Such data will probably not be available until an effective system of taxation is developed. In the meantime, we can give only a synoptic view of changes in this sector.

In the immediate postwar period, 1945–53, Thailand was preoccupied with recovery from the war and restoration of normal economic processes. The resumption of trade forced some war-induced plants out of business, and the booming commodity markets associated with the Korean war caused attention to be concentrated on facilitating production of traditional primary product exports. Nevertheless, even in this transition period, the momentum of the prewar nationalistic drive continued to exert an influence.[8] One objective was to increase the economic role of the Thai vis-à-vis Chinese and other foreigners. In the absence of initiative and entrepreneurship from the Thai private sector, it was natural to look to government. Furthermore, the postwar preoccupation with "economic development" had also reached Thailand, and there was increasing awareness of the need to shift the structure of the economy and to reduce the dependence upon agriculture and a few primary products. This of course meant it was necessary that an industrial sector be developed.

This need became more acute when the Korean boom ended and export prices dropped. The upshot was that in this period, 1953 to 1958, government tried to assume the entrepreneurial role. Over a hundred manufacturing enterprises were launched to produce textiles, glass, chemicals, cement, iron and steel products, pottery, etc. Some of these were set up within regular ministries, but many were established as state enterprises—separate legal entities.[9]

Unfortunately, the new enterprises proved to be inefficient, poorly managed, and prey to all the ills that had plagued government-operated industries prior to the war. They did not meet output targets; they could not compete with imports. Far from generating revenue for the government, as had been hoped, they became a net drain on the treasury. In a study of over 100 state enterprises, Artamanoff found that in 1964 the treasury received income of 603 million baht compared with disbursements of 698 million baht, but nearly

[8] T. H. Silcock (ed.), *Thailand: Social and Economic Studies in Development* (Canberra, 1967). Chs. 1 and 11 contain an interesting, brief account of this period.

[9] Appendix A in Silcock, *Thailand*, contains a description of the organizational structure of these enterprises.

all the income (567 million baht) came from five monopolies that required *no*
treasury disbursement.[10] These included the Tobacco Monopoly, the Lottery
Organization, and the Bank of Thailand. All the remaining state enterprises
combined thus required net disbursements of over 600 million baht. It soon
became apparent that this strategy of development was not working. There
had in fact been dissent and criticism all along, especially from the Bank of
Thailand. It was argued that the government should devote its limited resources and energies to social overhead facilities—power, transportation, education. A combination of factors led to a distinct shift in economic policy in
the late 1950's—a shift away from government entrepreneurship in manufacturing and toward reliance upon the private sector. These factors included
the poor performance of government-operated factories, growing recognition
that the government's administrative abilities would be stretched to the limit
merely to provide essential social overhead facilities and services, the impact
of the World Bank report with its criticism of public enterprises and its ad-
monition to strengthen the private sector, and the accumulating evidence that
foreign capital, both public and private, would be available in larger quantities
if the government limited its economic role. We have already mentioned
(Chapter 11) that Thai concern about Chinese economic domination had been
somewhat allayed by a *modus vivendi* in which Thai government officials
shared control (and profits) of business firms. Finally, Field Marshal Sarit
Thanarat became Prime Minister in 1959. He was strongly opposed to the
expanded government role in industry, and he wielded near-absolute power
in Thailand from 1959 to 1964.

Investment Promotion

In any case, a sharp change in economic policy did occur in the late 1950's.
The government concentrated its efforts on social overhead investment and
began actively to promote private investment in manufacturing industry. In
1959 the Board of Investment was created and given responsibility for imple-
menting the existing "Act on the Promotion of Industries."[11] Since 1959, investment promotion has been an important influence on industrial investment,
and the Board of Investment has played a prominent role in the development
of manufacturing industry.

The investment promotion legislation contained several incentives designed
to encourage private investment, both domestic and foreign. These included
guarantees against nationalization and competition from state enterprises,
right to own land (foreigners are ordinarily not allowed to own land), right
to repatriate profits and capital, right to bring in technical and managerial

---

[10] George Artamanoff, "State-owned Enterprises of Thailand" (mimeo., USOM-AID, Bangkok, 1965).

[11] This measure, enacted in 1954, had been until 1959 practically a dead letter. New Acts
were adopted in 1960 and 1962, and several subsequent amendments have been made, but the
Board of Investment has continued as the responsible agency for implementation.

personnel, exemption from import duties and business taxes on imports of capital equipment to be used in a new plant, exemption from income tax for a five-year period, exemption from import duties and business tax on imports of raw materials and inputs for a five-year period (full exemption for Group A industries, 50 percent exemption for Group B industries, and up to 33⅓ percent exemption for Group C industries).[12] At the discretion of the Board of Investment (or higher authority) a promoted firm might also be assisted by a tariff increase on competing imports or even by a ban on such imports, and it could be exempted from export duty, if any.

These incentives proved sufficiently attractive to induce a flow of applications, but at first the Board of Investment was hesitant, uncertain, and slow to act on them. It lacked a set of guiding principles; it also needed time to develop a staff and gain some experience. By the mid-1960's, applications were being processed more rapidly.

No really clear and explicit criteria were developed to form the basis for a decision to award promotion privileges to a firm, although some implicit criteria underlay the classification of industries into Groups A, B, and C. Those in Group A were considered to be the most "vital and necessary" to the Thai economy, those in Group B somewhat less "vital and necessary," while Group C included all other industries deemed worthy of promotion. In addition to type of product, the Board of Investment often stipulated a minimum size of plant and the technology to be utilized. Typically, Board approval was required for machinery and equipment, and its emphasis was upon use of "modern" technology and equipment. Other factors that have been considered pertinent include use of domestic raw materials, provision of employment, saving foreign exchange, and presence of linkages (backward or forward) to other sectors of the economy.

Broadly speaking, Group A industries included basic metals (smelting), chemicals, several types of metal manufactures (spare parts, pumps, bicycles, electrical appliances, agricultural machinery), and special cases such as tires, condensed milk, and kraft paper. Several Group B industries were simply the *assembly* stage of Group A industries— e.g., water pump manufacture is in Group A, water pump assembly in Group B. Otherwise, no clear rationale for the assignment of industries to these groups seemed to exist.[13]

Actually, these group assignments were not of great importance in any case. The only advantage a Group A industry had was the larger exemption from import duties and business taxes on raw materials for a five-year period. A Group C industry might well be able to obtain an equivalent degree of effective protection through an increase in the tariff on its product—and this protection could last much longer than five years!

[12] *Promotion of Industrial Investment Act, B.E. 2505 (1962)*, Board of Investment, Thailand, July 1966. Incentive provisions have varied over the past decade.

[13] Professor Silcock concluded that the more highly capital-intensive industries were in Group A (*Thailand*, pp. 269–71).

Although criteria for specific industry choices are elusive, the general thrust of promotion policy has clearly been toward import substitution. Nearly all of the firms awarded promotion certificates have proposed to produce goods for the domestic market, to replace imports. Few of them have made any significant contribution to exports.

This fact exposes an inherent contradiction in Thailand's investment promotion policy. On the one hand, the Thai market is small. Imports consist of a wide variety of goods, but a rather small quantity of each. When domestic production is undertaken merely to replace imports, the scale of output must be small, at least by modern industrial standards. On the other hand, economics of scale appear to be important in manufacturing, and government does not want to use special, temporary incentives to call forth a number of small-scale, high-cost factories that will be forever dependent on a sheltered market. Hence the emphasis by the Board of Investment upon minimum size of plant, use of modern technology and equipment, and international standards of quality. It was hoped that these requirements would increase the chance that the new factories would eventually become competitive with imports. The danger is that these requirements will not be enough to produce large-scale modern plants, but that they will be enough to prevent creative innovations and adaptations of small-to-medium scale operations to fit Thai factor costs and managerial capabilities, thus precluding an evolution of industry after the Japanese pattern.[14] In that event it would be a sounder strategy to give promotional incentives only to firms that propose to produce for export. Such firms would need no tariff protection, and they could choose their scale of operation without regard to size of the domestic market.

Investment promotion really began in 1959. From 1954 to 1958, only eleven firms were approved (three of them state-owned), and only seven new enterprises were actually created.[15] From 1959 to 1969, by contrast, 607 promotion certificates were issued and about 350 firms actually began to operate. They covered nearly every industrial category listed as eligible for promotion privileges, including many categories added during the 1960's.

Unfortunately, the Board of Investment has not developed an effective reporting system even for firms issued promotion certificates, and it is therefore impossible to evaluate their performance and analyze their characteristics as comprehensively as one would like. In view of the importance to the economy of the investment promotion policy, the lack of data is indeed regrettable.

The first part of Table XXXVI contains some summary figures for the entire period 1959 to 1969. Of 607 firms awarded promotion certificates, 112 were in Group A, 43 in Group B, and 452 in Group C. Total registered capital

---

[14] G. Ranis, "Factor Proportions in Japanese Economic Development," *American Economic Review*, Sept. 1957.

[15] Waytin Mallikamas, "Industrial Promotion in Thailand" (University of Wisconsin, 1967), p. 45.

TABLE XXXVI
Promotion Certifications and Registered Capital

Category	1959–65	1966–69	Total
Promoted Firms: Summary Data			
Number of promotion certificates issued..	337	270	607
Breakdown by group:			
Class A industries	66	46	112
Class B industries	21	22	43
Class C industries	250	202	452
Total registered capital (million baht) ...	2,532	3,648	6,180
Thai capital (million baht)	1,680	2,447	4,127
Foreign capital (million baht)	852	1,201	2,053
Total investment (million baht)	7,933	12,757	20,690
Machinery (million baht)	4,469	7,365	11,833
Approximate number of Thai workers ...	55,200	40,600	95,800
Registered Capital, by Source (Million Baht)			
Nationality of investor:			
Thailand	1,725.5	2,422.7	4,148.2
Japan	374.6	283.7	658.3
United States	87.7	245.4	333.1
China (Taiwan)	160.6	140.4	301.0
United Kingdom	28.9	77.3	106.2
Malaysia	26.8	60.3	87.1
Netherlands	6.3	43.9	50.2
West Germany	25.8	21.0	46.8
Denmark	22.5	5.8	28.3
Hong Kong	4.7	26.4	31.1
Singapore	—	26.4	26.4
Switzerland	9.6	12.8	22.4
India	16.1	2.6	18.7
Australia	14.5	—	14.5
Sweden	—	14.0	14.0
Italy	11.7	—	11.7
Portugal	6.3	5.1	11.4
Philippines	.9	10.0	10.9
Israel	7.0	—	7.0
Indonesia	5.5	—	5.5
Norway	—	3.6	3.6
Argentina	3.0	—	3.0
Panama	—	3.0	3.0
Burma	1.8	—	1.8
Other	37.4	235.5	272.9
Total	2,577.2	3,639.8	6,217.0

Source: Board of Investment.

of these firms was 6.2 billion baht, about a third of which was foreign, the rest Thai.[16] The breakdown of registered capital by nationality is shown in the second part of Table XXXVI. Japan was the largest source of foreign capital. In nearly all cases, foreign capital was associated with Thai capital in joint ventures. The government has preferred to have a controlling interest in Thai hands.[17] Equity capital comprised only a small part of the total investment of promoted firms, but no reliable data exist on total investment. The figures in Table XXXVI for total investment and machinery come from the application form and bear little relation to actual outlays. Besides that, the figures in this table pertain to all firms that were awarded promotion certificates, not to those that have actually carried out their investment and begun to operate.[18] Data for this latter, more significant group, are scarcer still.

A search for information on promoted industries turned up a few scattered statistics, but after examining and comparing these we concluded that the contradictions and obvious errors were so serious that these data could not be used. In 1970 an Asian Development Bank mission began a study and evaluation of industrial promotion in Thailand. Perhaps that mission will be able to obtain the data necessary for a comprehensive evaluation.

In the absence of operating data, to indicate the range and scope of investment promotion we show in Table XXXVII a list of industries awarded certificates from 1959 to 1969.

Even though we cannot provide an exact account of their operations, the 300-odd promoted firms that have begun production clearly were established primarily to produce goods competitive with imports. This fact can be shown indirectly by examining changes in imports. Many commodities show marked *decreases* in import value from 1960 to 1969, despite the fact that national income more than doubled and total imports nearly tripled in this period. A number of illustrative examples are shown in Table XXXVIII. In every case, one or more promoted firms began to produce domestically between 1960 and 1969.

A rough estimate of the magnitude of such import substitution was obtained as follows. We identified all items whose import value decreased from 1960 to 1969 and calculated the total value of imports for such items, as follows: 1960, 3,600 million baht; and 1969, 1,150 million baht.

If imports of these items had increased in proportion to the rise in money income, their import value in 1969 would have been 8,750 million baht; hence one could say that import substitution of 7,600 million baht has occurred

---

[16] "Registered capital" figures are based on the firm's application and do not represent actual investment. Indeed, these figures have little, if any, significance.

[17] In the negotiations preceding Board approval of a promotion certificate for a petrochemical complex in 1970, percentage of foreign (Japanese) ownership became a central issue. The eventual compromise was a 50-50 division, leaving control somewhat in doubt!

[18] Other problems with the data: promotion certificates are issued for expansion of plants as well as for new ventures, promotion certificates may lapse or be withdrawn, and firms may fail, but we cannot separate any of these categories.

TABLE XXXVII

Promotion Certificates, by Industry, April 1959–Dec. 1969

Industry	Number of Certificates	Industry	Number of Certificates
Food and agricultural:		Watch and parts............	1
Agricultural product curing .	9	Manganese and lead	3
Pearl oyster culture.........	4	Steel making	4
Slaughter house	1	Total	113
Edible milk	10	Chemical products:	
Food canning	5	Carbon dioxide	2
Sugar	13	Chemical fertilizer	2
Gourmet seasoning powder ..	3	Chemicals	16
Plantation oil	10	Ink	1
Tea	4	Paint	9
Animal feed	8	Pharmaceutical	5
Cold storage	24	Plastic powder	2
Edible flour	11	Petrochemicals	1
Ice	2	Total	38
Total	104	Electrical products:	
Textile and related:		Dry cell battery	9
Spinning, weaving, dyeing...	108	Storage battery	2
Cotton products	4	Electrical appliances	28
Gunny bag	3	Electric communication	4
Fishing net	2	Phonograph records	5
Coconut fiber	4	Electric motors, electrodes...	5
Carpet yarn	2	Total	53
Rope	2	Other:	
Synthetic fiber	1	Wood flooring, curing	30
Garment	1	Rattan and bamboo	4
Button and zipper	4	Paper	12
Artificial leather	2	Fiber and gypsum board	2
Total	133	Rubber products	17
Metal products and machinery:		Tires: auto and cycle........	7
Pipe (iron, plastic, etc.)	9	Glass	5
Welding rod	1	Ceramic	15
Tin plate, galvanized iron,		Cement	11
wire	17	Quarry	6
Petrol drum	1	Mineral products, mining ...	4
Aluminum products	5	Oil refining	3
Steel working (nails, nuts,		Grease	1
etc.)	27	Crude oil exploration	6
Agricultural tools	3	Deep sea fishing...........	7
Container tubes and cans	4	Spectacle lenses............	2
Sewing machine	1	Feather selection	4
Water pump	1	Ship building	3
Mechanics' tools	1	Sea transportation	3
Auto, truck, and tractor		Internal boat transportation..	2
assembly	13	Air transportation	1
Vehicle parts	14	Hotels	61
Motorcycle and bicycle	8	Total	206
		Grand total[a]	647

[a] The discrepancy between this total and that in Table XXXVI exists in the original sources.
Source: Board of Investment.

TABLE XXXVIII

IMPORT RESPONSE TO INVESTMENT PROMOTION: SELECTED PRODUCTS

(Million Baht)

	1960	1969		1960	1969
Imports of Products Produced by Promoted Firms			Imported Inputs for Promoted Firms[a]		
Condensed milk	230	100	Dry milk, blocks and powder	32	210
Wheat flour	69	29	Wheat, unmilled	1	82
Tea dust	17	8			
Gourmet seasoning	29	1			
Gasoline	319	112			
Benzine for airplane	52	10	Crude petroleum	—	749
Kerosene	105	24			
Diesel oil	297	77			
Soap powder and detergent	79	30			
Bicycle tires and tubes	33	14			
Paper for printing and writing	72	38	Wood pulp	—	91
Cotton yarn and thread	133	66	Raw cotton	59	200
Cotton fabrics	651	194	Yarn of man-made fibers	14	241
Ropes and nets	100	59			
Gunny bags	121	—			
Blankets and towels	71	27			
Iron universal plates	39	2			
Galvanized iron sheets and plates	204	4			
Aluminum plates and sheets	34	24	Aluminum unwrought	4	57
Barbed wire	9	1			
Nails	57	6	Nail wire	—	24
Sewing machines, treadle	35	19	Sewing machine heads	14	27
Batteries, flashlight and radio	25	4			
Electric bulbs, domestic	12	8			
Bicycles	41	16	Bicycle parts	34	52
Fountain pens	15	10			

[a] These inputs include only a few examples in which the connection is fairly obvious.

Source: Thailand Department of Customs, *Annual Statement of Foreign Trade*, 1960, 1969.

(8,750 — 1,150 million baht).[19] This calculation measures only import substitution at the final product level (if that); it does not measure *net* import substitution. Actually, many of these new firms relied upon imported raw materials, parts, etc., and the declining imports of the products they produced were accompanied by rising imports of these intermediate goods. Unfortunately, the data do not permit a complete comparison of these two elements, but we show a few examples in Table XXXVIII. The cases of petroleum, milk, and cotton dramatically illustrate the shift toward imported inputs for domestic producers.

Another rough measure of the magnitude of import substitution can be obtained by using some estimates of imports and total supply of manufactures (domestic production plus imports minus exports), by industry. With such estimates for 1960 and 1968, we can observe the extent to which the imported share of total supply rose or fell. Following Maizels, we can then define import substitution as the reduction in manufactured imports relative to what these imports would have been if they had grown proportionately to domestic utilization of manufactured goods.[20] This calculation is shown in Table XXXIX. The outcome depends upon the level of aggregation. The share of total manufactures supplied by imports of manufactures declined only slightly from 1960 to 1968 (from 0.34 to 0.32), which indicates that overall import substitution was small (1.2 billion baht), and that imports of manufactures grew almost in proportion to total domestic utilization. However, if we look at specific industries, the picture is different. In textiles, for example, proportionate growth would have increased textile imports 1.5 billion baht, whereas actual imports were only 0.4 billion baht, indicating import substitution of 1.1 billion baht in this one industry. Import substitution was largest in petroleum. It was

[19] This calculation assumes that income elasticity of demand for these goods is unity, which of course may not be correct.

[20] Alfred Maizels, *Industrial Growth and World Trade* (Cambridge: Cambridge University Press, 1963), pp. 150–61. The logical basis for the calculations in Table XXXIX is as follows:

S_t = total supply of manufactures available in year t—namely, production + imports − exports

M_t = imports of manufactures in year t

$m_t = M_t / S_t$

dM = change in imports = $m_1 S_1 - m_0 S_0$

To bring out the extent of import substitution, the expression for dM can be rewritten as $dM = S_1(m_1 - m_0) + m_0(S_1 - S_0)$, where the first term, $S_1(m_1 - m_0)$, is defined as "gross import substitution," and the second term, $m_0(S_1 - S_0)$, is defined as "expansion of imports due to the rise in home demand."

The sense of this distinction is that as GNP increases and domestic utilization of manufactures increases, *imports* of manufactures may rise more or less than proportionately to the rise in domestic utilization. If imports rise in exactly the same proportion as domestic utilization, then $m_1 = m_0$, and the first term is *zero*. There is no "import substitution." If imports rise less fast than domestic utilization, then $m_1 < m_0$, and the first term is negative. The negative magnitude measures import substitution—the amount that actual imports are less than they would have been, given the original proportion (m_0). Thus "import substitution" means the reduction in manufactured imports relative to what these imports *would have been* if they had grown in the same proportion as domestic utilization of manufactured goods.

TABLE XXXIX
IMPORT SUBSTITUTION IN MANUFACTURES: DOMESTIC PRODUCTION AND IMPORTS, 1960–68
(Million Baht)

Item	Imports 1960 M_0	Imports 1968 M_1	Domestic Utilization[a] 1960 S_0	Domestic Utilization[a] 1968 S_1	Change in Imports dM	= Import[b] Substitution $S_1(m_1-m_0)$ +	+ Expansion of Imports Due to Rise in Home Demand $m_0(S_1-S_0)$
Consumer goods:							
Food	589.0	821.4	8,980.9	17,741.0	232.3	−342.4	574.7
Beverages	12.8	29.2	823.7	2,169.1	16.5	−4.3	20.8
Tobacco	2.4	3.8	1,359.6	2,362.4	1.3	−.5	1.8
Clothing and footwear	69.1	191.7	1,203.5	2,517.9	122.5	47.1	75.4
Furniture and fixtures	11.5	34.0	205.8	797.1	22.5	−10.5	33.0
Textiles	1,279.3	1,700.8	2,310.4	5,099.4	421.4	−1,122.9	1,544.3
Printing and publishing	63.9	164.0	590.3	1,271.0	100.0	26.3	73.7
Subtotal	2,028.0	2,944.9	15474.2	31,957.9	914.7	−1,246.4	2,161.0
Intermediate goods:							
Wood and wood products	10.1	35.5	375.2	1,702.6	25.5	−10.2	35.7
Paper and paper products	265.6	625.2	372.3	950.4	359.6	−52.8	412.4
Leather and leather products	19.1	13.1	123.5	186.2	−6.0	−15.7	9.7
Rubber and rubber products	250.2	399.9	405.6	884.7	149.7	−145.9	295.6
Chemicals	973.6	2,914.9	2,116.1	5,465.6	1,941.2	400.1	1,541.1
Petroleum and its products	1,018.8	1,071.6	932.8	5,472.7	52.3	−4,905.7	4,958.0
Nonmetalic minerals	124.0	311.1	600.9	2,358.4	187.0	−175.7	362.7
Subtotal	2,661.4	5,371.3	4,926.4	17,020.6	2,710.5	−3,822.8	6,533.3
Capital goods:							
Basic metals	850.1	2,285.1	887.1	2,428.4	1,435.0	−42.0	1,477.0
Metal products	395.0	1,084.6	570.8	1,991.2	689.6	−293.3	982.9
Machinery, nonelectrical	1,259.4	4,027.9	1,302.6	4,586.2	2,768.7	−405.9	3,174.6
Electrical machinery	504.7	1,975.4	612.1	2,494.6	1,470.8	−81.3	1,552.1
Transport equipment	830.3	3,260.4	1,584.9	6,106.6	2,430.0	61.0	2,368.9
Subtotal	3,839.5	12,633.4	4,957.5	17,607.0	8,793.4	−1,003.6	9,797.0
Miscellaneous	222.3	966.2	354.8	1,409.0	743.8	83.3	660.5
Total	8,751.2	21,915.8	25,712.9	67,994.5	13,164.5	−1,223.9	14,388.4

[a] Production plus imports minus exports.
[b] Equations $m_0 = M_0/S_0$; $m_1 = M_1/S_1$.
Source: National Economic Development Board. See also Maizels, *op. cit.* and note 20.

small in capital goods, as expected. Overall, there was a shift from imports of consumer goods to capital goods.

We conclude that the primary effect of investment promotion in Thailand has not been a substitution of domestic production for imports, but a substitution of one kind of imports for another—in particular, a substitution of imported raw materials, components, and capital goods for imports of the products now turned out by promoted firms. Exceptions do exist, however.

Even with the special incentives they receive, promoted firms have sometimes found it difficult to compete with imports. Such firms, especially those whose five-year concessional rates on raw material imports had expired, frequently sought additional, more permanent tariff benefits. That is, they asked for increases in the tariff rates on their products and decreases in the tariff rates on their imported inputs. Since 1960 numerous tariff changes have been made, many of them designed to assist promoted industries. The Thai tariff structure has shifted toward higher rates on goods produced domestically, lower rates on imported inputs, thus increasing effective protection. A few specific examples are shown in Table XL.

In some cases, import quotas and import prohibition have been used to guarantee promoted firms a market. Specific items have been placed on the import control list when deemed necessary to provide protection for domestic firms. Recognizing that this confers monopoly power, the Board of Investment has tried to ameliorate it by awarding several promotion certificates (which fragments a small market), or by fixing maximum prices for the product.

TABLE XL

EXAMPLES OF THE THAI TARIFF STRUCTURE[a]

Commodity	1960 Tariff Ad valorem (Percent)	1960 Tariff Specific (Bahts/kg.)	1969 Tariff Ad valorem (Percent)	1969 Tariff Specific (Bahts/kg.)
Wood, unmanufactured	27.5%		10%	
Plywood	30.0		40	
Toothpicks	30.0			75.00
Pulp	27.5		10	
Paper	10		30	
Pig iron	10		5	
Galvanized iron plates	—	.35	30	1.25
Nails		.30	30	1.10
Motor for air cond.	55		15	
Air cond. machine, complete	55		60	
Woven fabric of man-made fibers	40	16.50	60	40.00

[a] When both ad valorem and specific rates are stated, the one requiring the larger amount of duty is applicable.

In summary, Thailand's investment promotion program from 1959 to 1970 has primarily stimulated firms to capture the small, tariff-sheltered domestic market. The incentives offered, plus existing protection, offered an opportunity for profit. However, some promoted firms required an increased degree of protection, especially when the five-year concessions expired, and the Thai tariff structure has become progressively more protective.

The industrial structure created by such a general policy pattern has certain undesirable aspects. First, promoted firms tend to design their plants to produce only for the sheltered domestic market, which means that they build small-scale plants. In those lines of production in which significant economies of scale exist, small plants mean high costs per unit. (Board insistence upon modern technology may exacerbate this problem by preventing the use of factor proportions appropriate to small-scale industry in Thailand.) Second, such firms will obviously not export their products, but the high prices they must charge for their output will impair the competitive position of potential exporters in other lines of production. If Thai exporters must pay higher prices than their foreign competitors for inputs (nails, plywood, paper, etc.), they will be at a disadvantage. In this way industrial promotion may handicap exports.

As we would expect in view of the foregoing discussion, exports of manufactures have remained small. Despite the growth of manufacturing in the past decade, only five manufactured products exceeded 20 million baht ($1 million) in 1969:[21]

	Million Baht		Million Baht
Cut gems	137	Silk fabrics	39
Gunny bags	74	Cotton fabrics	25
Cement and lime	40		

If we drop down to 10 million baht, we can add only four more items:

	Million Baht		Million Baht
Iron and steel tubes and pipes	18	Ropes and nets	11
Clothing	16	Iron sheets and plates	11

We can safely conclude that Thai industrial promotion has fostered the growth of a manufacturing sector that produces for the domestic market.[22]

During the 1960's the Thai balance-of-payments position was strong despite

[21] Thailand Department of Customs, *Annual Statement of Foreign Trade, 1969*. Tin metal could be listed as a manufactured export; value-added in tin-smelting is about 10 percent of the value of tin exports.

[22] In 1970, the Ministry of Economic Affairs prohibited the export of iron rods and bars, thus destroying a foreign market that was showing promise of growth. This action makes it more difficult for the industry to expand to a scale at which decreasing costs might operate. Such an expansion might never have occurred, but this kind of bureaucratic interference certainly is the kiss of death. Too many such obstacles handicap exporters—e.g., the interminable red tape required to obtain tariff drawbacks on exports.

the rapid increase in imports. Since reserves were steadily rising, the growing excess of merchandise imports over exports, and the failure of the industrial sector to produce goods for export, did not arouse much concern. However, in 1969 and 1970, when a deficit appeared in the balance of payments, much attention was focused on this matter. Investment promotion policy was criticized for having fostered a manufacturing sector incapable of competing in export markets and dependent upon a rising volume of imported inputs.

In response to this criticism, the Board of Investment announced that no more Group A and B certificates would be awarded, and then declared that no more tariff exemptions for raw material inputs would be granted. Priority would be given to firms using domestic raw materials or to firms contemplating production for the export market. Thus it appears that Thailand's investment promotion program has entered a new phase. Whether the government is prepared to take the steps necessary to make Thailand an attractive base of operations for international corporations remains to be seen. The experience of Taiwan and Hong Kong, and the recent success that Singapore has enjoyed in attracting foreign capital, have certainly been remarked, but Thailand may not be willing to allow foreign firms as much freedom as they require in such matters as control, import of foreign technicians and management personnel, and freedom from bureaucratic entanglements. The existing industrial structure may itself represent a hindrance because of noncompetitive prices.

GOVERNMENT FINANCE

The conduct of public finance in Thailand since 1950 has been marked by a high degree of continuity with the past. As we have seen, the government has experimented with publicly operated industries and it has been more active and energetic than before in provision of various types of social overhead investment, but in most respects the generally conservative financial policy has continued. The dominant characteristics of the public finances have remained much the same as in the pre-1950 period. The major change has been an increased reliance upon deficit financing, both domestic and external (loans and grants).

The general structure of government revenue has changed very little since 1950. Indirect taxes still account for the bulk of government revenue (81 percent in 1969). The largest of these are import duties, excise taxes, and a form of sales or turnover tax (called the "business tax" in Thailand). The share of export duties, though still significant, has declined in recent years. See Table XLI for some details of revenue by type of tax for selected years.

Since land and capitation taxes were abolished prior to World War II, the only direct taxes of any consequence have been income taxes on personal and corporate incomes. These taxes have proved difficult to collect, but their share in government revenue has risen slowly—to about 11 percent in 1969. The difficulties of enforcing income taxes in Thailand are well known; neverthe-

TABLE XLI
SOURCES OF GOVERNMENT REVENUE
(Million Baht)

Category	1951	1955	1960	1965	1969
Personal income	n.a.	173	375	642	1,181
Corporate income	n.a.	108	207	492	850
Total direct taxes	127	281	582	1,134	2,031
Import duties	729	1,296	2,061	2,830	5,437
Export duties	382	794	1,233	1,570	1,506
Excise and sales taxes	1,143[a]	853	1,531	3,556	6,095
Other indirect		535	795	1,297	1,735
Total indirect taxes	2,254	3,478	5,620	9,253	14,773
Sales and charges		339	228	328	372
Government enterprises	150[b]	70	150	232	617
Other		212	197	397	529
Total revenue	2,531	4,380	6,777	11,344	18,322

[a] For 1951, excise and sales taxes and other indirect sources of revenue were not broken down.
[b] For 1951, sales and charges, government enterprises, and other sources of government revenue were not broken down.
Sources: 1951, Thailand Department of Commerce and Statistics, *Statistical Yearbook of Thailand*, No. 22; 1955–69, Bank of Thailand, *Monthly Report*.

less, one suspects that the main obstacle may be a lack of determination in the top levels of government. The nominal tax rates are high enough; the problem is that few people report their incomes and pay the income tax. Despite the real estate and construction boom in Thailand, no property taxes exist. The failure to introduce direct taxes poses a serious problem for the future. Efforts to check imports, for example, will tend to reduce revenue and increase government deficits.

The so-called business tax has become an important source of revenue in recent years. This is a tax levied on the gross sales of business enterprises at all levels—retail, wholesale, manufacturing, services, etc. It is therefore a kind of turnover tax. The rate varies from one kind of business to another. No doubt this tax is collected unevenly, but it is much easier to enforce than the income tax because it is based simply on gross sales and requires no accounting for expenses and net income. The business tax is also collected on imports (in addition to import duties per se). It is likely that the business tax is collected more effectively on imports than on domestically produced goods, which tends to increase the dependence of the tax system on the flow of foreign trade.

Unlike the broadly based business tax, excise taxes are derived from a small number of commodities. The biggest revenue producers are alcoholic beverages, tobacco, and petroleum products.

Despite the fact that its structure has scarcely changed, the revenue system has generated steadily increasing revenues for the government, as may be seen in Table XLI. The bouyancy of revenue is demonstrated by the fact that the ratio of total revenue to GNP has risen, from 8 percent in 1951 to 12.5 percent in 1960 and to 13.7 percent in 1969.

With such a large share of revenue derived from tariffs, excises, and turn-over taxes, the tax system is closely linked to expenditure. This characteristic, together with high tax rates on luxury items, tends to encourage saving. We have no data on the share of taxes paid by persons at different income levels, but most economists believe the tax system to be regressive, especially when the rice premium is taken into account.

As in the past, virtually all tax revenue accrues to the central government. The only tax of any importance collected by local government is the "local development tax," which is in fact a land tax. The rates are low and the total revenue was less than one billion baht in 1969. Local governments receive some transfers from the central government, but most governmental activities are still financed, operated, and controlled by the central government.

Government revenue has continued to exceed current expenditures, but not by a margin large enough to cover capital expenditures (see Appendix B for annual figures). The government has resorted to borrowing to cover that part of capital expenditures not covered by ordinary revenues. The treasury issues bonds which are purchased chiefly by the Bank of Thailand, the Government Savings Bank, and commercial banks. Such bond issues are at once a means of financing government deficits and a means of influencing the supply of money. Bonds sold to the Bank of Thailand tend to increase the supply of money; bonds sold to commercial banks tend to restrain it when the treasury uses the proceeds to increase its cash balance at the Bank of Thailand. Internally held government debt increased steadily after 1950, as the following figures show:

End of Year	Government Debt (Millions of Baht)	
	Domestic	External[23]
1950	1,370	204
1955	4,790	550
1960	6,380	2,150
1965	10,010	5,300
1969	19,490	6,180

In the early 1950's, the Bank of Thailand accumulated exchange profits from the multiple-exchange rate system, and Treasury borrowings from the Bank could be regarded simply as transfers of this revenue, not as true deficit financing. After multiple-exchange rates were abolished in 1955, revenue from export duties (on rice, rubber, etc.), which replaced them, accrued directly to the government, thus reducing the need to borrow. During the 1960's the

[23] Including guarantee obligations. Source: Bank of Thailand, *Annual Report, Monthly Report.*

TABLE XLII
CENTRAL GOVERNMENT EXPENDITURES[a]
(Million Baht)

Year	Total Expenditures	Functional Classification				
		Economic	Social	Defense	Gen'l Admin.	Other
1959	6,443	1,460	1,755	1,420	1,297	511
1960	6,703	1,429	1,885	1,379	1,508	502
1961	7,727	1,925	2,127	1,461	1,597	617
1962	8,472	2,069	2,312	1,581	1,738	772
1963	9,589	2,400	2,674	1,661	1,977	877
1964	10,772	2,678	3,135	1,767	2,195	1,000
1965	12,449	3,382	3,635	1,979	2,195	1,258
1966	14,028	4,155	3,766	2,225	2,694	1,188
1967	17,333	5,528	4,446	2,694	2,752	1,913
1968	19,485	5,157	4,635	2,998	3,028	3,667
1969	21,613	6,216	5,601	3,733	3,149	2,914

[a] Appropriated in National Budget. Includes both current and capital expenditures, but not expenditures financed by foreign grants and loans.
Source: Bank of Thailand, *Monthly Report.*

Treasury deficit rose steadily as government expenditures, both current and capital, were increased in accordance with the requirements of the first two national economic plans (1961–66 and 1967–71).

Beginning in 1959, a functional classification of expenditures is available. Annual figures, which include both current and capital expenditure, are presented in Table XLII.[24] The largest increases have occurred in the "economic" and "social" categories. The former includes agriculture, irrigation, transportation, industry, etc., while the latter includes education, health, and welfare. Defense expenditures have risen, but their share in total expenditure declined from 22 percent in 1959 to 17 percent in 1969.

The government employs a large number of persons (about 290,000 civilians in 1967, of whom 140,000 were teachers). The civil service is a high-status occupation, and many persons seek government positions even though salaries may be lower than those available in the private sector. (Security and lesser pressures may contribute to this preference.) Civil service salaries have not kept pace with increases in the cost of living, and large numbers of government employees supplement their incomes by moonlighting. Low salaries are also blamed for the prevalence of the "tea money" system—payment of small bribes to expedite transactions with the various government offices.[25] It seems clear

[24] The figures in Table XLII and Appendix B do not include expenditures financed by foreign grants and loans. Neither do they include external military aid.

[25] Two interesting series of articles on "Prebendalism" and on the civil service and its problems appeared in the *Bangkok Magazine* under the pseudonym "GNP"—issues for July 26, Aug. 2, Oct. 25, and Nov. 1, 1970.

TABLE XLIII
External Grants and Loans
(Millions of U.S. Dollars)

Year	Grants U.S.[a]	Grants Other[b]	Grants Total	Loans Direct	Loans Government-guaranteed	Loans Total
1950				$18.0	—	$18.0
1951	$7.2	n.a.	$7.2	—	—	—
1952	6.0	n.a.	6.0	—	—	—
1953	5.9	n.a.	5.9	—	—	—
1954	10.6	n.a.	10.6	—	—	—
1955	40.3	n.a.	40.3		12.0	12.0
1956	26.7	n.a.	26.7	10.0	3.3	13.3
1957	26.4	n.a.	26.4	10.8	66.0	76.8
1958	24.9	n.a.	24.9	6.9	—	6.9
1959	24.4	n.a.	24.4	—	35.8	35.8
1960	25.1	n.a.	25.1	.7	—	.7
1961	25.3	4.6	29.9	1.9	41.0	42.9
1962	25.9	7.5	33.4	41.3	34.2	75.5
1963	17.3	7.3	24.6	27.1	18.6	45.7
1964	12.7	8.4	21.1	22.0	1.0	23.0
1965	18.9	9.2	28.1	7.4	11.7	19.1
1966	44.5	11.8	56.3	40.2	3.4	43.6
1967	56.6	15.2	71.8	34.6	6.0	40.6
1968	50.3	13.3	63.6	29.0	16.6	45.6
Total	$449.0	$77.3	$526.3	$249.7	$255.6	$505.3

Source of Loans

	Direct	Government-guaranteed	Total
World Bank	$170.0	$114.5	$284.5
United States	51.3	45.6	96.9
West Germany	28.8	29.6	58.4
Others	1.0	66.1	67.1
Total[c]	$251.1	$255.8	$506.9

[a] AID obligations, fiscal year. Military aid is *not* included in this table.

[b] "Other" grants not available on annual basis prior to 1960, but some grant assistance was received, mostly from the United Nations and the Colombo Plan.

[c] Discrepancies in totals appear in original sources.

Source: Thailand Department of Technical and Economic Cooperation, Ministry of National Development.

that many government offices are greatly overstaffed, and the marginal productivity of labor is close to zero—if indeed it is not negative. (This circumstance casts doubt on the validity of national income estimates, which include the full cost of government payrolls as value-added and hence as part of the national product. A substantial part of the government payroll could more

TABLE XLIV

CONSOLIDATED FINANCIAL ACCOUNT FOR THE PUBLIC SECTOR[a]

(Billions of Baht)

Category	1961/62	1962/63	1963/64	1964/65	1965/66	1966/67	1967/68	1968/69
Revenue	8.85	9.52	10.78	12.73	14.55	16.54	18.62	21.24
Current expenditure[b] ...	−7.13	−7.86	−8.40	−9.13	−10.71	−13.11	−14.71	−16.30
Capital expenditure	−3.62	−4.24	−4.72	−5.60	−5.74	−6.71	−8.66	−9.69
Deficit	−1.90	−2.58	−2.34	−2.00	−1.90	−3.28	−4.75	−4.75
Financed by:								
External loans	.92	.84	.52	.67	.13	.27	—	−.13
External grants	.67	.94	.62	.66	.89	1.02	1.27	1.46
Domestic sources[c]	.29	.80	1.03	.68	.88	1.99	3.48	3.42

[a] Includes central government, local government, and state enterprises.
[b] Certain transfers and adjustments have been combined with current expenditures.
[c] Includes extra-budgetary treasury receipts and certain adjustments.
Source: Bank of Thailand.

properly be treated as a transfer payment. The workers are "unproductive labor" in the classical sense.) A thoroughgoing reorganization of the civil service could reduce employment and raise salary levels at no increase in total outlay, but it is unlikely to occur.

Since 1950 Thailand has received a significant amount of external assistance in the form of foreign grants and loans. Table XLIII contains annual figures for the period 1950 to 1968. The United States has been the principal source of grants, providing a total of about $450 million in this period.[26] United States economic aid has been used for a wide variety of purposes, the most important of which have been highways, health, education, and police administration. In recent years primary emphasis has been placed on activities in the Northeastern region—accelerated rural development.

Foreign loans, including direct and guaranteed, have about equaled foreign grants over the whole period, as may be seen in Table XLIII. The World Bank has been the largest lender, followed by the United States and West Germany. These figures represent the gross amount of new loans; repayment has not been allowed for. In December 1969, external debt outstanding amounted to $300 million, which implies that about $200 million had been repaid. Loan funds have been used mainly for power, irrigation, port development, and transportation.

During the whole period 1950–68, foreign grants and loans amounted to about $1,000 million, or 21 billion baht. In that same period, government capital expenditures not including those financed by foreign grants and loans amounted to 39 billion baht (from Appendix B). External assistance thus comprised a significant addition to Thailand's investible resources. This comparison is not entirely appropriate, because not all of the foreign grants and loans were used for capital expenditures, but it is suggestive. On the other side, critics have argued that external assistance is not as beneficial as its size might indicate because it is not allocated to projects with the highest marginal rate of return. It is even argued that foreign aid can be harmful because it draws domestic resources into nonoptimal activities. In particular, some of the brightest, most energetic young officials in government may be assigned as "counterparts" to foreign experts, an assignment that may hamper the development of initiative, creativity, and a feeling of responsibility. Other domestic resources are also drawn into foreign aid projects. Because these external grants have significant effects upon the allocation of domestic resources and upon the course of economic development, Thailand should scrutinize them carefully and make certain they reflect the national priorities.

It is difficult to obtain an overall, comprehensive picture of government finance in Thailand. The regular accounts omit expenditures financed from external grants and loans; government enterprises may not be incorporated; local government is treated separately, etc. One would like to have a consoli-

---

[26] The figures in Table XLIII represent AID obligations by fiscal year, not the sums actually spent; but for the entire period the two values should be approximately the same.

dated account of the government sector compiled on a consistent basis. Such an account was developed (or estimated) by the World Bank Mission and it has been continued in subsequent reports to the World Bank. A summary of this account for the period 1961/62 to 1968/69 is presented in Table XLIV.

As expected, capital expenditures loom larger in this consolidated account than in the regular accounts, since most external loans and grants are used for capital expenditures. The size of the overall deficit has increased sharply since 1965, but a larger proportion of the total deficit is being financed domestically. This greater reliance upon internal debt has of course contributed to recent inflationary pressures and to the swing toward a deficit in the balance of payments. Net foreign debt has scarcely increased at all since 1965. If the government could put the funds to productive uses, foreign loans should provide a partial solution for the balance-of-payments difficulties that seem to lie ahead. Thailand's debt, both domestic and external, is still quite small, especially in comparison with foreign exchange reserves.

Money and the Balance of Payments

Since 1950 the supply of money (currency and demand deposits held by the private sector) has risen steadily. Monetization of the economy, still geographically uneven, has proceeded further, facilitated by general economic development in these two decades, especially by the extension of transportation and the spread of banking offices.

The rise in the money supply approximately kept pace with the rise in gross national product, which means that the income velocity of money (GNP $\div S_m$) remained fairly stable. Table XLV contains annual data showing that income velocity varied only from 5.2 to 6.4 in the period 1952 to 1969. It first declined (1952–60) and then rose (1960–69), a pattern that may result from changes in the relative sizes of demand and time deposits during these periods.

The share of currency in the money supply declined steadily, from 73 percent in 1952 to 54 percent in 1969 (see Table XLV, col. 4). This change also reflects the spread of banking services throughout the country. In 1952, there were 84 bank offices in 24 changwats; in 1969 there were 604 bank offices in 71 changwats.[27] Foreign-chartered banks continue to play an important role in Bangkok, the commercial and financial center, but domestic banks have greatly increased their relative importance; and it is they who have created branch offices throughout the country, if only because foreign banks are not allowed to establish provincial branches.

Rozental presents figures showing that in 1966 the provincial branches accounted for about one-third of total deposits (demand plus time) but only one-sixth of total loans.[28] He concludes that these branches are collecting rural

[27] Bank of Thailand, *Annual Economic Report*, 1952, 1969. These numbers refer to commercial banks only.

[28] Alek Rozental, *Finance and Development in Thailand* (New York, 1970), pp. 178ff.

savings and funneling them into the Bangkok-Thonburi area, and he recommends that commercial banks be prodded and persuaded to expand their lending activities in rural areas.

Perhaps the most dramatic monetary change since 1950 is the remarkable growth in time deposits. Beginning at a near-zero level in 1950, time deposits rose slowly during the 1950's, reaching only 1.66 billion baht in 1959, but they then grew rapidly to 20.07 billion baht in 1969. By 1969 time deposits were approximately equal to the total money supply. As may be seen in Table XLV, the great majority of time deposits are held in commercial banks, but the Government Savings Bank alone held nearly 4.0 billion baht in 1969. This phenomenal increase in privately held time deposits reflects the increasing monetization of the economy, but more than that it indicates a growth in private saving and public confidence in both the baht and the banking system. The interest rates obtainable on time deposits (7 percent) have made them more attractive than gold ornaments or currency as a form in which to hold savings, especially since interest on time deposits is exempt from income tax. Gold shops still exist, and many people still use gold, silver, jewelry, and currency as stores of wealth, but these forms of hoarding have probably declined in relative importance in recent years. The growth of time deposits has been encouraged by the Bank of Thailand through its reserve requirements, and by the government through its issuance of bonds (tax-exempt until 1969), which offer commercial banks a safe and convenient source of interest income. These bonds can also be counted as part of the reserves of the banks, up to 50 percent (formerly 25 percent). However, the presence of a *demand* for time deposits—a desire to hold such deposits on the part of firms and individuals possessing liquid assets—is the primary reason for their rapid growth. Given that demand, the banking institutions have been able to respond to it.[29]

The growth in time deposits represents an important mobilization of private saving, and it has of course greatly increased the lending power of the banking system. Except for their holdings of government bonds, Thai commercial banks are primarily engaged in financing foreign and domestic trade through short-term loans.

Prior to World War II, the primary determinant of the money supply in Thailand was the balance of payments (see Chapter 7). With no central bank (until 1942), a government budget in approximate balance, and a currency issue directly linked to foreign exchange reserves, changes in the money supply occurred largely in response to the balance-of-payments position. A payments surplus increased reserves and the money supply; a payments deficit reduced them.

The external balance has continued to play a prominent role in the determination of the money supply, but central bank credit, government finance,

[29] Rozental (p. 108) suggests that the reported rise in time deposits may be accounted for, in part, by a change in classification of deposits.

TABLE XLV
Selected Monetary Statistics

	(1)	(2)	(1)+(2)=(3)	(1)÷(3)=(4)	(5)	(6)	(5)+(6)=(7)	(8)	(9)
			Money Supply Held by Public (Billions of Baht)			Time Deposits (Public) (Billions of Baht)			Foreign Exchange Reserves (Million U.S. Dollars)
End of Year	Currency	Demand Deposits	Money Supply	Percentage of Currency	Commercial Banks	Government Savings Bank	Total	Income Velocity (GNP÷S_m)	
1952	3.68	1.40	5.08	73%	.10	0.32	0.42	6.1	$354
1953	4.02	1.84	5.86	69	.12	0.38	0.50	5.8	308
1954	4.55	1.89	6.44	71	.14	0.49	0.63	5.2	283
1955	5.18	2.05	7.23	72	.17	0.61	0.78	5.8	297
1956	5.42	2.30	7.73	70	.35	0.66	1.01	5.5	316
1957	5.57	2.62	8.20	68	.44	0.78	1.22	5.5	321
1958	5.50	2.95	8.45	65	.62	0.84	1.46	5.6	302
1959	5.78	3.29	9.08	64	.77	0.89	1.66	5.5	309
1960	6.05	4.04	10.09	60	1.03	1.06	2.09	5.3	353
1961	6.51	4.56	11.08	59	1.49	1.23	2.72	5.4	432
1962	6.57	4.52	11.09	59	3.15	1.39	4.54	5.7	495
1963	6.70	5.18	11.88	56	4.26	1.53	5.79	5.7	540
1964	7.29	5.63	12.92	56	5.37	1.68	7.05	5.8	609
1965	8.18	6.15	14.33	57	6.41	2.03	8.44	5.9	691
1966	9.44	7.22	16.66	57	8.83	2.57	11.40	6.1	850
1967	9.91	7.96	17.87	55	10.98	3.11	14.09	6.1	900
1968	10.69	8.71	19.41	55	13.24	3.54	16.78	6.1	922
1969	11.01	9.29	20.30	54	16.10	3.97	20.07	6.4	874

Source: Bank of Thailand, *Monthly Report*, *Annual Economic Report*.

Treasury cash balances, and other factors now also influence the outcome.[30] Table XLVI contains annual data, 1956–69, for factors affecting the money supply. (We omit the years 1950–55 because they involve complications arising from the multiple-exchange system.)

One striking point that appears in Table XLVI is the close relationship between the change in foreign assets and the change in money supply when these are *averaged* for the whole period. Thus, the average annual change in foreign assets was 839 million baht, compared with an average annual change in money supply of 935 million baht. Since the change in foreign assets is a measure of the balance-of-payments surplus or deficit, it is clear that the external balance still exerts a powerful influence on the money supply in Thailand.

However, we can also observe in Table XLVI that year-to-year changes in foreign assets can and do differ greatly from changes in the money supply. Since the final outcome depends, among other things, upon the amount of bank credit extended to the public sector and upon government deposit holdings, there is scope for policy decisions to affect the money supply. The actual figure is not entirely the result of an automatic mechanism, but is to some extent chosen by the policy makers. The most dramatic example is the latest year, 1969, when foreign assets *declined* by 998 million baht while the money supply *increased* 904 million baht, largely because of the sharp rise in bank credit extended to the public and private sectors. "During the year [1969], bank credit extended to the Government amounted to Baht 4,268.8 million, an exceptionally large amount compared with Baht 1,211.8 million in 1968.... A large portion of this credit was provided by the Bank of Thailand."[31]

Those who make decisions about Thai financial policy do not provide us with explanations of their monetary policy decisions. In fact, it is not even clear exactly how and where these decisions are made. The Bank of Thailand must have some voice, though it appears to make little use of its authority to regulate reserve requirements, and open-market operations are not feasible in the Thai money market.[32] Thus, the initiative appears to lie elsewhere, with the real monetary control coming through the determination of the amounts of government bonds and Treasury bills to be offered, and the size and location of government cash balances. For example, when the Treasury sells bonds to commercial banks and builds up its deposit in the Bank of Thailand, it exerts deflationary pressure on the economy.

In any event, since 1950 Thailand has continued its long tradition of gen-

[30] For a detailed analysis and discussion of postwar monetary policy in Thailand, see a series of papers by Paul B. Trescott, "Causes and Consequences of Monetary Change in Thailand, 1946–1967" (mimeo., Bangkok, *ca.* 1968).

[31] *Annual Economic Report, 1969*, Bank of Thailand, p. 43. The net figure shown in Table XLVI is smaller because government deposits also rose.

[32] See Silcock, *Thailand*, Ch. 8, for an interesting discussion of the *political* aspects of banking in Thailand.

TABLE XLVI
FACTORS AFFECTING THE MONEY SUPPLY
(Million Baht)

Year	(1) Bank Credit Extension To Government[a]	(2) To Private Sector	(3) Change in Time Deposits	(4) Other Factors	(5) Total Domestic Factors (1)+(2)−(3)−(4)	(6) Change in Foreign Assets	(7) (5)+(6)=(7) Change in Money Supply
1956	464	565	428	304	+297	+204	+501
1957	397	493	297	249	+345	+123	+468
1958	376	641	315	47	+655	−400	+255
1959	341	559	157	77	+666	−42	+624
1960	−377	849	448	−96	+121	+891	+1,012
1961	−496	825	678	234	−585	+1,572	+987
1962	95	1,205	1,775	699	−1,174	+1,192	+18
1963	215	1,117	1,378	8	−55	+843	+788
1964	−546	1,664	1,453	497	−832	+1,875	+1,043
1965	−183	2,058	1,417	750	−292	+1,705	+1,413
1966	377	2,089	2,968	462	−964	+3,289	+2,326
1967	827	2,342	2,754	248	+168	+1,048	+1,216
1968	2,139	2,767	2,723	1,098	+1,084	+447	+1,531
1969	2,824	3,090	3,267	745	+1,902	−998	+904
Average, 1956–69					+96	+839	+935

[a] Changes in government deposits are netted out.

Sources: T. H. Silcock (ed.), *Thailand: Social and Economic Studies in Development*, p. 198; Bank of Thailand, *Annual Economic Report*, 1969.

erally conservative monetary policy. Increases in the money supply have kept pace with, but not exceeded, the growth in national output. Government deficits have been financed largely through bond issues placed with commercial banks, and through foreign loans and grants. Consequently, Thailand has enjoyed exceptional price stability since 1952. The wholesale price index rose only 1.5 percent per year from 1952 to 1969, one of the lowest rates in the world in this period.[33] Price increases appear to have accelerated from 1966 to 1969.

Another aspect of Thailand's traditionally conservative financial policy is the relatively large holdings of foreign exchange reserves, which rose from $352 million in 1952 to $922 million at the end of 1968. At the latter date, foreign exchange reserves expressed in baht totaled 19.2 billion baht, an amount almost equal to the total money supply. The nation's external debt, about $300 million, was only about one-third as large as its holdings of gold and short-term dollars. It is clear that Thailand could have financed from its own resources the projects for which it borrowed from the World Bank, the United States, and elsewhere. To the extent that interest rates on these long-term loans exceeded interest rates on short-term dollar assets held in the reserves, this policy involved a net loss to Thailand.[34] However, it was recognized that important corollary benefits accompanied foreign loans: supervision, close accounting control that could restrain avaricious officials, and technical assistance in planning and executing complex capital projects. Over and beyond these undoubted advantages of foreign loans, however, there was the traditionally conservative view of financial policy in the Thai government. Thai authorities apparently *wanted* to accumulate foreign reserves, and the reserve level was not considered excessive even in 1968. The decline of $50 million in 1969 seemed to cause great anxiety and concern within the power structure.

The larger question is whether Thailand could have made productive use of these resources at home. Given the scarcity of capital in the domestic economy, the marginal productivity of capital should have been substantially higher than the interest yield on foreign reserves. To make effective use of additional increments of capital, however, it may be necessary to have additional quantities of other resources—skilled labor, managerial talent, technical knowledge, transport, power, etc. Aside from their conservative financial bias, Thai economic decision makers may have concluded that the economy did not possess sufficient amounts of these cooperating resources to warrant an expansion in investment.

We have no basis on which to evaluate this judgment, though the high rate

[33] This index refers to Bangkok-Thonburi. A consumer price index (1962 = 100) rose from 96 in 1960 to 117 in 1969. Price indexes are of doubtful reliability in Thailand, however.

[34] Actually, this loss was probably small. Some foreign loans were at nominal interest rates, and even World Bank loans were well below the rates Thailand would have had to pay in the capital market. In recent years, Thailand has benefited from the high short-term interest rates prevailing in world capital markets.

TABLE XLVII
Share of Principal Exports, 1950–69
(Million Baht)

Year	Rice	Rubber	Tin[a]	Teak	Total of Four Commodities	Total Merchandise Exports	Share of Four Commodities (Percent)	Share of Rice alone (Percent)
1950	1,672	726	257	143	2,798	3,473	81%	48%
1951	1,824	1,469	187	158	3,638	4,413	82	41
1952	2,629	1,009	224	97	3,959	4,619	86	57
1953	3,747	751	300	133	4,931	5,772	85	65
1954	3,087	1,108	373	211	4,779	6,177	77	50
1955	3,133	1,802	441	264	5,640	7,120	79	44
1956	2,861	1,526	507	306	5,200	6,923	75	41
1957	3,622	1,406	531	262	5,821	7,540	77	48
1958	2,968	1,326	255	239	4,788	6,447	74	46
1959	2,576	2,236	464	244	5,520	7,560	73	34
1960	2,570	2,579	537	356	6,042	8,614	70	30
1961	3,598	2,130	617	252	6,597	9,997	66	36
1962	3,240	2,111	685	170	6,206	9,529	65	34
1963	3,424	1,903	741	137	6,205	9,676	64	35
1964	4,389	2,060	961	179	7,589	12,339	62	36
1965	4,334	1,999	767	201	7,301	12,940	56	34
1966	4,001	1,861	1,315	243	7,420	14,310	52	28
1967	4,653	1,574	1,822	194	8,243	14,166	58	33
1968	3,774	1,816	1,406	169	7,165	13,679	52	28
1969	2,945	2,664	1,658	166	7,433	14,722	50	20

[a] Tin ore until 1965; tin metal thereafter.

Source: Thailand Department of Customs, *Annual Statement of Foreign Trade.*

of growth actually achieved, especially from 1960 to 1969, suggests that the Thai economy was at or near its maximum capacity to absorb capital. That having been said, it is still remarkable that a country in Thailand's stage of development was in effect a capital exporter from 1950 to 1970. Its short-term foreign assets exceeded its long-term debts, both public and private (including direct investment).

Another reason why Thai authorities pursued such a conservative policy with respect to foreign exchange reserves may have been that they regarded the balance-of-payments surplus as a temporary phenomenon that could quickly be transformed into a large deficit. This view was particularly pertinent from 1966 onward because of the large dollar receipts that accompanied the United States' military activities in Thailand.

But even if one takes a longer view, there was a legitimate basis for concern. As early as 1953, the traditional export surplus on merchandise account had given way to an import surplus (reversed only in 1955 and 1956), which steadily increased thereafter. The rise in merchandise imports did not appear to be easily reversible. Although industrial investment was creating a manufacturing capacity and replacing imports of certain finished goods, it was also generating a demand for imports of raw materials, parts, and capital goods. In the meantime, exports were lagging behind, and the market prospects for several export products were uncertain at best. It was easy to project import and export trends, allow for reduced U.S. military expenditures, and obtain "predictions" of large payments deficits that could quickly melt away the foreign exchange reserve. Even at the peak level of those reserves, high officials were issuing warnings that the nation's reserves were equal to "only 9–10 months supply of merchandise imports." Many countries would be glad to have reserves equal to three months' imports!

Still, the outlook for exports is gloomy, even though Thailand has developed several important new exports since 1950. The share of the four traditional export products (rice, rubber, tin, and teak) declined from 86 percent in 1952 to 50 percent in 1969. Table XLVII contains the details. The share of rice alone declined from 57 percent in 1952 to 20 percent in 1969. The new exports that have emerged include corn, cassava, kenaf, oilseeds, beans, shrimp, and other primary products, mostly agricultural. The new exports listed in Table XLVIII for selected years have, in total, exceeded rice exports for several years, an indication of their rapid growth from near-zero levels in 1950. The rapid growth of output of these products has been encouraging, but their markets have also been unstable. For example, kenaf exports declined from 1,613 million baht in 1966 to 866 million baht in 1967. As the residual supplier of nations that produce these items for themselves, Thailand must be prepared for wide fluctuations in specific products.[35] It needs to develop a flexible agri-

---

[35] Agricultural protection in other countries aggravates this problem. The subsidized U.S. export of rice is one of the bitterest examples for Thailand, but there are many others.

TABLE XLVIII
New Export Products, Selected Years
(Million Baht)

Commodity	1950	1960	1966	1969
Fish (mostly shrimp)	21	16	235	321
Maize, unmilled	—	551	1,520	1,674
Cassava	25	273	561	864
Tobacco	—	21	115	149
Oilseeds	93	170	277	224
Kenaf and jute	—	230	1,613	781
Beans and peas	12	56	185	243
Precious and semiprecious stones..	19	20	97	150
Gunny bags	—	—	48	74
Total	170	1,337	4,651	4,480

Source: Thailand Department of Customs, *Annual Statement of Foreign Trade.*

culture, capable of shifting quickly from one crop to another as market conditions warrant. It also needs to develop nonagricultural exports, as we have seen above. Among the services, only tourism offers much promise as a source of foreign exchange earnings.

During the past two decades, Thailand has developed a deficit in its merchandise trade balance. This shift to an excess of merchandise imports represents a profound change in its external economic position, for in the preceding century (1850–1950) Thailand consistently had an export surplus on merchandise account (see Chapter 10). The excess of imports appeared in the 1950's, and until recently it caused little concern. It was relatively small, it showed no strong upward trend, and it was more than covered by foreign aid and capital inflows so that Thailand actually had an overall balance-of-payments surplus. However, from 1966 to 1969 the merchandise trade deficit rose very rapidly, and policy makers began to worry about the ability of the nation to finance such a large excess of imports. See Table XLIX for a summary of balance-of-payments statistics from 1951 to 1969.

In 1965, merchandise exports were 12.7 billion baht, imports 15.2 billion baht, thus producing an excess of imports of 2.5 billion baht. By 1969, exports had risen only 1.7 billion baht, to 14.4 billion baht, while imports had risen 10.3 billion baht to 25.5 billion baht. The excess of merchandise imports over exports thus rose to 11.1 billion baht. What especially alarmed some officials was that in 1969 a deficit appeared in the overall balance of payments for the first time since the early 1950's. Foreign exchange reserves declined $48 million from December 1968 to December 1969, but still remained very high by most standard measures of reserve adequacy. This drop in reserves, the uncertain market prospects for export products, the expected decline in United States' military expenditures, and the continuing strong growth in imports all combined to create apprehension about the nation's external financial condition. In June 1970 the government sharply increased tariff rates on a large number of imports, especially luxury goods, and raised other taxes as well, in an effort to check the growth of imports and improve the balance of payments.

It is of course well understood in Thailand that one should not consider the merchandise trade balance by itself. We have done so above only because that balance has changed so dramatically in the last twenty years.

Thailand has consistently shown a surplus in its trade in services. Consequently, the "current account" deficit has been smaller than the merchandise trade deficit (see Table XLIX for annual figures). From 1966 to 1969, the receipts side of the services account increased sharply because of the inclusion there of U.S. military expenditures in Thailand. This item rose from 0.9 billion baht in 1965 to 2.6 billion baht in 1966, and reached a peak of 4.9 billion baht in 1968. These expenditures produced a large credit balance in services, and also had a substantial impact on the Thai economy. However, even when one allows for trade in services, the deficit on current account has increased sharply in recent years.

Actually, the swing toward a deficit on merchandise trade and on current account is easily accounted for. It is indeed a normal, expected development, given the changes in capital movements and in foreign aid and other transfers. One relatively minor cause of this swing is the shift in private remittances from an outflow (debit balance) to an inflow (credit balance). Traditionally, part of Thailand's export proceeds were used to pay remittances to foreign relatives of Chinese and other immigrants. These sums were therefore not spent on imports, either directly or indirectly. Since 1950, the outflow of remittances has declined, and has even been exceeded by inflows of such payments from abroad (see line B.1 in Table XLIX). The net inflow of private remittances serves to provide funds for a small part of merchandise imports, thus financing part of the trade deficit.

Foreign aid and capital movements (both private and official) have a similar effect. A foreign grant may provide the direct foreign exchange cost of imported machinery to be used in a given project; private direct investment may also be used in part for the purchase of imported capital goods. Alternatively, the effect on imports can be an indirect one. A foreign loan may be converted into baht and spent for local labor and materials, in which case the rise in money incomes will spill over into a demand for imports.

Since 1950, Thailand has received an increasing inflow of such transfers: foreign aid, private direct investment, official loans, and private loans. Foreign aid and official loans have already been discussed briefly, above. Private direct investment has been a small item until recently, but it has increased rapidly since 1965 (see line C.1, Table XLIX). Other long-term private capital has

TABLE XLIX

Balance of Payments, 1951–69

(Million Baht)

Item	1951	1952	1953	1954	1955	1956	1957	1958	1959
A. Current Account Balance	670.1	−350.0	−1,043.9	−1,376.0	403.8	−325.2	−772.5	−1,644.7	−1,474.8
1. Trade Balance	733.8	−143.8	−674.0	−1,021.7	4.6	−33.5	−406.2	−1,663.0	−1,413.4
1.1. Merchandise exports, f.o.b.	4,918.4	5,983.0	5,800.8	6,021.8	7,160.4	7,481.7	8,067.3	6,412.7	7,533.5
1.2. Merchandise imports, c.i.f.	−4,184.6	−6,126.8	−6,474.8	−7,043.5	−7,155.2	−7,515.2	−8,473.5	−8,075.7	−8,946.9
2. Services: Receipts	112.6	275.1	235.0	167.3	517.6	553.5	739.3	854.0	793.4
2.1. Freight and insurance } 2.2. Other transportation }	7.2	84.5	88.4	54.2	72.9	90.8	175.0	214.3	124.6
2.3. Travel		56.4	38.6	45.8	73.5	54.4	56.1	88.1	110.4
2.4. Investment income	53.0	68.9	27.9	11.8	64.2	88.4	109.9	125.7	104.4
2.5. Govt.: military services[a]	14.8	39.8	46.5	36.6	157.9	154.4	213.9	250.6	278.8
2.6. Govt.: n.i.e.	37.6	25.5	33.6	18.9	149.1	165.5	184.4	175.3	175.2
2.7. Other services									
3. Services: Payments	−176.3	−481.3	−604.9	−521.6	−926.0	−845.2	−1,105.6	−835.7	−854.8
3.1. Freight and insurance } 3.2. Other transportation }	−11.8	−143.1	−139.4	−127.4	−126.6	−116.5	−183.3	−130.0	−113.6
3.3. Travel	−41.2	−128.0	−139.1	−133.2	−165.9	−209.2	−262.1	−212.5	−211.5
3.4. Investment income	−4.9	−41.0	−91.9	−58.4	−177.9	−248.1	−362.7	−275.9	−240.6
3.5. Government, n.i.e.	−118.4	−72.9	−88.5	−97.0	−219.2	−114.1	−95.7	−60.6	−82.0
3.6. Other		−96.3	−146.0	−105.6	−236.4	−157.3	−201.8	−156.7	−207.1
B. Unrequited Transfers, net	49.7	58.8	−13.3	−14.7	127.8	373.5	529.3	501.1	936.3
1. Private	41.0	1.7	−95.0	−150.6	−176.1	−186.7	−195.3	−27.7	65.9
2. Government	8.7	57.1	81.7	135.9	303.9	560.2	724.0	528.8	870.4
C. Long-term Capital, net	−661.7	1,111.7	181.3	5.2	420.0	303.8	483.0	310.3	272.9
1. Private, direct					50.0	50.0	50.0	70.0	72.0
2. Private loans and other	13.0	−1.2	−1.2	−1.3	309.5	180.2	369.1	293.1	338.9
3. Official[b]	−674.7	1,112.9	182.5	6.5	60.5	73.6	63.9	−52.8	−138.0
D. Short-term Capital, net	−343.6	−556.5	784.0	460.6	−620.7	−298.2	−159.3	402.1	38.6
1. Private (nonmonetary)					−4.4				
2. Official (monetary)[c]	−343.6	−556.5	784.0	460.6	−616.3	−298.2	−159.3	402.1	38.6
E. Errors and Omissions	285.5	−264.0	91.9	924.9	476.7	53.9	−80.5	431.2	227.0

Item	1960	1961	1962	1963	1964	1965	1966	1967	1968	1969
A. Current Account Balance	−842.1	51.0	−1,454.2	−2,430.8	−1,228.0	−1,112.5	−372.3	−2,237.1	−4,501.5	−5,499.0
1. Trade Balance	−956.3	−269.1	−1,962.6	−3,117.0	−1,960.6	−2,556.3	−4,479.4	−8,150.2	−10,650.0	−11,070.0
1.1. Merchandise exports, f.o.b.	8,541.9	9,922.7	9,434.5	9,577.7	12,165.0	12,663.5	13,817.2	13,808.1	13,227.6	14,390.0
1.2. Merchandise imports, c.i.f.	9,498.2	10,191.8	11,397.1	12,694.7	14,125.6	15,219.8	18,296.6	21,958.3	23,877.6	25,460.0
2. Services: Receipts	1,037.9	1,332.9	1,617.6	1,848.4	2,262.1	3,249.1	6,200.3	8,432.3	9,421.2	9,101.0
2.1. Freight and insurance	132.7	179.0	158.7	157.4	258.0	392.1	511.3	541.0	397.3	276.0
2.2. Other transportation	66.8	79.4	137.6	158.2	164.4	154.1	175.7	230.7	182.5	208.0
2.3. Travel	114.4	159.7	183.0	206.8	241.2	358.8	832.3	1,211.7	1,417.2	1,485.0
2.4. Investment income	138.6	179.2	213.7	265.1	388.3	526.0	675.6	942.6	1,052.5	1,285.0
2.5. Govt: military services[a]		77.2	204.6	361.1	438.7	922.1	2,584.1	4,107.1	4,920.7	4,444.0
2.6. Govt.: n.i.e.	363.1	370.8	436.0	370.9	486.6	569.4	973.1	770.9	701.1	598.0
2.7. Other services	222.3	287.6	284.0	328.9	284.9	326.6	448.2	628.3	749.9	805.0
3. Services: Payments	−923.7	−1,012.8	−1,109.2	−1,162.2	−1,529.5	−1,805.3	−2,093.2	−2,519.2	−3,272.7	−3,530.0
3.1. Freight and insurance	−79.0	−99.6	−88.7	−69.8	−87.3	−117.5	−172.5	−143.9	−167.6	−142.0
3.2. Other transportation	−41.1	−36.1	−26.3	−21.2	−31.9	−63.1	−100.6	−76.2	−115.4	−121.0
3.3. Travel	−267.4	−257.7	−335.8	−355.4	−461.0	−508.6	−565.7	−715.3	−1,035.6	−1,071.0
3.4. Investment income	−237.7	−272.5	−312.1	−305.5	−467.0	−537.1	−683.8	−775.1	−780.3	−1,059.0
3.5. Government, n.i.e.	−111.1	−147.3	−137.0	−155.6	−180.7	−182.7	−194.4	−259.3	−527.6	−482.0
3.6. Other	−187.4	−199.6	−209.3	−254.7	−301.6	−396.3	−376.2	−549.4	−646.2	−655.0
B. Unrequited Transfers, net	770.3	541.0	910.9	1,138.2	775.1	796.4	982.7	1,198.2	1,547.5	1,250.0
1. Private	52.2	97.8	106.0	144.9	130.9	146.2	216.3	173.8	140.4	89.0
2. Government	718.1	443.2	804.9	993.3	644.2	650.2	766.4	1,024.4	1,407.1	1,161.0
C. Long-term Capital, net	342.7	794.8	1,490.2	1,665.9	1,607.3	1,201.8	1,005.9	2,104.5	2,225.3	2,478.0
1. Private, direct	66.9	120.9	156.0	346.8	374.2	590.8	541.3	755.1	1,217.4	1,080.0
2. Private loans and other	328.2	563.0	1,344.0	1,287.7	1,003.3	349.8	171.6	903.1	457.1	1,138.0
3. Official[b]	−46.4	110.9	−9.8	31.4	229.8	261.2	293.0	446.3	550.8	260.0
D. Short-term Capital, net	−890.1	−1,582.3	−1,289.3	−969.6	−1,394.0	−1,511.6	−2,929.0	−1,204.7	−351.3	1,084.8
1. Private (nonmonetary)	59.6	72.7	5.6	−20.9	36.3	185.4	358.3	68.8	95.7	87.0
2. Official (monetary)[c]	−949.7	−1,655.0	−1,294.9	−948.7	−1,430.3	−1,697.0	−3,287.3	−1,273.5	−447.0	997.8
E. Errors and Omissions	619.2	195.5	342.4	596.3	239.6	625.9	1,312.7	139.1	1,080.0	686.2

[a] Included in 2. 6, "Government: n.i.e.," until 1961.   [b] Includes small amounts of official short-term capital.

[c] Includes changes in short-term foreign position of commercial banks.

Source: Bank of Thailand, *Monthly Report*, 1961–69. Early figures (1951–60) supplied by the Bank of Thailand.

fluctuated greatly from year to year, but in total the net inflow has exceeded official borrowings in the past twenty years. One could argue that U.S. military expenditures should also be included in this group of "autonomous" transfer of funds. Although the motivation of these expenditures is clearly different, their short-run effect upon the balance of payments is very similar to that of capital inflows.

This rising inflow of capital and transfers, both private and official, tends to cause an increase in imports of goods and services. Thus it tends to produce a deficit balance on current account. The excess of imports over exports of goods and services is in fact the *real* transfer of capital from the outside world into Thailand; the current account deficit is therefore a normal and necessary aspect of the capital inflow.

In the theory of international trade, an extensive literature has developed to analyze and explain the mechanics and operation of the transfer process. Aside from the direct increase in imports, it is generally agreed that an increase in the level of transfers operates through both price effects and income effects to bring about a current account deficit in the receiving country. When a capital inflow occurs, for example, domestic expenditures increase, incomes rise, and part of the increased income will be spent for imports. The rise in expenditure may also put upward pressure on domestic prices, thus increasing the attractiveness of imports.[36] These forces may also tend to reduce exports. This influence may account, in part, for the sluggish growth of exports in recent years, but a more important explanation probably lies in certain economic policies, which have inhibited production for export (rice premium, the export duty on rubber, the import substitution bias of investment promotion, etc.).

In the literature, one issue has been whether or not the transfer will be complete—that is, whether the deficit on current account will be large enough to effect the real transfer of capital. In the Thai case, the data show that during this period, 1951–69, the sum of the current account deficits was *less than* the sum of the aid and capital items. The transfer was incomplete, with the difference accounted for by increases in foreign exchange reserves. (Clearly, if a more expansionary monetary policy had been followed in Thailand, imports would have been larger and a smaller reserve accumulation would have occurred.)[37] In 1969, however, the balance swung the other way, and the transfer was *over*-complete. Reserves declined.

The relationship between "transfers" and "current account deficit" is depicted in Chart X for the years 1961 to 1969. For this purpose we have treated U.S. military expenditures as part of "transfers" instead of treating them as

---

[36] We are assuming throughout that the exchange rate is fixed within narrow limits, as has been the case in Thailand.

[37] We do not suggest that this outcome would have been a better one, in any sense.

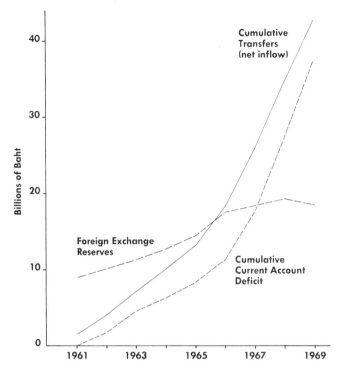

Chart X. Transfers, current account deficit, and reserves (cumulative, 1961–69). Source: Table XLIX.

part of the current account. This change is not essential for the argument, but it has a certain logic. The items included in "transfers" may be regarded as "autonomous" in Meade's sense; they do not occur in response to changes in other items in the balance of payments, but they tend to cause changes in the other items.[38]

The figures plotted in Chart X are cumulative totals. The excess of transfers over the current account deficit was largely offset by additions to foreign exchange reserves. Chart X shows that the current account deficit is closely related to total transfers; our argument is that transfers cause, or give rise to, the current account deficit.[39]

[38] The analytical concept of an autonomous item in the balance of payments is rarely found in pure form in real life. However, the items we have included in "transfers" come close to satisfying Meade's definition: ". . . the distinguishing feature of autonomous payments is that they take place regardless of the size of the other items in the balance of payments." James Meade, *The Balance of Payments* (London, 1951), p. 11.

[39] These relationships are definitional, of course. The only item left out of account is the "errors and omissions" term in the balance of payments. This item consistently showed a credit balance from 1961 to 1969.

This point is a simple one, well recognized in international economics. We have discussed it here for two reasons. First, some observers and even some government officials have expressed alarm at the large deficits on merchandise trade and on current account that have emerged in Thailand in recent years. The above discussion is reassuring because it suggests that these deficits are a normal and even necessary counterpart to the inflows of aid, capital, and other transfers in recent years. Second, this argument also implies that a reduction in the level of transfers will bring about a decline in the current account deficit. Thai authorities seem to fear that, when the planned reductions in U.S. military expenditures occur, the level of imports of goods and services will remain the same (or continue rising at the same rate), thus increasing the current account deficit. Actually, when the inflow of transfer declines, some direct reduction in imports of goods and services will occur, and a further indirect reduction will occur *unless* the authorities deliberately offset the domestic impact of the reduced transfer.

This last point is of course the real problem. Thailand desires to maintain its momentum of growth, and it does not wish to see a pause or slackening of that growth when transfers decline. If government expenditures expand to take up the "slack," or if monetary expansion is allowed in the face of a decline in reserves, then the current account deficit might indeed fail to decline. In that event foreign exchange reserves would be drawn down to cover the resulting overall payments deficit. The government would soon have to choose one of several alternative policies (or a combination of them) to provide a more basic solution.

First, the government could attempt to restore or increase the level of transfers, either by taking steps to attract an increased volume of private capital or by seeking additional foreign aid and official loans. In 1970 the government began to pursue both these courses.[40] Some changes in regulations were made to improve the investment climate and encourage private foreign investment, and the World Bank Consultative Group was convened to discuss external resource requirements of the Third Economic Plan and the resources that might be made available by donor countries.

Second, the government could attempt to reduce Thai purchases of goods and services from abroad by raising tariffs, imposing quotas, and otherwise restricting trade. If such measures are accompanied by expansionary fiscal and monetary policies, they are unlikely to accomplish much of an improvement in the balance of payments, especially in a small, open, market-oriented economy. Tariffs and quotas stimulate domestic production of the specific protected commodities, but they also stimulate imports of raw materials and parts.

---

[40] We should note that this blurs the definition of transfers as "autonomous" items in the balance of payments. The government is attempting, through policy, to induce a larger inflow of transfers.

Domestic prices tend to rise when expansionary fiscal and monetary policies are pursued at the same time that import supplies are reduced. As domestic prices rise, some renewed demand for imports will appear as consumers find import prices relatively more attractive despite the higher tariffs. The domestic price increases will also tend to reduce exports. Consequently, total trade will be reduced, but the *balance* of trade may not be much affected by such restrictions. A further practical point is that when tariff rates become very high and domestic prices are significantly higher than world prices, the rewards for smuggling and corruption become large. With its long coastline, limited administrative capacity, and intensely individualistic marketing system, Thailand faces a definite limit on its ability to restrict imports by higher tariff rates, import quotas, and other such devices.

The above discussion has assumed the maintenance of a fixed exchange rate for the baht. A third alternative would be to devalue the baht in an effort to stimulate exports and reduce imports. The immediate impact of a devaluation might be in the desired direction. That is, it would tend to stimulate exports and check imports, but if accompanied by expansionary fiscal and monetary policies it would also tend to cause a rise in domestic prices that would offset or reverse this impact effect. The real danger would be that a further devaluation would soon be necessary, and that the public would lose confidence in the baht. Since Thailand probably could not enforce an effective exchange control, a capital flight could seriously damage the nation's financial position. In view of the long tradition of conservative financial policy, it seems quite unlikely that the government will experiment with this alternative, except for modest changes in the baht parity.[41] Since 1955, the value of the baht in terms of the U.S. dollar has remained stable, except for small changes in the official parity. See Appendix D.

We have so far been considering short-term solutions and expedients, and we have assumed that government feels compelled to maintain the momentum of growth. A longer-term, more basic solution may lie in economic policies to encourage a shift in the structure of the economy—particularly toward expansion of the capacity to export. This structural solution is consistent with the first alternative mentioned above—namely, to seek an increased flow of foreign capital.

In the meantime, the government may be forced to accept a slowdown or pause in the growth momentum of the economy. In view of the high import content of domestic investment and the sensitive response of imports to changes in income, deflationary policies should have quick and substantial effects upon the trade balance. In other words, the income multiplier is low. A reduction in investment of 100 million baht will reduce income by about

---

[41] This point applies, *a fortiori*, to the use of a floating or fluctuating exchange rate for the baht.

175 million baht and reduce imports by about 56 million baht.[42] Thus, decreases in investment and income lead to quick and sizable improvements in the trade balance.

The trouble is that *any* reduction in income is unwelcome. If the level of transfers can be maintained, perhaps income need not fall. But if net transfers decline, and the current account deficit must therefore be reduced, deflationary financial policy may be the least painful of the available alternatives. Prior to World War II, when exports were the dominant element of autonomous expenditure, fluctuations in export income set in motion a prompt and apparently smooth adjustment mechanism through which imports were brought into line with exports. This mechanism appeared to operate without severe economic distress.

Perhaps the changes brought about by twenty years of virtually uninterrupted growth have weakened this capacity to adjust. However, the subsistence base of the economy still provides a large cushion. When U.S. military expenditures decline, for example, the service industries in nearby towns will release workers from employment, but most of these persons can return to their villages. Their money incomes will fall, and imports will decline.

If this process is allowed to operate—that is, if government allows some deflationary pressures to appear and does not attempt to counteract them through expansionary fiscal and monetary policies—then it is possible that a basic solution will arrive more quickly. Such policies will preserve domestic and international confidence in the baht and will also hold down the costs of production in Thailand. Consequently, domestic capital flight will be less likely to occur and capital inflows will be encouraged. Production for export should be promoted as vigorously as possible. The basic objective, in an open economy, is to correct the payments deficit by expanding trade and capital inflows in order to preserve the benefits that accrue from positions of comparative advantage. At the same time, some drawing down of foreign exchange reserves could ease the stress and strain of this adjustment.

[42] This estimate is based upon the values obtained in Chapter 11:
$\Delta I_m/\Delta I = 0.35; \Delta C_d/\Delta Y = 0.63; \Delta C_m/\Delta Y = 0.12$.

If $\Delta I = -100$, then $\Delta I_m = -35$

$$\Delta Y = (\Delta I - \Delta I_m) \cdot \left(\frac{1}{1 - C_d}\right)$$

$$\Delta Y = [-100 - (-35)] \cdot \left(\frac{1}{1 - .63}\right) = -65(2.7)$$

$$\Delta Y = -175$$

$$\Delta C_m = 0.12(-175) = -21$$

Then the total change in imports is: $\Delta M = \Delta I_m + \Delta C_m = -35 + (-21) = -56$.

APPENDIXES

Regions in Thailand

THE REGIONAL BOUNDARIES used in this study have been dictated largely by the classifications used in reporting statistics. A general idea of the regional division may be obtained from the map in the front of the book. A more exact definition is given in this Appendix.

Since 1932 the country has been divided into 70 (now 71) *changwats* (or provinces), and statistics of population, area cultivated, and production are published by changwats. Therefore, it is convenient to use a regional boundary which does not cut across changwat boundaries.

From 1894 to 1932 the country was divided into larger administrative units called *monthons*. The number of these varied from ten to eighteen, but fortunately each monthon was composed of an integral number of the present changwats.

In order to ensure continuity and comparability, the regional boundaries used in this study have been chosen in such a way as to include the same area for all years and at the same time to include an integral number of monthons or changwats. (As monthons were progressively reduced in number, each one eliminated was added to another, and not split between two or more others.)

The system used here has made it necessary to include somewhat more in the "Central Region" than is desirable, but there was no alternative.

The following classification has been used to define the regional boundaries used in this study. Official spellings are those given in the *Royal Gazette*.

CENTER

MONTHONS

Krung Thep	Ratchaburi	Chanthaburi
Prachin	Nakhon Chaisi	Phitsanulok
Ayutthaya	Nakhon Sawan	

CHANGWATS

Phra Nakhon	Chanthaburi	Chonburi
Thonburi	Trat	Nakhon Nayok
Nonthaburi	Rayong	Prachinburi
Samut Prakan	Chachoengsao	Chainat

325

Changwats (*Continued*)

Nakhon Sawan	Nakhon Pathom	Pichit
Uthai Thani	Samut Sakhon	Phitsanulok
Pathum Thani	Suphanburi	Phetchabun
Ayutthaya	Kanchanaburi	Sukhothai
Lopburi	Prachuap Khiri Khan	Uttaradit
Singburi	Phetchaburi	Kamphaeng Phet
Angthong	Ratchaburi	Tak
Saraburi	Samut Songkram	

NORTH

Monthons

Bayab	Maharat

Changwats

Chiangrai	Phrae	Lampang
Chiangmai	Mae Hong Son	Lamphun
Nan		

NORTHEAST

Monthons

Ubon Ratchathani	Nakhon Ratchasima	Udon Thani
Roi Et		

Changwats

Si Sa Ket	Roi Et	Loei
Chaiyaphum	Surin	Sakon Nakhon
Nakhon Ratchasima	Ubon Ratchathani	Nongkhai
Buriram	Khonkaen	Udon Thani
Maha Sarakham	Nakhon Phanom	

SOUTH

Monthons

Surat	Nakhon Si Thammarat	Phuket
Pattani		

Changwats

Chumphon	Trang	Pattani
Phatthalung	Phuket	Krabi
Songkhla	Nakhon Si Thammarat	Phang-nga
Narathiwat	Satun	Ranong
Yala	Surat Thani	

APPENDIX B

Government Receipts and Expenditures

ANNUAL FIGURES for government revenues and expenditures from 1892 to 1969 are given below. The basic sources for these figures are the *Statistical Year Book of Thailand, Reports of the Financial Advisers,* and *Annual Reports,* Bank of Thailand.

Changes have been made from time to time in the method of accounting for certain items, and an effort has been made to choose the figures according to a consistent system of classification. This has not been entirely possible because some inconsistencies are buried in the figures, but certain major adjustments have been made, including the following:

1. "Capital" expenditures included in "ordinary" expenditures have been deducted from the latter and added to the former, wherever possible.

2. Defense expenditures included in "capital" expenditures have been deducted from the latter and added to "ordinary" expenditures.

3. Certain other noncapital items of expenditure have been deducted from "capital" expenditures and added to "ordinary" expenditures.

4. In certain recent years, the "extraordinary" expenditures have been split between "capital" and "ordinary" expenditures, according to the nature of each item.

Even after these adjustments have been made, "ordinary" expenditures still include some "capital" expenditure, but it is not possible to segregate them. Expenditures for the construction of buildings, roads, canals, telegraph system, and many others were often charged to "ordinary" expenditures, especially in the earlier years.

GOVERNMENT REVENUES AND EXPENDITURES
(*All Figures in Millions of Baht*)

Year[a]	Ordinary Revenue	Adjusted Ordinary Expenditures	Surplus (Deficit) on Ordinary Account[b]	Adjusted Capital Expenditures
1892	15.38	12.80	2.58	2.12
1893	17.39	17.05	0.34	1.13
1894	17.33	11.06	6.27	1.43
1895	18.07	11.16	6.91	1.53
1896	20.65	16.89	3.76	1.59
1897	24.81	20.81	4.00	3.19
1898	28.50	20.37	8.13	3.42
1899	29.92	24.13	5.79	2.92
1900	35.61	28.34	7.27	3.50
1901	36.16	32.29	3.87	4.36
1902	39.15	36.46	2.69	2.79
1903	43.46	40.84	2.62	3.07
1904	46.05	46.64	(0.59)	4.99
1905	50.46	48.83	1.63	4.22
1906	55.52	55.34	0.18	5.58
1907	54.28	54.96	(0.68)	6.43
1908	58.92	56.44	2.48	4.29
1909	60.69	56.85	3.84	4.70
1910	61.36	56.92	4.44	5.96
1911	59.46	61.99	(2.53)	6.70
1912	64.78	61.54	3.24	10.31
1913	72.09	60.91	11.18	11.15
1914	71.15	62.78	8.37	11.39
1915	74.36	67.09	7.27	9.64
1916	79.50	67.55	11.95	8.52
1917	82.46	70.44	12.02	6.52
1918	87.81	85.55	2.26	7.84
1919	90.68	81.75	8.93	10.27

[a] Until 1939, the years refer to the period April through March. The year 1939 refers to the period April–September 1939, while the year 1940 as used here refers to the period October 1939 to December 1940. After 1940, the years run from January through December until 1960, after which the fiscal year runs from October 1 to September 30.

[b] The Surplus (Deficit) column refers only to the balance on *ordinary* account. Before 1925, most capital expenditures were made from loan funds, but since 1925 they have come from ordinary revenues. The over-all surplus or deficit of the government is therefore quite different from that given above, in many cases.

(*All Figures in Millions of Baht*)

Year[a]	Ordinary Revenue	Adjusted Ordinary Expenditures	Surplus (Deficit) on Ordinary Account[b]	Adjusted Capital Expenditures
1920	80.34	80.36	(0.02)	14.69
1921	79.63	79.39	0.24	12.50
1922	78.08	80.43	(2.35)	9.03
1923	81.60	84.23	(2.63)	4.59
1924	85.18	89.67	(4.49)	7.57
1925	92.71	94.65	(1.94)	7.93
1926	100.59	100.55	0.04	5.78
1927	117.44	112.13	5.31	5.26
1928	106.96	101.70	5.26	5.22
1929	108.12	98.62	9.50	8.48
1930	96.32	91.66	4.66	7.97
1931	78.95	82.90	(3.95)	6.18
1932	79.65	70.23	9.42	3.51
1933	83.73	73.64	10.09	3.79
1934	94.00	75.82	18.18	3.96
1935	94.66	85.08	9.58	7.07
1936	119.49	98.14	21.35	12.41
1937	109.41	107.66	1.75	17.78
1938	118.23	110.71	7.52	22.22
1939	59.61	60.78	(1.17)	13.42
1940	178.36	165.83	12.53	1.15
1941	160.99	167.99	(7.00)	37.12
1942	147.37	178.74	(31.37)	21.27
1943	211.65	207.61	4.04	53.46
1944	286.01	332.19	(46.18)	58.53
1945	314.68	412.26	(97.58)	12.94
1946	628.48	544.26	84.22	75.28
1947	993.65	967.37	26.28	67.34
1948	1,658.23	1,496.39	161.84	165.49
1949	1,905.21	1,617.61	287.60	410.09
1950	2,138.58	1,964.29	174.29	341.03

(*table continued on next page*)

Year[a]	Ordinary Revenue	Adjusted Ordinary Expenditures	Surplus (Deficit) on Ordinary Account[b]	Adjusted Capital Expenditures
1951	2,531	2,445	86	970
1952	3,347	3,355	−8	953
1953	3,941	3,848	93	1,042
1954	4,266	4,143	123	1,351
1955	4,380	3,932	448	1,093
1956	5,100	4,568	532	899
1957	5,183	4,947	236	908
1958	5,527	5,041	486	935
1959	6,037	5,268	769	1,175
1960	6,777	5,505	1,272	1,198
1961	7,449	6,143	1,306	1,584
1962	8,002	6,548	1,454	1,924
1963	8,819	7,326	1,493	2,263
1964	9,957	8,177	1,780	2,598
1965	11,344	8,859	2,485	3,590
1966	12,901	9,827	3,074	4,201
1967	14,780	11,536	3,244	5,797
1968	16,889	14,485	2,404	5,000
1969	18,322	15,062	3,260	6,551

APPENDIX C

Statistics of Foreign Trade

AVAILABLE TRADE FIGURES probably vary a great deal in accuracy from year to year, but it is not possible to evaluate the reliability of the figures in any very useful way. A few notes may help to guard against misuse of the figures, however.

1. Prior to 1920/21, the figures refer to the port of Bangkok only. This port probably accounted for 80–85 percent of the total foreign trade of Thailand, however. The largest omission was the trade of southern Thailand, consisting largely of tin exports and consumer-goods imports. There was also some border trade with Burma and Indochina, which was omitted before 1920/21.

2. Prior to 1896, the trade figures apparently include coastwise trade with the port of Bangkok, even though such trade was not foreign trade. The amount of such coastal trade was quite small relative to the total, however, and it probably amounted to no more than one or two percent.

3. In a number of the early years, imports are understated because government imports were omitted from the returns. The practice varied in this respect, however, and in any case no adjustment can be made for this item.

4. In some of the early years, trade figures were reported in Straits dollars or pounds sterling. In such cases, the baht values have been obtained by using available information on exchange rates. See Appendix D.

5. "Treasure" includes coin, bullion, and gold leaf. In some years the figures are not given for the separate items, so we have combined them in all years. Sometimes imports of gold leaf have filled a monetary role, but in most years such imports probably should be treated as a commodity. Gold leaf is widely used for religious and ceremonial purposes, and most imports are intended for this purpose, although in some years gold leaf was sent to Bangkok to settle monetary debts.

6. Imports have probably been undervalued throughout the period covered, although in varying degrees. In the early years, customs duties were collected by a "tax farmer," who probably reported imports on the low side in order to conceal his true revenue and thus to hold down the purchase price of his "farm." Importers also had an interest in undervaluing imports because of the ad valorem duties. In recent years specific duties have tended to replace ad valorem duties, but, while this removes the merchant's incentive

to undervalue, it also reduces the customs department's concern about accurate valuation.

7. From 1947 to 1955, import statistics are questionable because it is not known with certainty exactly how imports were valued: that is, whether at the official or open-market exchange rate. Officially, the rule was that if the accompanying invoice was accepted as valid, the shipment was valued at the foreign price times the *official* rate of exchange; but if the invoice was questioned, the local wholesale price of the article concerned (less the duty) was used as the value. The latter method meant in effect that the shipment was valued at the open-market rate. When the article was subject to a specific duty, however, the customs officials did not concern themselves with the accuracy of the invoice, and they simply accepted the declared valuation. As a result the import statistics published by customs for these years are a confusing mixture as far as valuation is concerned.

8. The valuation problem is much simpler for exports from 1947 to 1955. About 80 percent of total exports were under exchange control, and these commodities (rice, tin, and rubber) were valued at the official rate in the figures given below. The remaining exports were under no exchange controls, and the valuation of the exporter was accepted. In most cases, this was given at the open-market exchange rate.

9. In some earlier years, two or three estimates, all official, are available for the same period. Sometimes these estimates vary widely. We have no sound basis for selecting one set rather than another, although we have done so for the sake of simplicity.

10. Exports include a small amount of re-exports in many years.

Subject to qualifications made in the above notes, the table given in the following pages summarizes available statistics on the value of the foreign trade of Thailand. For years since 1952, see Table XLIX, pp. 316–17.

STATISTICS OF FOREIGN TRADE
(Millions of Baht)

Year	Commodity Imports	Treasure	Total Imports	Commodity Exports	Treasure	Total Exports
1850	4.33		4.33	5.59		5.59
1859	2.74	1.29	4.03			
1862	2.88	1.82	4.70			
1863	4.92	1.38	6.30			
1864	6.36	2.98	9.34	10.50		10.50
1865	3.78	0.38	4.16	4.20		4.20
1866	6.08	0.24	6.32	7.40		7.40
1867	6.03	0.31	6.34	7.65	0.46	8.11

(*Millions of Baht*)

Year	Commodity Imports	Treasure	Total Imports	Commodity Exports	Treasure	Total Exports
1870	6.31	1.60	7.91	10.78	0.27	11.05
1871	6.16	1.35	7.51	9.60	0.32	9.92
1872	7.61	1.14	8.75	10.56	0.58	11.14
1873	6.58	0.23	6.81	6.55	1.15	7.70
1874	7.37	0.34	7.71	9.27	0.54	9.81
1875	7.12	3.52	10.64	13.46	0.58	14.04
1876	8.78	3.02	11.80	13.54	0.32	13.86
1877	7.97	1.91	9.88	14.60	0.66	15.26
1878	7.85	1.86	9.71	13.85	0.93	14.78
1879	8.46	2.36	10.82	17.01	1.00	18.01
1880	8.85	1.72	10.57	15.43	0.74	16.17
1881	9.20	1.26	10.46	16.42	0.02	16.44
1882	10.89	0.94	11.83	14.61	1.56	16.17
1883	8.22	0.39	8.61	14.37	0.97	15.34
1884	9.10	1.21	10.31	18.09	0.57	18.66
1885	9.49	1.89	11.38			15.73
1886	9.00	3.30	12.30			17.29
1887	9.90	6.68	16.58			26.00
1888	11.00	7.12	18.12			27.24
1889	14.12	1.81	15.93			22.86
1890	16.36	9.95	26.31			32.10
1891	13.81	1.56	15.37			18.00
1892	14.96	0.75	15.71	16.81		16.81
1893	20.35	8.80	29.15	57.50		57.50
1894	21.06	7.41	28.47	41.10		41.10
1895	23.35	8.96	32.31	39.37	2.93	42.30
1896	23.83	10.86	34.69	45.83	1.67	47.50
1897	25.09	15.88	40.97	49.92	1.06	50.98
1898	29.00	16.15	45.15	55.47	2.22	57.69
1899	34.60	8.73	43.33	53.21	0.25	53.46
1900	37.71	5.68	43.39	51.70	0.30	52.00
1901	43.48	5.05	48.53	74.76	0.78	75.54
1902	47.65	17.77	65.42	86.14	1.26	87.40
1903	51.33	14.09	65.42	73.34	1.12	74.46
1904	66.99	11.32	78.31	99.88	1.51	101.39

(*table continued on next page*)

(*Millions of Baht*)

Year	Commodity Imports	Treasure	Total Imports	Commodity Exports	Treasure	Total Exports
1905/6	61.05	7.83	68.88	106.57	0.39	106.96
1906/7	66.78	10.28	77.06	105.56	0.30	105.86
1907/8	66.51	12.18	78.69	97.84	1.90	99.74
1908/9	66.82	10.00	76.82	100.05	0.71	100.76
1909/10	62.61	7.20	69.81	100.95	1.62	102.57
1910/11	61.92	6.29	68.21	108.69	0.22	108.91
1911/12	68.21	4.93	73.14	83.77	0.86	84.63
1912/13	72.39	3.84	76.23	81.71	0.26	81.97
1913/14	83.62	7.17	90.79	115.43	0.09	115.52
1914/15	71.76	6.72	78.48	100.96	0.68	101.64
1915/16	71.75	3.70	75.45	105.22	0.76	105.98
1916/17	84.36	3.49	87.85	121.15	0.33	121.48
1917/18	93.39	3.69	97.08	122.05	1.75	123.80
1918/19	98.56	4.53	103.09	160.99	1.04	162.03
1919/20	123.28	15.16	138.44	174.96	2.34	177.30
1920/21	152.44	7.24	159.68	89.79	0.70	90.49
1921/22	134.20	10.34	144.54	183.47	0.15	183.62
1922/23	133.30	10.95	144.25	169.86	0.60	170.46
1923/24	142.02	7.84	149.86	200.29	1.26	201.55
1924/25	158.97	10.40	169.37	202.48	0.60	203.08
1925/26	168.79	12.59	181.38	244.09	0.64	244.73
1926/27	179.18	17.34	196.52	238.56	0.71	239.27
1927/28	188.68	12.40	201.08	276.06	0.21	276.27
1928/29	180.86	8.93	189.79	252.43	0.05	252.48
1929/30	198.45	8.26	206.71	219.59	0.18	219.77
1930/31	149.46	5.55	155.01	159.88	1.64	161.52
1931/32	97.18	2.73	99.91	116.91	17.30	134.21
1932/33	87.69	1.81	89.50	129.23	23.29	152.52
1933/34	92.42	0.54	92.96	129.79	14.29	144.08
1934/35	101.35	0.37	101.72	161.04	11.56	172.60
1935/36	108.55	0.20	108.75	149.31	8.91	158.22
1936/37	109.08	0.96	110.04	179.38	4.98	184.36
1937/38	111.12	0.70	111.82	165.93	3.56	169.49
1938/39	127.22	2.41	129.63	176.76	27.66	204.42
1939/40	128.19	66.41	194.60	212.79	3.76	216.55

Year	Commodity Imports	Treasure	Total Imports	Commodity Exports	Treasure	Total Exports
1940	123.47	0.78	124.25	182.63	3.21	185.84
1941	155.21	13.63	168.84	290.00	0.09	290.09
1942	100.64	0.16	100.80	137.71		137.71
1943	193.13	9.63	202.76	115.73		115.73
1944	151.68	4.99	156.67	94.24		94.24
1945	107.61	1.72	109.33	89.46		89.46
1946	564.64	0.81	565.45	449.86		449.86
1947	1,112.79	270.96	1,383.75	1,091.34		1,091.34
1948	1,754.20	0.39	1,754.59	2,484.35		2,484.35
1949	2,271.85	4.15	2,276.00	2,981.01		2,981.01
1950			2,881.00			3,922.00
1951			3,714.00			4,413.00
1952			5,678.00			4,619.00

Sources: 1850, D. E. Malloch, *Siam, Some General Remarks on Its Productions*; 1859, *Bangkok Calendar for 1862*; 1862–91, *Annual Diplomatic and Consular Reports from H.M.'s Consuls in Siam, 1864–1892*, Great Britain, Foreign Office; 1892–95, *Comparative Statement of the Imports and Exports of Siam, 1892–1901*; 1896–1945, *Statistical Year Book of Thailand*. Treasure figures for the years 1896–1904 were obtained from *Statistics of Import and Export Trade of Siam*, Thailand, Dept. of Customs, 1901–4; 1946–49, *Report of the Financial Adviser, 1941–50*, Thailand, Ministry of Finance, pp. 8–11, except for the export figures which were supplied by the Exchange Control Division, Bank of Thailand; 1950–52, *Annual Statement of Foreign Trade*, 1957.

APPENDIX D

Exchange Rates, 1850–1970

THE EXCHANGE RATES given here will suffice to indicate the general nature of the changes during the period 1850 to 1969, but they are not precise figures, nor are they entirely comparable with each other. Some refer to the rates quoted by commercial banks, others to the buying or selling rates of the Treasury.

From 1850 to 1890 the rates are largely based on the annual reports of British consuls in Bangkok. In these reports an "average" rate is frequently given, but it is not always clear what these averages refer to. In many years the consul reports the value of Thailand's trade in Straits or Mexican dollars, and sometimes he quotes a dollar/sterling rate without mentioning the baht/sterling rate at all. In such cases we have converted to a baht/sterling rate by using the fixed ratio of 5 baht to $3.

Silver prices began to drop in terms of gold after 1870, but the baht/sterling exchange rate does not appear to have been affected until about 1880. The reason for this is not known.

The rates from 1908 to 1941 are the Treasury par rates in most cases. As usual, there was a slight spread between buying and selling rates, and commercial rates are slightly different, but we have ignored these refinements.

From 1947 to 1955, Thailand had a system of multiple exchange rates. The detailed regulations were modified from time to time, but the broad outlines of the system remained the same during the period 1947–55. An "official" rate was fixed for certain specified transactions, and it was changed only once between 1947 and 1955. The "official" rates were as follows:

Year	Baht/Pound Sterling	Baht/U.S. Dollar
1947–49	35.00–40.00	9.925–12.50
1949–55	35.00	0.025–12.50

All dealings in foreign exchange other than those specifically designated at the official rate were transacted at the open-market rate. This rate was fixed by the forces of the free market, although the Bank of Thailand did exert some influence on it. The open-market rates for the period 1947–55 are included in the table, below.

336

Year	Baht per Pound Sterling[a]	Year[b]	Baht per Pound Sterling	Baht per U.S. Dollar
1850–79	8.00	1930	11.00	2.30
1880	—	1931	10.13	2.35
1881	—	1932	9.95	2.81
1882	—	1933	11.00	2.68
1883	9.23	1934	11.00	2.24
1884	9.57	1935	11.00	2.25
1885	10.00	1936	11.00	2.20
1886	10.00	1937	11.00	2.22
1887	10.00	1938	11.00	2.27
1888	10.00	1939	11.00	2.60
1889	10.90	1940	11.00	3.07
1890	10.00	1941	11.00	2.85
1891	10.67	1947	75.80	24.10
1892	12.10	1948	60.20	20.00
1893	12.90	1949	60.00	21.70
1894	16.67	1950	57.00	22.30
1895	15.60	1951	54.00	21.60
1896	16.67	1952	46.95	18.87
1897	16.67	1953	50.00	18.37
1898	17.40	1954	59.16	21.42
1899	17.10	1955	59.63	21.59
1900	16.75	1956	57.56	20.78
1901	17.30	1957	57.57	20.77
1902	19.30	1958	58.60	20.99
1903	19.00	1959	58.63	20.99
1904	17.80	1960	59.47	21.18
1905	17.15	1961	59.02	21.06
1906	15.60	1962	58.55	20.62
1907	13.70	1963	58.27	20.84
1908–18	13.00	1964	58.17	20.84
1919	9.54–13.00	1965	58.26	20.83
1920	9.54	1966	58.10	20.80
1921	9.54	1967	50.07	20.80
1922–29	11.00	1968	49.73	20.85
		1969	50.00	21.00
		1970	50.10	21.00

[a] Dash indicates that figures are not available.

[b] Since 1947 these rates refer to the open-market rate.

Sources: *Annual Diplomatic and Consular Reports from Her Majesty's Consuls in Siam, 1864–1909*, Great Britain, Foreign Office, 1865–1910; *Statistical Year Book of Thailand*, 1916–44; Exchange Control Division, Bank of Thailand; "The Currency History of Siam," *The Record*, Thailand, Ministry of Commerce, October 1923, pp. 3–14; January 1924, pp. 7–20; Bank of Thailand, *Monthly Report*, 1961–70.

Selected Bibliography

Abraham, William I. "Report to the Government of Thailand by the National Income Adviser." Mimeo. Bangkok, August 1963.

Andrews, James M. *Siam, 2nd Rural Economic Survey, 1934–1935*. Bangkok, 1935.

Antonio, J. *Guide to Bangkok and Siam*. Rev. by W. W. Fregen. Bangkok, 1904.

Artamanoff, G. "State-owned Enterprises of Thailand." Mimeo. Bangkok: USOM-AID, 1965.

Asian Development Bank. *Regional Seminar on Agriculture*. 1969.

Ayal, Eliezer B. "Some Crucial Issues in Thailand's Economic Development," *Pacific Affairs*, Summer 1961.

Bacon, George B. *Siam, Land of the White Elephant*. New York, 1892.

Bangkok Calendar. Annually, 1859–72.

Bank of Thailand. *Annual Report*, 1942–69. *Monthly Report*, 1961–69.

——— "IMF Consultation Papers." Mimeo. Selected years, 1954–70. Documents and statistical tables prepared for annual consultations with the International Monetary Fund.

Barnett, J. C. *Report of the First Annual Exhibition of Agriculture and Commerce*. Bangkok: Ministry of Agriculture, 1910.

Bau, David H. "Agricultural Economic Survey of Sarapee District, Chiengmai Province, Thailand." Mimeo. Bangkok: United Nations, FAO, July 1, 1951.

Bauer, P. T. *The Rubber Industry*. Cambridge, Mass., 1948.

Behrman, Jere. *Supply Response in Underdeveloped Agriculture: A Case Study of Four Major Annual Crops in Thailand, 1937–63*. Amsterdam, 1968.

Bell, Peter F., and Janet Tai. "Markets, Middlemen, and Technology: Agricultural Supply Response in the Dualistic Economies of Southeast Asia," *Malayan Economic Review*, April 1969.

Bliss, Don C. *Market for American Foodstuffs in Siam*. U.S. Bureau of Foreign and Domestic Commerce, Trade Information Bulletin 610. Washington, D.C., 1929.

Bock, Carl. *Temples and Elephants*. London, 1884.

Bond, Billy, *et al.* "A Report on the Thailand Fertilizer Situation and Potential." Mimeo. AID, Bangkok, May 10, 1966.

Bourke-Borrowes, D. "The Teak Industry of Siam," Technical and Scientific Supplement to *The Record*, VII (October 1927).

Bowring, Sir John. *The Kingdom and People of Siam*. 2 vols. London, 1857.

[Bradley, D. B.] *Siamese Laws and Customs on Slavery*. Published as part of the *Bangkok Calendar* for 1861.

The Burney Papers. Printed by order of the Committee of the Vajiranana Library. 4 vols. Bangkok, 1910.

Callis, H. G. *Foreign Capital in Southeast Asia*. New York, 1942.

Campbell, J. G. D. *Siam in the Twentieth Century*. London, 1902.

Carter, A. Cecil, ed. *The Kingdom of Siam*. New York, 1904.

Chancellor, William J. *Survey of Tractor Contractor Operations in Thailand and Malaysia*. University of California at Davis, August 1970.

Child, Jacob T. *The Pearl of Asia*. Chicago, 1892.

Chuchart, Chaiyong, and Sopin Tongpan. *The Determination and Analysis of Policies to Support and Stabilize Agricultural Prices and Incomes of Thai Farmers (with Special Reference to the Rice Premium)*. Bangkok, May 1965.

Clark, Colin. *The Conditions of Economic Progress*. 2d ed. London, 1951.

Collet, Octave-J-A. *Étude politique et économique sur le Siam moderne*. Bruxelles, 1911.

Colquhoun, Archibald Ross. *Across Chrysê*. 2 vols. London, 1883.

—— *Amongst the Shans*. New York, 1885.

Comparative Statement of the Imports and Exports of Siam, 1892–1901. Extracts from Thai Customs Reports. Bangkok, n.d.

Cook, Sir E. "The Building of Modern Siam," *Asiatic Review*, October 1930.

Cort, Mary L. *Siam, or the Heart of Farther India*. New York, 1866.

Crawfurd, John. *Journal of an Embassy to the Courts of Siam and Cochin-China*. London, 1828.

Credner, W. *Siam: Das Land der Tai*. Stuttgart, 1935.

"The Currency History of Siam, 1902–23," *The Record*, III (October 1923), 3–14; IV (January 1924), 7–20.

Curtis, Lillian J. *The Laos of North Siam*. Philadelphia, 1903.

Debect, Henry. *La question Siamoise et le Traité de 1896*. Paris, 1904.

Dilock, Prinz von Siam. *Die Landwirtschaft in Siam*. Tübingen, 1907.

Donner, Wolf, and Banlu Puthigorn, *The Marketing of Fertilizer in Thailand*. FAO, Preliminary Economic Report, Bangkok, 1970.

DuPlatre, Louis. *Essai sur la condition de la femme au Siam*. Lyon, 1922.

Finlayson, George. *The Mission to Siam, and Hué, the Capital of Cochin-China, in the Years 1821–2*. London, 1826.

Frankfurter, Dr. Oscar. *Die Rechtlichen und Wirtschaftlichen Verhaltnisse in Siam*. Guben, Germany, 1895.

—— "King Mongkut," *Journal of the Siam Society*, I (1904), 191–207.

Freeman, J. H. *An Oriental Land of the Free*. Philadelphia, 1910.

Gajewski, Peter. "The 1963 Census of Agriculture and the National Income Accounts." Mimeo. Bangkok, 1965.

Gerini, G. E. *Siam, Its Production, Arts, and Manufactures*. Hertford, Eng., 1912.

Golay, Frank, *et al. Underdevelopment and Economic Nationalism in Southeast Asia*. Ithaca, N.Y., 1969.

Gordon, Robert. "The Economic Development of Siam," *Journal of the Society of Arts*, XXXIX (1891), 283–98.

Gould, Joseph S. "Estimates of Gross National Product and Net National Income of Thailand, 1938/39, 1946, 1947, and 1948." Mimeo. Bangkok, 1950.

—— "Preliminary Estimates of the Gross Geographical Product and Domestic National Income of Thailand, 1938/39, 1946–50." Mimeo. Bangkok: National Economic Council, 1952.

—— "Thailand's National Income and Its Meaning." Mimeo. Bangkok: National Economic Council, 1953.

Graham, W. A. *Siam*. 3d ed. 2 vols. London, 1924.

Great Britain. Foreign Office. *Annual Diplomatic and Consular Reports on Trade and Finance from H.M.'s Consuls in Siam, 1864–1937*. This is a composite title, since the titles of the reports vary frequently. London, 1865–1938.

—— [Foreign Office.] *Correspondence Respecting the Affairs of Siam*. Published by order of the House of Commons. London, 1894.

—— Foreign Office. *Report on Teak Trade in Siam*. Miscellaneous Series, No. 357, Reports on Subjects of General and Commercial Interest. London, 1895.

—— India Office. *East India (Treaty with the King of Siam)*. London, 1874.

Gréhan, M. A. *Le royaume de Siam*. Paris, 1869.

Guyon, René. *The Work of Codification in Siam*. Paris, 1919.

Haas, Joseph. *Siamese Coinage*. Shanghai, 1880.

Hagrup, J. F. "Report on Investigation of Hydro-Electric Power Sources in Siam." Royal State Railways. Mimeo. Bangkok, 1932/33.

Hallett, Holt S. *A Thousand Miles on an Elephant in the Shan States*. Edinburgh, 1890.

Haring, Joseph E., and Larry Westphal. "Financial Policy in Postwar Thailand," *Asian Survey*, May 1968.

H.H. Prince Damrong's Miscellanies. Published under the auspices of the Jotekasthira family for presentation on the occasion of the cremation of Phya Dharmacharya. In Thai language. Bangkok, 1947.

Hirschman, Albert O. *A Strategy for Economic Development*. New Haven, 1958.

Hoeylaerts, H. *Le royaume de Siam*. Bruxelles, 1892.

H.R.H. The Prince of Chandaburi—His Record as Minister of Finance. In Thai language. Bangkok, 1931.

International Development, 1966. Dobbs Ferry, N.Y.: Oceana Publications, 1967.

Inukai, Ichirou. "Farm Mechanization, Output, and Labor Input," *International Labour Review*, May 1970.

Isarangkun, Chirayu. "Manufacturing Industries in Thailand." Ph.D. thesis, Australian National University, Canberra, 1969.

Johnson, Webster. *Agricultural Development of Thailand with Special Reference to Rural Institutions*. Dept. of Land Development, Bangkok, 1969.

Journal of the Siam Society. Vols. 1–39 (1904–52).

Jumsai, M. L. Manich. *Compulsory Education in Thailand*. Studies on Compulsory Education VIII. Paris: UNESCO, 1951.

Kanchananaga, Nai Thuan. *The Commercial and Economic Progress of Thailand, 1949*. Bangkok: Thai Commercial Development Bureau, 1949.

Kanchananaga, Nai Thuan, comp. *Report on Commercial and Economic Progress of Thailand, 1939–40*. Bangkok, 1941.

Khumbkan, Chote. *Siams Wirtschaftlicher Aufbau, Aussenhandel und Zahlungsbilanz*. Leipzig, 1932.

Kridakara, M. C. Sithiporn. *Some Aspects of Rice Farming in Siam*. Bangkok, 1970.

Krisanamis, Phairach. *Paddy Price Movements and their Effect on the Economic*

Situation of Farmers in the Central Plains of Thailand. (Ph.D. thesis, Indiana University, 1967.) Bangkok, 1967.

Kuznets, Simon. "The State as a Unit in Economic Growth," *Journal of Economic History*, XI, Winter 1951.

Lailaksana, Police-Lieutenant Sthier, ed. *Annual Collections of Laws.* 52 vols. in Thai language. Bangkok, 1935–40.

Landon, K. P. *The Chinese in Thailand.* New York, 1941.

———— *Siam in Transition.* Shanghai and Chicago, 1939.

Lasker, Bruno. *Human Bondage in Southeast Asia.* Chapel Hill, N.C., 1950.

Le May, Reginald. *The Coinage of Siam.* Bangkok, 1932.

Lewis, W. A. "Economic Development with Unlimited Supplies of Labour," *Manchester School*, May 1954.

Lingat, R. *L'Esclavage privé dans le Vieux droit Siamois.* Paris, 1931.

Loftus, Captain A. J. *A New Year's Paper on the Development of the Kingdom of Siam.* Bangkok, 1890.

Long, Millard. "Interest Rates and the Structure of Agricultural Credit Markets," *Oxford Economic Papers*, July 1968.

MacDonald, Alexander. *Bangkok Editor.* New York, 1949.

McDonald, N. A. *Siam: Its Government, Manners, Customs, etc.* Philadelphia, 1871.

Maitri, Phya Kalyan (Francis B. Sayre), ed. *Siam: Treaties with Foreign Powers, 1920–1927.* Published by order of the Royal Siamese Government. Norwood, Mass., 1928.

Maizels, Alfred. *Industrial Growth and World Trade.* Cambridge, Eng., 1963.

Mallikamas, Waytin. "Industrial Promotion in Thailand." Ph.D. thesis, University of Wisconsin, Madison, 1967.

Malloch, D. E. *Siam, Some General Remarks on Its Productions.* Calcutta, 1852.

Maprasert, Lamduan. *The Domestic Product of Thailand and Its Regional Distribution.* (Ph.D. thesis, University of London, 1965.) Bangkok, 1967.

Martin, Aymé. *Siam mouvement économique du Laos Siamois (Monthons Isan et Oudon).* France, Ministry of Commerce and Industry, Rapports Commerciaux des Agents Diplomatiques et Consulaires de France, No. 865. Paris, 1910.

"Monograph on Sugar in Siam," *The Record*, II (January 1922), 6–17.

Moore, R. A. "An Early British Merchant in Bangkok," *Journal of the Siam Society*, XI (1914–15), 21–39.

Motooka, Takeshi. "The Conditions Governing Agricultural Development in Southeast Asia," *The Developing Economics*, V (1967), No. 3.

Mousny, André. *The Economy of Thailand.* Bangkok, 1964.

Muscat, Robert. *Development Strategy in Thailand.*

Myrdal, Gunnar. *Asian Drama.* New York, 1968.

Nathabanja, Luang. *Extraterritoriality in Siam.* Bangkok, 1924.

Neale, F. A. *Narrative of a Residence in Siam.* London, 1852.

Nunn, W. "Some Notes upon the Development of the Commerce of Siam," *Journal of the Siam Society*, XV (1922), 78–102.

Nuprapath, Chao Phya Wongsa. *History of the Ministry of Agriculture.* In Thai language. Bangkok, 1941.

Pallegoix, Mgr. *Description du Royaume Thai ou Siam.* 2 vols. Paris, 1854.

Pendleton, R. L. *Thailand, Aspects of Landscape and Life.* New York, 1962.

Pitkin, Wolcott H. *Siam's Case for Revision of Obsolete Treaty Obligations Admittedly Inapplicable to Present Conditions.* Bangkok, 1919.

Platenius, Hans. *Evaluation of the Agricultural Program for Thailand.* Bangkok, NEDB, 1964.

Pramoj, M. R. Kukhrit, and M. R. Seni Pramoj. "The King of Siam Speaks." Unpublished manuscript, n.d.

Pringle, Richard. "Report on Cooperatives in Thailand." U.S. Special Technical and Economic Mission to Thailand. Mimeo. Bangkok, 1951.

A Public Development Program for Thailand. International Bank for Reconstruction and Development. Baltimore, Md., 1959.

Purcell, Victor. *The Chinese in Southeast Asia.* London: Oxford University Press, 1951.

Rachaton, Phya Anuman. *Government Revenue and Royal Trading in Ancient Times.* In Thai language. Bangkok, 1947.

———— *The Life of the Farmer.* In Thai language. Trans. by William J. Gedney, in MS form. Bangkok, 1948.

Rajanubhab, H.H. Prince Damrong. *True Stories of Past Events.* 5th ed. In Thai language. Bangkok, 1951.

Ranis, G. "Factor Proportions in Japanese Economic Development," *American Economic Review*, September 1957.

Records of the Relations Between Siam and Foreign Countries in the 17th Century. 5 vols. Copies of papers preserved at the India Office. Printed by order of the Council of the Vajiranana National Library. Bangkok, 1916.

Reeve, W. D. *Public Administration in Siam.* London, 1951.

Report of the Second Exhibition of Agriculture and Commerce Held in Bangkok, April 1911. London, 1911.

Reports upon the Effect Which the Proposed Irrigation Scheme Is Likely to Have upon the Proposed Water-Works Scheme for Bangkok. Bangkok, 1903.

Royal State Railways of Siam, Fiftieth Anniversary, 1897–1947. Bangkok, 1947.

Rozental, Alek A. *Finance and Development in Thailand.* New York, 1970.

Sanittanont, Sura. *Thailand's Rice Export Tax: Its Effects on the Rice Economy.* (Ph.D. thesis, University of Wisconsin, 1967.) Bangkok, 1967.

Santitwongse, Yai S. *An Outline of Rice Cultivation in Siam.* Ministry of Agriculture. Bangkok, 1911.

Sarasas, Phra. *My Country Thailand.* 2d ed. Bangkok, 1950.

Satow, Sir Ernest M. *Essay Towards a Bibliography of Siam.* Singapore, 1886.

Scherzer, Karl von. *Fachmännische Berichte über die Österreichisch-ungarische Expedition, 1868–71.* Stuttgart, 1872.

Scoville, W., and A. Thieme. *Agricultural Development in Thailand.* USOM, Bangkok, 1964.

Seth, A. N. "Report on Land Reforms in Thailand." Mimeo. FAO Regional Office, 1968.

Seventy Years Trade in Bangkok, 1856–1926. Bangkok, 1926.

Shenoy, B. R. "The Currency, Banking and Exchange System of Thailand," International Monetary Fund, *Staff Papers,* I (1950), 289–314.

Siam, General and Medical Features. Bangkok, 1930.

The Siam Repository. 6 vols. 1869–74.

Silcock, T. H. *The Economic Development of Thai Agriculture.* Canberra, Australia, 1970.

Silcock, T. H., ed. *Thailand: Social and Economic Studies in Development.* Canberra, Australia, 1967.

Sitton, Gordon. "The Role of the Farmer in the Economic Development of Thailand." Council of Economic and Cultural Affairs, New York, 1962.

Sivaram, M. *New Siam in the Making.* Bangkok, 1936.

Skinner, G. W. *Leadership and Power in the Chinese Community in Thailand.* Ithaca, N.Y., 1958.

Smith, Samuel J. *Brief Sketches of Siam from 1833 to 1909.* Bangkok, 1909.

Smyth, H. Warington. *Five Years in Siam.* 2 vols. New York, 1898.

Snidvongs, Mom Luang Dej. *Die Entwicklung des siamesischen Aussenhandels.* Bern, 1926.

State Papers of the Kingdom of Siam, 1664–1886. London, 1886.

"Statistics, Memoranda, and Documents Submitted to the International Monetary Fund and the World Bank Missions, 1949–50." Mimeo. Bangkok, n.d.

Suwanakijboriharn, Amnuey. "The Administration of Foreign Aid in Thailand." Ph.D. thesis, Indiana University, 1968.

Suwankiri, Trairong. "The Structure of Protection and Import Substitution in Thailand." M.A. thesis, University of the Philippines, 1970.

Thailand Electric Power Study, December 1966. Royal Government of Thailand and USOM, Bangkok, 1967.

Thailand Farm Mechanization and Farm Machinery Market. A Coordinated Industry Study Project. Royal Government of Thailand and USOM, Bangkok, 1969.

THAILAND GOVERNMENT PUBLICATIONS
(Printed in Bangkok unless otherwise noted)

Board of Investment. *Promotion of Industrial Investment Act, B.E. 2505 (1962),* July 1966.

Central Statistical Office. *Thailand Population Census, 1960.*

Department of Commerce and Statistics [later National Statistical Office]. *Statistical Year Book of Thailand.* Title varies. I–XXIX (1916–69). 1917–69.

Department of Customs. *Annual Statement of Foreign Trade of Thailand.* 1951–69.

Department of Land Development. *Land Tenure Situation in 26 Changwats in the Central Plain Region.* 1969.

Department of Mines. "Mining Statistics of Thailand for the Months of March, April, May 1951." Mimeo. 1951.

Department of Ways. "Memorandum Concerning the Policy and Programme of Highways." Mimeo. 1923.

Fiscal Committee (temporary), "Report Suggesting the Basis for Raising Revenues for the Year B.E. 2475 (1932/33) and Probably Future Years." Mimeo. 1931/32, pp. 38–42.

His Majesty's Customs. *Statistics of the Import and Export Trade of Siam.* Annually, 1900–1946.

Ministry of Agriculture. *Agricultural Statistics of Thailand.* Annual.

—— *Annual Report for the Year 1950 to the FAO of United Nations.* 1951.

—— *Land Utilization in Thailand, 1965.* 1968.

—— *Planted Area, Harvested Area, Production and Yield by Changwats, 1937–65.* Kasetsart University. N.d.

—— *Summarized Report on Fertilizer Experiments and Soil Fertility Research.* 1966.

—— National FAO Committee. *Thailand and Her Agricultural Problems.* Rev. ed. 1950.

Ministry of Commerce. *The Record.* A quarterly journal. 19 vols. 1921–40.

Ministry of Commerce and Communications. *The Economic Conditions of North-Eastern Siam.* Prepared by R. S. Le May. 1932.

—— *Siam, Nature and Industry.* 1930.

Ministry of Communications. *Annual Reports on the Administration of the Department of Ways.* 1918/19–1928/29. Title varies.

—— *Annual Reports on the Administration of the Royal State Railways.* 1897/98–1938/39. Title varies.

Ministry of Defence. *Reports on the Operations of the Royal Survey Department.* 1899/1900–1930/31. Title varies.

Ministry of Economic Affairs. Department of Commerce. *Commercial Directory for Siam, 1939.* 4th ed. 1939.

Ministry of Finance. *Report of the Financial Adviser.* Annually, 1901–50. Some reports cover more than one year.

—— Correspondence, memoranda, and documents in the files of the Financial Advisers pertaining to the period 1896–1950.

Ministry of Industry. *History of the Activities and Functions of the Ministry of Industries from 1942 to 1951.* In Thai language. Bangkok, 1951.

—— *Industrial Development and Investment in Thailand, 1966.*

Ministry of Interior. *Yearbook of Labour Statistics, 1965.*

Ministry of National Development. *Thailand, An Official Handbook.* 1970.

National Economic Council. Central Statistical Office. *Monthly Bulletin of Statistics,* No. 1, June 1952.

National Economic Development Board. *Economic Progress of Thailand General Indicators, 1968.*

—— *Evaluations of the First Six-Year Plan, 1961–66.* 1967.

—— *National Income Statistics of Thailand.* 1964 edition.

—— *National Income of Thailand.* 1965 edition. 1966.

—— "National Income of Thailand, Revised Estimates, 1960–69." Mimeo. August 1970.

—— *Performance Evaluation of Development in Thailand for 1965 Under the National Economic Development Plan, 1961–66.* June 1966.

—— *The Second National Economic and Social Development Plan, 1967–71.* N.d.

National Statistical Office. *Census of Agriculture, 1963—Whole Kingdom.*

—— *Household Expenditure Survey, B.E. 2506* (1963).

—— *Income and Expenditure of Farmers, 1963.*

—— *Report of Crop Cutting Survey, 1968.* 1970?

—— *Report of the 1964 Industrial Census.* 1968.

——— *Statistical Year Book of Thailand*, XXII–XXVIII (1952–69).
Royal Department of Mines. *Notes on Mining in Siam with Statistics to March 31st, 1921.* 1921.
Royal Irrigation Department. *Administration Report for the Period, 2457 B.E.– 2468 B.E. (1914/15–1925/26).* 1927.
——— *Project Estimate for Works of Irrigation, Drainage and Navigation to Develop the Plain of Central Siam.* 4 vols. 1915.
——— *Report on the Benefits Which Have Already Accrued to the State by Irrigation Works Already Completed, and What Benefit May Be Expected from Works Still to Be Undertaken.* 1929.
——— *Report on the Farm Management Survey.* Land Consolidation Project Phase II. Netherlands Engineering Consultants, November 1969.

*

Thisjamondol, Pantum, Virach Arromdee, and Millard Long. *Agricultural Credit in Thailand: Theory, Data, Policy.* Bangkok: Kasetsart University, 1965.
Thompson, Virginia M. *Labor Problems in Southeast Asia.* New Haven, 1947.
——— *Thailand, the New Siam.* New York, 1941.
Thornely, P. W. *The History of a Transition.* Bangkok, 1923.
Trescott, Paul B. "Causes and Consequences of Monetary Change in Thailand, 1946–1967." Mimeo., Bangkok, ca. 1968.
——— "Measurement of Thailand's Economic Growth, 1946–1965," *Warasan Sethasat* (Thai Economic Journal), IV (1969), No. 1.
——— "Rice Yields and Productivity: Evidence and Analysis," *Warasan Sethasat* (Thai Economic Journal), III (1968), No. 1.
Ungphakorn, Puey. "Economic Development in Thailand, 1955–64." Mimeo. Bangkok: Bank of Thailand, August 27, 1965.
United Nations. Economic Commission for Asia and the Far East (ECAFE). "Financial Institutions and the Mobilization of Domestic Capital in Thailand." Research and Statistics Series, Trade and Finance Paper No. 3. Mimeo. Bangkok, 1950.
——— *Statistical Yearbook for Asia and the Far East.* 1968.
United Nations. FAO. *Report of the FAO Fisheries Mission for Thailand.* Washington, D.C., December 1949.
——— *Report of the FAO Mission for Siam.* Washington, D.C., 1948.
U.S. Department of Commerce. *Report on Indochina Rubber Industry and Siamese Rubber Production Outlook.* Washington, D.C., 1946.
Usher, Dan. "The Economics of the Rice Premium." Mimeo. Bangkok, 1965?
——— "Equalizing Differences in Income and the Interpretation of National Income Statistics," *Economica*, XXXII (1965), 253–68.
——— "Income as a Measure of Productivity: Alternative Comparisons of Agricultural and Non-Agricultural Productivity in Thailand," *Economica*, XXXIII (1966).
——— *The Price Mechanism and the Meaning of National Income Statistics.* New York, 1968.
——— "The Thai National Income at United Kingdom Prices," *Bulletin of Oxford University Institute of Statistics*, 1963.
——— "Transport Bias in Comparisons of National Income," *Economica*, XXX (1963).

Van der Heide, J. H. "The Economical Development of Siam During the Last Half Century," *Journal of the Siam Society*, III (1906), 74–101.

—— *General Report on Irrigation and Drainage in the Lower Menam Valley.* Bangkok, 1903.

Van Roy, Edward. "The Pursuit of Growth and Stability through Taxation of Agricultural Exports: Thailand's Experience," *Public Finance*, XXIII, No. 3, 294–317.

Vincent, Frank, Jr. *The Land of the White Elephant.* London, 1873.

Wagner, Melvin, and Sopin Tongpan. *Structure of Thai Rice Prices.* Mimeo., Bangkok, 1965?

Waithayakon, H.R.H. Prince Wan. *A History of the Thai Diplomatic Service.* In Thai language. Bangkok, 1943.

Wales, H. G. Quaritch. *Ancient Siamese Government and Administration.* London, 1934.

Wickizer, V. D., and M. K. Bennett. *The Rice Economy of Monsoon Asia.* Stanford, Calif., 1941.

Williamson, W. J. F. "Finance," in A. Wright and O. T. Breakspear, eds., *Twentieth Century Impressions of Siam.* London, 1908, pp. 112–20.

Wilson, George W., ed. *The Impact of Highway Investment on Development.* Washington, D.C., 1966.

Wisakul, Ake. *Commercial Navigation in Thailand.* In Thai language. Bangkok, 1949.

Wood, W. A. R. *A History of Siam.* London, 1926.

Wright, Arnold, and Oliver T. Breakspear, eds. *Twentieth Century Impressions of Siam.* London, 1908.

Yang, S. C. *A Multiple Exchange Rate System.* Madison, Wis., 1957.

Yano, Toru. "Land Tenure in Thailand," *Asian Survey*, October 1968.

Young, Ernest. *The Kingdom of the Yellow Robe.* Westminster, 1898.

Zelinsky, Wilbur. "The Indochinese Peninsula: A Demographic Anomaly," *Far Eastern Quarterly*, IX (1950), 115–45.

Zimmerman, Carle C. *Siam, Rural Economic Survey, 1930–31.* Bangkok, 1931.

Index